FTCE

FLORIDA TEACHER CERTIFICATION EXAMINATIONS

ELEMENTARY EDUCATION K-6
(060)

WITHDRAWN

Rhonda Atkinson, Ph.D.
Professor of Education
Valencia College
Orlando, Florida

D1219466

Research & Education Association
Visit our website: www.rea.com

Research & Education Association
258 Prospect Plains Road
Cranbury, New Jersey 08512
Email: info@rea.com

**Florida FTCE Elementary Education K–6
with Online Practice Tests, 3rd Edition**

Printed in the United States of America

Library of Congress Control Number 2016934649

ISBN-13: 978-0-7386-1208-9
ISBN-10: 0-7386-1208-1

The competencies presented in this book were created and implemented by the
Florida Department of Education and Pearson Education, Inc. For further information
visit the FTCE website at *www.fl.nesinc.com*.

Cover Image © istockphoto.com/damircudic

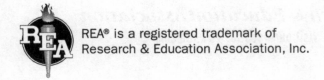

REA® is a registered trademark of
Research & Education Association, Inc.

Contents

Chapter 5: Mathematics

FTCE Elementary Education K-6 Practice Test 1

FTCE Elementary Education K-6 Practice Test 2

Index

About Our Author

Rhonda Atkinson, Ph.D., has an extensive background in reading and psychology, and a deep understanding of how people learn. She has applied this knowledge to a variety of content areas and learner needs, and is an expert in instructional design.

After earning her doctorate in curriculum and instruction from Louisiana State University, Dr. Atkinson went on to become a faculty member and administrator in post-secondary education programs in Louisiana, Missouri, and Florida. Along the way, she has created courses and workshops to meet different content and learner needs in online, face-to-face, and hybrid formats.

She has also developed educational materials for Northrop Grumman, the Institute for Healthcare Advancement, Novartis, the Public Broadcasting Corporation, the Louisiana Office of Elder Affairs, the Louisiana Office of Nutrition Education, and the Louisiana Department of Education.

Dr. Atkinson is the co-author of seven college textbooks—many of them in multiple editions—in reading and learning strategies. She currently serves as a professor of education at Valencia College, Orlando, Florida, where she teaches undergraduate education courses in student success and technology as well as post-graduate certification courses in education.

About REA

Founded in 1959, Research & Education Association (REA) is dedicated to publishing the finest and most effective educational materials—including study guides and test preps—for students of all ages.

Today, REA's wide-ranging catalog is a leading resource for students, teachers, and other professionals. Visit *www.rea.com* to see a complete listing of all our titles.

Acknowledgments

In addition to our authors, we would like to thank REA's Larry B. Kling, Vice President, Editorial, for supervising development; Pam Weston, Publisher, for setting the quality standards for production integrity and managing the publication to completion; John Paul Cording, Vice President, Technology, for coordinating the design and development of the REA Study Center; Diane Goldschmidt, Managing Editor, for coordinating development of this edition; Eve Grinnell for page design; Ellen Gong for proofreading; and Kathy Caratozzolo of Caragraphics for typesetting this edition.

Getting Started

Congratulations! By taking the FTCE Elementary Education K–6 (060) test, you're on your way to a rewarding career as a teacher of young students in Florida. Our book, and the online tools that come with it, give you everything you need to succeed on this important exam, bringing you one step closer to being certified to teach in Florida.

This FTCE Elementary Education K–6 test prep package includes:

- A **complete overview** of the FTCE Elementary Education K–6 (060) test

- A **comprehensive review** for all four subject tests in the FTCE Elementary Education K–6 test battery

- **End-of-chapter review questions**

- An **online diagnostic test** to pinpoint your strengths and weaknesses and focus your study

- **Two full-length practice tests:** one in the book and an additional test online that comes with powerful diagnostic tools to help you personalize your prep

How to Use This Book + Online Prep

About Our Review

The review chapters in this book are designed to help you sharpen your command of all the skills you'll need to pass the FTCE Elementary Education K–6 test. The test is composed of four competencies. Each of the skills required for all of the competencies is discussed at length to optimize your understanding of what the test covers.

Keep in mind that your schooling has taught you most of what you need to know to answer the questions on the test. Our content review is designed to reinforce what you have learned and show you how to relate the information you have acquired to the specific competencies on the test. Studying your class notes and textbooks together with our review will give you an excellent foundation for passing the test.

About the REA Study Center

We know your time is valuable and you want an efficient study experience. At the REA Study Center (*www.rea.com/studycenter*), you will get feedback right from the start on what you know and what you don't know to help make the most of your study time.

Here is what you will find at the REA Study Center:

- **Diagnostic Test**—Before you review with the book, take our online diagnostic test. Your score report will pinpoint topics for which you need the most review, to help focus your study.

- **2 Full-Length Practice Tests***—These practice tests give you the most complete picture of your strengths and weaknesses. After you've studied with the book, test what you've learned by taking the first of two online practice exams. Review your score reports, then go back and study any topics you missed. Take the second practice test to ensure you've mastered the material.

Our online exams simulate the computer-based format of the actual FTCE test and come with these features:

- **Automatic scoring**—Find out how you did on your test, instantly.

- **Diagnostic score reports**—Get a specific score tied to each competency, so you can focus on the areas that challenge you the most.

---

* *Note:* Practice Test 1 is also available in this book.

- **On-screen detailed answer explanations**—See why the correct response option is right, and learn why the other answer choices are incorrect.

- **Timed testing**—Learn to manage your time as you practice, so you'll feel confident on test day.

An Overview of the Test

What is assessed on the FTCE Elementary Education K–6 test?

The FTCE Elementary Education K–6 test is a subject area examination constructed to measure the knowledge and skills that an entry-level educator in Florida public schools must have. The test is a requirement for candidates seeking an Elementary Education K–6 certificate. Because it's a computer-administered test, the FTCE Elementary Education K–6 test is available throughout the year at numerous locations across the state and at select locations nationally. To find the test center near you, visit *www.fl.nesinc.com*.

Below is an outline of the Elementary Education K–6 exam's four subject tests. The table shows the number of questions in each subject, as well as the time allocated for each section of the test.

A Snapshot of the FTCE Elementary Education K–6 Test

Subject	Number of Items	Time Allotted
Language Arts and Reading (601)	60	1 hour and 5 minutes (65 minutes)
Social Science (602)	55	1 hour and 5 minutes (65 minutes)
Science (603)	55	1 hour and 10 minutes (70 minutes)
Mathematics (604)	50	1 hour and 10 minutes (70 minutes)
TOTAL	220	4 hours and 30 minutes

What is the format of the FTCE Elementary Education K–6 test?

The test includes a total of 220 multiple-choice items. Your test may include questions that are being evaluated for future administrations. These items will not count toward your score and you won't know which is which, so they aren't worth worrying about. Your final scale score will be based only on the scorable items.

When should the test be taken?

Traditionally, teacher preparation programs determine when their candidates take the required tests for teacher certification. These programs will also clear you to take the examinations and make final recommendations for certification to the Florida Bureau of Educator Certification.

A candidate seeking K–6 certification may take the appropriate test at such time as his or her Educator Preparation Program (EPP) determines the candidate's readiness to take the test, or upon successful completion of the EPP, whichever comes first. The EPP will determine readiness through benchmarks and structured assessments of the candidates' progress throughout the preparation program.

Taking the appropriate FTCE examinations is a requirement to teach in Florida, so if you are planning on being an educator, you must take and pass these tests.

How do I register for the test?

To register for the FTCE Elementary Education K–6 test, you must create an account in the FTCE/FELE online registration system. Registration will then be available to you online, 24/7.

How should I prepare for the test?

It is never too early to start studying for the FTCE. The earlier you begin, the more time you will have to sharpen your skills. Do not procrastinate. Cramming is not an effective way to study, since it does not allow you the time needed to learn the test material. It is important for you to choose the time and place for studying that works best for you. Be consistent and use your time wisely. Work out a study routine and stick to it.

When you take REA's diagnostic test and practice tests, simulate the conditions of the actual test as closely as possible. Turn your television and radio off, and go to a quiet place free from distraction. Read each question carefully, consider all answer choices, and pace yourself.

As you complete each test, review your score reports, study the diagnostic feedback, and thoroughly review the explanations to the questions you answered incorrectly. But don't overdo it. Take one problem area at a time; review it until you are confident that you have mastered the material. Give extra attention to the areas giving you the most difficulty, as this will help build your score.

FTCE Elementary Education K–6 Study Schedule

Week	Activity
1	Take the online Diagnostic Test at the REA Study Center (*www.rea.com/studycenter*). Your detailed score report will identify the topics where you need the most review.
2–3	Study the review chapters. Use your score report from the Diagnostic Test to focus your study. Useful study techniques include highlighting key terms and information and taking notes as you read the review. Learn all the competencies by making flashcards and targeting questions you missed on the Diagnostic Test.
4	Take Practice Test 1 either in the book or online at the REA Study Center. Review your score report and identify topics where you need more review.
5	Reread all your notes, refresh your understanding of the test's competencies and skills, review your college textbooks, and read class notes you've taken. This is also the time to consider any other supplementary materials that your advisor or the Florida Department of Education suggests.
6	Take Practice Test 2 online at the REA Study Center. Review your score report and restudy the appropriate review section(s) until you are confident you understand the material.

Are there any breaks during the test?

If you take at least 3 of the FTCE Elementary Education K–6 subtests, you will receive a 15-minute break which is built into the test. Instructions will appear on the computer screen at the appropriate time. During a scheduled break you are permitted to access personal items and you may leave the test center. You will need to show identification when leaving or re-entering the testing room. After finishing your break, the test administrator will check your ID and escort you back to your seat so you can resume your test.

If you need to take an unscheduled break during the FTCE Elementary Education K–6 test, the exam clock will *not* stop. The test administrator will set your workstation to "break" mode before you leave the room. During an unscheduled break, you are not permitted to access personal items (other than food, drink, or medications) and you are not allowed to leave the test center. After your break, the test administrator will check your ID and escort you back to your seat so you can continue your test.

What's the passing score?

The FTCE Elementary Education K–6 test is a pass/fail test. Immediately after testing, you will receive an *unofficial* pass/non-pass status. Official score reports are released within 4 weeks of testing.

On your official score report you will see "Pass" or "Not Pass." Your raw score and percentage of correct answers on the test are converted to what is called a scale score. The minimum passing scale score for each subtest on the FTCE Elementary Education K–6 test is 200. The following table shows the approximate percentage of questions you need to get correct in order to pass:

Subtest	Approx. Number of Correct Answers Needed to Pass
Language Arts and Reading	44
Social Science	38
Science	39
Mathematics	35

What if I don't pass each subject area subtest?

You must pass all parts of the FTCE Elementary Education K–6 test in order to meet the examination requirement for FTCE Elementary Education K–6 certification. If you don't do well on every part of the test, don't panic. You can retake the individual subject area subtests after a 31-day waiting period after the first and subsequent attempts.

If you did not pass one of the FTCE Elementary Education K–6 subtests, your score report will include a numeric score as well as a detailed performance analysis report that indicates the number and percentage of multiple-choice questions you answered correctly by applicable competency. Use this information to determine the sections of the test in which your performance was weakest, and then plan to do some additional studying in those areas.

What else do I need to know about test day?

The day before your test, check for any updates in your testing account. This is where you'll learn of any changes to your reporting schedule or if there's a change in the test site.

On the day of the test, you should wake up early after a good night's rest. Have a healthy breakfast and dress in layers that can be removed or added as the conditions in the test center require.

Arrive at the test center early. This will allow you to relax and collect your thoughts before the test, and will also spare you the anguish that comes with being late. As an added incentive to make sure that you arrive early, keep in mind that no one will be admitted into the test center after the test has begun.

Before you leave for the testing site, carefully review your registration materials. Make sure you bring your admission ticket and two unexpired forms of identification. Primary forms of ID include:

- Passport
- Government-issued driver's license
- State-issued ID card
- Military ID card

You may need to produce a supplemental ID document if any questions arise with your primary ID or if your primary ID is otherwise valid but lacks your full name, photo, and signature. Without proper identification, you will not be admitted to the test center.

You may not bring watches of any kind, cellphones, smartphones, or any other electronic communication devices or weapons of any kind in the testing room. Scrap paper, written notes, books, and any printed material is prohibited.

No smoking, eating, or drinking is allowed in the testing room. Consider bringing a small snack and a bottle of water to keep you sharp during the test.

Test-Taking Tips

1. Guess Away

One of the most frequently asked questions about the FTCE Elementary Education K–6 test is: Can I guess? The answer: absolutely! There is no penalty for guessing on the test. That means that if you guess incorrectly, you will not lose any points, but if you guess correctly, you will gain points. Thus, while it's fine to guess, it's important to guess smartly, or as the strategy is called: use process of elimination (see Strategy No. 2). Your score is based strictly on the number of correct answers. So answer all questions and take your best guess when you don't know the answer.

2. Process of Elimination

Process of elimination is one of the most important test-taking strategies at your disposal. Process of elimination means looking at the choices and eliminating the ones you know are wrong, including answers that are partially wrong. Your odds of getting the right answer increase from the moment you're able to get rid of a wrong choice.

3. All in

Review all the response options. Just because you believe you've found the correct answer—or, in some cases, answers—look at each choice so you don't mistakenly jump to any conclusions. If you are asked to choose the *best* answer, be sure your first answer is really the best one.

4. Choice of the Day

What if you are truly stumped and can't use the process of elimination? It's time to pick a fallback answer. On the day of the test, choose the position of the answer (e.g., the third of the four choices) that you will pick for any question you cannot smartly guess. According to the laws of probability, you have a higher chance of getting an answer right if you stick to one chosen position for the answer choice when you have to guess an answer instead of randomly picking one.

5. Use Choices to Confirm Your Answer

The great thing about multiple-choice questions is that the answer has to be staring back at you. Have an answer in mind and use the choices to *confirm* it. For the Math test, you can work the problem and find the match among the choices, or you may want to try the opposite: *backsolving*—that is, working backwards—from the choices given.

6. Watch the Clock

Among the most vital point-saving skills is active time management. The breakdown and time limits of each section are provided as you begin each test. Keep an eye on the timer on your computer screen. Make sure you stay on top of how much time you have left for each section and never spend too much time on any one question. Remember: Most multiple-choice questions are worth one raw point. Treat each one as if it's the one that will put you over the top. You never know, it just might.

7. Read, Read, Read

It's important to read through all the multiple-choice options. Even if you believe answer choice A is correct, you can misread a question or response option if you're rushing to get through the test. While it is important not to linger on a question, it is also crucial to avoid giving a question short shrift. Slow down, calm down, read all the choices. Verify that your choice is the best one, and click on it.

8. Take Notes

If the test site provides you with scratch paper, use it to make notes to work toward the answer(s). If you use all the scratch paper you're initially given, you can get more.

9. Isolate Limiters

Pay attention to any limiters in a multiple-choice question stem. These are words such as *initial, best, most* (as in *most appropriate* or *most likely*), *not, least, except, required,* or *necessary*. Especially watch for negative words, such as "Choose the answer that is *not* true." When you select your answer, double-check yourself by asking how the response fits the limitations established by the stem. Think of the stem as a puzzle piece that perfectly fits only the response option(s) that contain the correct answer. Let it guide you.

10. It's Not a Race

Ignore other test-takers. Don't compare yourself to anyone else in the room. Focus on the items in front of you and the time you have left. If someone finishes the test 30 minutes early, it does not necessarily mean that person answered more questions correctly than you did. Stay calm and focus on *your* test. It's the only one that matters.

11. Confirm Your Click

In the digital age, many of us are used to rapid-clicking, be it in the course of emailing or gaming. Look at the screen to be sure to see that your mouse-click is acknowledged. If your answer doesn't register, you won't get credit. However, if you want to mark it for review so you can return later, that's your call. Before you click "Submit," use the test's review screen to see whether you inadvertently skipped any questions.

12. Creature of Habit? No Worries.

We are all creatures of habit. It's therefore best to follow a familiar pattern of study. Do what's comfortable for you. Set a time and place each day to study for this test. Whether it is 30 minutes at the library or an hour in a secluded corner of your local coffee shop, commit yourself as best you can to this schedule every day. Find quiet places where it is less crowded, as constant background noise can distract you. Don't study one subject for too long, either. Take an occasional breather and treat yourself to a healthy snack or some quick exercise. After your short break—5 or 10 minutes can do the trick—return to what you were studying or start a new section.

13. Knowledge is Power

Purchasing this book gave you an edge on passing the FTCE Elementary Education K–6 test. Make the most of this edge. Review the sections on how the test is structured, what the directions look like, what types of questions will be asked, and so on. Take our practice tests to familiarize yourself with what the test looks and feels like. Most test anxiety occurs because people feel unprepared when they are taking the test, and they psych themselves out. You can whittle away at anxiety by learning the format of the test and by knowing what to expect. Fully simulating the test even once will boost your chances of getting the score you need. Meanwhile, the knowledge you've gained will also will save you the valuable time that would have been eaten up puzzling through what the directions are asking As an added benefit, previewing the test will free up your brain's resources so you can focus on racking up as many points as you can.

14. B-r-e-a-t-h-e

What's the worst that can happen when you take a test? You may have an off day, and despite your best efforts, you may not pass. Well, the good news is that a test can be retaken. In fact, you may already be doing this—this book is every bit for you as it is for first-timers. Fortunately, the FTCE Elementary Education K–6 test is something you can study and prepare for, and in some ways to a greater extent than other tests you've taken throughout your academic career. Yes, there will be questions you won't know, but neither your teacher education program nor state licensing board expects you to know everything. When unfamiliar vocabulary appears or difficult math problems loom, don't despair: Use context clues, process of elimination, or your letter of the day to make your choice, and then press ahead. If you have time left, you can always come back to the question later. If not, relax. It is only one question on a test filled with many. Take a deep breath and then exhale. You know this information. Now you're going to show it.

Good luck on the FTCE Elementary Education K–6 test!

CHAPTER 2

Language Arts and Reading

Competency 1: Knowledge of the Reading Process

For most people, reading is a natural process used to gain understanding. Most adults have been readers for so long that they have assimilated the process and read without really thinking much about it. But teachers, especially teachers who teach grades K–6, need to think consciously about what occurs when students read. That is, they need to focus on the reading process itself. It is critical that teachers know how the process works so they can identify where students are in the process and intentionally and strategically help them develop, practice, and refine reading skills as they become more able readers.

What is reading? Reading occurs when a reader decodes print symbols to understand or comprehend the writer's meaning. Reading is a complex interaction in which the reader brings background knowledge, motivation, and skills to the process. The text provides content in the form of written language. According to the National Reading Panel (National Institute of Child Health and Human Development, 2000), teaching the process of reading focuses on the following:

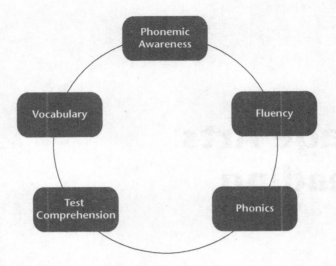

The focus of Competency 1 is the reading process.

Skill 1.1: Identify the Content of Emergent Literacy

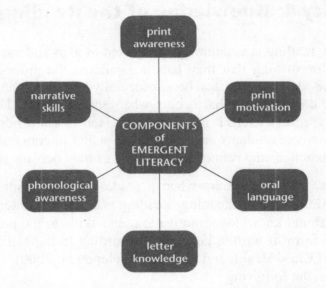

Emergent literacy, a term coined by Marie M. Clay (1966), consists of reading-related knowledge and skills that children develop prior to formal instruction in reading. There are six basic components of emergent literacy:

- **print motivation**—interest in and enjoyment of printed materials

- **print awareness**—interest and interaction with print; pretending to read

- **listening and oral vocabularies**—words understood when heard; words used in speech

- **narrative skills**—ability to retell stories or describe events

- **letter knowledge**—understand letter names and shapes

- **phonological awareness**—ability to understand the sound of language and manipulate or play with speech sounds

Educators often associate emergent literacy with children up to about age 5. Most young children are exposed to a print-rich environment from an early age through books, magazines, advertisements, and other sources of print they encounter at home, in daycare or preschool, and on outings. Through this exposure, they learn something about reading without actually being able to read. Here are some examples of what they learn:

- Print differs from other visual patterns.

- Books contain print.

- Readers glean information from print.

- Print can be translated into speech.

- Reading follows certain conventions (e.g., in the U.S., book pages are turned from right to left, and print runs from left to right and from top to bottom).

It is important for children's interest in reading-related and literacy-related activities to be supported at this time, as emergent literacy forms the foundation of future reading and writing development. Some experts suggest that emergent literacy is a transitional period without sharp boundaries during which a child gradually transforms from a nonreader to a beginning reader while others suggest that emergent literacy is a stage reflected in a particular set of skills such as reading readiness. In either case, emergent literacy is understood to develop at individual rates. This raises the question of when children can be considered ready for formal reading instruction. Some educators suggest that if a child is not ready to read, the teacher should focus on instilling readiness and delay formal reading instruction until the child is ready. Many educators believe that certain criteria should determine whether or not a child is ready for reading instruction. These criteria include concepts of print, oral language development, and understanding of the alphabetic principle: the relationship between letters (graphemes) and the sounds they represent (phonemes).

Concepts of Print

Marie M. Clay (1966) developed a formal procedure for observing a child's behavior with books to determine the extent of a child's print-related concepts. For instance, her assessment checks whether a child can find the title of a book, show where to start reading it, and locate the last page or end of the book. These components may differ from those typically considered essential before children can begin to read, like discriminating between sounds and finding likenesses and differences in print. To assess concepts of print, a teacher or parent might hand a book to a child in a horizontal position with the back of the book facing the child. The adult would then ask questions like, "Where is the name of the book?," "Where does the story start?," and "If the book has the words *the end,* where might I find those words?"

Another critical pre-reading skill is being able to indicate the directionality of print. The reader in the U.S. must start at the left side of the page and read to the right. This skill is not inborn but rather acquired, as some languages require the reader to progress from right to left (e.g., Hebrew), both left to right and right to left (e.g., some ancient Greek texts), or top to bottom (e.g., some Japanese texts). Teachers or parents can also model directionality by passing their hands or fingers under the words or sentences as they read aloud.

Oral Language Development

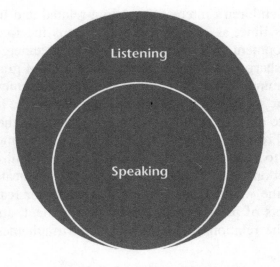

Oral Language Components

Language has four dimensions: speaking, listening, reading, and writing. Oral language is a subset of language and has two dimensions: speaking and listening. Listening is the precursor of speaking because children have to hear language before they can speak it. Oral language is important because it provides the mental framework for what words mean and how language works. This provides the foundation for making the connection between oral and written language. Oral language starts in the home. Researchers Hart and Risley (1995) investigated the number and kind of words children heard in terms of socioeconomic status level (SES).

Average Number of Words Heard in an Hour by Socioeconomic Status (SES)

	Average Words per Hour
Low SES	616
Working Class SES	1251
Professional Career SES	2153

While the average numbers of words heard per hour for different SES groups show significant differences within themselves, multiplying those by the number of hours a child is awake per day and the number of days in a year results in dramatically different amounts. Thus, although all of the children who enter kindergarten might be roughly the same age, their knowledge of language and how it works could be very different based on their exposure.

Components of oral language:

- **Phonological awareness** is defined as a broad understanding of the sound of language and occurs as children begin to hear speech sounds and play with them.

- **Semantic understanding** involves understanding the morphology or meanings of words: vocabulary.

- **Syntactic understanding** involves the rules for using words in sentences: grammar.

- **Pragmatics** is defined as understanding the social and cultural use of language.

Phonological and Phonemic Awareness

Phonological awareness has several subskills. First, children should be able to distinguish spoken language from other environmental sounds. This includes locating the source of a sound, recognizing similar and different sounds, remembering sounds, ordering sounds and understanding the meaning of sounds. Phonological awareness also focuses on the structure of syllables in words (e.g., Which word is longer: *spaghetti* or *cat*? How many word parts do you hear in the word *apple*? What part of *television* and *telephone* are the same? In the word *potato*, what is the first/last sound you hear?) and on onset/rime tasks (Do these words rhyme: *men* and *ten?* Which word does not rhyme: *Cat, dog, rat?* Tell me two words that rhyme). As phonological awareness increases, children begin to develop phonemic awareness, the ability to think about and manipulate the smallest units of speech: phonemes. A phoneme is represented as a letter within slashes (e.g., */b/*). Phonemic awareness can be demonstrated in different ways as the chart below shows.

Examples of Phonemic Awareness

Type	Definition	Example
Phonemic isolation	Recognition of individual sounds	What is the first sound in *top*?
Phonemic identification	Recognition of same sounds	What sound is the same in these words? (*Top, ten, tall*)
Phonemic categorization	Recognition of similar sounds and choosing the different sound	Which word doesn't belong? (*Dip, dime, sun*)
Phonemic Addition/ Subtraction	Making a new words by adding or subtracting a phoneme	What word is *stop* without */s/*? What word do you get if you add */s/* to the beginning of top?
Phonemic Blending	Combining phonemes into a word	What word is */c/ /a/ /t/*?
Phonemic segmentation	Breaking words into separate phonemes	How many sounds are in *stop*?
Phonemic substitution	Replacing one phoneme with another to make a new word	What word is formed if the */t/* in *tap* is replaced with */m/*?

Alphabet Knowledge: The Alphabetic Principle

Once children understand how oral language works, they begin to connect that knowledge to print. Being able to recognize the connection between the spoken word and the written word is part of children's emerging reading and writing skills. During the emergent literacy period, children begin to understand that the printed word represents speech or can be examined and "turned into" speech. Shared reading can help children gain this understanding. As an adult reads aloud, children can join in with words, phrases, repetitions and sentences they recognize. In this way, they begin to make the connection between words printed in the book and the words they and the adult are saying.

Eventually, children realize that the funny squiggles—letters—on a page have individual meanings in terms of speech sounds. Alphabet knowledge involves understanding

the relationship between letters and sounds. This is called the **alphabetic principle**, or graphophonemic awareness. It refers to the understanding that written words are composed of letters (**graphemes**) and that groups of letters represent the sounds of spoken words. There are approximately 44 phonemes in the English language; however, since the alphabet consists of only 26 letters, there is not an exact one-to-one correspondence between letters and sounds. Some sounds can be made by more than one grapheme (e.g., *ph* and *f* both represent /f/), and the 26 letters combine in different ways to produce the needed sounds. For example, the letter *a* has different sounds in *pan*, *wan*, and *cane*. Alphabet knowledge is a precursor to **decoding**.

Decoding

Since the letters of the alphabet are used to encode speech sounds (words), decoding, then, is the application of the alphabetic principle to correctly say or read written words with understanding. Until children recognize and remember a word, they use word identification strategies to decode new words.

Word Identification Strategies for Decoding

Strategy	Definition
Phonics	Application of the alphabetical principle; using letter/sounds relationships
Analogical Word Reasoning	Use of words with the same onset or rime as examples
Syllabication	Breaking words into syllables
Morphemic Awareness	Dividing words into units of meaning

Ease of decoding contributes to comprehension. If students decode sentences one word at a time, they often lose track of meaning. Reading materials for emerging readers often has repeated words and short sentences to allow them to read with meaning.

Motivation

Motivation is defined as enthusiasm or the reason for a behavior. In terms of emergent literacy, it is both and is demonstrated when children show interest in print materials and enjoy them. Children are motivated to read when they understand that reading has a purpose. As a result, they then have more enthusiasm or desire to read. Motivators for emergent literacy include attitude of family and other adults, a sense of community and rewards. For example, when children see adults reading for information or pleasure, they are more inclined to copy that behavior. If they see other children reading or playing with books, they want to be able to read or play as well. If they get a feeling of success or enjoyment from literacy experiences, they are more likely to continue.

Text Structure

Books read aloud to young children are more likely to be fictional narrative stories rather than nonfiction informational text. As a result, the first text structure that children understand is narrative story structures, sometimes referred to as story grammar. Knowledge of narrative story structure includes understanding that a story has a beginning (e.g., *Once upon a time. . . .*) and an end (e.g. . . . *and they lived happily ever after.*). A story also has a setting, plot, characters, theme, and style. Understanding these text structures provides a framework for comprehension.

Written Language Development

As children make the connection between letters and reading, they begin to see that they can express their own ideas by writing letters. At first, they begin to notice that writing differs from drawing and they may randomly scribble on a page to emulate writing. Eventually, the scribbles will more closely approximate text in that they may be in rows that start at the top of the page and move from left to right. As children gain hand-eye coordination, they may begin to form random crude letters in groups to form an approximation of words. They may even be able to "read" what they wrote. Eventually, with assistance and practice, the letters become more regular. Children learn to copy words (e.g., their names) in preparation for copying patterned sentences (*I see a cat. I see a dog. I see a house.*).

Skill 1.2: Identify the Processes, Skills, and Stages of Word Recognition that Lead to Effective Decoding

How do children recognize words? Three models can be used to understand the processes, skills and stages of word recognition.

Bottom-Up Model of Word Recognition

Before children recognize words in print, they must recognize sounds (**phonological awareness**) and that some sounds represent speech (**pre-alphabetic stage**). As their ability to identify and manipulate speech sounds increases (**phonemic awareness**), they begin to realize that the sounds of words match the look of words (**partial-alphabetic**). Children eventually realize that the entire alphabet is the code for all speech sounds (**full-alphabetic**). **Phonics**, also called **graphophonemic** understanding, is the recognition that written letters (**graphemes**) represent sounds (**phonemes**). In the bottom-up model, children start on the page at the letter level. For example, combining /b/ /a/ /t/ forms the word *bat*. This method, in isolation, is slow and laborious.

Top-Down Model of Word Recognition

The top-down model suggests that decoding doesn't start on the page. Rather it starts in the reader's brain as the reader decodes connected text (e.g., sentences) rather than words in isolation. The reader uses background knowledge of how language works (syntactic understanding) and the "look" of words and meanings (**morphemes**) to decode meaning. Look at the following graphic to see how this works.

Did you read *I love Paris in the Springtime*? In reality, the sentence is *I love Paris in THE THE Springtime* with the word *the* written twice. If you missed the second *the*, you demonstrated top-down reading. No sentence in English uses the word *the* consecutively. You decoded the words in the sentence based on what made sense. Thus, reading started at the top with thinking rather than at the bottom with letters.

Interactive Model of Word Recognition

As readers increase their skills and abilities to decode words, they use both top-down and bottom-up processes in an interactive model. They "sample" enough text to gain meaning though the use of syntactic and semantic meaning: how language works and what meanings make sense in context. This allows the reader to gain speed and automaticity. However, the reader now uses a new skill—**metacognition**, or the ability to recognize when you understand and when you do not understand. If the reader (in top-down model) suddenly realizes that something was misread and doesn't make sense, the reader will reread more slowly and carefully (bottom-up) to check if the words that were "sampled" were actually correct.

Skill 1.3: Select and Apply Instructional Methods for the Development of Decoding Skills

Decoding skills involve **phonics** (blending sounds together), sight words (words that cannot be phonetically decoded) and **chunking** (breaking words into manageable parts for decoding).

Instructional Method: Phonics

Phonics emphasizes the association between the **grapheme** (the written symbol) and the **phoneme** (the speech sound). The phonics method also relates spelling rules to this process. Scientifically based research on reading instruction (National Institute of Child Health and Human Development, 2000) indicates that phonics instruction must be systematic (planned) and explicit (directly taught). Phonics gives children tools for decoding, or figuring out, how to read and pronounce words that they do not immediately recognize. Because the phonics approach involves phoneme-grapheme associations, auditory learners, those who learn best through the sense of sound, often prefer to read using phonics. Auditory learners can usually hear a sound and associate it easily with its printed symbol. The emphasis of phonics on sound-symbol relationships allows phonics readers to transfer their skills to spelling. Spelling involves associating sounds with letters. In a sense, it is the opposite of phonics, which associates symbols with sounds. Phonics readers often become good spellers.

Methods of Phonics Instruction

To help children learn phonics, many teachers find certain techniques for teaching the method helpful. Students should have opportunities to practice phonics rules and generalizations in context, and instructors should make every effort to illustrate the transfer of the phonics rules and generalizations to everyday materials and to other subjects.

In the beginning, students may read slowly as they decode words. Reading may be very slow as they laboriously sound their way through words in sentences. By the time they get to the end of the sentence, they may focus on the decoding to the detriment of comprehension. As students begin to commit high-frequency words to memory, reading speed and, in turn, comprehension will increase.

The following types of phonics instruction can be used in combination.

Types of Phonic Instruction

Synthetic Phonics	Converting letters into sounds and blending the sounds to form recognizable words
Analytic Phonics	Analyzing letter-sound relationships in previously learned words rather than pronouncing sounds in isolation
Analogy-Based Phonics	Using parts of already-known word families to identify new words with similar parts
Phonics Through Spelling	Segmenting words into phonemes and making words by writing letters for phonemes
Embedded Phonics	Learning phonics in the context of connected text rather than in isolation. *NOTE: This method is neither explicit nor systematic and should be used in combination with other methods.*
Onset-Rime Phonics	Identifying the sound of the letter or letters before the first vowel (the onset) in one syllable words and the sound of the remaining part of the word (the rime)

Sight Words

Sight words are generally defined as high-frequency words in reading. Some sight words are function words that are used to connect meaning (e.g., *a, the, to, what, could, then, there, was, were, an, which*). These are difficult to learn in isolation because their meanings are abstract. For example, *cloud* is easy to visualize whereas *could* is more abstract. Other high frequency words are commonly used words (*I, we, they, you, see, like*). Sight words can also be words that are not phonetically regular (e.g., *cough, tough, through, though, thorough, thought*). Direct instruction and practice of sight words (e.g., flash cards, context, word walls) are good ways for students to learn these high frequency words.

Chunking

Breaking a word into its parts is called chunking. By dividing a word into its syllables and sounding out smaller parts, students are often able to pronounce longer, unknown words that they previously did not recognize. There are many rules for dividing words into syllables; some of these rules are widely consistent across words, while other rules are not.

Children do not use all rules for chunking in their early years. Most add word endings to words that are already part of their sight vocabulary or word families. Some of the endings that children encounter first are the suffixes: *-ed, -s, -es,* and *-ing.* Experts have pointed out that six suffixes are responsible for a large percentage of structural variance across words: *-ed, -s, -er, -ly, est,* and *-ing.*

Examples of Simple Chunking

Separating the prefix and/or the suffix from the root word is an example of chunking. After separating these word parts, the child may be able to sound out the word. Examples include "untie" (un-tie), "repeat" (re-peat) and "ringing" (ring-ing).

Another important rule for chunking is the compound word rule. With this rule, the child divides a compound word into its parts. The child and the teacher can work together to sound out each part. Examples include "cowgirl" (cow-girl) and "baseball" (base-ball).

Two essential rules for chunking are *v/cv* and *vc/cv.* Teachers introduce these rules and encourage students in the later stages of reading development to employ these attack skills. To use the rules successfully, the child must first determine if each letter in a word is a vowel (v) or a consonant (c). The child can write the label over each letter in the word. Looking for the *v/cv* or *vc/cv* pattern, the child separates the word at the appropriate place.

Examples of the *v/cv* rule are "oven" (o-ven) and "body" (bo-dy). Examples of the *vc/cv rule* are "summer" (sum-mer) and "igloo" (ig-loo).

Examples of Complex Chunking

Rules of chunking such as the following are complex, useful, and best for older readers:

1. When *-le* comes at the end of the word and a consonant comes before it, the consonant goes with the *-le,* as in the words "purple" (pur-ple) and "bubble" (bub-ble). (An exception to this rule occurs when the word contains a *ck,* because one would not separate the *c* and the *k,* as in the word "pick-le.")

2. *-ed* forms a separate syllable if *d* or *t* comes before the *-ed,* as in "skidded" (skidd-ed) and "misted" (mist-ed).

Skill 1.4: Distinguish Among the Components of Reading Fluency

The Language Arts Florida Standards define *fluency* as "reading with sufficient accuracy and fluency to support comprehension." These are interrelated skills. The ability to read depends on quickly grasping the meaning of text, and the ability to grasp the meaning depends on the ability to quickly and accurately decode the words. Fluency involves four components: **accuracy**, **automaticity**, **rate**, and **prosody**.

Accuracy and Automaticity

Accuracy is the ability to both pronounce or sound out a word and also know the word's meaning. **Automaticity** occurs when a reader can identify words without conscious effort. Automaticity in word recognition can be thought of as a continuum that begins with the slow, struggling word recognition of a beginning reader and extends to the rapid, effortless word recognition of the skilled reader. Readers progress gradually along this continuum as a result of both instruction and practice. When a reader recognizes a word accurately on the first attempt, the reader can focus on the broader meaning of a passage rather than concentrating on decoding an individual word.

Rate

Rate refers to the speed at which a reader can read a specific text and generally refers to silent reading rate. Rate differs from automaticity in that rate can, and should, be a more conscious process. For young readers, their rate will be more constant because the levels of reading materials written for them may be very similar. However, as readers develop, they should be taught that background knowledge, difficulty of the reading content, and purpose also affect rate. Grade-level reading equivalents (e.g., 1st grade level; 4th grade level) often are determined by word and sentence length. Reading materials with longer words and sentences are, theoretically, harder to read than materials with shorter words and sentences. Purpose also affects rate in that skimming for a general idea and scanning for specific information are faster processes than reading deeply for critical understanding.

Prosody

Prosody refers to the rhythm, stress patterns, and intonations of speech. Expressive reading reflects skillful use of prosody. A fluent reader is able to stress key words, introduce pauses in appropriate places, raise or lower his/her pitch appropriately, and in many other ways bring a written passage to life when reading out loud.

Skill 1.5: Choose and Apply Instructional Methods for Developing Reading Fluency

Fluency can only occur through practice as readers move through the continuum of developing a reading vocabulary and automaticity. Fluency in reading aloud occurs through direct instruction and practice.

Initially, teachers might focus on developing fluency in reading single words (e.g., flashcards), sentence strips, easily decodable text (e.g., *The Cat in the Hat*), and immediate repeated readings of the same content. Oral verbal practice to develop fluency should use relatively easy and short passages so that the word recognition process is automatic. Depending on the content of the reading and a student's decoding skills, the student may be able to read on his or her own (**independent level**), with assistance (**instructional level**), or with difficulty (**frustration level**).

Level of Reading	Accuracy in word recognition	Instructional Implication
Independent	95% success (struggles with or misses an average of 1 word in 20)	Good choice for fluency practice
Instructional	90% success (struggles with or misses an average of 1 word in 10)	Can be used with teacher's or other adult reader's assistance
Frustration	< 90% success (struggles with or misses an average of more than 1 word in 10)	Should not be used for fluency work

There are a variety of instructional methods for developing fluency.

Methods for Developing Fluency

Teacher Modeling	Teacher demonstrates reading with automaticity and prosody as students follow along in their books or on projected content.
1-1 Reading	Student reads aloud to an adult.
Choral Reading	Students read aloud in unison from books or from projected content.
Recorded Reading	Students can record themselves digitally using a phone or software and playback to review their work. This is also a good way to help older readers who need to practice with simpler text. For example, a 5th grade teacher with struggling readers would partner with a kindergarten class. The 5th grade students would practice reading and recording simpler texts in order to provide an authentic service (digital recordings for kindergarten children to hear).
Partner Reading	Students read aloud to each other.
Readers' Theater	Students practice reading short plays or text rich in dialog. Depending on the number of "parts" in the material, this could be done in small groups with final performances for the whole class or another class.

While a teacher only knows if a student is reading fluently when the student reads aloud, silent reading also involves fluency and the goal of oral practice is to facilitate future silent reading. For some children, the act of reading aloud is more stressful than reading silently and they will make mistakes as a result of that stress rather than a lack of ability. No matter if reading occurs aloud or silently, the goal is always comprehension. If a student reads silently and can answer questions about what was read, the student was also reading fluently.

Although students should be encouraged to read when they complete their work or other spare moments, most classroom work should focus on oral reading for fluency practice. Teachers can allow students to choose books for reading at home. While the teacher should provide books at the appropriate grade level and guide students in selecting those that are at their independent levels, some children may select books that seem "too hard." Keep in mind that desire is a powerful motivator and, with assistance at home, the child may be able to read the book successfully.

■ Skill 1.6: Identify and Differentiate Instructional Methods and Strategies for Increasing Vocabulary Acquisition Across the Content Areas

The words of a language are its vocabulary. There are different types of words. Some words are general vocabulary words. Their meanings are the same for any subject. Examples of **general vocabulary** include *there*, *girl*, and *door*. General vocabulary can be further divided into well-known words and **academic vocabulary** (more complex words) such as *ignite, commit*, and *significant*. Some words are **technical vocabulary**. They apply to specific subjects. Examples of technical vocabulary in science would be *ion, atom*, and *phylum*. Still other words are general vocabulary words that have specific meanings in different subjects. These are called **specialized vocabulary**. For example, the word *set* has different meanings in math (*closed set*); drama (a *stage set*), astronomy (*sunset*). Thus, **content vocabulary** includes both technical and specialized vocabulary.

Additionally, all vocabulary a person knows can be divided into two broad groups: **receptive vocabulary** (words a person knows when they see or hear them) and **expressive vocabulary** (words a person uses in speaking or writing). A word must be in a student's receptive vocabulary before it can be used in his or her expressive vocabulary. In general, a person's listening vocabulary is largest because we are surrounded by speech. That's why a print-rich environment and environmental print are so important for young readers. It helps them link reading vocabulary words with listening vocabulary words.

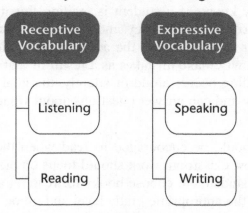

Vocabulary instruction consists of more than memorizing definitions. Vocabulary instruction includes efforts to make connections with the backgrounds of the students. Repeating vocabulary words and using them in meaningful sentences, as well as encouraging independent reading, will also enhance students' vocabulary development.

A variety of strategies should be used for vocabulary development. These include word walls as reminders of new vocabulary words as well as lessons about idioms, the use of dictionaries and glossaries, multiple meanings of words, figurative meanings, and categories of words such as antonyms, synonyms, and homonyms.

Although a lot of vocabulary is learned indirectly through listening and reading, direct instruction of both individual words and word learning strategies is critical to the development of content and academic vocabulary. Students acquire vocabulary best when the teacher explains the meanings of new words in context. Students should have ample opportunities and multiple exposures to review and use newly acquired vocabulary words, especially across different contexts and contents. Thus, students need several structured opportunities to use the words in speaking, writing, and reading. This allows them to progress from no knowledge of a word to a general understanding of a word, to the ability to use a word correctly in writing or speaking.

In many cases, there may be more words that could be taught than you have time to address with sufficient depth. You should probably focus on a solid understanding of a few words than a shallow understanding of many words. The key to successful vocabulary instruction is identifying which words to teach directly. To do so, ask the following questions:

1. Is the word important and necessary for understanding the content?

2. Does the word exemplify academic vocabulary?

3. Is the word repeated numerous times throughout the content?

4. Is the word's meaning difficult to understand?

5. Are students learning a new meaning for a known word or expanding the meaning of a word they already know?

6. Do students have strategies (e.g., structural analysis, context) that can help them identify the meanings of unknown words? If not, is this a good opportunity to teach or reinforce a strategy?

Word/Structural Analysis

Structural analysis is the understanding that words have parts that fit together and contribute to meaning. **Bases** or **roots** (e.g., *ject*-throw, *rupt*-break, *graph*-write; *bio*-life) form the essential meanings of words and generally have Greek or Latin origins. **Affixes** affect the meaning of the base. **Prefixes** (e.g., *un*-not, *dis*-apart, *re*-again) occur at the beginning of a word and change the meaning of the base. **Suffixes** (e.g. *tion*-state of, *er*-one who) occur at the end of a word and changes the word's part of speech. For example, the word *disruption* is the state of being broken apart. A *biographer* is one who writes about a person's life.

As a teacher identifies vocabulary words for direct instruction, the teacher can choose vocabulary with the same word part. For example, a reading passage that includes *formation, reaction,* and *communication* allows a teacher to point out the common suffix *tion* and then develop a vocabulary activity around that word part.

Context Clues

Context consists of the surroundings of an unknown word and context often provides clues to the meaning of the word. Each type is signaled by specific clue words.

Type	Clues	Examples
Punctuation	Commas, parentheses, brackets, dashes	Cognitive (mental) processes include analysis and evaluation.
Definition	*To, was, are, means, involves, seems, is called, that is, i.e., which resemble*	Peer tutoring involves students helping each other learn.
Comparison	*Similarly, both, as well as, likewise*	Federal as well as state and local taxes must be paid on time.
Contrast	*However, on the other hand, on the contrary, while, but, instead of, although, nevertheless, yet*	Digital natives grew up using technology; however, technology is new to digital immigrants.
Example	*Such as, like, for example, e.g.*	Graphic organizers, such as webs or fishbones help students organize ideas.

Author's Word Choice

'When I use a word,' Humpty Dumpty said in rather a scornful tone, 'it means just what I choose it to mean—neither more nor less.' 'The question is,' said Alice, 'whether you can make words mean so many different things.'

—Lewis Carroll, *Through the Looking Glass*

Author word choice is an important part of vocabulary development. For example, the words *fragrant, musty, pungent, rank, stinking* all describe odors, but in entirely different ways. There are also shades of meaning. For example, how are the words *humans, people, individuals,* and *persons* the same? How are they different? The exact word a writer uses can communicate important variations of a concept. Thus, students need to be aware of word use and how an author's choice of words impacts meaning. This concept can also be transferred to listening, speaking, and writing activities.

Skill 1.7: Identify and Evaluate Instructional Methods and Strategies for Facilitating Students' Reading Comprehension

Comprehension, or understanding, is the goal of reading. Comprehension instruction is an ongoing process that occurs before, during and after reading. Instructional methods should include direct instruction, modeling, application of skills in guided and independent practice, and cooperative learning. Additionally, teachers should encourage flexible use of the strategies individually and in combination.

Before readers begin a passage the teacher can help them identify purposes for reading and activate background knowledge. The teacher may also preview vocabulary or other parts of the text (e.g., title, graphics, setting, characters) and help readers make predictions about content based on the preview. As students read, the teacher can remind them to use comprehension and comprehension monitoring strategies. This will help students stay on track as they read. Teachers can periodically stop readers to ask questions or ask students to pose questions or call attention to text content or features. This helps students make connections within the text and between their background knowledge and text content. It also allows the teacher and students to check understanding for what is read. After students complete reading, the teacher can guide discussion of the content in terms of analyzing and evaluating content as well as applying and extending learning to other readings or real life situations. Finally, the teacher can ask students to summarize what they read verbally or in writing or complete graphic or semantic organizers.

The National Reading Panel identifies six instructional strategies, supported by research, that contribute to the development of comprehension Panel (National Institute of Child Health and Human Development, 2000). The teacher should provide direct instruction for each strategy with opportunities to apply, practice, refine, and assimilate the skill.

Comprehension Monitoring and Think Alouds

As active readers, students should always test what they understand against what makes sense. This requires them to think about their thinking and recognize when they are understanding what is read and when comprehension fails. This is called **metacognition.** For example, students are monitoring understanding if they can specify where comprehension fails (*I understood the first paragraph, but I got lost in the second paragraph.*) or if they can identify what aspect of comprehension is problematic (*I don't know the meaning of a _____ in the paragraph.*). Students also need to know how to resolve and "fix up" comprehension failures.

Fix up strategies include

- rereading at a slower pace to find specific information,

- looking up unknown words in a dictionary or identifying their meaning through context or structural analysis,

- restating what is read in one's own words, or

- reading on to see if additional information clarifies understanding.

Since comprehension is an invisible process, teachers can "think aloud" to model examples of comprehension failure and the use of fix up strategies. For example, the teacher could say, "I understood the first paragraph, but I got lost in the second paragraph. I will reread and summarize the first paragraph to make sure I understood it. Then I will reread the second paragraph more slowly to see if it makes sense. That helped, but I am still a little confused. Let me read on for a few paragraphs to see if the author clarified the meaning." Or, the teacher might say, "I don't know the meaning of a _____ in the paragraph. Let me look at the context and see if I can figure out the meaning."

Graphic and Semantic Organizers

If you've ever heard the phrase, *A picture is worth a thousand words*, you know the value of graphic and semantic organizers. **Graphic organizers** visually depict complex concepts and relationships among concepts. **Semantic organizers** also focus on relationships are a subset of graphic organizers. Although they are still pictorial, the focus of the relationships is on word meanings (semantics). Readers need to analyze and interpret the information within a graphic organizer. They can also complete blank organizers to structure their reading and thinking.

Examples of graphic organizers include:

- Maps

- Charts

- Graphs

- Diagrams

- Semantic Maps (also called concept maps or semantic webs)

- Clusters

Example of graphic organizer:

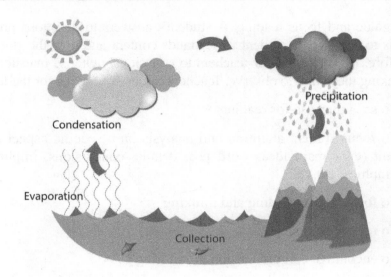

Example of semantic organizer:

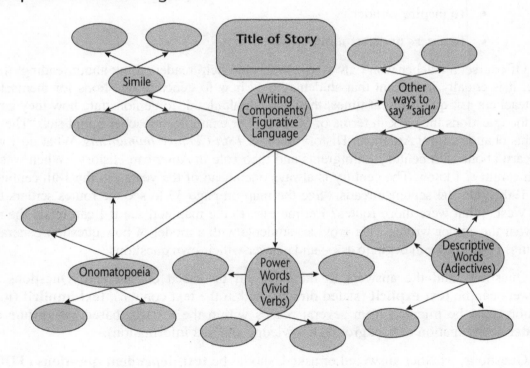

Questions: Answering and Generating

Questions guide and focus reading. A student's answers to questions provide a teacher with insights as to how well a student understands content and how the student is thinking about it; therefore, it's important for teachers to consciously choose questions according to the kind of thinking they want to observe. Teachers can use questions for the following goals:

- To set a purpose for reading

- To focus student attention and analysis on a specific aspect of content (e.g., main idea, word use, details, conclusions, implications, graphics, etc.)

- To foster active reading and thinking

- To review content

- To encourage comprehension monitoring

- To relate content to background knowledge

- To inspire wonder

- To assess understanding

Of course, a teacher won't always be around to help readers think about reading; therefore, it is equally important that students know how to generate questions for themselves. As teachers ask questions, at times, they can "think aloud" to demonstrate how they generate the questions they ask in terms of purpose. For example, a teacher might say, "The title of this chapter in my American History book is *18th Century Immigrants.* What do I want to learn about 18th century immigrants and their role in American History? When was the 18th century? I know. The century is always one ahead of the years. So the 18th century is the 1900s. Or, the sentence reads, "See the map on page 35 to see the routes settlers took out West. What were those routes? Let me turn to the map and see if I can relate the map to what the author wrote." This provides students with a model of how question generating occurs. Then, they can begin to ask—and answer—their own questions.

Questions and the answers to them should be based on the text. Questions and answers can be **text explicit** (stated directly within the text content), **text implicit** (information must be inferred from several places within the text) or based on **author and reader** (combination of background knowledge and text information).

Questions, whether answered or asked, should be **text-dependent questions (TDQs)**; that is, the student must use what is in the text to respond to or ask a question. In other words, if the student reads the poem *Casey at the Bat*, questions would focus on the information in the poem as contrast to asking, "*Have you ever played baseball? What was your experience?*" This is not to say that a teacher doesn't activate background knowledge. A teacher could ask those questions but follow up by asking, "*What was similar or different between your experience and Casey's?*"

Summarizing

Summarizing is a retelling of reading content in either written or oral form. This requires that readers understand the content and vocabulary, identify the main idea and key details and then, restate it in their own words. Teaching readers to summarize includes the following:

- How to find main ideas

- How to identify important information that relates to and supports the main idea

- How to eliminate redundant or unimportant details

- How to organize and remember ideas

Narrative Story Structure

"Once upon a time. . . . and they lived happily ever after—The end." These are some of the words that signal that a person is reading a story. Understanding the structure of a story helps readers organize the content of what they read. This helps them identify main ideas and supporting details. It also helps them ask and answer valid and relevant questions. Narrative stories include the following components:

- **Sequence** (organization with a defined beginning, middle, and end)

- **Characters** (real or imaginary; major and minor)

- **Setting** (location)

- **Plot** (what occurs)

- **Conflict** (problem to solve)

- **Climax** (high point of the story)

- **Resolution** (how the conflict is resolved)

- **Theme** (central meaning or application beyond the reading)

Expository Structures

Expository text is used to describe or reveal subject area content, such as math, history, science and other subjects. As students progress through grades, they encounter fewer readings with narrative story structures and more readings with expository text structures.

There are three types of expository structures:

1. **Sequence** shows facts, information or steps that occur in a specific order or time. Text clues include numbers, bullets, letters, or word clues, such as *first, second, then, next*, and *finally*.

2. **Cause-Effect/Problem-Solution** shows that one thing has an impact on or results in something else or a way or ways to resolve an issue or problem. Text clues include *because, resulting in, why* and *consequently*.

3. **Comparison/Contrast** shows similarities and/or differences among two or more things. Text clues indicating comparison include *like, same as, similar,* and *as well as*. Text clues indicating contrast include *differ, however, on the other hand,* and *opposite of.*

Skill 1.8: Identify Essential Comprehension Skills

Regardless of the content, readers need to possess several essential comprehension skills to read effectively. Finding **main ideas** allows students to identify the key point, whether stated or unstated. Readers can use narrative story, expository structures, and graphic and semantic organizers to help identify main ideas. Readers also need to know how to locate important **details and facts** directly or explicitly stated in the text. These are pieces of specific information that communicate or support the main idea and may include key vocabulary and other content. Drawing **conclusions** (also called **inferring**) allows a reader to read implicitly by making connections among different pieces of the text or between the text and what the reader already knows. Identifying the **author's point of view** is another important skill that contributes to comprehension. For example, authors write to inform, entertain, persuade or communicate in some other way. This changes the way a reader approaches the text and contributes, in part, to the reader's purpose for reading.

Skill 1.9: Determine Appropriate Uses of Multiple Representations of Information for a Variety of Purposes

Graphics represent information to visually organize and show relationships in data and facts. They also explain or make written information more clear. In some cases, graphics provide information in a format that would be hard to explain without their use.

Charts, tables, graphs, pictures, and other graphics are examples of materials writers use to present information. It is not unusual to find literally hundreds of graphic aids in a single textbook. Because printing a book is expensive, the reader should realize that the purpose of visual content is to organize and present complex or detailed information and to encourage interpretation.

A graphic can expand a concept, serve as an illustration, support a point, summarize data, organize facts, add a dimension such as humor to the content, compare information, demonstrate change over time, or otherwise extend information in the text. Graphics can also arouse and sustain interest, although the very features that do so may also prove distracting in some cases. The questions that teachers use to guide student reading can positively impact students' ability to focus on and clarify the information derived from graphics.

Many students initially skip over graphic aids or give them a cursory look. These students may not have been taught how to use multiple representations of information, in which case they may not appreciate how graphics extend the text. Even students who have some training in the use of graphic information may not transfer that knowledge to other content areas or they may have trouble going from print to graphics and back to print.

Teachers can help students use multiple representations of information by means of direct instruction and guided reading. Making use of overhead projectors or PowerPoint presentations can be helpful, as can pausing a video to discuss a particular graphic.

Types of Graphics

Type	Purpose
Table	Show relationships in information organized and labeled in rows and columns
Bar Graph	Compare and contrast quantitative values by showing the amount or quantity any item possesses
Line Graph	Shows quantitative trends for an item over time with each line on a graph representing one item
Circle Graph	Shows how a whole unit is divided into parts
Diagram	Depicts a simplified drawing of the appearance, structure, or functioning of something
Venn Diagram	Shows comparison/contrast relationships between or among sets of information
Flowchart	Show arrangement in terms of hierarchy of ideas or steps in a process
Timeline	Shows order in which events occur
Physical Map	Provides information about the topography or surface characteristics of a location (elevation, rivers, lakes, and so on)
Political Map	Shows location of constructed features such as capital and other cities, state or county boundaries or international borders; however, political maps also can show significant physical features such as oceans, mountains and/or large lakes and rivers
Photograph	Provide authentic, real-life views of a specific, time, place, object, event, or process

Skill 1.10: Determine and Analyze Strategies for Developing Critical-Thinking Skills Such as Analysis, Synthesis, and Evaluation

In 1956, Benjamin Bloom led a group of educational psychologists, who developed a classification or taxonomy of cognitive behavior important to learning. In 2001, one of Bloom's former students, Lorin Anderson, and his colleagues updated the taxonomy to reflect its relevance to the 21st century learning environment. The most significant change was the use of verbs instead of nouns to describe the different levels. Each level in the taxonomy depends on the one(s) below it. Although the higher levels involve critical thinking, the teacher should foster and develop critical thinking at all levels.

Bloom's Cognitive Taxonomy: Levels of Thinking

1. *Remembering:* This level concerns the literal representation of information in a text. Words that often elicit recall or memorized answers are *who, what, when, which,* and *where.*

2. *Understanding:* This level involves comprehension and concerns the meaning of both literal and inferred information.

3. *Applying:* This is a higher level of thinking that demonstrates the ability to use what is read in new and/or different situations.

4. *Analyzing:* This level concerns the ability to break down the parts or components of what is written.

5. *Evaluating:* This level involves making value judgments or decisions and very often involves the question "Why?" or a request to "Justify your answer."

6. *Creating:* This level involves putting information together in new, creative ways to synthesize knowledge.

A number of strategies are available to teachers for developing critical-thinking skills in the context of reading and reading instruction. The following strategies can be used to develop critical thinking skills:

- **Socratic Questioning:** This strategy is a method of questioning that focuses on aspects of thinking, such as clarification, assumptions, reasons and evidence, point of view, or implications and consequences.

- **Reciprocal Teaching:** In this strategy, students take the role of the teacher in small group reading sessions. Teachers model four strategies: summarizing, question generating, clarifying, and prediction;

then, students take turns assuming the role of the teacher in group discussions and practice of the strategies.

- **Literature Circles:** This strategy is a structured and student-centered version of book clubs for adults in which students read the same book and work collaboratively to discuss and analyze reading content. Groups are formed by book choice and use the book for application of reading and writing skills. Although the group is student-guided, the teacher can help structure the group by suggesting roles (e.g., summarizer, figurative language finder, fact-finder, illustrator, questioner, etc.) and by modeling skills for students to practice.

- **Problem-Based Learning:** Problem-based learning, also known as inquiry-based learning, starts with a question or problem provided and explained by the teacher. Students, usually in cooperative groups, explore and choose a strategy for resolution of the problem.

- **Contextual Learning:** In this strategy, information is presented using practical experience or simulations rather than theoretical perspectives so students apply what is learned to real-life situations.

- **Project-Based Learning:** In this strategy, students work for an extended period of time to investigate and work through a complex question, problem or challenge.

Skill 1.11: Evaluate and Select Instructional Methods to Teach a Variety of Informational and Literary Text

The Florida Standards for English Language Arts for elementary grades K-6 address both literary and informational text and are organized into clusters. The clusters that address text are the same for informational and literary formats. Any of the following cluster tasks can be used to teach informational or literary text. Grade-level standards inform the selection of specific strategies for a given grade level. Teaching readers how to accomplish each task involves direct instruction, scaffolding, guided and independent practice with a variety of texts and formative as well as summative assessment. Strategies should be applied in both print and digital formats, incorporate diverse learning styles, and include opportunities to speak and write.

Methods for Teaching Literary and Informational Texts

Cluster	Literary Text	Informational Text
Key Ideas and Details	• Ask and answer questions • Identify main idea and supporting details • Retell and summarize a story • Identify and describe character, setting, plot and other literary elements • Identify causes and effects within a story (e.g., character motivation, feelings) • Demonstrate literal and inferred meaning	• Ask and answer questions • Identify main idea or topic and supporting details • Retell and summarize information • Identify and describe aspects of text structure (e.g., comparisons/contrasts, causes/effects, sequence and so on • Identify connections within the text • Demonstrate literal and inferred meaning • Differentiate between firsthand and secondhand accounts
Craft and Structure	• Use context to identify word meaning • Recognize and differentiate among types of literary text (e.g., stories, poetry, drama) in terms of their structures • Identify role of author and illustrator in a story • Identify point of view and differences among points of view and how that influences the description of events • Ask and answer questions to clarify meaning of words and phrases • Identify how word choice supplies rhythm and meaning • Compare two or more versions of the same story, theme, topic, or genre • Distinguish literal from figurative or metaphorical use of language • Make connections between print and visual or performance versions of the same content • Quote accurately from a text	• Use context to identify word meaning • Describe difference between literary and informational text • Identify how to use text features (e.g., headings, table of contents, glossary) to locate information • Use print and digital text to locate information • Identify author's purpose • Identify meaning of general academic and domain-specific words • Distinguish their own point of view from that of the author • Quote accurately from a text • Analyze multiple accounts of the same information

Cluster	Literary Text	Informational Text
Integration of Knowledge and Ideas	• Describe book features or relationships between illustration and story • Compare and contrast elements of a story	• Identify reasons an author gives to support points in a text • Compare, contrast and evaluate information within a single text or between two texts on the same topic in order to respond in writing or speaking • Identify how graphics contribute to and clarify text • Describe connections within text • Interpret information presented visually, orally, or quantitatively and how it contributes to a topic • Use digital resources to find and answer questions or solve problems
Range of Reading and Level of Text Complexity	• Read prose (e.g. stories, poetry, drama, fiction) at grade level with purpose and understanding	• Read expository text (e.g., math, science, social studies, technical materials) at grade level with purpose and understanding

Competency 2: Knowledge of Literary Analysis and Genres

The power and versatility of language is reflected in literature. Novels, poetry, plays, essays, and other forms of literature are objects of study in their own right as well as a means of learning important information and ideas. The focus of Competency 2 is on the elements of literature and literary analysis.

Skill 2.1: Differentiate Among Characteristics and Elements of a Variety of Literary Genres

Fiction is a form of writing that describes imaginary people and events. **Nonfiction** is informational and based on factual accounts or opinion pieces on real events and people.

Differentiating among characteristics and elements of literary genres is important in the K–6 classroom because many reading materials in today's classrooms are **multi-genre** and include a variety of reading formats. For early readers, teachers need to describe the type of material that would be read. For example, the teacher might say, "Our story today is *The Cat in the Hat*. *The Cat in the Hat* is a fictional story. That means that it describes imaginary—or pretend—people or events. As I read the story and show you the pictures, try to figure out what makes it fiction." Intermediate readers might need a reminder of the type. For example, the teacher could say, "Today we are reading *Where the Wild Things Are*. Look at the pictures. Do you think this is going to be fiction or nonfiction? Yes. It is fiction. I will tell you that it is one of three types of fiction: It is either *historical fiction, fantasy,* or *realistic fiction*. By the end of the story, try to figure out which one it is." Scaffolding could help more advanced readers analyze content and draw conclusions about its genre. For example, "Today you will start reading *Charlotte's Web*. I am giving you a blank story concept map to help you determine the type or genre of the book. As you read the first chapter, identify who you think are the main characters. Identify the setting and time of the book. Make a prediction of whether you think it is fiction or nonfiction and explain your reasoning. Write a one-sentence summary of Chapter 1. This will be the start of your summary of the book. As you read each chapter, add another sentence. Finally, identify the theme of the book and the genre."

Fiction Formats, Descriptions/Elements and Examples

Type	Description/Elements	Example
Drama/Play	Writing in prose or verse for performance in a theatrical or reader's theater setting; emotions and actions are expressed through dialogue. Drama/play often enact well-known stories or books.	*Tiny Tim's A Christmas Carol; The Princess and the Pea*
Fictional Verse	Stories or novels in which the narrative is in the form of blank or other verse forms	*The Raven* by Edgar Allan Poe; *The Song of Hiawatha* by Henry Wadsworth Longfellow
Novel	Writing with a relatively long and complex plot developed through the thoughts and actions of characters; often divided into chapters and without art	*Harry Potter series; Charlotte's Web*
Picture Books	Illustrated story for children generally written in a simple and straightforward style	*Curious George; Where the Wild Things Are*
Poetic Verse	Literary works written in verse (rhythmical style or one distinguished by groups of lines arranged together in a single unit)	*A Light in the Attic; Winnie-the-Pooh stories; Green Eggs and Ham*
Prose	Writing or speech that is in a normal continuous form without the rhythmic or visual line structure of poetry	*The Velveteen Rabbit; Alexander and the Terrible, Horrible, No Good, Very Bad Day*

Type	Description/Elements	Example
Short Story	Differentiated from novels in terms of length; may vary in length.	*Jack and the Beanstalk; Cinderella; The City Mouse and the Country Mouse*
Classic literature	Literature that has become part of accepted literary canon and is widely taught in schools	*Huckleberry Finn; Goodnight, Moon; The Cat in the Hat*
Comic/Graphic Novel	Scripted story told in sequential, paneled pictures and speech bubbles	*Lunch Lady Series; Diary of a Wimpy Kid*
Fable	Use of animals who speak as humans to demonstrate a useful truth or moral	*Aesop's Fables (e.g., The Tortoise and the Hare; The Goose Who Laid the Golden Eggs)*
Fairy Tale	Story of fairies or other magical creatures	*The Ugly Duckling; Little Red Riding Hood*
Fantasy	Use of strange or otherworldly characters or settings	*Where the Wild Things Are; Alice's Adventures in Wonderland; Bridge to Terrabithia; Harry Potter Series*
Folktale/Folklore	Songs, stories, myths, and proverbs of a people or "folk" as handed down by word of mouth	*Goldilocks and the Three Bears; The Three Billy Goats Gruff*
Historical Fiction	Fictional characters in real, historical settings	*Island of the Blue Dolphins, Johnny Tremain*
Horror	Writing that causes feelings of dread, fear, or terror in the reader or the characters	*R.L. Stein's Goosebumps Series; Something Wicked This Way Comes*
Humor	Writing that is comical, absurd, or witty; meant to entertain or cause laughter	*Diary of a Wimpy Kid; Amelia Bedelia*
Legend	Imaginative old story, often passed down for generations, which may or may not feature a historical national or folk hero	*Casey Jones; Johnny Appleseed*
Mystery	Story that involves discovery of secrets or of unsolved crimes	*Encyclopaedia Brown, Boy Detective; From the Mixed-Up Files of Mrs. Basil E. Frankweiler*

(continued)

Fiction Formats, Descriptions/Elements and Examples

(continued)

Type	Description/Elements	Example
Mythology	Writing based on a culture's legends or traditional narratives about their ancestors, heroes, gods and other supernatural being; characters often reveal the cause and/or effect of human behavior and natural phenomena through symbolism	*The Myth of King Midas and the Gold; The Myth of Daedalus and Icarus*
Realistic Fiction	True to life writing that could actually occur	*Ramona Quimby; Because of Winn Dixie*
Science Fiction	Writing based on impact of actual, imagined, or potential science, usually set in the future or on other planets	*The Giver; A Wrinkle in Time*
Tall Tale	Humorous story with unbelievable or exaggerated elements described as if they were factual or true	*Paul Bunyan; Pecos Bill*

Nonfiction Formats, Descriptions/Elements and Examples

Type	Description/Elements	Example
Autobiography	True story of a person's life written by that person	*The Diary of Anne Frank; I Am Rosa Parks*
Biography	True story of a person's life written by another individual	*Neil Armstrong; Kobe Bryant*
Essay	Short composition reflecting the author's outlook or opinion	*Letter from a Birmingham Jail* by Dr. Martin Luther King, Jr., *Advice to Youth* by Mark Twain
Narrative nonfiction	Factual information presented in the form of a story	Little House Series; *Amelia Lost: The Life and Disappearance of Amelia Earhart*
Speech	Public address	*The Gettysburg Address;* Dr. Martin Luther King's *I Have a Dream Speech*
Reference Book	Writing used for information and facts about a word or subject organized alphabetically or by topic	Dictionary; Thesaurus, Encyclopedia; Atlas; Almanac

Skill 2.2: Identify and Analyze the Terminology and Intentional Use of Literary Devices

Literature (e.g., short story, drama, novel, poetry) is characterized by essential and nonessential elements. Literature must include theme (central idea), plot (events or action), setting (place of the action), character(s) (people or animals), and style (vocabulary and syntax).

These elements can be developed in a variety of ways. Helping students learn and use these words provides them with the tools for discussing or writing about what they read. As they read, they can analyze how the elements are developed. Understanding and using the terms also helps students become more precise in their thinking and writing.

Theme

The theme is the main point of a story. Three of the most common themes in traditional literature can be called the survival of the unfittest theme, the picaresque theme, and the reversal of fortune theme.

- *The survival of the unfittest theme* involves characters who face life-threatening situations yet manage to survive. Examples include the 18th century classics *Gulliver's Travels* and *Robinson Crusoe*.

- *The picaresque theme* features a roguish character (*picaro* is Spanish for "rogue"). Typically lowborn but clever, the rogue wanders in and out of adventures that take place at all social levels. Often punctuated by humor, picaresque stories are often intended to convey social satire. Examples include the classics *Don Quixote*, *Tom Jones*, and *Moll Flanders*.

- *The reversal of fortune theme* concerns the changing circumstance of a character or characters. Examples include the classics *Heidi* and *The Old Man and the Sea*.

Skilled writers often employ motifs to help unify their works. A motif is a story detail that recurs throughout the work and helps convey the theme. The *Nancy Drew* books, for example, rely on motifs such as lonely roads, ticking clocks, shadows, and empty houses. These motifs help convey to the reader the challenges and perhaps even dangers facing the detective as she tries to solve the mystery.

Plot

In most fictional genres, including novels, short stories, and plays, the plot is one of the most important elements. The events of the plot may or may not occur in chronological order. In some narratives, the plot carries the reader from the present to the past by means of a flashback. In other narratives, there may be hints of future events expressed by means of foreshadowing.

Plots can be described as either progressive or episodic:

- *Progressive plots* are observed when the reader must finish reading the entire work to find out how key developments in the plot are resolved.

- *Episodic plots* are observed when units in the narrative, such as chapters, constitute complete stories unto themselves.

Conflict is essential to interesting plots. The conflict can be with self, others, society, or nature. For example, in *Where the Lilies Bloom*, Vera and Bill Cleaver present a family of children who are fighting society and its rules in order to remain together. In *The Chocolate War*, the main character, Jerry, faces conflicts with himself as well as with the rest of the school community over whether to sell chocolate.

A plot will also be interesting if there is an element of suspense, such that the reader is unaware of the outcome of the story until the end. For instance, in *The Island of the Blue Dolphins*, the reader does not know until the end of the book whether the main character, Karana, will stay on the island.

Sensationalism is when the plot turns on a series of exciting and unusual events. *Hansel and Gretel* is an example of sensationalism in traditional literature, in that the plot turns on the abandonment of children, the prospect of their being eaten by a witch, and so on.

The plot of a narrative leads to a denouement or the ending of the narrative. There are two types. A closed denouement occurs when all of the reader's questions about the plot are answered, while an open denouement occurs when key questions are unanswered.

Setting

Narratives in every genre of fiction and most genres of nonfiction present a setting. The setting—the time and place of a narrative—may be realistic or fictional, unusual or ordinary. In addition, settings may either be backdrop or integral.

- A *backdrop setting* is not essential to the plot. For example, the setting in many of the Nancy Drew books is a backdrop setting because the plot could have unfolded in almost any American city.

- An *integral setting* is essential to the plot. In *The Life of Pi*, the story would not make sense unless most of the events took place out on the open ocean.

Settings can also be used in a symbolic way. In *Lord of the Flies,* the setting of the island has symbolic importance to the themes Golding develops about human nature. Being remote from civilization, the island becomes a stage where "human nature" gradually expresses itself.

Characters

Characters are the individuals in literature. They are most often people or animals; however, they can be imaginary creatures or even inanimate objects (e.g., cars, houses, robots) who have human attributes. They may be major characters who play a significant role in the plot or they may be minor characters who provide detail to the plot. Following are some key distinctions in the treatment of characters:

1. *Round versus flat.* A round character is fully developed, meaning that much is known about the character's external and internal life. A flat character is not extensively developed; consequently readers know little about him or her.

2. *Dynamic versus static.* A dynamic character undergoes some kind of change during the course of the story. Static characters do not change in significant ways.

3. *Protagonist versus antagonist.* In a narrative, the protagonist struggles for someone or something, while the antagonist is the enemy or rival that the protagonist is struggling against.

Stock characters exist because the plot demands them. For instance, the ball scene in *Cinderella* must include many men and women who do nothing more than attend the dance.

A character can be a stereotype, without individual characteristics. For instance, in many fairy tales, the oldest daughter is ugly and mean, while the youngest daughter is beautiful—outside and inside. A sheriff in a small southern town, a football player who is all brawn, a librarian clucking over her prized books, or the cruel commandant of a prisoner-of-war camp might all be stereotypic.

Characters often serve as foils for other characters, serving to help the reader see the novel's other characters more clearly. A classic example is in Mark Twain's *The Adventures of Tom Sawyer*. Tom is the romantic foil for Huck Finn's realism. In Harper Lee's *To Kill a Mockingbird*, Scout serves as the naive observer of events that her older brother, Jem, comes to understand from the perspective of the adult world.

Some characters are allegorical, standing for qualities or concepts rather than for actual personages. In C.S. Lewis's *The Lion, the Witch, and the Wardrobe*, the Lion stands for goodness rather than representing a specific lion.

Writers use a variety of means to reveal characters to the reader:

1. The writer may tell the reader directly about the character.

2. The writer may describe the character in his or her natural surroundings.

3. The writer may show the character in action.

4. The writer may provide examples of the character's distinctive manner of speaking.

5. The writer may reveal the inner thoughts and feelings of the character.

6. The writer may describe the character's outward appearance.

7. The writer may quote others from the story discussing the character.

8. The writer may show how others react to the character.

Whatever methods are used to reveal character, the careful writer avoids stereotyping. Stereotyping is typecasting someone by characteristics such as nationality, religion, size, age, or gender. In traditional literature, for example, female characters engage in less critical problem solving, lead more placid lives, and depend on males for support and survival, particularly in times of crisis. Some teachers who discover stereotyping in a juvenile book may wish to exclude it from the required reading lists for their classrooms. Other teachers may make a point of including such books as a way of helping students become aware of stereotyping and encouraging students to critically evaluate what they read.

Style

Stories can be differentiated according to their plots, characters, topics, themes, motifs, and settings, as well as by the style of the writing. Stylistic differences are easy to spot when comparing relatively diverse writers such as Jane Austen (formal and mannered), Mark Twain (casual and colloquial), and Ernest Hemingway (spare and driven).

Analysis and identification of intentional use of style is complex because most authors use a variety of **literary devices** within a single piece of writing to develop their work. Literary devices are techniques for varying form and word choice in writing. Just as understanding the elements of fiction allows readers to think and communicate more exactly, understanding the literary devices that affect style provides students with additional tools for understanding an author's meaning and other ways to communicate that understanding in writing and speaking. Style is affected by form and word choice.

Form affects the organization of writing. An author may vary **syntax** (grammar) depending on the target age group. Writing for young children uses simpler sentence structures, whereas writing for more advanced readers includes more complex and compound sentences. The level of details is another way that writers vary form. This can, in some cases, make literature more complex and difficult to understand. Authors can use a straightforward narrative form or include **dialogue** (spoken speech of characters). **Narrative voice** or **point of view** allows a writer to tell a story from different perspectives. For example, in **first person voice**, a story is told from the perspective of a single character using *I/We* or *me/us* as pronouns and the content is based on what that person knows, thinks, does, sees, or hears from another character. In **third person voice**, the story is told from the point of view of someone who narrates the story based on what is seen, heard or experienced. The narrator cannot tell anything about the thoughts of the characters; however, an **omniscient voice** does have knowledge of the thoughts of other characters.

Word choice and usage also impacts style. Writers choose **literal language** when they want to use words according to their proper meanings. Words that are used literally have standard meanings in different contexts. The intended meaning is the same as the actual meaning. However, **figurative language** allows writers to add variety and interest through the use of words as an intentional departure from their standard meaning.

Common Types, Descriptions, and Examples of Figurative Language and Literary Devices

Type	Description/Elements	Example
Alliteration	Repeated use of words with same initial sound	"The *wicked witch* of the *west went without* a *whimper*."
Allusion	Brief reference to a subject matter such as a place, event, or literary work by way of a passing reference. It is up to the reader to make a connection to the subject being mentioned.	"I tried a lot of different chairs: *some were too big; some were too small, but I finally found one that was just right!*"
Euphemism	Use of a milder or more positive phrase rather than a more literal or harsh phrase	*"This was not your best work on the test"* versus "You flunked the exam."
Hyperbole	Extreme exaggeration	"I'm so tired I could *sleep for a 100 years!*"
Imagery	Use of words to engage the senses	The lush, green landscape was dotted with blooming flowers whose aroma perfumed the air.
Irony/Sarcasm	Use of words or phrases whose intended meaning is the opposite of the literal meaning.	The mom looked at the puddle of spilled milk on the floor and thought, *"Great! This is just what I needed today!"*
Metaphor	Comparison in which one thing is described as another.	That dog is *a real gem*.
Onomatopoeia	Use of words whose sound is representative of that made by an object	The bee *buzzed*. The boy rang the doorbell, *ding-dong*.
Personification	Inanimate object is given human characteristics	The *sun smiled* on the little village.
Rhythm	A pattern of stressed and unstressed words	A government *of the people, by the people, for the people*.
Simile	Comparison using the word *like* or *as*	Paul looks *like a rumpled pile of sheets* in the morning. The day was *as hot as a firecracker*.
Symbolism	Use of a word or phrase that has come to stand for an idea or concept	*Green* represents freshness, newness, or inexperience. The *bald eagle* represents the United States. The *dove* represents peace.

Skill 2.3: Evaluate and Select Appropriate Multicultural Texts Based on Purpose, Relevance, Cultural Sensitivity, and Developmental Appropriateness

Literature for children is a window through which they view the world. For this reason, it is desirable for children's literature to reflect the diversity of the world's peoples in terms of culture: values, way of life, beliefs and patterns of thinking (Jenkins and Austin, 1987). Multicultural diversity also takes the form of gender, age, sexual orientation, socioeconomic group, or other factors. The variety and kind of multicultural literature has increased in availability so teachers now have to make informed choices about what multicultural readings to use in their classroom. Choice is based on **purpose, relevance**, **cultural sensitivity,** and **developmental appropriateness**.

One of the first factors in evaluating and selecting multicultural literature depends on the purpose or objective a teacher wants to achieve by its use. Purposes and objectives are varied; however, a teacher might want to increase awareness, promote feelings of community, or provide opportunities for students to see the world from other perspectives. Purpose is also related to relevance or importance of the material. A school librarian or other teachers can often share examples of what has worked best for specific age groups. You can also refer to published book lists and reviews for advice. Cultural sensitivity is another consideration in choosing multicultural literature. Cultural sensitivity is the awareness that no culture is superior to another culture and that that differences among peoples or cultures is not positive or negative or right or wrong. Finally, any form of literature should be developmentally appropriate in reading level, complexity, and content. The focus of multicultural literature for young children might be about folktales from different countries or stories with characters who are approximately the same age as the children in the class. Multicultural literature for upper elementary students could address more serious or complex issues, such as war, oppression, or discrimination.

The following questions can help a teacher determine what to select:

1. Does the reading provide insights into groups or individuals in different historical times or places as well as in contemporary situations?

2. Would reading literature that mirrors a specific group or culture represented in the teacher's class give students opportunities to relate to similar experiences and backgrounds, develop strategies to cope with similar problems, identify with and increase pride or interest in their inherited culture or identity?

3. Does the material help students learn more about shared likenesses and differences?

4. Does the material help students understand world diversity and cultural contributions of different groups and individuals?

5. Will the materials contribute to a sense of shared pride as members of a family, community, and the world?

6. Does the material portray realistic, authentic, and objective understandings of another group or culture rather than a stereotypical or inaccurate representation?

7. Does the material represent the extent of diversity in the United States and the contributions of other cultures as assets to American society?

8. Can the material be used to demonstrate the cultural origins of folktales, legends, songs, or other concepts?

9. Do illustrations and artwork support accurate and representative reading or advocate stereotypical and inaccurate interpretations?

10. Is this material the most relevant choice?

11. Is this material culturally sensitive?

12. Is this material developmentally appropriate?

Use of Multicultural Literature

Cultural pluralism involves the acceptance of the distinctive characteristics of all cultures, including one's own. Teachers can heighten students' appreciation of cultural pluralism through literature-related activities such as the following:

1. Give students the opportunity to examine a situation through several viewpoints. For example, *Faithful Elephants* requires the reader to consider war through its impact on animals, particularly the animals in Japan. *Sadako and the Thousand Paper Cranes* enables the reader to consider war through the eyes of an innocent child. *Maniac Magee* asks the reader to consider prejudice in America through a child's eyes.

2. Invite members of the class and community to share their diverse backgrounds.

3. Establish a cooperative work environment in the classroom and school.

4. Explore the history of rhymes, riddles, superstitions, customs, symbols, chants, songs, foods, dances, and games reflecting a variety of different cultures.

5. Identify and read authors who describe different cultures.

6. Compare and contrast the "melting pot" view with the "salad bowl" view of American society.

7. Study successful individuals who represent various cultural groups.

8. Engage in culturally specific activities after reading stories of other cultures. For example, experiment with writing Haiku or make origami cranes after reading *Sadako and the Thousand Paper Cranes* or experiment with rope rhymes after reading Eloise Greenfield's poem "Rope Rhyme."

Exceptionalities and Children's Literature

Schools have progressed from ignoring children with special needs, to isolating children with special needs in special schools, to providing separate classrooms for these students within public schools, to mainstreaming the students into regular classrooms, and finally to including those with exceptionalities in the "regular" class. Because biases and prejudices sometimes exist as a result of or even before inclusion, teachers must help construct a working environment that meets each student's basic needs, including a feeling of belonging, a feeling of safety, and a place where each student feels loved and accepted.

Children's literature can show others how it feels to be different in some way and can emphasize that everyone has the same basic needs. For instance, "Crow Boy" helps students understand what it is like to be excluded because of being "different." "The Flunking of Joshua T. Bates" explores the impact that failing a class has on a student. "Discoveries" provides numerous biographical sketches of successful people who are deaf. The book establishes effective role models, discourages labeling, and presents individuals who have overcome obstacles in their lives.

Bibliotherapy—giving the right book to the right child at the right time or treating problems with books—can be helpful in constructing a cooperative classroom. Students might read and discuss books such as *I Have a Sister; My Sister Is Deaf* or *The Summer of the Swans*, which concern deafness and academic problems, respectively. These books and others can serve as springboards for discussions of exceptionalities.

Multicultural Poems and Poets

Teachers can include poetry of all cultures in their classrooms. For example, Cynthia Rylant has written many poems on growing up in the Appalachian Mountains. Charlotte Pomerantz writes about her winters in Puerto Rico. Louise Bennett writes of Jamaica. Javaka Steptoe emphasizes the African American experience. The Japanese Haiku is a type of poetry that is particularly suited to the elementary classroom because of its brevity.

Sexism

Despite Title IX and substantial publicity on the topic, students and teachers sometimes witness or perpetuate sex discrimination in educational settings. To keep students from taking discrimination for granted, it is helpful to raise their consciousness about sexism in American society.

Useful activities in this regard include role playing, having students look at key situations through several viewpoints, inviting successful community members of both sexes to visit the classroom, establishing a cooperative work environment in the classroom, and exploring the contributions of males and females in history. Books like *Focus on Women* provide activities, biographical sketches, and insight into the contributions of women to America.

Exploring the contributions of individual women to society is another valuable tool in handling sexism. One of many examples is *Harriet Quimby: America's First Lady of the Air*. When coupled with the suggested activities in the accompanying activity book, the class can engage in lively discussions and learning experiences.

Another helpful tool is recognizing that sexism may play a role in older children's books that are still used in educational settings. In the early 1970s, Suzanne Czaplinski conducted a study of picture books that won the Caldecott Medal. The researcher counted each appearance of a male or female in the text and in the pictures and calculated the number of males and females in each. Among Czaplinski's findings were that males outnumbered females both in the text (65% vs. 35%) and in the pictures (63% vs. 37%). Surprisingly, the percentage of females in the books decreased from 1950 (51%) through the 1960s (23%).

To find out if there had been changes since Czaplinski's study, Davis and McDaniel conducted a study with the help of their students based on the prediction that females would appear more frequently in Caldecott Medal winners after 1972, the year that Congress passed Title IX as part of a federal law to promote (if not guarantee) sex equity in education. Furthermore, sex discrimination was an emerging political issue in American life, feminism was on the rise, publishers were issuing guidelines for sex-neutral language, and women were outpacing men in college (and professional) school admissions as well as in academics. Surely, Caldecott winners from 1972 through 1997 would reflect a quarter century of social change.

When Davis, McDaniel, and their students compared their results to the earlier study conducted by Czaplinski, they discovered the following:

- There was very little change in the percentage of male vs. female characters in the text of Caldecott winners from 1972 through 1997. The percentages were 61% vs. 39%, respectively, as compared with Czaplinski's finding of 65% vs. 35%.

- There was also very little change in the percentage of males vs. females in the pictures of Caldecott winners from 1972 through 1997. The percentages were 65% vs. 35%, respectively, as compared with Czaplinski's finding of 63% vs. 37%.

- In the 1990s, 39% of characters in Caldecott winners were females, a slight decrease from the 1980s.

- The percentage of females appearing in texts of Caldecott winners never exceeded that of the decade of the 1950s, when 51% of the characters were females.

Davis, McDaniel, and their students were perplexed that the decade of the 1950s remains the golden era for representation of females in the text of Caldecott winners. The findings show that, in some ways, sexism is still a part of children's literature. The mere awareness of this fact can raise teachers' and students' consciousness and serve a purpose. The informed teacher can help make students aware of sex discrimination, modify the curriculum, and teach acceptance of others.

Skill 2.4: Identify and Evaluate Appropriate Techniques for Varying Student Response to Texts

Some students spontaneously connect with literature, while others make connections only after some degree of scaffolding and encouragement. The following eight comprehension strategies may not only help students understand what they read but also promote thoughtful and useful responses to the reading:

1. *Predicting.* Making predictions requires readers to develop informed guesses about what will happen; they can then determine whether their predictions were accurate or not.

2. *Connecting.* Making connections requires readers to relate texts to their own lives, to the world, and to other materials.

3. *Visualizing.* Visualization requires students to create mental images of what they are reading.

4. *Questioning.* Questioning activities requires students to answer literal, interpretive, critical, and creative questions that they ask themselves or that their teachers might ask.

5. *Identifying.* Identification requires students to recognize major points of information as they read, such as plot, topic, and theme.

6. *Summarizing.* Summarization requires students to restate key points in concise summaries, reports, dioramas, posters, plays, or other forms of expression.

7. *Monitoring.* Monitoring is performed by teachers and the students themselves to ensure that the latter understand what they are reading and can use the appropriate techniques (decoding, context clues, picture clues, sight words, etc.) if they are having difficulty.

8. *Evaluating.* Evaluation activities require students to think about and evaluate what they read as well as the experience of reading.

9. *Representing.* Using graphic or semantic organizers to represent elements and relationships provides a scaffold for students to use when making sense of content.

10. *Dramatizing.* Readers Theatre and role playing provides a kinesthetic way for students to respond to reading.

11. *Making Art and Music.* Students can create two- and three-dimensional representations (e.g., drawing, collages, sculptures) when responding to what they read. They can also write or choose songs to express reactions to what they read.

12. *Creating Content Using Multimedia and Digital Tools.* As digital natives, today's students frequently create and share digital content using infographics, presentations, animation, comic generators, blogging, wikis, and other Web 2.0 tools.

Competency 3: Knowledge of Language and the Writing Process

At one point, reading was thought to be primarily a precursor of writing; however, the development of reading and writing are now more closely linked. As a result, instruction in one area necessarily involves skills and experiences of relevance to the other. Competency 3 focuses on the writing process.

Skill 3.1: Identify and Evaluate the Developmental Stages of Writing

If you ever compared the writing of a first-grade student to that of a sixth-grade student, you've noticed they differ vastly. The difference is the result of writing development that occurs through physical growth in cognitive and motor skill development. Some of the physical characteristics involve the following:

- **Small Motor Development** of muscles in the fingers and hand to form letters or use a keyboard

- **Mental Attention** to the task and monitoring of how a writer thinks and focuses on ideas

- **Semantic and Syntactic Language Knowledge** based on listening and reading experiences and instruction

- **Memory** in terms of the writer recalling experience to express it in writing

- **Thinking Skills** for synthesizing, analyzing, and evaluating information for writing and refining what is written

Children progress through the stages of writing development at different rates depending on physical and other personal characteristics including effects of teaching and practice. In general, writing develops in stages.

Developmental Stages of Writing

At each stage, the student should demonstrate grade-level appropriate skills with increasingly complex writing assignments for diverse genres and subject areas as follows:

- Writing clearly and effectively

- Writing in various forms for different audiences and purposes

- Applying the steps in the writing process

As students develop, they gain greater understanding and use of the **six traits of writing:**

- **Ideas:** Knowledge of content to fit the task

- **Organization:** Structure of ideas to fit various forms, audiences, and purposes

- **Voice:** Individual style

- **Word Choice:** Effective communication of meaning with general, specialized, technical and academic vocabulary; use of precise words, figurative language and transitional phrases

- **Sentence Fluency:** Flow and sentence variety

- **Conventions:** Usage of correct spelling, punctuation, and grammar

Writing requires other language arts skills: speaking, listening, and reading. Understanding the general progression of writing skills and the grade-level state standards for writing in language arts enables teachers to screen for potential writing difficulties, pinpoint specific problems, and intervene accordingly. The following table outlines the general progression of stages of writing by grade level:

Approximate Grade Level	Stage Description
Pre-K (age 1–3)	Children may make random marks or drawings on a page as "writing," but the marks have no meaning.
Pre-K (age 4–5)	As children make the connections between sounds and letters (alphabetic principle), they begin to try to copy or write letters.
K–1	Students realize that writing shows communication of thoughts. They understand the meaning of "author" and can write the alphabet in isolation and use the alphabet to write words and simple sentences. They can also dictate stories to be written and read.
1–2	Students increase fluency of writing and can write paragraphs using semantic and syntactic knowledge.
2–3	Students continue to increase in fluency and can analyze and evaluate their own writing in terms of the 6 traits of writing.
4	Students can vary writing style according to task, purpose, and audience.
5	Students can demonstrate all writing traits and edit for those traits. They can also narrow or expand writing content as needed.
6	Students can demonstrate mastery of writing traits across content areas and complete complex writing tasks including research and synthesis of ideas.

Skill 3.2: Differentiate Stages of the Writing Process

In the early 1970s, teachers were very concerned with spelling and punctuation in students' papers. The teacher did all the "correcting" and watched carefully for grammatical, spelling, and punctuation errors. In the late 1970s, many writing experts argued that students' compositions were too dull. The schools began to foster creative writing and encouraged teachers to provide students with regular opportunities to do so. However, many teachers began to view creative writing activities as lacking in structure. Process writing has since become a popular alternative to unstructured writing. The stages of process writing are often described as follows:

1. *Prewriting Stage.* During the first stage of the writing process, students begin to collect information for the writing that they will do. The student selects a topic, considers the audience and purpose, and begins brainstorming lists of events, experiences, and/or key details. The student will also engage in organizational activities.

2. *Drafting Stage.* During this stage, the student begins to compose. The student should ask whether the writing fits the intended audience and purpose. The class resembles a laboratory at this point. Students may consult with one another and use various books and materials to create their drafts. At this stage, the students should not worry about spelling and mechanics.

3. *Revising Stage.* During the revising stage, the student will polish and improve the composition. The student can continue to ask whether the writing fits the audience and purpose, whether his or her thoughts and feelings are conveyed, whether the organization is appropriate, and whether the composition flows smoothly when read aloud.

4. *Editing Stage.* During the editing stage, students correct their own writing as well as the works of others. After self-evaluations, as well as evaluations and constructive criticism from classmates and teachers, the students rewrite their compositions.

5. *Publishing.* In some classes the students publish their own works and even have an author's chair from which they can share some things about themselves, discuss their writing process, and read their compositions aloud. Research studies suggest that the most effective writing process includes at least the pre-writing, composing, revising, and editing stages.

Skill 3.3: Distinguish Among Modes of Writing

Writers choose their mode of writing based on the kind of impact they hope to have on their audiences. Writing can serve many different authorial needs, including narration (personal and fictional), description, exposition, and persuasion. Students need to be aware of, and to practice, these modes of writing.

Mode	Purpose	Description
Personal Narrative	To entertain or interest	Fictional or nonfictional account of an individual's feelings or experience typically written in first-person and in chronological order
Fictional or Creative Narrative	To entertain or interest	Writing created from imagination which has a typical plot structure and features; can also include descriptive writing and use of dialogue
Descriptive	To inform	Information about a fictional or nonfictional person, place, thing, event or idea
Expository	To inform	Information about a content topic such as math, history, science and so on
Persuasive	To convince	Information written to prove or argue a point, to select someone or something, or to support or challenge an idea or statement

Skill 3.4: Select the Appropriate Mode of Writing for a Variety of Occasions, Purposes, and Audiences

The writer must consider the audience, the occasion, and the purpose when choosing the mode of writing.

Audience

The teacher can designate an audience for students' writing. Knowing who will read their work allows students to think about modifying the writing to suit their intended readers. For instance, a fourth-grade teacher might suggest that the class take their compositions about a favorite animal to second graders and allow the younger children to read or listen to the works. The fourth graders will realize that they need to employ simple vocabulary, to avoid grammatically complex sentences, and to use print-writing rather than cursive when they write for their younger audience. The fourth graders would produce somewhat different compositions for the teacher or an administrator at a local zoo.

Occasion

The occasion also has an impact on the elements of the writing. The language of a piece of writing should fit the occasion. Formal writing is needed for formal occasions, while a casual tone is suitable for casual occasions. Young writers will learn that particular words may have certain effects, such as evoking sympathy or raising questions about an opposing point of view. Students can work together and/or work with their teachers to think about the kinds of language and organization that are suitable for each occasion.

Purpose

As noted earlier, the purpose of a piece of writing helps to determine the mode (narrative, expository, descriptive, persuasive, or speculative) as well as other aspects of the writer's language. Students will learn about the differences between writing a business letter, a communication with the residents of a retirement center, and a thank-you note to parents, for example.

In selecting the mode of writing as well as the content, the writer might ask the following:

- How interested is the audience in the topic?

- How controversial or emotionally charged is the topic?

- What would the audience need to know to understand you or to be persuaded your position?

- What is the audience most likely to disagree with?

- What common knowledge does the audience share with you?

- What background information do you need to share with the audience?

The teacher might wish to have the students practice selecting the mode and the language by adapting forms, organizational strategies, and styles for different audiences and purposes.

Skill 3.5: Identify and Apply Instructional Methods for Teaching Writing Conventions

The purpose of writing is the same as speaking: communication; however, in the beginning stages, children sometime find writing frustrating because their writing skills lag significantly behind speaking skills. In other words, they often know what they want to write but lack the fine motor skills, memory, or knowledge of spelling or other conventions to translate that into writing.

Writing instruction should always be provided as precursor skills. Before writing letters, a child must recognize letters. Before spelling a word, a child must arrange letters into a word or recognize the correct spelling of a word from given choices. Before learning capitalization, a child must understand how speech works (e.g., a proper name, what is a sentence, titles) and recognize and produce visually different uppercase and lowercase letters. Before using appropriate grammar and word choice, a child must hear or read content that demonstrates appropriate usage and word choice.

In general, writing instruction should be taught as a form of communication in sync with the other language arts (reading, speaking, and listening) with practice embedded in social contexts. While practice is critical, it should be meaningful and authentic. For example, language experience (using the students' own language and experience to generate writing) is a good means of scaffolding writing practice that integrates reading, listening, and speaking. This approach usually follows a shared class experience (e.g., a field trip, a stormy day, hands-on lab, classroom visitor) in which the teacher writes what students say to form a story or description. Students can then read or reread the story and copy or add details. Collaborative and cooperative learning incorporates other language arts skills so children are writing, reading aloud (speaking), listening, editing, and reviewing for each other. Technology is a great way to incorporate writing by having students write a blog or journal entry, use web 2.0 tools, and write the character equivalent (140 characters) of tweets.

Conventions are commonly accepted rules of appropriate behavior; therefore, writing conventions apply the following standard rules of spelling, capitalization, punctuation, syntax, and word usage.

Spelling. Spelling can taught through a combination of phonics and sight words with direct instruction of specific spelling rules and mnemonics (*i before e except after c or when sounded like a as in neighbor and weigh*). Encourage students to use a variety of sensory modes to practice spelling (looking at the letters, saying letters aloud, listening to someone spell the word aloud, writing the letters) followed by visualization. Word walls, banks, and lists provide spelling support as well.

Capitalization. Although some children may figure out which words should be capitalized through observation and reading, most require direct instruction of capitalization rules such as capitalizing proper names, first words of sentences, important words in titles and so on.

Punctuation. Although some children may discern the function of some forms of punctuation, most students will not. The abstract nature of punctuation makes it ideal for direct instruction and wall posters, desk notes, or bookmarks that provide examples of usage.

Syntax. Each language has its own syntax (also called grammar): written and unwritten rules for arranging words into sentences. While writing can reflect regional variations or dialect, the goal of writing is standard English. Learning proper use of syntax in writing standard English depends on exposure to proper use of standard English when listening, speaking, and reading. Syntax is generally based on the parts of speech.

Parts of Speech	Use	Examples
Noun	Name of person, place, thing, idea	*teacher, town, car, freedom*
Pronoun	Replaces nouns	*I, we, you, they, us, them*
Verb	Shows action or being	*run, count, is, were*
Adjective	Describes a noun or pronoun	*big, red, hot, sad*
Adverb	Describes a verb	*quickly, smoothly, completely*
Article	Determiner that precedes a noun	*a, an, the*
Conjunction	Join ideas	*and, but, or*
Preposition	Shows relationships between nouns and other parts of a sentence	*in, on, out, to*
Interjection	Expresses surprise or emotion	*oh! ah, wow,*

Word Usage. Word usage requires reading and listening vocabulary. Students can't use words they don't know. After learning vocabulary words, students need to apply them in meaningful ways through writing and speaking.

Skill 3.6: Apply Instructional Methods for Teaching Writer's Craft Across Genres

Writing has no content of its own; rather, writers must write about something. Beginning writers often write short stories and descriptive writings based on familiar experiences or imagination. However, as students progress into upper grades, they increasingly read more diverse genres and expository information with technical, specialized, academic, and general vocabulary. This knowledge must be reinforced and reflected in writing opportunities within different subject areas and genres to allow students to refine their skills for using precise language (e.g., using the word *stanza* rather than *paragraph* in describing poetry), figurative language (e.g., similes, metaphors, personification), and dialogue.

Complexity of writing should increase as students incorporate transitional phrases (e.g., linking words to add detail, reference, summarize, draw conclusions or serve other functions) and temporal words to show the progression of time, movement, or sequence.

Craft is defined as skill proficiency. Students cannot increase writing skills without an opportunity to read and listen to content from different genres and content areas. They must also have meaningful and authentic practice with timely and valid feedback. Students must realize that writing is a skill that can be learned, practiced, and improved and that proficient writing rarely results from a first draft. Students should see competent writers (e.g., the teacher) think aloud as they work through the stages of the writing process.

Competency 4: Knowledge of Literacy Instruction and Assessments

Based on Florida's Language Arts Standards, literacy instruction focuses on development of speaking, listening, reading, writing, and language. Teachers identify learning outcomes and create lessons based on standards. Assessment determines the success of past instruction by meeting learning outcomes and informing future instruction of daily practice and long-term planning. Given a variety of instructional methods and styles, there are many ways to assess learning. Competency 4 focuses on understanding both assessment and literacy instruction.

Skill 4.1: Distinguish Among Different Types of Assessments and Their Purposes and Characteristics

With a variety of purposes and characteristics, assessments can be categorized in many ways. The following sections describe assessments in terms of timing and purpose.

Initial Assessments

Screening assessments are often given either individually or as a group before a student begins a course or grade. The results determine if the student is cognitively or academically ready to succeed and if additional programming or support will be needed. **Diagnostic tests** are standardized tests that pinpoint a student's specific reading strengths or weaknesses. These are usually administered based on teacher observation or screening test results to determine if additional support or remediation is required.

Formative Assessments

Formative assessments are ongoing and informal, such as quizzes, exit-ticket, feedback prompts (*The muddiest point. . . . ; My biggest question about today's lesson. . . .*), student response to informal questions, classroom or individual discussions, results of practice or homework, and teacher observation. Their purpose is to provide immediate real-time feedback to the teacher and learner about the status of learning so instruction can continue as planned or be modified. Most formative assessments are either ungraded, used for participation points, or have comparatively small point values. Informal assessments are also described as **criterion-referenced** (demonstrates mastery of learning objectives) or **performance-based/authentic** (application and demonstration of skill beyond traditional testing through completion of a complex task, such as a longer writing assignment, science project, speech, presentation, or performance). These are not normed exams and are used to determine if learners met identified instructional goals and standards. As such, formative assessments are integral to the instructional cycle. To be useful, formative assessments should clearly align with standards and lesson outcomes. Teachers should analyze and use the results to provide specific feedback to students and to inform and guide future instruction.

Summative Assessments

Summative assessments take place at the end of a unit or grade to determine if instructional goals and learning outcomes were met. While a **unit exam** might be created by a teacher or from textbook supplements, a **common exam** might be created by a group of teachers for the same content or grade. Most summative assessments are **formal, standardized assessments.** These are commercial assessments that have been consistently tested with controlled populations. Such tests are **norm-referenced,** meaning that the assessment was tested with a variety of socioeconomic levels and at different geographical areas so that the average scores represent the **norm.** Standardized tests measure overall achievement in a specific area, such as reading, and are used to draw statistically valid conclusions about group and individual performance in reference to the norming group. Results are reported as **standard scores** such as **percentile rankings.** For example, if a student scores at the 90 percentile, that means the student scored better than 89% of the population used for standardization, with 10% of the testing population scoring better than the student. **Stanine scores,** similar to the percentile ranking concept, divides scores into nine ranges: midrange scores of 4–6 indicate average skills; 1–3 are below average; 7–9 are above average. **High-stakes tests** are summative assessments whose purpose is accountability. Results from such tests are used at the federal, state, or local level to decide whether a school and its teachers are effective and if students have reached learning goals.

Skill 4.2: Select and Apply Oral and Written Methods for Assessing Student Progress

There are a variety of formative assessments for evaluating student progress in various elements of literacy. Monitoring progress on a frequent and ongoing basis helps teachers identify where instructional modifications and/or interventions need to occur for individuals, small groups, or the class as a whole. This fosters increased student achievement in literacy skills.

Pretests

When given to a class of students before a lesson or unit, pretests determine a student's starting point, or baseline, on a specific topic or skill. The pretest is not calculated in the student's grade because it may or may not be content the student knows. Rather, the results help the teacher determine if the skill needs to be retaught, refined, or omitted from instruction. Results can be compared with post-test assessments to determine progress.

Informal Reading Inventories (IRI)

Given individually, an IRI provides specific information about a student's skills in terms of word recognition in isolation, oral reading and fluency, silent reading, comprehension, and listening comprehension. This allows the teacher to customize reading instruction to meet the student's individual strengths and weaknesses. The IRI can be given at the beginning of the year to refine instructional goals or at the end of the year to monitor progress. It should also be given to transfer students or to students who are demonstrating reading problems. Although commercial IRIs are available, teachers can also create them from typical reading materials; however, the inventory should include fiction and nonfiction passages and content both above and below grade level. The assessment should begin with a word list or passage that the student demonstrates mastery. This allows the teacher to identify a student's independent, instructional, and frustration levels. Because the test is administered individually, the teacher gains qualitative information from a **miscue analysis** as well as quantitative information about results. For example, a word or phrase that is incorrect (**miscue**) but doesn't change the meaning is not the same kind of error as a word or phrase that does not semantically or syntactically make sense. A student who makes a mistake and then self-corrects is demonstrating metacognitive skills. A student who demonstrates better comprehension of fiction than of a content-specific passage might have deficits in technical or specialized vocabulary.

Level	Characteristics
Independent	• Student can read without teacher assistance. • Oral reading is fluent with word accuracy of 99% or above. • Silent reading is free from finger-pointing and subvocalization. • Comprehension is 90% or higher.
Instructional	• Student can read without teacher assistance. • Oral reading is 85% accurate for grades 1–2 or 95% accurate for grades 3–6. • Comprehension is 75% or higher for both oral and silent reading.
Frustration	• Oral reading lacks fluency and student cannot read without teacher assistance. Body language may indicate difficulty or tension. • Word recognition in isolation or passages is less than 85% in grades 1–2 or less than 90% in grades 3–6. • Comprehension is less than 50%.
Capacity/Potential	• In listening comprehension, capacity indicates the level at which a student's comprehension is 75% or higher.

Fluency Check

Fluency checks are administered individually to assess oral reading in terms of accuracy, rate, and prosody. They can either be timed readings of statements followed by true-false questions for comprehension or 1-minute readings. The result is either words per minute (WPM = # words × 60/number of seconds or words correct per minute (WCPM = number of words – number of errors (X-E) × 60/number of seconds. WCPM targets are estimates for fluency development. While oral reading fluency is important, an individual student's fluency performance may be affected by anxiety or other factors.

Sample Fluency Targets by Grade

Grade	Beginning of Year WCPM	End of Year WCPM
1	50	80
2	50	90
3	80	115
4	100	120
5	100	130

Story Retelling

Before students learn to read, they are often asked to retell a story as a measure of listening comprehension. Story retelling uses that principle with stories that the student reads orally or silently. Additionally, the teacher should provide feedback by **active listening** during the retelling and occasionally paraphrasing what students say to check comprehension and understanding.

Portfolios

Portfolios are collections of student work over a period of time. In literacy, this would include formative and summative examples of writing and reading (e.g., writing based on fiction and nonfiction reading) and demonstrating different styles (e.g., narrative, descriptive, persuasive), spelling, writing samples, graphic organizers, and other tests. Portfolios often provide a more balanced view of student performance because they are based on various artifacts. Additionally, they can exemplify student progress. Portfolios of work and student grades or results of formal assessments are useful for family-teacher conferencing.

Running Records

A running record is a quick individual assessment of oral reading fluency in which the teacher codes each word the child reads. Using a separate page for each student, the teacher marks the page as the student reads aloud. This provides a graphic representation of a student's miscues for analysis. For example, correct words might be designated with a check mark and repeated words with an "R."

Anecdotal Records

Anecdotal records are a form of informal assessment based on observation. They include notes about a student's behavior and should be made during or shortly after the observation. The notes may provide clues for analyzing student performance. For example, you might note that a student demonstrates good fluency when reading from a page, but does not demonstrate fluency when reading information posted on a wall or a board. Or, you could notice that the child is always sleepy and performs poorly on Monday but not on other days of the week. Without judgments or conclusions, you can bring this to the attention of a parent or a fellow school professional. For example, perhaps the child reading from the board across the classroom needs glasses for distance vision. Perhaps the sleepy child stays up late on weekends but has a regular bedtime on other days.

Rubrics

A rubric is both a checklist to help writers identify writing objectives and a tool for grading or scoring writing according to the objectives. Rubrics identify key elements of the assignment as levels of competency across each element and assign scores or point values to the levels. This allows the teacher to clearly set standards and then determine if students reach those. The rubric provides teachers with a consistent format for assessing qualitative work to reach a quantitative score.

Writing rubrics differ according to grade level and writing task. For example, an element for assessing writing for a kindergarten student might be accurate letter formation, whereas that would not be a relevant element for most upper-elementary students. Typical writing rubrics generally focus on developmentally-appropriate aspects of the 6 writing traits.

 ## Skill 4.3: Analyze Assessment Data to Guide Instructional Decisions and Differentiate Instruction

Assessment data is a key component of the Florida State Department of Education "Just Read, Florida!" program. The goal is for every student to read at or above grade level based on the **Florida Formula for Reading Success** which is:

$$6+4+ii+iii = \textbf{No Child} \text{ Left Behind}$$

The components of the formula are:

6 Instructional Components: (1) *Oral Language*, (2) *Phonemic awareness*, (3) *Phonics*, (4) *Fluency*, (5) *Vocabulary*, and (6) *Comprehension*

4 Forms of Assessment to Guide Instruction: (1) *Screening* to identify students who need additional instruction; (2) *Progress monitoring* to determine if children are making adequate progress within the current instructional environment (3) *Diagnosis* to determine their specific instructional needs; and (4) *Outcome measures* to guide instruction.

(ii) Initial Instruction in All K–3 Classrooms. Initial instruction in reading within elementary classrooms should integrate the six components. Instruction should be differentiated according to the needs of individual students in terms of background knowledge, motivation, and skills. The classroom should maintain a print-rich environment and instruction should be explicit and systematic. The teacher should scaffold instruction and emphasize connections among the language arts: reading, writing, listening, and speaking.

(iii) Immediate Intensive Intervention. As the result of ongoing monitoring through formative and other assessments, the classroom teacher or other instructional personnel should provide additional and/or different instruction and practice as soon as possible. This prevents a child from falling behind and can include interventions, such as extended time, flexible grouping, instructional accommodations, and additional monitoring or diagnostic testing.

■ Skill 4.4. Analyze and Interpret Students' Formal and Informal Assessment Results to Inform Students and Stakeholders

Assessment results aren't just for teachers to use in planning instruction. They also help students and stakeholders (e.g., parents, guardians, etc.) understand progress toward and attainment of learning outcomes. This requires that teachers create a system of ongoing communication and strategies to ensure that results are communicated in meaningful ways.

Providing Informal Assessment Results

Informal assessments of content such as quizzes, essays, projects, and other work are created by the teacher or obtained from textbook resources. Results usually take the form of a letter grade (e.g., A, B, C, D, F), numerical score (e.g., percentages, items correct), graded rubric, and/or written comments about an assignment.

Results and feedback always should be shared with students using language appropriate for the grade. This includes the purpose of the assessment and how it contributes to the learning outcomes and overall grade. If the majority of the students did well on an informal assessment, the teacher can complete an item analysis to determine which specific questions were missed and review those missed items with the entire class. However, if some students experienced significant problems on an assessment, the teacher should discuss the results with each student individually. This allows the teacher to gain insights about the student's strategies and lets students learn from their mistakes. Additionally, individual feedback should include information about what the student did well and what the student needs to do to improve.

At the beginning of the year, the teacher should establish the method(s) by which informal assessment results will be communicated to stakeholders. This can include work sent home, notes on student planners, electronic grades on a district or school grade management system, email and/or text messaging.

Providing Formal Assessment Results

Formal assessments include state exams, results from diagnostic tests, or other standardized tests. Results are often provided online or in more technical individual reports. Because their results are often reported in less familiar ways, the teacher may need to explain results. Thus, the teacher needs to understand fully assessment terminology and scoring. Teachers may need to conference with stakeholders and their students individually to discuss results and implications of formal assessments. When meeting with stakeholders and students, the teacher should:

- start with information that shows a student's strengths or relative strengths before addressing the student's weaker areas.

- connect student performance on informal assessments to scores on formal assessments.

- provide specific and concrete suggestions for improving content success (learning strategies) or testing performance (e.g., test anxiety; preparation).

Skill 4.5: Evaluate the Appropriateness of Assessment Instruments and Practices

Because students are individuals, there's no one-size-fits-all assessment. A single assessment often provides incomplete information about a student's knowledge and abilities because individual students may have personal variables (e.g., family instability, social issues, anxiety, illness and so on) that affect performance on a single test on a given day. Thus, multiple forms of assessing skills over time are better than a single assessment given on a specific day and time. Assessments should always be aligned to standards and reflect instructional context. As in the story of *Goldilocks and the Three Bears*, the goal is to use an assessment that is "just right" and provides information that can be used for confirmation or change of instructional practices. Once the assessment is completed, there should be little delay between evaluating the work and providing feedback to students and modifying instruction.

Assessments of any type should be **reliable** and **valid**. Reliability refers to the consistency of results. Validity refers to how well a test measures what it is supposed to measure. Formal, norm-referenced tests are carefully assessed to determine that the results they give are both reliable and valid. However, these are considerations for classroom teachers as well. Perhaps a teacher decides to create two forms of a test to prevent cheating. If students who randomly get Form A score significantly better than students who randomly take Form B, reliability could be an issue in that the tests were not equivalent.

Or, if a teacher's objective is for students to identify main ideas, a test over the details or vocabulary of the plot would not be valid because what was measured was not what was taught or learned.

 ## Skill 4.6: Select Appropriate Classroom Organizational Formats for Specific Instructional Strategies

With a goal of 90 instructional minutes devoted to reading, teachers should have a variety of organizational formats depending on instructional purpose and student needs. Using a single organizational format neither engages students for the full length of time nor differentiates instruction appropriately.

Whole Group Instruction

Whole group instruction is a good way to start a lesson, but should be brief based on the age group of the students. Attention span is generally about the same as the age of the learners. Thus the attention span of a first grade student might be 5–7 minutes, while the attention span of a fifth-grade student might be 10–12 minutes. Whole group instruction within an appropriate timeframe might become more of a mini-lesson that includes a brief introduction, activation of prior knowledge, direct instruction, and use of media (e.g., video clip).

Small Group Instruction

Small group instruction, generally 5–7 students, should focus on additional or different instruction, guided practice, reinforcement, and review. To do small group instruction, students should be in a cluster around the teacher who can see the entire class past the small group. Grouping should be flexible so one individual might be in one group to work on advanced vocabulary, but a different group for work on writing errors. A teacher doesn't want a student to always be in the "low" group.

Reading Workshops

Reading workshops build on the writing workshop tradition of instruction. Reading workshops develop skills and reading enjoyment. They also integrate writing with reading instruction. As in the writing workshop model, a reading workshop begins with a direct instruction mini-lesson (whole or small group) that focuses on a single strategy or skill termed the "*teaching point*." This lasts 10–15 minutes depending on student age and attention span. Following direct instruction, students are actively engaged by practicing the skill independently or with partners. The teacher conferences with individual students or partners to coach skills and provide feedback on practice. The workshop concludes with written responses to the workshop in the form of journaling, reflection, demonstration of skill, or formative assessment.

Literacy Centers

Classroom centers are specific classroom locations (e.g., designated tables) created for the purpose of guided or independent practice. Most classrooms have several centers. The centers can focus on different subject areas (e.g., math center, science center, etc.) or they can focus on different areas of literacy development (reading center, writing center, listening center). Centers can be changed throughout the year as new topics are introduced and mastered or as students need additional practice and review. After instruction (e.g., whole group, small group, workshop), students are assigned to a center for a specific time period while the teacher works with a small group.

Learning Partners/Reading Buddies

Learning partners are usually peers within the same grade who may or may not be on the same reading level. They work together on the development and practice of skills and often focus on oral reading. Reading buddies uses the same principle, but with students from different grades. For example, a fifth-grade student's buddy might be a first-grade student. Before partnering older and younger students, make sure that the older student wants to participate and that the older student has been given guidelines about how to work with the younger student.

Literature Circles

Literature circles for children are like book clubs for adults. They provide natural opportunities for student-guided and independent practice through discussion of the book's content. A circle is a temporary group of approximately 5–7 students defined by what the students want to read. A classroom might have several circles of varying size with each group reading a different book. Students in the circle have regular times to meet and discuss what has been read. The teacher serves as a facilitator, not an instructor. However, students may assume or be assigned specific roles (e.g., *word finder* for new vocabulary; *fact checker* for information; *interrogator* to ask questions, *linker* to draw conclusions, *recorder* to take minutes or summarize thoughts; and a *facilitator* to lead discussions) that rotate each time the group meets. The roles allow students to separate those processes and work on them one at a time with group feedback. Assessment is based on teacher observation and student self-reflections.

Skill 4.7: Evaluate Methods for the Diagnosis, Prevention, and Intervention of Common Emergent Literacy Difficulties

Emergent literacy, as defined in Section 1, consists of reading-related knowledge and skills that develop prior to formal reading instruction and include print motivation, print awareness, listening and oral vocabularies, narrative skills, letter knowledge and phonological awareness. Problems with emergent literacy consist of gaps or limited skills in one or more of the literacy components due to lack of exposure, language differences, or developmental disability. Because these skills form the foundation of future reading success, early childhood professionals, and kindergarten teachers should be proactive in identifying children at risk through observation and informal assessments. For example, a teacher should immediately notice if a student seems unfamiliar with using books, does not identify letter names, cannot write his or her name, is unable to retell a simple story, or follow up with an assessment to diagnose specific reading problems. Structured opportunities to develop these skills should focus on both the sound and look of language and also integrate reading and writing. Reading and writing should be both environmental (natural exposures in authentic contexts), and the focus of direct instruction, or repeated and intensive practice.

Competency 5: Knowledge of Communication and Media Literacy

Language arts skills include speaking and listening as well as reading and writing. Additionally, 21st century learners must be able to use these skills in digital as well as traditional formats. Competency 5 focuses on both communication and media literacy.

Skill 5.1: Identify Characteristics of Penmanship

With the increase of digital formats for writing, there is growing debate about the efficacy of penmanship instruction; however, the ability to use fluent and legible handwriting skills is still part of the Florida Language Arts Standards. Penmanship in early grades depends on eye-hand coordination and use of small motor movements. Handwriting will predictably be labored and imperfect in appearance as students learn to decode and encode the symbols of language.

Teacher feedback and practice in meaningful communication formats improves the following characteristics of penmanship.

- **Alignment**—horizontal placement on the page from left to write with a common base

- **Letter formation**—use of shapes of the alphabet (circles, horizontal lines, vertical lines, and slanted lines) in creating letters

- **Line quality**—consistency in smoothness, color and pressure without obvious visual differences (too light, too dark, pressing too hard on the page)

- **Spacing**—consistency of space between among letters, words, sentences, and lines

- **Size**—uniformity in writing uppercase and lowercase letters

Skill 5.2: Distinguish Between Listening and Speaking Strategies

The importance of listening and speaking are emphasized by their specific inclusion in the Florida Language Arts Standards:

- **Cluster 1:** Collaboration and Comprehension

- **Cluster 2:** Presentation of Knowledge and Ideas

The first standard in Cluster 1 requires students to *prepare for and participate effectively in a range of conversations and collaborations with diverse partners, building on others' ideas and expressing their own clearly and persuasively.* Speaking and listening are key skills in that they allow an individual to both receive information and communicate ideas. The strategies that support one tend to support the other, and effective use of one typically requires effective use of the other.

Listening

Listening is the process of making sense of oral language. It is a process of constructing meaning by attending, anticipating, predicting, focusing, visualizing, making connections, generalizing, and evaluating.

Listening is not a passive process. Effective listeners actively engage what they hear, isolate key points, and make note of anything that seems incomplete, confusing, and/or contradictory. A good listener can identify the general nature, as well as the details, of what the speaker is saying in order to prepare an appropriate response.

Active Listening. Active Listening is the single most useful and important listening skill. Active Listening, as the name suggests, is not the mere acknowledgment that someone else is talking. Rather, during Active Listening, one indicates genuine interest in what the other person is thinking and feeling. Active Listening involves restating or paraphrasing what the other person is saying. This allows one to check whether the other person has been understood, and it allows the other person to verify or correct the listener's understanding. It also allows the speaker to feel understood and thus more confident in expressing him- or herself.

Speaking

Speaking allows students to express themselves, to negotiate relationships, to give definition to their thoughts, and to learn about language, themselves, and their world. Following are some of the most important speaking skills:

1. Questioning. Good questions are the key to good communication, as they support both speaking and listening.

2. Paraphrasing. The goal of paraphrasing is to restate an idea in your own words while retaining the meaning of the original idea. Although paraphrasing is a speaking skill, it plays a key role in listening (as in the case of Active Listening), and effective listening is required in order to generate accurate paraphrases.

3. Extemporizing. Through extemporaneous speech, individuals express their own thoughts and feelings rather than asking about or restating the thoughts and feelings of others. Effective listening is required in order to know when extemporaneous speech is appropriate and to determine the appropriate length and content of what is said. Good extemporaneous speech also requires a mastery of vocabulary, grammar, and diction.

Promoting Voice

In oral expression, voice refers to the effective use of such elements as diction, tone, syntax, unity, coherence, and audience to create a clear and distinct "personality" as one speaks.

To promote the development of voice, students can be encouraged to pay attention to the basics of oral expression. For example:

*   Say it so we can hear it.

*   Look at the people you are talking to.

*   Say it so that it is exciting.

*   Say some parts fast and some slow.

*   Stop at the right places.

To illustrate these basic principles, teachers can read one or two paragraphs to their students in a soft monotone, with poor expression, averted gaze, and inappropriate pauses. Students can then be asked whether the presentation was interesting or enjoyable to listen to, and they can brainstorm ideas for improving the quality of the reading.

Skill 5.3: Identify and Apply Instructional Methods (Collaborative Conversation, Collaborative Discussion, Presentation) for Developing Listening and Speaking Skills

Listening and speaking instruction is often overlooked since students already know how to hear and talk. However, listening differs from hearing and speaking differs from talking. Both are active processes of communication involving thinking as well as intention.

Several factors affect a student's willingness and ability to communicate in listening and speaking. These include the following:

- Lack of instruction
- Unclear directions
- Lack of background knowledge, vocabulary, or grammar skills
- Effect of emotions (shyness, fear, intimidation)

Strategies for promoting listening and speaking include the following:

Games

Verbal games such as *I Spy*, *Pass the Whisper*, *20 Questions*, *Role Play*, and *Simon Says* help younger students learn through play.

Collaborative or Partners Learning

Small-group or partner learning are good strategies for students who feel uncomfortable speaking up in the entire classroom. It is important that group size and membership or partners change frequently. This helps students learn to communicate with different speakers and listeners, and prevents one partner or group member from overtaking the conversation. Additionally, students need more direction than "Get in a group and do this activity." They need to know how they are expected to interact with each other in order to complete the activity. This may be a good opportunity to develop skills such as turn-taking (an object used as a talking stick held by the speaker; timer), asking good questions, contributing or elaborating on an idea, and appropriate use of body language and voice (e.g., no eye-rolling or raised voices, nodding to show agreement, eye contact). The teacher can also assign group roles (notetaker, summarizer, questioner, leader, fact checker and so on) which should be rotated for each activity. Once a small group or partners complete their work, one person from the team can verbally report to the rest of the class.

Informal and Formal Presentations

Informal and formal presentations share more commonalities than differences. Many students panic when they think of formally presenting to the class. This fear can continue throughout their lives. Speaking, both formally and informally, should be natural. Informal presentations can start with group reports and paired reports before students are asked to give individual reports. Students might gain confidence in presenting to small audiences (e.g., one small group or team presenting to another).

Avoid "putting students on the spot." That is, students should have some confidence that what they say is correct. Teachers can pre-teach vocabulary and provide incomplete outlines to help students scaffold ideas before speaking. Students can also write responses before sharing them.

Using Guided Imagery

When students listen to presentations that include visual images, they can be encouraged to form mental pictures that help them remember while listening. This process of creating and updating mental images is a useful listening skill.

LAPS

The acronym LAPS stands for listen, ask, picture, and summarize. LAPS is a simple listening strategy that involves both listening and writing. Before students listen to a speaker, they generate two or three questions and record them. They picture what they hear in response to their questions and quickly sketch that out. They then summarize what they have heard in a paragraph.

SLANT

Another simple listening strategy is referred to by the acronym SLANT, which stands for sit, lean, ask, nod, and track. To use this strategy, students are taught to sit up straight, lean forward slightly, ask questions, nod their heads, and track the teacher. This strategy engages the student in the listening process at a variety of levels.

Listening Guides

Providing students with a framework or guide for listening can help them focus on the listening task and the purpose for listening. These guides can be prepared by the teacher or by both the teacher and the students and tailored to the specific purpose for listening.

Partner Retells

For partner retells, students form groups and read a story independently. Each member thinks about the key elements of the story and one member is designated to retell the story to the group. After the storyteller finishes, the listeners go through their books and place a note on any pages or details that the storyteller included in the retell.

Following are some general strategies that teachers can use to promote oral expression:

- Engage students in oral communication activities that reflect a variety of settings: small group, one-to-many, one-to-one, and so on.

- Create oral communication activities designed to achieve specific purposes, such as to inform, persuade and/or solve problems.

- Guide students in oral communication activities that exercise basic competencies needed for everyday life: giving directions, asking for help, requesting clarification, brainstorming, discussing class topics, and so on.

Paraphrasing Activities. Teachers can ask students to use their own words to restate the main ideas, themes, etc., of various kinds of writing. The teacher can also place a limit on the number of words to be used by students. For example, students can be asked to describe the main character of a story in 20 to 25 words. Students may work on these activities individually or in small groups.

Oral Storytelling

Storytelling often relies on familiar verses, stories, riddles, and jokes with humor and surprise endings. Students can retell these stories aloud, make up different endings to old favorites, or extend the stories with new events. They may also prepare and share a favorite story that is unfamiliar to the class or a personal or family story.

When students tell stories, they can be taught to consider their facial expression, their body language, their intonation of voice, and their strategies for engaging audience interest. They can be encouraged to choose words and literary devices (such as repetition and pauses) to convey feelings and create mood. Explicit instruction, modeling, and guided practice help students create mood as they tell their own and others' stories. They should read or hear stories several times and get a feel for the basic components.

RAP

RAP is an acronym that stands for read, ask, and put. In a RAP, students first read a paragraph silently thinking about the meanings of the words as they read. After they are finished reading, they ask themselves what are the main ideas and details of the paragraph. They may look back quickly over the paragraph to isolate the ideas and details. Finally, they attempt to put the main idea and details into their own words. They should try to generate at least two details related to the main idea.

Think, Pair, Share

In a Think, Pair, Share activity, students first listen to a presentation, watch a video, or read a text. They work individually to record their ideas (in notes, on a diagram, or in a guide) and then team with a partner or two sets of partners to discuss their ideas. The groups can add to the ideas that they generated individually. "Squares" (i.e., two sets of partners) can share the ideas with the whole class. Another variation is to have students practice retelling the story or sharing the main ideas with a partner.

Skill 5.4: Select and Evaluate a Wide Array of Resources for Reseach and Presentation

A wide array of informational and media resources are available for use as tools of communication in the classroom. As technology advances, the need for students to be technologically savvy is becoming increasingly important. It is important that teachers make information technology resources available to students and both model and provide explicit instruction in their use. Literacy education is no longer limited to reading printed text; students need to also develop reading skills in the context of using various forms of multimedia. From an educator's perspective, the wealth of information readily available to teachers and students is a mixed blessing. On the one hand, the goals of education are advanced by the quantity of information available as well as the elative ease of access. On the other hand, the sheer volume of information on any topic is overwhelming, and thus a key component of informational literacy is to be able to identify information of greatest relevance to one's needs and to be able to evaluate the sources of the information. Evaluation of sources begins with a distinction between types: primary and secondary.

Primary Sources

Primary sources consist of first-hand accounts of events, practices, or conditions about which one is seeking information. Generally speaking, these are documents or other records created by witnesses. They may include journalistic accounts, diaries, letters, essays, financial records, memos, websites, blogs, photographs, videos, audio recordings, and so on. The most reliable primary sources are usually considered to be those created closest to the time period in question.

The advantage of primary sources for obtaining information is that they are relatively untouched by others' interpretive or editing activities. This advantage also constitutes a disadvantage, in that primary sources may be difficult to understand without knowing something about the time, place, and event about which information was recorded.

Secondary Sources

Secondary sources are interpretations or paraphrases of primary sources. Each secondary source therefore represents someone else's view of the primary source. These sources consist of books, reviews, critical summaries, and, in some cases, they may include journalistic accounts, diaries, and the other materials indicated under Primary Sources above. The key to distinguishing a letter, for example, as a primary or secondary source is whether the letter pertains to the letter-writer's own experience (primary) or the experience of someone else about whom the letter-writer is reporting (secondary).

The advantage of secondary sources is that background information about the time, place, writer, and situation tend to help make these sources understandable to readers. The disadvantage is that the reader experiences the topic second-hand, filtered through the eyes of someone else, rather than directly.

Multimedia Resources

In the twenty-first century, information comes to students in a variety of forms, including print, text, audio, and multimedia (a combination of the previous) in print and digital formats. The Center for Media Literacy (2011) defines *media literacy* as the ability to access, analyze, evaluate, and create media in a variety of forms. Ultimately, the goals of media literacy are essentially the same as those for information learned in a traditional classroom: students should identify key themes and concepts, make connections between themes, ask questions that elicit additional information, critically evaluate the information, and formulate an opinion or response.

Multimedia presentations are available to students on stand-alone resources, such as CD-ROMs, as well has on the Internet. The Internet is a global information system that facilitates electronic communication and information gathering through both private and public channels. In essence, the Internet is a worldwide system of computer networks through which users of any one computer can, if they have permission, obtain information from any other computer.

Multimedia-related instruction helps students understand and communicate by means of technologies such as the following:

- Websites

- Podcasts

- Streaming video

- Blogs

- PowerPoint and other digital presentations

- Digital editing software

- Mobile technologies and apps

Familiarity with these and other forms of multimedia will give students access to the tools that can help them thrive in increasingly multimedia-rich environments. For example, with a teacher's guidance, students can use social networks and other Internet resources to work collaboratively with peers on shared projects and perhaps even to create their own websites to present the results of their work.

Multimedia Literacy

Multimedia literacy involves the following:

- Understanding the differences between different types of multimedia resources, including their purpose, their advantages, and their disadvantages

- Understanding how to obtain information efficiently from different types of multimedia resources

- Understanding how to evaluate information obtained from various forms of multimedia

- Understanding how to use multimedia as a means of personal expression

Evaluating Multimedia Resources. In many but not all respects, the evaluation of multimedia resources involves the same processes as print resources. For example, Florida Diagnostic and Learning Resources (2011) remind educators to ask themselves five questions about an Internet resource:

1. Who created the website and what is their expertise?

2. What does the creator of the website say about the purpose of the site?

3. When was the website created and when, if ever, was it updated?

4. Where does the information on the website come from?

5. Why is the information on the website useful?

Skill 5.5: Determine and Apply the Ethical Process for Collecting and Presenting Authentic Information While Avoiding Plagiarism

Educators are expected to model professionalism in the gathering and presentation of information. Professionalism in this regard includes working with information in an ethical manner.

Perhaps the first lesson students need to learn is the concept of intellectual property. Teachers should explicitly discuss plagiarism, help students recognize when a source is or is not plagiarized, and teach the use of citations and other methods for avoiding plagiarism when using others' materials.

For example, the Center for Social Media (2011) identifies five principles of acceptable practices for the fair use of copyrighted media materials:

- Employing copyrighted material in media literacy lessons

- Employing copyrighted material in preparing curriculum materials

- Sharing media literacy curriculum materials

- Allowing student use of copyrighted materials in their own academic and creative work

- Developing audiences for student work

Skill 5.6: Identify and Evaluate Current Technology for Use in Educational Settings

Today's technology provides new formats for teaching and learning that appeal to the digital natives in today's classrooms. However, while teachers should use available technology for classroom teaching and learning, teachers should also realize that some children may not have access to digital tools at home. As a result, their lack of exposure to computers and online information may put them at a disadvantage if teachers assume they already know how to find and use online content. Teachers should be sure to provide explicit instruction in computer use including online safety. Teachers also should be cautious in assigning homework that requires use of computers or online sites. Some children may not be able to complete the assignment due to lack of availability rather than lack of effort.

Computer-related technology can be classified as hardware, software, online, and mobile tools. Smart boards are also important classroom computer-related technologies.

Hardware

The physical parts of technology are termed **hardware.** These include desktop computers, notebook computers, tablets, and even mobile technologies. These are generally networked to provide online access. Other peripheral hardware (e.g., printers, USB drives, disk drives) work with computers to input or output information. Other classroom technologies include document cameras, student response systems (clickers) and, in some cases, hardware to provide access and accommodations for students with disabilities.

Software

The programs used to direct the operation of a computer are known as *software.* Software is often classified as either application software (programs that do the work users are interested in) or system software (which includes operating systems and any program that supports application software).

Application software used in schools can generally be categorized in the following ways:

Administrative—Administrative software helps teachers manage students and information. Administrative software is usually a kind of learning management system which can be used to organize and record data such as attendance, grades, electronic communications, budgets and so on.

Productivity—Productivity software allows teachers to use tools to increase efficiency and time management. Productivity tools typically include word processors, spreadsheet, databases, and presentation software. Newsletter, rubric, puzzle and other software generators also increase productivity.

Instructional—Instructional software supports classroom teaching and learning. Examples include tutorial, drill and practice, simulations, problem-based, concept mapping/outlining, and instructional games. Productivity tools such a newsletter generators, word processors, and other tools can also be used by students for instructional purposes.

Online Tools

The Internet allows users to find and use information from around the world. Common web-based content include websites, reference materials (e.g., dictionaries, maps, atlases, and encyclopedias), video tutorials, screen readers, webquests, and other resources.

Web 2.0 tools allow users to create and share content across the internet. Web 2.0 are diverse with numerous options and tools within each type. Common online Web 2.0 tools include wikis, blogs, concept-mapping, curation, email, monitored social networking, video tools, audio tools, comic and graphic generators and digital storytelling.

Mobile Tools

Many of the tools available as software or online use are also available for use on tablets and mobile devices. Many mobile apps are designed for older infants and toddlers so children are often familiar with using apps and manipulating screen content when they get to school. Just as care should be taken in deciding what online content is appropriate, care should also be taken in terms of which apps should be available for student use. While there is a voluminous quantity of available apps, they vary in quality.

Interactive Whiteboards

In the past, lessons taught using chalkboards or whiteboards were lost when old information was erased and replaced with new content. Interactive whiteboards allow what is written on the board to be saved. Additionally, interactive whiteboards permit manipulation of content on the board as the teacher and/or students write, draw, highlight, click, drag, hide, and save work digitally. Teachers can retrieve information and use it for review with the entire class, small groups, or individual students.

References

Anderson, L.W., Krathwohl, D.R., Airasian, P.W., Cruikshank, K.A., Mayer, R.E., Pintrich, P.R., Raths, J., Wittrock, M.C. (2001). *A Taxonomy for Learning, Teaching, and Assessing: A revision of Bloom's Taxonomy of Educational Objectives*. New York: Pearson, Allyn & Bacon.

Bloom, B.S. (Ed.). Engelhart, M.D., Furst, E.J., Hill, W.H., Krathwohl, D.R. (1956). *Taxonomy of Educational Objectives, Handbook I: The Cognitive Domain*. New York: David McKay Co Inc.

Clay, M. (1966). Emergent reading behavior. Unpublished doctoral dissertation, University of Auckland, New Zealand.

National Institute of Child Health and Human Development. (2000). *Report of the National Reading Panel. Teaching children to read: An evidence-based assessment of the scientific research literature on reading and its implications for reading instruction* (NIH Publication No. 00-4769). Washington, D.C.: U.S. Government Printing Office.

Review Questions

1. Which of the following consists of the correct components of emerging literacy?

    (A) print awareness, basic writing skills, reading and writing vocabularies, expository skills, letter knowledge, syntactic awareness

    (B) graphical understanding, logical reasoning, listening and oral vocabularies, narrative skills, abstract thinking, structural analysis

    (C) shape differentiation, sight word vocabulary story structure awareness, semantic knowledge, phonological awareness

    (D) print motivation, print awareness, listening and oral vocabularies, narrative skills, letter knowledge, phonological awareness

2. Mrs. Jackson's second-grade class is working on the following skills: accuracy, automaticity, rate, and prosody. What aspect of language arts are they learning?

    (A) fluency

    (B) comprehension monitoring

    (C) analysis of graphics

    (D) structural analysis

3. Which type and example of figurative language are correctly matched?

    (A) Alliteration: *BRRRRR! It's cold.*

    (B) Onomatopoeia: *The sun smiled on the sleepy village.*

    (C) Simile: *She was like a bull in a china shop.*

    (D) Personification: *He was the picture of health.*

4. Lucy selected a book to read. The book uses animals as characters and ends with a moral. What type of book did Lucy read?

    (A) tall tale

    (B) fable

    (C) legend

    (D) myth

5. Caroline's teacher told her that she needed to work on the *conventions of writing*. What does her teacher want her to do?

    (A) work with other students to practice writing skills

    (B) work on handwriting fluency

    (C) improve spelling, grammar or punctuation

    (D) develop her ability to write creatively in a narrative form

6. First-grade student Luis wrote the following sentence: *He runned up the hill.* The use of the word *runned* is an error of _____.

    (A) semantics

    (B) narrative style

    (C) voice

    (D) syntax

7. Mr. Thompson is using a formative assessment with his 3rd grade class. What is Mr. Thompson most likely to be using?

(A) a high stakes test at the end of the year

(B) anecdotal records

(C) a diagnostic reading test

(D) a feedback prompt

8. Mr. Stelly is using a tool to grade his students' writing assignments. The tool provides a way to grade or score writing according to the objectives of the assignment. Mr. Stelly is most likely using a(n) _____.

(A) rubric

(B) running record

(C) anecdotal record

(D) portfolio

9. Ms. Carson wants to provide her sixth grade language arts students with a listening guide. What would be her best choice?

(A) extemporizing

(B) RAP

(C) SLANT

(D) Think, Pair, Share

10. What is an example of a primary source?

(A) a diary entry from 1792

(B) a letter written to a soldier in World War II

(C) an opinion article in today's newspaper

(D) a textbook on American history

Answer Key and Explanations

1.　**(D)**

While the other choices include some of the components of emerging literacy, they also more advanced literacy skills such as sight word vocabulary, reading and writing vocabularies, abstract thinking, expository structures graphical awareness, syntactic awareness, and semantic knowledge. *For more information, see Competency 1.*

2.　**(A)**

Choice B is incorrect because comprehension monitoring is the use of background knowledge and text information to make sure that what is read is understood. Choice C is incorrect because analysis of graphics involves interpretation, analysis, and evaluation skills. Choice D is incorrect because structural analysis is the study of word parts. *For more information, see Competency 1.*

3.　**(C)**

Choice A is incorrect because alliteration is using several words with the same onset (e.g., She sells seashells down by the seashore). Choice B is incorrect because onomatopoeia is the formation of words that imitate sounds. Choice D is incorrect because personification is giving inanimate objects characteristics of a human. *For more information, see Competency 2.*

4.　**(B)**

Choice A is incorrect because a tall tale tells a humorous story with exaggerated elements. Choice C is incorrect because a legend is an imaginative old story, often passed down for generations, which may or may not feature a historical national or folk hero. Answer D is incorrect because a myth is an example of a culture's legends or traditional narratives about their ancestors, heroes, gods and other supernatural being. *For more information, see Competency 2.*

5.　**(C)**

The conventions of writing consist of the mechanics of writing: grammar, spelling and punctuation. *For more information, see Competency 3.*

6.　**(D)**

Choice A is incorrect because semantics involves meaning. Choice B is incorrect because narrative style is a kind of writing, not a writing error. Choice C is incorrect because voice refers to individual style. *For more information, see Competency 3.*

7.　**(D)**

Choice A is incorrect because high-stakes tests are summative tests used for accountability. Choice B is incorrect because anecdotal records reflect behavior rather than learning progress. Choice C is incorrect because a diagnostic reading test is used to identify a student's strengths and weaknesses. *For more information, see Competency 4.*

8.　**(A)**

Choice B is incorrect because running records are quick assessments of reading fluency. Choice C is incorrect because anecdotal records reflect behavior rather than learning progress. Choice D is incorrect because a portfolio is a collection of work over time. *For more information, see Competency 4.*

9.　**(C)**

Choice A is incorrect because extemporizing is a kind of informal speaking. Choice B is incorrect because RAP is strategy based on reading. Choice D is incorrect because Think, Pair, Share is not a listening guide. *For more information, see Competency 5.*

10.　**(A)**

The rest of the responses are secondary sources. *For more information, see Competency 5.*

Social Science

Knowing what social science concepts and processes to teach and knowing the most effective way to communicate those to students differ. Competency 1 identifies effective practices and assessment of the social sciences.

Skill 1.1: Select Appropriate Resources for Instructional Delivery of Social Science Concepts, Including Complex Informational Text

The world—and the concepts of elementary social sciences—are both at your fingertips and complex in nature. This section addresses resources for delivering social science concepts.

Educational Technology

In addition to traditional print materials and textbooks, educational technology—the effective use of technology tools in learning—is critical for learning social sciences. Educational technology includes the use of media to deliver text, audio, images, animation, and streaming video, and includes technology applications and processes such as audio or video, satellite TV, CD-ROM, and computer-based learning, as well as web-based learning. This allows teachers to use recordings and live streaming of speeches and events, maps, simulations, and real-time data in social studies teaching and learning. Such materials should be carefully curated and scaffolded for student understanding and use. For example, in using a video, the teacher might create a viewing guide with specific stopping points for reflection and discussion.

Complex Informational Text

The first materials children read or hear are typically story-type narrative texts. In the past, narrative text materials and simple expository texts often dominated K–6 classrooms. Florida Standards now require increasing the use of complex informational texts in the teaching of social studies and other content subjects.

Three elements define complex informational texts. Qualitative features of text include type and depth of vocabulary, levels of meaning, language conventions and clarity and knowledge demands. Quantitative features include readability levels and measures of complexity. Matching reader to text and task focuses on reader variables (such as motivation, knowledge, and experiences) and task variables (such as purpose and the complexity generated by the task assigned and the questions posed).

Using complex informational texts often involves the combination of multiple sources, print and digital, primary and secondary. The questions teachers ask of students should be text dependent questions (TDQs); that is, the questions must require students to read, interpret, analyze, and evaluate content. For example, after reading Martin Luther King's *I Have a Dream* speech, teachers often ask something like *Have you ever had a dream?* or *What is your dream for the future?* Text-dependent questions would be: *What was King's dream?* or *How did the dream contrast to the reality in which King and other African Americans of the time lived?* The first pair of questions can be answered without even reading the content. The second pair of questions depends on deep understanding in order to respond.

Realia

Realia consists of objects or activities that teachers can use to relate classroom content to real life. While a variety of content is available online, actual artifacts that students can touch and hold connect students to concepts in powerful ways. For example, teachers can create collections of materials by theme or by time period. This could include pictures, clothing, flags, letters, or other memorabilia.

Human Resources

Parents and other members of the community can serve as experts from whom students can learn about any subject: economics from bankers, history from veterans, music from a specific period from local musicians or collectors, community history from local historians or librarians, business from owners of companies, and so on. Effective teachers ensure that any invited guest understands the purpose of the visit and the goals or objectives of the presentation. Preparation can make the class period more focused and meaningful. Students can create questions for the speaker which reflect understanding of previous content.

Community members can also interact with students in the context of a field trip. Field trips are excellent sources of information, especially about careers, the local community, and topics of contemporary interest. One field trip can yield assignments in a variety of subjects. Teachers can collaborate with each other to produce thematic assignments for the field trip or to coordinate the students' assignments.

 ## Skill 1.2: Identify Appropriate Resources for Planning for Instruction of Social Science Concepts

Planning for instruction provides the basis for effective use of instruction. Instruction should also be based on appropriate Florida standards for Social Sciences, Language Arts, and Math Practices. Additionally, teachers should plan for integration of social science concepts. The graphic organizer PERSIA can help teachers focus instruction and identify key questions for each concept. Then teachers can ask questions which combine concepts such as the following: *How does the political focus of a country affect the economy? How does geography impact economy? What is the relationship between what people believe and how they relate to each other and who they choose to lead them?*

	Focus	**Question**
P	Political	Who is in charge?
E	Economic	How do people make a living?
R	Religion	What do people believe?
S	Social	How do people relate to each other?
I	Intellectual/Arts	How do humans learn and express themselves?
A	Area/Geography	How does where humans live impact how they live?

Following are some recommendations for planning for effective use of resources in social science instruction:

- Use of a variety of educational resources (including people and technology) to enhance both individual and group learning

- Familiarity with the school library, the local public library, education service center resources, and the library of any college or university in the area

- Familiarity with relevant and valid online resources

- Use of a variety of resources in the classroom that relate to instructional objectives

- Previewing resources available from librarians or elsewhere before use in Instructional Strategies

There are many useful instructional strategies for the social studies classroom. Together these strategies convey content in a clear and engaging way, and prepare students to be citizens in a democratic society.

Teachers should consider the following in planning for social science instruction:

- Provide opportunities to gain knowledge through primary sources as well as concept development and attainment.

- Enhance skills through discovery learning, questioning, and inquiry learning.

- Focus on cause-effect aspects of and connections within social science concepts.

- Develop democratic dispositions through the fostering of multiple perspectives, the establishment of a democratic classroom, and efforts toward community building.

- Primary sources should be examined and discussed with guidance from the teacher.

- Concept development should be promoted by helping students analyze characteristics, group similar characteristics, and then identify the concept.

- Discovery learning should be implemented by helping students seek information through research, analysis, and interpretation in the context of problem-solving activities.

- Good questioning should be promoted to help students stay engaged, to learn, and to exercise critical-thinking skills.

- Inquiry learning should be implemented so that students participate in topic selection as well as the process of acquiring information, thereby enhancing motivation and learning.

- The development of multiple perspectives should be fostered, so that students from all backgrounds are respected and understood and so that students themselves can understand and respect others.

- A democratic classroom should be established, so that students understand the importance of participating in creating and maintaining the rules and so they are consequently more likely to respect and follow the rules.

- Community building should be fostered, so that students develop a sense of belonging and safety and can both support and disagree with each other.

Planning for use of these strategies throughout the social studies curriculum will enable students to develop their knowledge base, their critical-thinking skills, and their appreciation of diversity.

Skill 1.3: Choose Appropriate Methods for Assessing Social Science Concepts

The basic goals of assessment are to enhance teachers' knowledge of learners and their needs, to monitor students' progress toward goals and outcomes, and to modify instruction whenever needed.

Extensive discussion of assessment can be found in the Language Arts and Reading chapter. Although specific methods for the assessment of literacy skills, such as running records, are not suitable for social studies classes, the general principles, concepts, and strategies of assessment are the same. In addition, authentic assessments such as projects and portfolios are particularly important in social studies. Projects allow students to integrate and apply what they have learned and to exercise self-assessment skills as they evaluate their progress at each step of the project.

Skill 1.4: Determine Appropriate Learning Environments for Social Science Lessons

A teacher's vision and expectations of student learning shape and inform instruction and form the foundation of the learning environment. Teachers provide structure, scaffolding, inspiration, and support. A classroom has both physical and affective elements that affect learning. The layout of a classroom can promote discussion (e.g., small clusters of tables) or restrict it (traditional classroom rows and columns). Physical classroom elements also include lighting, availability and organization of resources, comfort, and traffic patterns. Affective elements include a sense of safety, inclusion, and community. The learning environment should differentiate instruction to meet student needs and accommodate learning differences. Particularly in social sciences, classroom discussions should foster open discussion and inquiry.

Competency 2: Knowledge of Time, Continuity, and Change

Social Science is a set of disciplines that provide knowledge about societies and people. When one teaches social studies in an elementary setting, the teacher takes on various roles, including historian, geographer, political scientist, economist, and, of course, educator. By intertwining these roles, the teacher helps the young students to become good citizens and to make good decisions. Competency 2 focuses on history, although other disciplines, such as anthropology and economics, play a role.

Skill 2.1: Identify and Analyze Historical Events that Are Related by Cause and Effect

History is the study of the past. As historians, teachers relate important information about past happenings, ensure that the information is authentic and accurate, and engage students in exploring evidence from various sources. By studying the past, students equip themselves with knowledge and skills that allow them to judge the present and make informed decisions about the future. Making history come alive by investigating historical artifacts will bring relevance and meaning to distant times and places. With recent technological advances and the wealth of information acquired through the Internet, our teachers, as historians, can produce hands-on resources and provide ample opportunities for investigation and exploration.

Cause-Effect Analysis

Knowledge of significant events, ideas, and people from the past is an important part of the social studies curriculum. This knowledge results from careful analysis of cause-effect relationships. For example, the causal forces responsible for each of the following eras can be used to frame the study of American history:

- Colonization and settlement (1585–1763)

- Revolution and the new nation (1754–1815)

- Expansion and reform (1801–1861)

- Civil War and Reconstruction (1850–1877)

- Development of the industrial United States (1870–1900)

- Emergence of modern America (1890–1930)

- Great Depression and World War II (1929–1945)

- Postwar United States (1945–1970)

- Contemporary United States (1968–1999)

- New Millennium (2000–present)

Cause-effect analysis may focus on broad events (e.g., causes of the Civil War) or on specific ones (e.g., causes of victory in one particular Civil War battle). As students learn the narratives of history, they will recognize that particular events and forces are both causes and effects. The Civil War, for example, represents an effect produced by many causes, but it, in turn, had a dramatic impact on all facets of our nation's development.

When teachers wish to introduce students to historical cause-effect relationships, they create lesson plans that tap into higher levels of critical thinking according to Level 4 of Webb's Depth of Knowledge and Bloom's taxonomy, such as analysis, synthesis, and evaluation. Tools that support causal analysis include the following:

- *Timelines* that present events in chronological order.

- *Charts* that compare and contrast or summarize causal relationships.

- *Graphs* that illustrate relationships between variables.

When synthesizing the information they learn, students may create drawings, blueprints, and models or use Web 2.0 tools to create and share content. Through evaluative activities, students may produce critical essays and editorials and participate in classroom debates or online discussions through which they express their points of view on historical topics.

Reading for and writing about causes and effects requires that students understand key words that signal them. These include the following:

Words That Show Causation	Words That Show Effect
• Because	• Consequently
• This leads to	• As a result
• For one thing	• For this reason
• Due to	• This leads to
• Hence	• One result is
• Cause	• Hence
• Reason	• Later
• Since	• Result
• So	• Therefore, thus
• On account of	• So
• If	• Then

Skill 2.2: Analyze the Sequential Nature of Historical Events Using Timelines

For many students, history seems to be an almost random collection of people, places, and events that happened at various points in the past. A timeline provides students with a visual chronological representation of history. This allows them to connect people and places to the eras in which they occurred. It also helps students see causal relationships and overlaps across the sequence. As a result, students can analyze specific elements within the same era or across various time periods. A timeline allows students to see where newly-learned historical content fits into the context of already-learned information. This forms the basis for thinking historically.

Skill 2.3: Analyze Examples of Primary and Secondary Source Documents for Historical Perspective

Evaluating primary sources is a relatively direct way to analyze and interpret the past. Unlike secondary sources, which are interpretations of historical materials, primary source documents are the materials themselves. These materials include eyewitness accounts, oral histories, paintings, clothing, letters, diaries, artifacts, photos, historical sites, and so on. It is through such materials that history can come alive. Although primary source documents may be difficult to understand without background information and commentary from the teacher or some other expert source, these documents can provide students with a unique perspective that may not be attainable through secondary sources. Primary sources should be examined in terms of the context (*who, what, when, where, why*) in which they were created as well as any biases or points of view that may affect the item or its context.

The U.S. Library of Congress makes available online a wide range of primary source documents, ranging from the *Declaration of Independence* and the *Constitution* to recordings and photographs created during the Great Depression. Many museums also have online resources that include primary documents which have been digitized for online access. Students examine the diaries, letters, and discharge papers that veterans or members of their families or communities may possess. Visits to local museums, libraries, and courthouses are also good places for students to examine primary source documents.

Secondary sources are based on primary sources. They generally provide more information about a primary source or explain it in some way. They often "connect the dots" by providing background and showing how events occurred within a context. Textbooks are good examples of secondary sources. They describe concepts in terms that students can understand. However, secondary sources can also be biased or lack accurate information.

Skill 2.4: Analyze the Impacts of the Cultural Contributions and Technological Developments of Africa, the Americas, Asia, Including the Middle East, and Europe

The impact of cultural contributions and technological developments from all areas of the earth are wide-ranging and numerous. Since today's classrooms represent diverse world cultures, it's important for children to understand the contributions of their ancestors.

	Contributions	**Impact**
AFRICA	The oldest bones of humans (homo sapiens) and closely related hominids were found in Africa which would make it the first place in which humans are known to have existed.	The migration of early humans from Africa to all parts of the world formed the basis for the nations and civilizations of today.

(continued)

(continued)

	Contributions	Impact
THE AMERICAS	Indigenous Native Americans contributed almanacs of meteorological and astronomical information, calendar, and agricultural domestication of plants and animals (maize, dog breeds, turkey, chocolate, tomatoes, peanuts). The United States was the first colony to gain independence from a mother country.	Understanding of astronomy contributed to the understanding of our place in the world. Domestication of plants and animals fostered agricultural endeavors that allowed civilizations to develop cities. Independence became an achievable goal for other colonies.
ASIA	Extensive trade routes developed within Asia and across Europe, which gave people access to spices and other rare goods.	The desire for a faster route to the East led many countries to send ships West, which resulted in the discovery of the Americas by European explorers.
MIDDLE EAST	Early humans in the Middle East created the first civilizations with tools, which led to achievements in building (e.g., the Great Pyramids) and craftwork with metals. Other hallmarks of civilization included the first system of alphabetic writing, mathematical principles (number system; algebra; basic geometry); agriculture, art, music and healing arts (surgery and use of medicine). The Jewish, Islamic, and Christian religions originated in the Middle East.	
EUROPE	Democracy was first established in Greece where education was valued and political theory debated. Middle Ages brought a Renaissance in art, music and architecture. European nations colonized the Americas as well as other areas of the world.	Educational and political concepts as well appreciation of the arts contributed to the development of colonies around the world.

Skill 2.5: Identify the Significant Historical Leaders and Events that Have Influenced Eastern and Western Civilizations

This section provides an overview of some of the events and leaders that have influenced eastern and western civilizations.

Prehistoric Period

The Earth is estimated to be approximately 4.5 billion years old. The earliest known humans, called hominids, lived in Africa 3 to 4 million years ago. Of the several species of hominids that developed, all modern humans descended from just one group, the Homo sapiens, who appeared in Africa several hundred thousand years ago.

Historians divide prehistory into three periods:

1. *Paleolithic*. The period from the emergence of the first-known hominids until approximately 10,000 BCE is known as the Paleolithic period, or Old Stone Age. During this period, human beings lived in very small groups of perhaps 10 to 20 nomadic people, constantly moving from place to place. Humans had the ability to make tools and weapons from stone and from the bones of animals they killed. Hunting large game such as mammoths, which were sometimes driven off cliffs in large numbers, was crucial to the survival of early humans, who used the meat, fur, and bones of the animals to survive. Early humans supplemented their diets by foraging for food. They took shelter in caves and other natural formations, and they painted and drew on the walls of caves. Cave paintings discovered in France and northern Spain, created during the Paleolithic period, depict scenes of animals such as lions, owls, and oxen. Around 500,000 years ago, humans began to use fire, which provided light and warmth in shelters and caves, and cooked meat and other foods. Human beings developed means of creating fire and improved techniques of producing tools and weapons.

2. *Mesolithic*. The Mesolithic period, or Middle Stone Age, extending from 10,000 to 7000 BCE, marks the beginning of a major transformation known as the Neolithic Revolution. During this time, humans domesticated plants and began to shift away from a reliance on hunting large game and foraging. Human beings had previously relied on gathering food where they found it and had moved almost constantly in search of game, wild berries, and other vegetation. During the Mesolithic age, humans were able to plant and harvest some crops and began to stay in one place for longer periods. Early humans also improved their toolmaking techniques and developed various kinds of tools and weapons.

3. *Neolithic.* During the Neolithic period, or New Stone Age, the "agricultural revolution" described above was complete, as humans now engaged in systematic agricultural practices and began domesticating animals. Although humans continued to hunt animals, to supplement their diet with meat, and to use skins and bones to make clothing and weapons, major changes in society occurred as a result of agricultural developments. Humans began to settle in farming villages or towns, the population increased, and communities grew. A more settled way of life led to a more structured social system, a greater level of organization within societies, the development of crafts such as the production of pottery, and an increase in exchanges of goods among groups.

Beginnings of Recorded History

Between 6000 and 3000 BCE, humans invented the plow, developed the wheel, harnessed the wind, discovered how to smelt copper ores, and began to develop accurate solar calendars. Small villages gradually grew into populous cities. Between 4000 and 3000 BCE, writing developed, and the towns and villages settled during the Neolithic period developed more complex patterns of existence. The existence of written records marks the end of the prehistoric period and the beginning of recorded history. The beginning of history coincides with the emergence of the earliest societies that exhibit characteristics enabling them to be considered as civilizations. The first civilizations emerged in Mesopotamia and Egypt.

Mesopotamia

The ancient civilization of Sumer (4000–2000 BCE) included the city of Ur. The Sumerians constructed dikes and reservoirs and established a loose confederation of city-states. They probably invented writing (called cuneiform because of its wedge-shaped letters). After 538 BCE, the peoples of Mesopotamia, whose natural boundaries were insufficient to thwart invaders, were absorbed into other empires and dynasties.

Egypt

Near the end of the Archaic period (5000–2685 BCE), at around 3200 BCE, Menes, or Narmer, probably unified upper and lower Egypt. The capital moved to Memphis during the Third Dynasty (ca. 2650 BCE). The pyramids were built during the Fourth Dynasty (ca. 2613–2494 BCE). After 1085 BCE, in the Post-Empire period, Egypt came under the successive control of the Assyrians, the Persians, Alexander the Great, and finally, in 30 BCE, the Roman Empire. The Egyptians developed papyrus and made many medical advances.

Palestine and the Hebrews

Phoenicians settled along the present-day coast of Lebanon (Sidon, Tyre, Beirut, Byblos) and established colonies at Carthage and in Spain. They spread Mesopotamian culture through their trade networks.

The Hebrews probably moved to Egypt around 1700 BCE and suffered enslavement until about 1500 BCE. The Hebrews fled Egypt under Moses and, around 1200 BCE, returned to Palestine. King David, who reigned circa 1012–972 BCE, defeated the Philistines and established Jerusalem as the capital of his kingdom. The poor and less attractive state of Judah continued until 586 BCE, when the Chaldeans transported the Jews to Chaldea as advisors and slaves, a time known as the Babylonian captivity. The Persians conquered Babylon in 539 BCE and allowed the Jews to return to Palestine.

Greece

During the Archaic period in Greece (800–500 BCE), Greek society organized around the polis, or city-state. Oligarchs (small combined groups of rulers) controlled most of the polis until the end of the sixth century, when individuals holding absolute power replaced them. By the end of the sixth century, democratic governments in turn replaced many of these tyrants. The fifth century BCE was the high point of Greek civilization and is known as the Classical Age. It opened with the Persian Wars (560–479 BCE), after which Athens organized the Delian League. Pericles (ca. 495–429 BCE) used money from the Delian League to rebuild Athens, including construction of the Parthenon and other buildings on the Acropolis. Athens' political and cultural dominance then led to war with Sparta. At the same time, a revolution in philosophy occurred in classical Athens. The Sophists emphasized the individual and the attainment of excellence through rhetoric, grammar, music, and mathematics. Socrates (ca. 470–399 BCE) criticized the Sophists' emphasis on rhetoric and developed a process of questioning, or dialogues, with his students as a means of obtaining knowledge and making ethical decisions. Like Socrates, Plato (ca. 428–348 BCE) and his student Aristotle (ca. 384–322 BCE) emphasized the importance of ethics in social and political decision-making. Aristotle made enduring contributions to philosophy and natural science and contended that to understand any object it is necessary to examine four factors: its matter, its form, its cause or origin, and its end or purpose.

Rome

The traditional founding date for Rome is 753 BCE. Between 800 and 500 BCE, Greek tribes colonized southern Italy, bringing their alphabet and religious practices to Roman tribes. In the sixth and seventh centuries BCE, the Etruscans expanded southward and conquered Rome. During the time of the early Republic, power was in the hands of the patricians (wealthy landowners). During the 70s and 60s BCE, Pompey (106–48 BCE) and Julius Caesar (100–44 BCE) emerged as the most powerful men. In 60 BCE, Caesar convinced Pompey and Crassus (ca. 115–53 BCE) to form the First Triumvirate. When Crassus died, Caesar and Pompey fought for leadership. In 47 BCE, the Senate proclaimed Caesar dictator and later named him consul for life. Brutus and Cassius believed that Caesar had destroyed the Republic. They formed a conspiracy and, on March 15, 44 BCE (the Ides of March), Brutus and Cassius assassinated Caesar in the Roman forum. Caesar's 18-year-old nephew and adopted son, Octavian, succeeded him. Octavian, who reigned from 27 BCE to 14 CE, gained absolute political control while maintaining the appearance of a republic. When he offered to relinquish his power in 27 BCE, the Senate gave him a vote of confidence and a new title, Augustus. He introduced many reforms, including new coinage, new tax collection, fire and police protection, and land for settlers in the provinces.

Origin of Christianity in the Middle East

Jesus was born in Bethlehem in what is now Palestine. Christianity is based on his life, teachings, death, and resurrection. The three major branches of Christianity are Roman Catholicism, Eastern Orthodoxy, and Protestantism.

At one time, much of history was dated by the birth of Jesus of Nazareth. The term *BC* was understood to mean "before Christ" and *AD* was the abbreviation *of Anno Domini* (Latin for *in the year of the Lord*). Although the presumed birth year of Jesus still forms the demarcation, the terms *BC* or *BCE* now mean Before Common Era and the term *CE* (Common Era) is what was formerly described as *AD*.

The Byzantine Empire

By the first century CE, Christianity, based on the teachings of Jesus and his followers, had spread throughout the Empire. Around 312 CE, Emperor Constantine converted to Christianity and ordered toleration in the Edict of Milan (ca. 313 CE). In 391 CE, Emperor Theodosius I (reigned 371–395 CE) proclaimed Christianity the Empire's official religion. Emperor Theodosius II (reigned 408–450 CE) divided his Empire between his two sons, one ruling the East and the other ruling the West. After the Vandals sacked Rome in 455 CE, Constantinople became the undisputed leading city of the Byzantine Empire. In 1453 CE, Constantinople fell to the Ottoman Turks.

Islamic Civilization in the Middle Ages

Mohammed was born about 570 CE. In 630 CE, he marched into Mecca. The Sharia (code of law and theology) outlines five pillars of faith for Muslims to observe.

Pillar One:	Muslims believe that there is one God and that Mohammed is his prophet.
Pillar Two:	The faithful pray five times a day
Pillar Three:	Faithful believers must perform charitable acts.
Pillar Four:	The faithful must fast from sunrise to sunset during the holy month of Ramadan.
Pillar Five:	The faithful must make a haj, or pilgrimage, to Mecca.

The Koran, which consists of 114 *suras* (verses), contains Mohammed's teachings. The Omayyad caliphs, with their base in Damascus, governed from 661–750 CE. They called themselves Shiites and believed they were Mohammed's true successors. Most Muslims were Sunnis, from the word *sunna*, meaning "oral traditions about the prophet." The Abbasid caliphs ruled from 750–1258 CE. They moved the capital to Baghdad and treated Arab and non-Arab Muslims as equals. Genghis (or Chingis) Khan (reigned 1206–1227 CE) and his army invaded the Abbasids. In 1258 CE, they seized Baghdad and murdered the last caliph.

Feudalism in Japan

Feudalism in Japan began with the arrival of mounted nomadic warriors from throughout Asia during the Kofun Era (300–710 CE). Some members of the nomadic groups formed an elite class and became part of the court aristocracy in the capital city of Kyoto, in western Japan. During the Heian Era (794–1185 CE), a hereditary military aristocracy arose in the Japanese provinces; by the late Heian Era, many of these formerly nomadic warriors had established themselves as independent landowners, or as managers of landed estates, or *shoen*, owned by Kyoto aristocrats. These aristocrats depended on the warriors to defend their shoen, and in response to this need, the warriors organized into small groups called *bushidan*. After victory in the Taira-Minamoto War (1180–1185 CE), Minamoto no Yorimoto forced the emperor to award him the title of shogun, which is short for "barbarian-subduing generalissimo." Yorimoto used this power to found the Kamakura Shogunate, a feudal military dictatorship that survived for 148 years. By the fourteenth century CE, the great military governors (*shugo*) had augmented their power enough to become a threat to the Karnakura, and in 1333 CE they led a rebellion that overthrew the shogunate. The Tokugawa shogunate was the final and most unified of the three shogunates. Under the Tokugawa, the *daimyo* were direct vassals of the shoguns and were under strict control. The warriors gradually became scholars and bureaucrats under the *bushido*, or code of chivalry, and the principles of neo-Confucianism. Under the Meji Restoration of 1868, the emperor again received power and the samurai class lost its special privileges.

Chinese and Indian Empires

In the third century BCE, the Indian kingdoms fell under the Mauryan Empire. The grandson of the founder of this empire, named Ashoka, opened a new era in the cultural history of India by embracing the Buddhist religion. The Buddha had disregarded the Vedic gods and the institutions of caste and had preached a relatively simple ethical religion that advocated two levels of aspiration—a monastic life of renunciation of the world and a high, but not too difficult, morality for the layman. Although the two religions of Hinduism and Buddhism flourished together for centuries in a tolerant rivalry, Buddhism virtually disappeared from India by the thirteenth century CE. Chinese civilization originated in the Yellow River Valley, only gradually extending to the southern regions. Three dynasties ruled early China: the Xia or Hsia, the Shang (ca. 1500 to 1122 BCE), and the Zhou (ca. 1122 to 211 BCE). After the Zhou Dynasty fell, China welcomed the teachings of Confucius; warfare between states and philosophical speculation created circumstances ripe for such teachings. Confucius held that the good order of society depends on an ethical ruler who receives advice from scholar-moralists like Confucius himself. In contrast to the Confucians, the Chinese Taoists professed a kind of apparent anarchism; the best kind of government was none at all. The wise man did not concern himself with political affairs but rather with mystical contemplation of the forces behind the rise and fall of earthly things.

African Kingdoms and Cultures

The Bantu peoples occupied large sections of Africa. Bantu societies lived in tiny chiefdoms, starting in the third millennium BCE, and each group developed its own version of the original Bantu language. The Nok people lived in the area now known as Nigeria. Artifacts indicate that they were peaceful farmers who built small communities consisting of houses of wattle and daub (poles and sticks). The Ghanaians lived about 500 miles from what is now Ghana. Their kingdom fell to a Berber group in the late eleventh century CE, and Mali emerged as the next large kingdom in the thirteenth century. The Malians lived in a huge kingdom that lay mostly on the savanna bordering the Sahara Desert. Timbuktu, built in the thirteenth century CE, was a thriving city of culture where traders visited stone houses, shops, libraries, and mosques. The Songhai lived near the Niger River and gained their independence from the Mali in the early 1400s. The major growth of the empire came after 1464 CE, under the leadership of Sunni Ali, who devoted his reign to warfare and expansion of the empire.

Civilizations of the Americas

The great civilizations of early America were agricultural; foremost among these were the Mayan people in Yucatan, Guatemala, and eastern Honduras. Farther north in

Mexico, a series of advanced cultures arose that derived much of their substance from the Maya. Peoples like the Zapotecs, Totonacs, Olmecs, and Toltecs evolved a high level of civilization. By 500 BCE, agricultural peoples had begun to use a ceremonial calendar and had built stone pyramids where they held religious observances. The Aztecs then dominated Mexican culture. A major feature of Aztec society was human sacrifice in repeated propitiation of their chief god. Aztec government was centralized, with an elected king and a large army. Andean civilization was characterized by the evolution of beautifully made pottery, intricate fabrics, and flat-topped mounds, or huacas. In the interior of South America, the Inca, who called themselves "Children of the Sun," controlled an area stretching from Ecuador to central Chile. As sun worshippers, they believed that they were the sun god's vice regents on Earth and more powerful than any other humans. They also believed that every person's place in society was fixed and immutable and that the state and the army were supreme. The Inca reached the apex of their power just before the Spanish conquest. In the present-day southwestern United States and northern Mexico, two varieties of ancient culture are still identifiable. The Anasazi developed adobe architecture, worked the land extensively, had a highly developed system of irrigation, and made cloth and baskets. The Hohokam built separate stone and timber houses around a central plaza.

Medieval Europe

The Frankish Kingdom was the most important medieval Germanic state. Under Clovis I (reigned 481511 CE), the Franks finished conquering France and the Gauls in 486 CE. Clovis converted to Christianity and founded the Merovingian dynasty. Charles the Great, or Charlemagne (reigned 768–814 CE), founded the Carolingian dynasty. In 800 CE, Pope Leo III named Charlemagne Emperor of the Holy Roman Empire. Through the Treaty of Aix-la-Chapelle (812 CE), the Byzantine emperor recognized Charles's authority in the West, thereby achieving the main purpose of the Holy Roman Empire. Charles's son, Louis the Pious (reigned 814–840 CE), succeeded him. On Louis's death, his three sons vied for control of the Empire. The three eventually signed the Treaty of Verdun in 843 CE. This treaty gave Charles the Western Kingdom (France), Louis the Eastern Kingdom (Germany), and Lothair the Middle Kingdom, a narrow strip of land running from the North Sea to the Mediterranean. During this period, manorialism—an essential part of feudalism—developed as an economic system in which large estates, granted by the king to nobles, strove for self-sufficiency. The lord and his serfs divided the ownership of the estates. The church was the only institution to survive the Germanic invasions intact. The power of the popes grew during this period. Gregory I (reigned 590–604 CE) was the first member of a monastic order to rise to the papacy. He advanced the ideas of penance and purgatory. He also centralized church administration and was the first pope to rule as the secular head of Rome. Monasteries preserved the few remnants of culture that survived the decline of antiquity. The year 1050 marked the beginning of the High Middle Ages. Europe was poised to emerge from five centuries of decline. Between 1000 and 1350, the population of Europe grew from 38 million to 75 million. New technologies, such as heavy plows, and a slight temperature rise produced a longer growing season and contributed to agricultural productivity.

The Holy Roman Empire

Charlemagne's grandson, Louis the German, became Holy Roman Emperor under the Treaty of Verdun in 843. His descendants governed the empire until 1024, when the Franconian dynasty assumed power, reigning until 1125. Under the leadership of William the Conqueror (reigned 1066–1087), the Normans conquered England in 1066. William stripped the Anglo-Saxon nobility of its privileges and instituted feudalism. He ordered a survey of all property of the realm; the *Domesday Book* (1086) records the findings. William introduced feudalism to England. Feudalism was the decentralized political system of personal ties and obligations that bound vassals to their lords. Serfs were peasants who were bound to the land. They worked on the *demesne*, or lord's property, three or four days a week in return for the right to work their own land. In 1215, the English barons forced King John I to sign the Magna Carta Libertatum, acknowledging their "ancient" privileges. The Magna Carta established the principle of a limited English monarchy. From 710 to 711, the Moors conquered Spain from the Visigoths. Under the Moors, Spain enjoyed a stable, prosperous government. The caliphate of Cordoba became a center of scientific and intellectual activity. The Reconquista (1085–1340) wrested control from the Moors. The fall of Cordoba in 1234 completed the Reconquista, except for the small state of Granada. Most of Eastern Europe and Russia was never under Rome control; Germanic invasions separated the areas from Western influence. In Russia, Vladimir I converted to Orthodox Christianity in 988. He established the basis of Kievian Russia. After 1054, Russia broke into competing principalities. The Mongols (Tartars) invaded in 1221. They completed their conquest in 125 and cut Russia's contact with the West for almost a century.

The Crusades

The Crusades attempted to liberate the Holy Land from infidels. Seven major crusades occurred between 1096 and 1300. Urban II called Christians to the First Crusade (1096–1099) with the promise of a plenary indulgence (exemption from punishment in purgatory). Younger sons who would not inherit their fathers' lands were also attracted. The Crusades helped to renew interest in the ancient world. However, the Crusaders massacred thousands of Jews and Muslims, and relations between Europe and the Byzantine Empire collapsed.

Scholasticism

Scholasticism represented an effort to reconcile reason and faith and to instruct Christians on how to make sense of the pagan tradition. The most influential proponent of this effort was Thomas Aquinas (ca. 1225–1274), who believed that there were two orders of truth. The lower level, reason, could demonstrate propositions such as the existence of God, but the higher level necessitated that some of God's mysteries, such as the nature of the Trinity, be accepted on faith. Aquinas viewed the universe as a great chain of being, with humans midway on the chain between the material and the spiritual.

The Black Death

The plague, also called the Black Death, was a rampant pandemic of the Middle Ages. Merchants helped bring the plague to Asia; carried by fleas on rats, the disease arrived in Europe in 1347. By 1350, the disease had killed 25 to 40 percent of the European population as well as about one-quarter of the world's population. Conditions in Europe further encouraged the quick spread of disease. Refuse, excrement, and dead animals filled the streets of the cities, which lacked any form of urban sanitation. Living conditions were overcrowded, with families often sleeping in one room or one bed; poor nutrition was rampant; and there was often little personal cleanliness. Western Europe would not regain the pre-plague levels of population until the beginning of the 16th century.

The Renaissance

The period known as the Renaissance (rebirth) witnessed a surge of interest in antiquity as well as a spirit of humanism and classically inspired innovation. The literature of the period was more secular and wide-ranging than that of the Middle Ages. Dante Alighieri (1265–1321) was a Florentine writer whose *Divine Comedy*, describing a journey through hell, purgatory, and heaven, shows that reason can take people only so far and that attaining heaven requires God's grace and revelation. Francesco Petrarch (1304–1374) encouraged the study of ancient Rome, collected and preserved works of ancient writers, and produced a large body of work in the classical literary style. The Italian Giovanni Boccaccio (1313–1375) wrote *The Decameron*, a collection of short stories intended more to amuse than to edify the reader. Artists also broke with medieval traditions, in both technique and content. Renaissance art sometimes explored religious topics but often dealt with secular themes or portraits of individuals. Oil paints, chiaroscuro, and linear perspectives produced energetic works in both two and three dimensions. Leonardo da Vinci (1452–1519) produced numerous works, including *The Last Supper* and *Mona Lisa*. Raphael Santi (1483–1520), a master of Renaissance grace and style, theory, and technique, deployed wide-ranging skills in his masterpiece *The School of Athens*. Michelangelo Buonarroti (1475–1564) produced enduring works in architecture, sculpture

(*David*), and painting (the ceiling of the Sistine Chapel). Michelangelo's work created a bridge to a new, post-Renaissance style known as mannerism. Renaissance scholars were more practical and secular than medieval ones. Manuscript collections enabled scholars to study primary sources and to reject or at least critically evaluate traditions established since classical times. Also, scholars participated in the lives of their cities as active politicians. Leonardo Bruni (1370–1444), a civic humanist, served as chancellor of Florence, where he used his rhetorical skills to rouse the citizens against external enemies. Niccolo Machiavelli (1469–1527) wrote *The Prince*, which analyzed politics from the standpoint of expedience rather than morality in the name of maintaining political power.

The Reformation

The Reformation undermined Western Europe's religious unity and introduced new ideas about the relationships among God, the individual, and society. Politics greatly influenced the course of the Reformation and led, in most areas, to the subjection of the church to the political rulers. Martin Luther (1483–1546), to his personal distress, could not reconcile the sinfulness of humans with the justice of God. During his studies of the *Bible*, Luther came to believe that personal efforts—good works such as a Christian life and attention to the sacraments of the church—could not "earn" the sinner salvation but that belief and faith were the only way to obtain grace. By 1515, Luther held that "justification by faith alone" was the road to salvation. On October 31, 1517, Luther nailed 95 theses, or statements, about indulgences (the cancellation of a sin in return for money) to the door of the Wittenberg church and challenged the practice of selling them. At this time he was seeking to reform the church, not divide it. In 1519, Luther presented various criticisms of the church and declared that only the *Bible,* not religious traditions or papal statements, could determine correct religious practices and beliefs. In 1521, Pope Leo X excommunicated Luther for his beliefs. In 1536, John Calvin (1509–1564), a Frenchman, arrived in Geneva, a Swiss city-state that had adopted an anti-Catholic position. In 1540, Geneva became the center of the Reformation. Calvin's *Institutes of the Christian Religion* (1536), a strictly logical analysis of Christianity, had a universal appeal. Calvin emphasized the doctrine of predestination, which indicated that God has determined who will obtain salvation before those people are born. Calvin believed that church and state should unite. Calvinism triumphed as the majority religion in Scotland, under the leadership of John Knox (ca. 1514–1572), and in the United Provinces of the Netherlands. Puritans in England and New England also accepted Calvinism.

The Thirty Years' War

Between 1618 and 1648, the European powers fought a series of wars. The reasons for the wars varied; religious, dynastic, commercial, and territorial rivalries all played a part.

The battles were fought over most of Europe and ended with the Treaty of Westphalia in 1648. The Thirty Years' War changed the boundaries of most European countries.

The Enlightenment

For the first time in recorded history, the eighteenth century saw the widespread appearance of a secular worldview: the Age of Enlightenment. The philosophical starting point for the Enlightenment was the belief in the autonomy of man's intellect apart from God. The most basic assumption was faith in reason rather than faith in revelation. René Descartes (1596–1650) sought a basis for logic and believed he found it in man's ability to think. "I think; therefore, I am" was his most famous statement. Benedict de Spinoza (1632–1677) developed a rational pantheism in which he equated God and nature. He denied all free will and ended up with an impersonal, mechanical universe. Gottfried Wilhelm Leibniz (1646–1716) worked on symbolic logic and calculus and invented a calculating machine. He, too, had a mechanistic view of the world and life and thought of God as a hypothetical abstraction rather than a persona. John Locke (1632–1704) pioneered the empiricist approach to knowledge, stressing the importance of the environment in human development. Locke thought reason and revelation were complementary and originating from God with respect to political and economic theory. Locke and Jean-Jacques Rousseau (1712–1778) believed that people were capable of governing themselves, either through a political (Locke) or social (Rousseau) contract forming the basis of society. Most philosophers opposed democracy, preferring a limited monarchy that shared power with the nobility. The assault on mercantilist economic theory was begun by the physiocrats in France, who proposed a laissez-faire (minimal governmental interference) attitude toward land usage that culminated in the theory of economic capitalism associated with Adam Smith (1723–1790) and his notions of free trade, free enterprise, and the law of supply and demand.

The French Revolution

Increased criticism directed toward governmental inefficiency and corruption as well as toward the privileged classes demonstrated the rising expectations of "enlightened" society in France. The remainder of the population (called the Third Estate) consisted of the middle class, urban workers, and the mass of peasants, who bore the entire burden of taxation and the imposition of feudal obligations. The most notorious event of the French Revolution was the so-called Reign of Terror (1793–1794), the government's campaign against its internal enemies and counterrevolutionaries. Louis XVI faced charges of treason, declared guilty, and executed on January 21, 1793. Later the same year, the queen, Marie Antoinette, met the same fate. The middle class controlled the Directory (1795–1799). Members of the Directory believed that through peace they would gain more wealth and establish a society in which money and property would become the only requirements for prestige and power. Rising inflation and mass public dissatisfaction led to the downfall of the Directory. The French and U.S. revolutions provided the model for future colonies (e.g., India, Canada, Belize, Pakistan, New Zealand) to also gain independence.

The Napoleonic Era

On December 25, 1799, a new government and constitution concentrated supreme power in the hands of Napoleon. Napoleon's domestic reforms and policies affected every aspect of society. French-ruled peoples viewed Napoleon as a tyrant who repressed and exploited them for France's glory and advantage. Enlightened reformers believed Napoleon had betrayed the ideals of the Revolution. The downfall of Napoleon resulted from his inability to conquer England, economic distress caused by the Continental System (boycott of British goods), the Peninsular War with Spain, the German War of Liberation, and the invasion of Russia. The actual defeat of Napoleon occurred at the Battle of Waterloo in 1815.

The Industrial Revolution

The Industrial Revolution was a period of transition when machines began to significantly displace human and animal power in methods of producing and distributing goods and when an agricultural and commercial society became an industrial one. Roots of the Industrial Revolution are evident in the following:

- The Commercial Revolution (1500–1700), which spurred the great economic growth of Europe and brought about the Age of Discovery and Exploration, which in turn helped to solidify the economic doctrines of mercantilism.

- The effects of the Scientific Revolution, which produced the first wave of mechanical inventions and technological advances.

- The increase in population in Europe from 140 million people in 1750 to 266 million people by the mid-nineteenth century (more producers, more consumers).

- The nineteenth-century political and social revolutions that began the rise to power of the middle class and that provided leadership for the economic revolution.

A transportation revolution ensued that distributed the productivity of machinery and delivery of raw materials to eager factories. This revolution led to the growth of canal systems, the construction of hard-surfaced "macadam" roads, the commercial use of the steamboat that Robert Fulton (1765–1815) demonstrated, and the railway locomotive that George Stephenson (1781–1848) made commercially successful. The Industrial Revolution created a unique new category of people who depended on their jobs for income and who needed job security. Until 1850, workers as a whole did not share in the general wealth produced by the Industrial Revolution. Conditions improved as the century wore on. Union action combined with general prosperity and a developing social conscience to improve the working conditions, wages, and hours of skilled labor first and unskilled labor later.

Socialism

The Utopian Socialists were the earliest writers to propose an equitable solution to improve the distribution of society's wealth. The name of this group comes from *Utopia*, Saint Thomas More's (1478–1535) book on a fictional ideal society. While they endorsed the productive capacity of industrialism, the Utopian Socialists denounced its mismanagement. Human society was ideally a community rather than a mixture of competing, selfish individuals. All the goods a person needed could be produced in one community. Scientific socialism, or Marxism, was the creation of Karl Marx (1818–1883), a German scholar who, with the help of Friedrich Engels (1820–1895), intended to replace utopian hopes and dreams with a militant blueprint for socialist working-class success. The principal works of this revolutionary school of socialism were *The Communist Manifesto* and *Das Kapital*.

Marxism has four key propositions:

1. An economic interpretation of history that asserts that economic factors (mainly centered on who controls the means of production and distribution) determines all human history.

3. The belief that there has always been a class struggle between the rich and the poor (or the exploiters and the exploited).

4. The theory of surplus value, which holds that the true value of a product is labor; because workers receive a small portion of their just labor price, the difference is surplus value "stolen" from workers by capitalists.

5. The belief that socialism is inevitable because capitalism contains the seeds of its own destruction (overproduction, unemployment, etc.). The rich grow richer and the poor grow poorer until the gap between each class (proletariat and bourgeoisie) becomes so great that the working classes rise up in revolution and overthrow the elite bourgeoisie to install a "dictatorship of the proletariat." The creation of a classless society guided by the principle "from each according to his abilities, to each according to his needs" will be the result of dismantling capitalism.

Skill 2.6: Determine the Causes and Consequences of Exploration, Settlement, and Growth on Various Cultures

Beginnings of European Exploration

Europeans were largely unaware of the existence of the American continent, even though a Norse seaman, Leif Eriksson, had sailed within sight of the continent in the eleventh century. Few other explorers ventured nearly as far as America. Before the fifteenth century, Europeans had little desire to explore and were not ready to face the many challenges of a long sea voyage. Just as developments led to changes and conflict in North America and produced an increasing number of distinct cultures and political systems, developments in Europe were about to make possible the great voyages that led to contact between Europe and the Americas. In the fifteenth and sixteenth centuries, technological devices such as the compass and astrolabe freed explorers from some of the constraints that had limited early voyages. Four primary factors—God, gold, glory, and goods—led to increased interest in exploration and eventually to a desire to settle in the newly discovered lands. European Christians wanted to spread religion. Gold and other riches were purported to be found in the new lands. The discovery of new worlds would result in fame. New worlds would provide new markets for European goods.

Early Challenges

Although Europeans such as Italians participated in overland trade with the East and sailed through the Mediterranean and beyond, it was the Arabs who played the largest part in such trade and who benefited the most economically. Prince Henry the Navigator, ruler of Portugal, sponsored voyages aimed at adding territory and gaining control of trading routes to increase the power and wealth of Portugal. Prince Henry also wanted to spread Christianity and prevent the further expansion of Islam in Africa. Henry the Navigator brought a number of Italian merchant traders to his court at Cape St. Vincent, and subsequently they sailed in Portuguese ships down the western coast of Africa. The initial voyages were extremely difficult owing to the lack of navigational instruments and any kind of maps or charts. Europeans had charted the entire Mediterranean Sea, including harbors and the coastline, but they had no knowledge or maps of the African coast.

The first task of the explorers was to create accurate charts of the African shoreline. The crews on these initial voyages did not encounter horrible monsters or boiling water, which had been rumored to exist in the ocean beyond Cape Bojador, the farthest point Europeans had previously reached. However, the explorers did discover that strong southward winds made it easy to sail out of the Mediterranean but difficult to return. Most people at the time believed that Africa and China were joined by a southern continent, eliminating any possibility of an eastern maritime route to the Indian Ocean. Portugal's Prince Henry, however, sent ships along the coast of Africa because he believed it was possible to sail most directly to Asia by sailing around the tip of Africa and then east across the Indian Ocean.

Technical Innovations Aiding Exploration

One of the reasons that the explorers sailing from Portugal traveled along the coast was to avoid losing sight of land. By the thirteenth century, explorers were using the compass, borrowed from China, to determine direction; it was more difficult to determine the relative position from the North and South poles and from landmasses or anything else. In the Northern Hemisphere, a navigator could determine the relative north-south position, or latitude, by calculating the height of the Pole Star from the horizon. South of the equator, one cannot see the Pole Star; until around 1460, captains had no way to determine their position if they sailed too far south.

Although longitude (relative east-west position) remained unknown until the eighteenth century, the introduction of the astrolabe allowed sailors to calculate their latitude south of the equator. Along with navigational aids, improvements in shipbuilding and in weaponry also facilitated exploration. Unlike in the Mediterranean, it was not possible to use ships propelled only by oarsmen in the Atlantic, because the waves there are high and the currents and winds are strong. Europeans had initially used very broad sails on ships that went out into the Atlantic. The ships were heavy and often became stranded by the absence of the favorable tailwinds upon which the ships and sailors depended. The Portuguese borrowed techniques from Arab and European shipbuilding and developed the Caravela Redondo. This ship proved to be more worthy of long voyages because it combined square rigging for speed with lateen sails that were more responsive and easier to handle. Other European states adopted the ship and also the practice of mounting artillery and other weapons on exploration vessels.

Main Elements of European Exploration

As the Portuguese began to trade and explore along the coast of Africa, they brought back slaves, ivory, gold, and knowledge of the African coast. It appeared that the Portuguese might find a route to the Indian Ocean, and it was clear that the voyages sponsored by Prince Henry were benefiting Portugal in many ways. Other European states wanted to increase their territory and wealth and to establish trade routes to the East. Although the desire for control of trade routes and wealth was a primary motive in launching voyages of exploration, it was not the only incentive. Europe in the fifteenth and sixteenth centuries, despite the increase in dissenting views, was still extremely religious. The Catholic Church continued to exert a tremendous influence, and some Christians were motivated to go on voyages of discovery to conduct missionary activities and spread the word of God.

After the beginning of the Reformation, many Lutherans, Calvinists, and other groups who had left the Catholic Church emigrated from Europe in hopes of settling where they would be free from religious persecution or violent conflicts. Younger sons of families in well-to-do Europe were often not able to find lucrative opportunities at home because the eldest son usually inherited lands and wealth. As a result, many younger sons often secure prominent positions in the church. The voyages of exploration, therefore, were a means of securing fame and fortune as well as spreading Christianity. Other individuals sponsored or participated in voyages in the hope of gaining wealth or increased opportunities.

Although the motivation of fame and fortune was often secondary to God and glory, many individuals were attracted to exploration by the possibility of adventure and by their desire to explore uncharted territory. These three factors—gold, God, and glory—operated on both individual and state levels; kings and heads of states were as interested as the seamen were in spreading their faith and increasing the wealth and prestige of their states. Portugal was the first European state to establish sugar plantations on an island off the west coast of Africa and to import slaves from Africa to labor there. It was the beginning of the slave trade. The level of trading was initially far less extensive and intense than during the later period of slave trade when Spain and England became involved. In an attempt to maintain control of the slave trade and of the eastern routes to India, the Portuguese appealed to the pope; he ruled in their favor and forbade the Spanish and others to sail south and east in an attempt to reach India or Asia.

Columbus

When Ferdinand and Isabella married and united the two largest provinces in Spain, Castile and Aragon, they not only began the process of uniting all of Spain but also agreed to sponsor Christopher Columbus in his voyage of exploration. Only the heads of states had the necessary resources and could afford the risk involved in sponsoring a major voyage across the oceans of the world, but most monarchs were unwilling to take such a risk. Columbus was an Italian explorer looking for a sponsor and had approached Ferdinand and Isabella after being turned down by the English government. He convinced the Spanish monarchs that a western route to the Indian Ocean existed and that it would be possible to make the voyage. However, Columbus had miscalculated the distance of the voyage from Europe to Asia. His estimate of the circumference of the earth was much less than it should have been for an accurate calculation, and no Europeans were aware of the existence of the American continents. One of the reasons that Ferdinand and Isabella were willing to support Columbus was that the previous agreements prevented all states but Portugal from sailing east to reach India. Therefore, the only chance for Spain to launch an expedition to India and to participate in trade and exploration was in the discovery of a western route to India.

In 1492, Columbus sailed from Spain with 90 men on three ships, the *Niña*, the *Pinta*, and the *Santa Maria* (though at least two of those names were probably nicknames). After a 10-week voyage, they landed in the Bahamas. On his second trip, Columbus reached Cuba, and then in 1498, during his third trip, he reached the mainland and sailed along the northern coast of South America. Columbus originally thought he had reached India; he referred to the people he encountered in the Bahamas and on his second landing in Cuba as Indians.

There is considerable debate over whether Columbus realized, either during his third voyage or just before his death, that he had landed not in India but on an entirely unknown continent between Europe and Asia. Another question is whether Columbus, who died in obscurity despite his fame for having discovered America, should receive credit for this discovery; earlier explorers had reached the American continent. However, because Columbus's voyages prompted extensive exploration and settlement of the Americas, it is accurate to state that he was responsible for the discovery of the New World by Europeans. Another result of Columbus's voyages was the increased focus of Spain on exploration and conquest. Nevertheless, the New World took its name from the Florentine merchant Amerigo Vespucci—not Columbus. Vespucci took part in several voyages to the New World and wrote a series of descriptions that not only gave Europeans an image of this "New World" but also spread the idea that the discovered lands were not a part of Asia or India. Vespucci, then, popularized the image of the Americas and the idea that the Americas were continents separate from those previously known.

Columbus is, however, remembered in the term *Columbian Exchange*. This was the start of an exchange between the old and new worlds. Although some exchanges such as ideas, foods, crops and populations resulted in benefits for both groups, other exchanges brought losses. Indigenous people were often seen as "inferior" and overthrown, subjugated, or killed. Diseases that were minimal in Europe ravaged indigenous groups that had no built-up immunities. Bows and arrows or spears were no match for gunpowder, spears, and cannons.

Balboa

Spanish explorer Vasco Nuñez de Balboa, who crossed the Isthmus of Panama and came to another ocean, which separates the American continents from China. Portuguese sailor Ferdinand Magellan, who sailed under the flag of both Spain and Portugal, discovered at the southern end of South America a strait that provided access to the ocean west of the Americas. Magellan named this ocean the Pacific because it was much calmer than the strait through which he had sailed to reach it. Later, he reached the Philippines and met his death in a conflict with the natives. Magellan's voyage, nevertheless, was the final stage of the process whereby Europeans completed the first-known circumnavigation of the globe. Although initially the Spanish were eager to find a route around the Americas that would enable them to sail on toward their original goal, the treasures of the Far East, they began to consider the Americas as a possible source of untapped wealth.

Cortez

Eventually the Spanish claimed all the New World except Brazil, which papal decree gave to the Portuguese. The first Spanish settlements were on the islands of the Caribbean Sea. It was not until 1518 that Spain appointed Hernando Cortez as a government official in Cuba.

Cortez led a small military expedition against the Aztecs in Mexico. Cortez and his men failed in their first attack on the Aztec capital city, Tenochtitlán, but were ultimately successful. A combination of factors allowed the small force of approximately 600 Spanish soldiers to overcome the extensive Aztec Empire. The Spanish were armed with rifles and bows, which provided an advantage over Aztec fighters armed only with spears. However, weapons and armor were not the main reason that the Spanish were able to overcome the military forces of the natives. The Aztec ruler, Montezuma, allowed a delegation, which included Cortez, into the capital city because the description of the Spanish soldiers in their armor and with feathers in their helmets was similar to the description in Aztec legend of messengers who would be sent by the chief Aztec god, Quetzcoatl. The members of Cortez's expedition exposed the natives to smallpox and other diseases that devastated the native population. Finally, the Spanish expedition was also able to form alliances with other native tribes that the Aztecs had conquered. These tribes were willing to cooperate to defeat the Aztecs and thus break up their empire.

Pizarro

Twenty years after Cortez defeated the Aztecs, another conquistador, Francisco Pizarro, defeated the Incas in Peru. Pizarro's expedition enabled the Spanish to begin to explore and settle South America. Spain funded the conquistadors, or conquerors, who were the first Europeans to explore some areas of the Americas. However, the sole purpose of the conquistadors' explorations was defeating the natives to gain access to gold, silver, and other wealth. Spain established mines in the territory it claimed and produced a tremendous amount of gold and silver. In the 300 years after the Spanish conquest of the Americas in the sixteenth century, those mines produced 10 times more gold and silver than the total produced by all the mines in the rest of the world.

Spanish Interest in the New World

Spain had come to view the New World as more than an obstacle to voyages toward India. Over time, Spain began to think that it might be possible to exploit this territory for more than just mining. It was the conquistadors who made it possible for the Spanish to settle the New World, but they were not responsible for forming settlements or for overseeing Spanish colonies in the New World. Instead, Spain sent officials and administrators from Spain to oversee settlements after their initial formation. Spanish settlers came to the New World for various reasons: some came in search of land to settle or buy, others came looking for opportunities that were not available to them in Europe, and priests and missionaries came to spread Christianity to the natives. By the end of the sixteenth century, Spain had established firm control over not only the several islands in the Caribbean, Mexico, and southern North America, but also the territory currently within the modern states of Chile, Argentina, and Peru.

Spanish Settlements in the New World

The first permanent settlement established by the Spanish was the predominantly military fort of St. Augustine, located in Florida. In 1598, Don Juan de Onate led a group of 500 settlers north out of Mexico and established a colony in what is now New Mexico. Onate granted *encomiendas* to the most prominent Spaniards who had accompanied him. Under the *encomienda* system, which the Spanish established in Mexico and parts of North America, these distinguished individuals had the right to exact tribute and/or labor from the native population, which continued to live on the land in exchange for the services it provided. Spanish colonists founded Santa Fe in 1609, and by 1680 about 2,000 Spaniards were living in New Mexico. Most of the colonists raised sheep and cattle on large ranches and lived among approximately 30,000 Pueblo Indians. The Spanish crushed a major revolt that threatened to destroy Santa Fe in 1680. Provoking the revolt were attempts to prevent the natives—both those who had converted to Catholicism and those who had not—from performing religious rituals that predated the Spaniards' arrival. The natives drove the Spaniards from Santa Fe, but they returned in 1696, crushed the Pueblos, and seized the land. Although the Spanish ultimately quelled the revolt, they began to change their policies toward the natives, who still greatly outnumbered the Spanish settlers. The Spanish continued to try to convert natives to Christianity and civilize them, but they also began to allow the Pueblos to own land. In addition, the Spanish unofficially tolerated native religious rituals, although Catholicism officially condemned all such practices.

By 1700, the Spanish population in New Mexico had increased and reached about 4,000; the native population had decreased to about 13,000 and intermarriage between natives and Spaniards increased. Nevertheless, disease, war, and migration resulted in the steady decline in the Pueblo population. New Mexico had become a prosperous and stable region, but it was still relatively weak and, as the only major Spanish settlement in northern Mexico, was isolated.

Effects of European-American Contact

One cannot underestimate the impact of Europeans on the New World, both before and after the arrival of the English and French. The most immediate effect was the spread of disease, which ravaged the native population. In some areas of Mexico, 95 percent of the native population died as a result of contact with Europeans and the subsequent outbreaks of diseases like smallpox. In South America, the native population was devastated not only by disease but also by deliberate policies instituted to control and in some cases eliminate native peoples. Although Europeans passed most diseases to the natives, the natives passed syphilis to the Europeans, who carried it back to Europe. The European and American continents exchanged plants and animals. Europeans brought over animals to the New World, and they took plants like potatoes, corn, and squash back to Europe, where introduction of these crops led to an explosion of the European population. The decimation of the native population and the establishment of large plantations led to a shortage of workers, and Europeans began to transport slaves from Africa to the New World to fill the shortage.

Skill 2.7: Interpret the Ways that Individuals and Events Have Influenced Economic, Social, and Political Institutions in the World, Nation, or State

World history is a story of causes and effects. Individual people and events have influenced the course of history and changed its course in many ways.

English Interest in the New World

In 1497, King Henry VIII of England sponsored a voyage by John Cabot to seek a northwest passage through the New World to the Orient. However, the English made no real attempt to settle in the New World until nearly a century later. By the 1600s, the English became interested in colonizing the New World. Several factors motivated their interest. Many people in England hoped to emigrate overseas because the country's population was increasing, and because the land was being used to raise sheep for wool rather than for growing foodstuffs for survival. The ability to buy land in England was scarce, another primary motivator for emigration.

Some people in England left their homeland because of the religious turmoil that engulfed England after the beginning of the Protestant Reformation. In addition to converts to Lutheranism and Calvinism, a major emigrating group was the Puritans, who called for reforms to "purify" the church. Mercantilism also provided a motive for exploration and for the establishment of colonies. According to mercantile theories, an industrialized nation needed an inexpensive source of raw materials and markets for finished products. Colonies provided a way to obtain raw materials and to guarantee a market for industrial goods. By the early 1800's it was said that "the sun never sets of the British Empire."

French and Dutch Settlements

Economic reasons, among others, motivated the French and the Dutch to explore and establish colonies in the New World. In 1609, the year after the first English settlement, the French established a colony in Quebec. Overall, far fewer French settlers traveled to the New World than did English settlers, but the French were able to exercise a tremendous influence through the establishment of strong ties with the natives. The French created trading partnerships and a vast trading network, they often intermarried with the local native population. The Dutch financed an English explorer, Henry Hudson, who claimed for Holland the territory that is now New York. The Dutch settlements along the Hudson, Delaware, and Connecticut rivers developed into the colony of New Netherlands and established a vast trading network that effectively separated the English colonies of Jamestown and Plymouth.

Roanoke

One reason that English settlements began to become more prominent after 1600 was the defeat of Spanish fleet, the supposedly invincible Armada, by the English in 1588. The changing power balance in the seas encouraged the English to increase their exploration and attempted colonization of the Americas. However, the first few colonies founded by the English in America did not flourish.

Sir Humphrey Gilbert, who had obtained a six-year grant giving him the exclusive rights to settle unclaimed land in America, was planning to establish a colony in Newfoundland, but a storm sank his ship. Instead, Sir Walter Raleigh received the six-year grant. Raleigh explored the North American coast and named the territory through which he traveled Virginia, in honor of the "Virgin Queen" Elizabeth I of England. In addition, Raleigh convinced his cousin, Sir Grenville, to establish a colony on the island of Roanoke. Roanoke was located off the coast of what later became North Carolina. The first settlers lived there for a year while Sir Grenville returned to England for supplies and additional settlers. However, when Sir Francis Drake arrived in Roanoke nearly a year later and found that Sir Grenville had not returned, the colonists left on his ship and abandoned the settlement. In 1587, Raleigh sent another group of colonists to Roanoke, but a war with Spain broke out in 1588 and kept him from returning until 1590. When Raleigh returned to Roanoke, the colonists had vanished. A single word, "Croatan," carved into a tree could have referred to a nearby settlement of natives. This suggested a number of possibilities in regard to the missing settlers; conclusive proof of their fate was never found.

The Jamestown Settlement

In 1606, King James I of England granted to the Virginia Company a charter for exploration and colonization. This charter marked the beginning of ventures sponsored by merchants rather than directly by the Crown. The charter of the Virginia Company had two branches. James I gave one branch to the English city of Plymouth, which had the right to the northern portion of territory on the eastern coast of North America, and he granted the London branch of the company the right to the southern portion.

Considerable difficulties prevented the English from founding and maintaining a permanent settlement in North America. The Plymouth Company failed to establish a lasting settlement. The company itself ran out of money, and the settlers who had gone to the New World gave up and abandoned their established Sagadahoc Colony in Maine. Having decided to colonize the Chesapeake Bay area, the London Company sent three ships with about 104 sailors to that area in 1607. The company's ships sailed up a river, which they named the James in honor of the English king, and they established the fort and permanent settlement of Jamestown. The London Company and the men who settled Jamestown were hoping to find a northwest passage to Asia, gold, and silver, or to be able to find lands capable of producing valuable goods, such as grapes, oranges, or silk. The colony at Jamestown did not allow the settlers to accomplish any of those things, and its location on the river, which became contaminated every spring, led to the outbreak of diseases such as typhoid, dysentery, and malaria. Over half the colonists died the first year, and by the spring of 1609, only one-third of the total number of colonists who had joined the colony was still alive.

The survival of Jamestown initially was largely accomplished through the efforts of Captain John Smith. Smith was a soldier who turned the colony's focus from exploration to obtaining food. Initially, Smith was able to obtain corn from the local Indians led by Powhatan and his 12-year-old daughter Pocahontas. Smith also forced all able men in the colony to work four hours a day in the wheat fields. Attempts by the London Company to send additional settlers and supplies encountered troubles and delays.

Demise of Jamestown

Thomas Gates and some 600 settlers, who left for Jamestown in 1609, ran aground on Bermuda and had to build a new ship. Although some new settlers did arrive in Jamestown, disease continued to shrink the population. When seriously-injured Smith had to return to England, his departure deprived the colony of its most effective and resourceful leader. It was not long after Smith left that the colonists provoked a war with Powhatan, who was beginning to tire of the colonists' demands for corn. Powhatan realized that the settlers intended to stay indefinitely and might challenge the Indians for control of the surrounding territory.

Gates finally arrived at Jamestown in June 1610 with only 175 of the original 600 settlers. He found only 60 colonists who had survived the war with the Indians and the harsh winter of 1610, during which they had minimal food and other resources. Gates decided to abandon Jamestown and was sailing down the river with the surviving colonists on board when he encountered the new governor from England, Thomas West, and Baron de la Warr. Gates and West returned to Jamestown, imposed martial law, responded to Indian attacks, and survived a five-year war with the Indians. Although the war did not end until 1614, when the colonists were able to negotiate a settlement by holding Pocahontas hostage, the situation in Jamestown began to improve in 1610.

Virginia Settlements

After this time, some of the Jamestown settlers relocated to healthier locations, and in 1613 one of them, John Rolfe, married Pocahontas. In 1614, the settlers planted a mild strain of tobacco, which gave them a crop they could sell for cash. The Crown issued two new charters that allowed Virginia to extend its borders all the way to the Pacific and made the London Company a joint-stock company. Changes in the company led to a new treasurer, Sir Edwin Sandy, who tried to reform Virginia.

Sandy encouraged settlers in Virginia to try to produce grapes and silkworms and to diversify the colony's economy in other ways. Sandy also replaced martial law with English common law. The colonists established a council to make laws, and settlers now had the right to own land. By 1623, about 4,000 additional settlers had arrived in Virginia. Attempts to produce and sell crops other than tobacco, however, failed, and the arrival of large numbers of new colonists provoked renewed conflict with the Indians. A major Indian attack launched in March 1622 killed 347 colonists. Investors in the London Company withdrew their capital and appealed to the king, and a royal commission visited the colony. As a result of this investigation, the king declared the London Company bankrupt and assumed direct control of Virginia in 1624. Virginia became the first royal colony, and the Crown appointed a governor and a council to oversee its administration.

Three trends continued after the Crown assumed control. The first was unrelenting conflict with the Indians. Through war and raids, by 1632 the colonists had killed or driven out most of the Indians in the area immediately around Jamestown. The other two trends were the yearly influx of thousands of new settlers and the high death rate in the colony.

Despite the high mortality rate, the population of the colony began gradually to increase. The expansion of tobacco production led to a demand for labor, and thousands of the young men who came were indentured servants. In exchange for their passage to America and food and shelter during their terms of service, these men were bound to work for their masters for four or five years. After that time, they gained their freedom and often a small payment to help them become established. Most of these men were not able to participate in the running of the colony even after they became free, but some were able to acquire land.

In 1634, the Crown divided Virginia into counties, each with appointed justices and the right to fill all other positions. Under this type of system, individuals from a few wealthy families tended to dominate the government. Most of the counties became Anglican, and the colony continued to elect representatives to its House of Burgesses, an assembly that met with the governor to discuss issues of common law. The king, however, refused to recognize the colony's House of Burgesses. After 1660, the colony became even more dominated by the wealthiest 15 percent of the population, and these individuals and their sons continued to be the only colonists to serve as justices and burgesses. Settlement of the colonies continued, primarily for religious and economic reasons. Conflict between the colonists and the natives was a constant.

Growth of the Slave Trade

The shortage of labor in the southern colonies and a drop in the number of people coming to the colonies as indentured servants forced the colonists to search for other sources of labor. Although the colonists began using African servants and slaves almost immediately after settling in the New World, the slave trade and the slave population in British North America remained small in the first half of the seventeenth century. Toward the end of the seventeenth century, increasing numbers of slaves from Africa became available, and the demand for them in North America further stimulated the growth of the transatlantic slave trade.

By the nineteenth century, millions of Africans had been forcibly taken from their native lands and sold into perpetual slavery. The Europeans sold slaves at forts the slave traders had established on the African coast; the Europeans packed the slaves as closely as possible into the lower regions of ships for the long journey to the Americas. Chained slaves traveled in deplorably unsanitary conditions and received only enough food and water to keep them alive. Many slaves died during this Middle Passage voyage. Plantation owners in the Caribbean, Brazil, or North America bought the slaves to do the work. It was only after 1697 that English colonists began to buy large numbers of slaves. By 1760, the slave population had reached approximately a quarter of a million with most of the slaves concentrated in the southern colonies. Slave labor replaced indentured servitude, and a race-based system of perpetual slavery developed. Colonial assemblies began to pass "slave codes" in the eighteenth century. These codes identified all nonwhites or dark-skinned people as slaves, made their condition permanent, and legalized slavery in British North America.

Salem Witch Trials

During this period of increasing tensions, several communities held witchcraft trials. In Salem, Massachusetts, a group of young girls accused servants from West India and older white members of the community, mostly women, of exercising powers that Satan had given to them. Other towns also experienced turmoil and charged residents with witchcraft. In Salem alone, the juries pronounced 19 people guilty; in 1692 after the execution of all 19 victims, the girls admitted their stories were not true.

The witchcraft trials illustrate the highly religious nature of the New England society, but they also suggest that individuals who did not conform to societal expectations were at risk of serious consequences. Most of the accused were outspoken women who were often critical of their communities, were older, and were either widows or unmarried. Some of these women had acquired property despite the accepted views and limitations regarding women's role in society.

Religion in the Colonies

The religious nature of colonial settlers did not lead to the kind of intolerance or persecution that had plagued Europe since the Reformation. Conflict among various religious groups did break out occasionally, but British North America enjoyed a far greater degree of religious toleration than anywhere else. Among the reasons this toleration existed were that several religious groups had immigrated to North America and that every colony, except Virginia and Maryland, ignored the laws establishing the Church of England as the official faith of the colony. Even among the Puritans, differences in religious opinion led to the establishment of different denominations.

Although there was some religious tolerance, Protestants still tended to view Roman Catholics as threatening rivals. In Maryland, Catholics numbered about 3,000, the largest population of all the colonies, and were the victims of persecution. Jews were often victims of persecution; they could not vote or hold office in any of the colonies, and only in Rhode Island could they practice the Jewish religion openly.

In addition to religious tolerance, the other main trends at the time were the westward spread of communities, the rise of cities, and a decline in religious piousness. This sense of the weakening of religious authority and faithfulness led to the Great Awakening.

The Great Awakening

The Great Awakening refers to a period beginning in the 1730s in which several well-known preachers traveled through British North America giving speeches and arguing for the need to revive religious piety and closer relationships with God. The main message of the preachers was that everyone has the potential, regardless of past behavior, to reestablish their relationship with God. This message appealed to many women and younger sons of landowners who stood to inherit very little. The best-known preacher during this period was Jonathan Edwards. Edwards denounced some current beliefs as doctrines of easy salvation. At his church in Northampton, Edwards sermonized about the absolute sovereignty of God, predestination, and salvation by grace alone.

The Great Awakening further divided religion in America by creating distinctions among New Light groups (revivalists), Old Light groups (traditionalists), and new groups that incorporated elements of both. The various revivalists, or New Light groups, did not agree on every issue. Some revivalists denounced education and learning from books while others founded schools in the belief that education was a means of furthering religion. While some individuals were stressing a need for renewed spiritual focus, others were beginning to embrace the ideas of the Enlightenment.

The Enlightenment in Colonial America

The Scientific Revolution had demonstrated the existence of natural laws that operated in nature, and enlightened thinkers began to argue that man had the ability to improve his own situation through the use of rational thought and acquired knowledge. Intellectuals of the Enlightenment shifted the focus from God to man, introduced the idea of progress, and argued that people could improve their own situations and make decisions on how to live rather than just having faith in God and waiting for a better life after death and salvation.

Enlightenment thought had a tremendous impact on the North American colonists, who began to establish more schools, encourage the acquisition of knowledge, and become more interested in gaining scientific knowledge. The colleges founded in North America taught the scientific theories held by Copernicus, who argued that planets rotated around the sun not the Earth, and Newton, who introduced the key principles of physics, including gravity. The colonists did not just learn European theories. Benjamin Franklin was among the colonists who began to carry out their own experiments and form their own theories. Franklin experimented with electricity and was able to demonstrate in 1752, by using a kite, that electricity and lightning were the same.

The perspective of the Enlightenment and scientific theories and research in particular also led to inoculations against smallpox. The Puritan theologian Cotton Mather convinced the population of Boston that injections with a small amount of the smallpox virus would build up their resistance to the disease and reduce the likelihood of reinfection. Leading theologians and scientists spread European scientific ideas and developed their own theories and applications using their acquired knowledge.

The Beginnings of the American Revolution

In 1764, George Grenville pushed through Britain's Parliament the Sugar Act (the Revenue Act), which aimed at raising revenue by taxing goods imported by Americans. The Stamp Act (1765) imposed a direct tax on the colonists for the first time. By requiring Americans to purchase revenue stamps on everything from newspapers to legal documents, the Stamp Act would have created an impossible drain on hard currency in the colonies.

Americans reacted to these parliamentary acts first with restrained and respectful petitions and pamphlets in which they pointed out that "taxation without representation is tyranny." The colonists began to limit their purchase of imported goods. From there, resistance progressed to stronger protests that eventually became violent. In October 1765, delegates from nine colonies met as the Stamp Act Congress and passed moderate resolutions against the act and asserted that Americans could not be taxed without the consent of their representatives. The colonists now ceased all importation.

In March 1766, Parliament repealed the Stamp Act. At the same time, however, it passed the Declaratory Act, which claimed the power to tax or make laws for the Americans "in all cases whatsoever." In 1766, Parliament passed a program of taxes on items imported into the colonies. The taxes came to be known as the Townsend duties, a name that came from Britain's Chancellor of the Exchequer, Charles Townsend. American reaction was at first slow, but the sending of troops roused them to resistance.

Again the colonies halted importation, and soon British merchants were calling on Parliament to repeal the Townsend duties. In March 1770, Parliament repealed all the taxes except that on tea; Parliament wanted to prove that it had the right to tax the colonies if it so desired. When Parliament ended the Tea Act in 1773, a relative peace ensued.

Resumption of Conflict

In desperate financial condition—partially because the Americans were buying smuggled Dutch tea rather than the taxed British product—the British East India Company sought and obtained from Parliament concessions that allowed it to ship tea directly to the colonies rather than only by way of Britain. The result would be that the East India Company tea, even with the tax, would be cheaper than smuggled Dutch tea. The company hoped that the colonists would thus buy the tea, tax and all, save the East India Company, and tacitly accept Parliament's right to tax them. The Americans, however, proved resistant to this approach. Rather than acknowledge Parliament's right to tax, they refused to buy the cheaper tea and resorted to various methods, including tar and feathers, to prevent the collection of the tax on tea. In most ports, Americans did not allow ships carrying the tea to land.

In Boston, however, the pro-British governor Thomas Hutchinson forced a confrontation by ordering Royal Navy vessels to prevent the tea ships from leaving the harbor. After 20 days, this would, by law, result in selling the cargoes at auction and paying the tax. The night before the time was to expire, December 16, 1773, Bostonians thinly disguised as Native Americans boarded the ships and threw the tea into the harbor. This was the Boston Tea Party. The British responded with four acts collectively titled the Coercive Acts (1774), in which they strengthened their control over the colonists. The First Continental Congress (1774) met in response to the acts. The Congress called for strict nonimportation and rigorous preparation of local militia companies.

The American War for Independence

British troops went to Massachusetts, which the Crown had officially declared to be in a state of rebellion. British General Thomas Gage received orders to arrest the leaders of the resistance or, failing that, to provoke any sort of confrontation that would allow him to turn British military might loose on the Americans. Americans, however, detected the movement of Gage's troops toward Concord, and dispatch riders, like Paul Revere and William Dawes, spread the news throughout the countryside.

In Lexington, about 70 minutemen (trained militiamen who would respond at a moment's notice) awaited the British on the village green. A shot was fired; it is unknown which side fired first. This became "the shot heard 'round the world." The British opened fire and charged, and casualties occurred on both sides. The following month, the Americans tightened the noose around Boston by fortifying Breed's Hill (a spur of Bunker Hill). The British determined to remove them by a frontal attack. Twice thrown back, the British finally succeeded when the Americans ran out of ammunition. There were more than 1,000 British casualties in what turned out to be the bloodiest battle of the war (June 17, 1775), yet the British had gained very little and remained essentially trapped in Boston.

Congress now put George Washington (1732–1799) in charge of the army, called for more troops, and adopted the Olive Branch Petition, which pleaded with King George III to intercede with Parliament to restore peace. However, the king gave his approval to the Prohibitory Act, declaring the colonies in rebellion and no longer under his protection. Preparations began for full-scale war against America.

In 1776, the colonists formed two committees to establish independence and a national government. One committee was created to work out a framework for a national government. The other was created to draft a statement of the reasons for declaring independence. This statement, called the *Declaration of Independence*, was primarily the work of Thomas Jefferson (1743–1826) of Virginia. It was a restatement of political ideas by then commonplace in America and an explanation of why the former colonists felt justified in separating from Great Britain. Congress formally adopted the *Declaration of Independence* on July 4, 1776.

The British landed that summer at New York City. General Washington, who had anticipated the move, was waiting for them, but the undertrained, underequipped, and badly outnumbered American army was no match for the British and had to retreat. By December, what was left of Washington's army had made it into Pennsylvania. With his small army melting away as demoralized soldiers deserted, Washington then decided on a bold stroke. On Christmas night, 1776, his army crossed the Delaware River and struck the Hessians (German mercenaries fighting for England) at Trenton. Washington's troops easily defeated the Hessians, still groggy from their hard-drinking Christmas party.

A few days later, Washington defeated a British force at Princeton. The Americans regained much of New Jersey from the British and saved the American army from disintegration. Hoping to weaken Britain, France began making covert shipments of arms to the Americans early in the war. These French shipments were vital for the Americans. The American victory at Saratoga convinced the French to join openly in the war against England. Eventually, the Spanish (1779) and the Dutch (1780) joined as well. The final agreement became known as the Treaty of Paris of 1783. Its terms stipulated the following:

1. The recognition by the major European powers, including Britain, of the United States as an independent nation.

2. The establishment of America's western boundary at the Mississippi River.

3. The establishment of America's southern boundary at 31 degrees north latitude (the northern boundary of Florida).

4. The surrender of Florida to Spain and the retainment of Canada by Britain.

5. The enablement of private British creditors to collect any debts owed by United States citizens.

6. The recommendation of Congress that the states restore confiscated loyalist property.

The Federalist Era

After the adoption of the *Articles of Confederation*, Congress adopted a new constitution and the Americans elected George Washington as President under the guidelines. George Washington received virtually all the votes of the presidential electors. John Adams (1735–1826) received the next highest number and became the vice president. After a triumphant journey from Mount Vernon, Washington attended his inauguration in New York City, the temporary seat of government.

To oppose the antifederalists, the states ratified 10 amendments—the *Bill of Rights*—by the end of 1791. The first nine spelled out specific guarantees of personal freedoms, and the Tenth Amendment reserved to the states all powers not specifically withheld or granted to the federal government.

Alexander Hamilton (1757–1804) interpreted the Constitution as having vested extensive powers in the federal government. This "implied powers" stance claimed that the government had all powers that the Constitution had not expressly denied to it. Hamilton's was the "broad" interpretation of the Constitution. By contrast, Thomas Jefferson and James Madison (1751–1836) held the view that the Constitution prohibited any action not specifically permitted in the Constitution. Based on this view of government, adherents of this "strict" interpretation opposed the establishment of Hamilton's national bank. Jeffersonian supporters, primarily under the guidance of James Madison, began to organize political groups in opposition to Hamilton's program. The groups opposing Hamilton's view called themselves Democratic-Republicans or Jeffersonians.

The Federalists, Hamilton's supporters, received their strongest confirmation from the business and financial groups in the commercial centers of the Northeast and from the port cities of the South. The strength of the Democratic-Republicans lay primarily in the rural and frontier areas of the South and West. Federalist candidate John Adams won the election of 1796. The elections in 1798 increased the Federalists' majorities in both houses of Congress that used their "mandate" to enact legislation to stifle foreign influences. For example, the Alien Act raised new hurdles in the path of immigrants trying to obtain citizenship, and the Sedition Act widened the powers of the Adams administration to muzzle its newspaper critics. Democratic-Republicans were convinced that the Alien and Sedition Acts were unconstitutional, but the process of deciding on the constitutionality of federal laws was as yet undefined.

The Jeffersonian Era

Thomas Jefferson and Aaron Burr ran for the presidency on the Democratic-Republican ticket, though not together, against John Adams and Charles Pinckney for the Federalists. Both Jefferson and Burr received the same number of votes in the Electoral College, so the election went to the House of Representatives. After a lengthy deadlock, Alexander Hamilton threw his support to Jefferson. Burr had to accept the vice presidency, the result obviously intended by the electorate.

The adoption and ratification of the Twelfth Amendment in 1804 ensured that a tie vote between candidates of the same party could not again cause the confusion of the Jefferson-Burr affair. Following the constitutional mandate, an 1808 law prevented the importation of slaves. An American delegation purchased the trans-Mississippi territory, 828,000 square miles in all, from Napoleon for $15 million in April 1803 (the Louisiana Purchase), even though they had no authority to buy more than the city of New Orleans.

The War of 1812

Democratic-Republican James Madison won the election of 1808 over Federalist Charles Pinckney, but the Federalists gained seats in both houses of Congress. The Native American tribes of the Northwest and the Mississippi Valley were resentful of the government's policy of pressured removal to the West, and the British authorities in Canada exploited their discontent by encouraging border raids against the American settlements. At the same time, the British interfered with American transatlantic shipping, including impressment of sailors and capture of ships. On June 1, 1812, President Madison asked for a declaration of war, and Congress complied. After three years of inconclusive war, the British and Americans signed the Treaty of Ghent (1815). It provided for the acceptance of the status quo that had existed at the beginning of hostilities, and both sides restored their wartime conquests to the other.

The Monroe Doctrine

As Latin American nations began declaring independence, British and American leaders feared that European governments would try to restore the former New World colonies to their erstwhile royal owners. In December 1823, President James Monroe (1758–1831) included in his annual message to Congress a statement that the peoples of the American hemisphere were "henceforth not to be considered as subjects for future colonization by any European powers."

The Marshall Court

Chief Justice John Marshall (1755–1835) delivered the majority opinions in several critical decisions in the formative years of the U.S. Supreme Court. These decisions served to strengthen the power of the federal government (and of the court itself) and restrict the powers of state governments.

Following are two key examples:

- *Marbury v. Madison* (1803) established the Supreme Court's power of judicial review over federal legislation.

- In *Gibbons v. Ogden* (1824), a case involving competing steamboat companies, Marshall ruled that commerce includes navigation and that only Congress has the right to regulate commerce among states, thereby voiding state-granted monopolies.

The Missouri Compromise

The Missouri Territory, the first territory organized from the Louisiana Purchase, applied for statehood in 1819. Because the Senate membership was evenly divided between slave-holding and free states at that time, the admission of a new state would give the voting advantage to either the North or the South. As the debate dragged on, the northern territory of Massachusetts applied for admission as the state of Maine. By combining the two admission bills, Maine came in as a free state and Missouri as a slave state. To make the Missouri Compromise palatable for the House of Representatives, an added provision prohibited slavery in the remainder of the Louisiana Territory north of the southern boundary of Missouri (latitude 36°30′).

Jacksonian Democracy

Andrew Jackson (1767–1845), the candidate of a faction of the emerging Democratic Party, won the election of 1828. Jackson was popular with the common man. He seemed to be the prototype of the self-made westerner: rough-hewn, violent, vindictive, with few ideas but strong convictions. He ignored his appointed cabinet officers and relied instead on the counsel of his "Kitchen Cabinet," a group of partisan supporters. He exercised his veto power more than any other president before him and, in one of many notable actions, he vetoed the renewal of the national bank.

Jackson supported the removal of all Native American tribes to an area west of the Mississippi River. The Indian Removal Act of 1830 provided for the federal enforcement of that process. One of the results of this policy was the Trail of Tears, the forced march under U.S. Army escort of thousands of Cherokee Indians to the West. One-quarter or more of the Cherokee, mostly women and children, perished on the journey.

The Early Antislavery Movement

In 1831, William Lloyd Garrison started his newspaper, *The Liberator*, and began to advocate total and immediate emancipation. He founded the New England Antislavery Society in 1832 and the American Antislavery Society in 1833. At around the same time, Theodore Weld pursued the same goals but advocated more gradual means. The antislavery movement then split into two wings: Garrison's radical followers and the moderates who favored "moral persuasion" and petitions to Congress. In 1840, the Liberty Party, the first national antislavery party, fielded a presidential candidate on the platform of *free soil* (preventing the expansion of slavery into the new western territories).

Manifest Destiny and Westward Expansion

The term *Manifest Destiny* was not coined until 1844, but the belief that the destiny of the American nation consisted of expansion all the way to the Pacific Ocean, and possibly even to Canada and Mexico, was older than that. A common conviction was that Americans should share American liberty and ideals with everyone possible and, if necessary, by force. During the 1830s, American missionaries followed the traders and trappers to the Oregon country and began to publicize the richness and beauty of the land. The result was the Oregon Fever of the 1840s, as thousands of settlers trekked across the Great Plains and the Rocky Mountains to settle the new Shangri-La.

Texas had been a state in the Republic of Mexico since 1822, following the Mexican revolution against Spanish control. The new Mexican government invited immigration from the North by offering land grants to Stephen Austin and other Americans. By 1835, approximately 35,000 "gringos" were homesteading on Texas land. When Mexican officials saw their powerbase eroding as the foreigners flooded in, they moved to tighten control through restrictions on immigration and through tax increases. The Texans responded in 1836 by proclaiming independence and establishing a new republic. In 1845, after a series of failed attempts at annexation, the United States Congress admitted Texas to the Union.

The Mexican War

Though Mexico broke diplomatic relations with the United States immediately after Texas's admission to the Union, there was still hope of a peaceful settlement. In the fall of 1845, President James K. Polk (1795–1849) sent John Slidell to Mexico City with a proposal for a peaceful settlement, but, like other attempts at negotiation, nothing came of it. Racked by coup and countercoup, the Mexican government refused even to receive Slidell. Polk responded by sending U.S. troops into the disputed territory. On April 5, 1846, Mexican troops attacked an American patrol. When news of the clash reached Washington, Polk sought and received from Congress a declaration of war against Mexico.

At the close of the war, peace was negotiated via the Treaty of Guadalupe Hidalgo on February 2, 1848. Under the terms of the treaty, Mexico ceded to the United States the southwestern territory from Texas to the California coast.

Seeds of the Civil War

The Mexican War had barely started when, on August 8, 1846, a freshman Democratic congressman, David Wilmot of Pennsylvania, introduced his Wilmot Proviso as a proposed amendment to a war appropriations bill. The bill stipulated that "neither slavery nor involuntary servitude shall ever exist" in any territory to be acquired from Mexico. The House passed the proviso, but the Senate did not; Wilmot introduced his provision again amidst increasingly acrimonious debate.

One compromise proposal called for the extension of the 36°30′ line of the Missouri Compromise westward through the Mexican cession to the Pacific, with territory north of the line closed to slavery. Another compromise solution was "popular sovereignty," which held that the residents of each territory should decide for themselves whether to allow slavery.

Having more than the requisite population and being in need of better government, California petitioned in September 1849 for admission to the Union as a free state. Southerners were furious. Long outnumbered in the House of Representatives, the South would find itself, should Congress admit California as a free state, similarly outnumbered in the Senate. At this point, the aged Henry Clay proposed what would be known as the Compromise of 1850. For the North, Congress would admit California as a free state; the land in dispute between Texas and New Mexico would go to New Mexico; popular sovereignty would decide the issue of slavery in the New Mexico and Utah territories (all of the Mexican cession outside of California); and there would be no slave trade in the District of Columbia. For the South, Congress would enact a tougher Fugitive Slave Law, promise not to abolish slavery in the District of Columbia, and declare that it did not have jurisdiction over the interstate slave trade; the federal government would pay Texas's $10 million pre-annexation debt.

The Kansas-Nebraska Act

All illusion of sectional peace ended abruptly in 1854 when Senator Stephen A. Douglas of Illinois introduced a bill in Congress to organize the area west of Missouri and Iowa as the territories of Kansas and Nebraska on the basis of popular sovereignty. The Kansas-Nebraska Act aroused a storm of outrage in the North, which viewed the repeal of the Missouri Compromise as the breaking of a solemn agreement, hastened the disintegration of the Whig Party, and divided the Democratic Party along North-South lines. Springing to life almost overnight as a result of northern fury at the Kansas-Nebraska Act was the Republican Party. This party included diverse elements whose sole unifying principle was banning slavery from all the nation's territories, confining slavery to the states where it already existed, and preventing the further spread of slavery.

The *Dred Scott* Decision

In *Dred Scott v. Sandford* (1857), the Supreme Court attempted to settle the slavery question. The case involved a Missouri slave, Dred Scott, whom the abolitionists had encouraged to sue for his freedom on the basis that his owner had taken him to a free state, Illinois, for several years and then to a free territory, Wisconsin. The Court attempted to read the extreme southern position on slavery into the Constitution, ruling not only that Scott had no standing to sue in federal court but also that temporary residence in a free state, even for several years, did not make a slave free. In addition, the Court ruling signified that the Missouri Compromise (already a dead letter by that time) had been unconstitutional all along because Congress did not have the authority to exclude slavery from a territory nor did territorial governments have the right to prohibit slavery.

The Election of 1860

As the 1860 presidential election approached, the Republicans met in Chicago, confident of victory and determined to do nothing to jeopardize their favorable position. Accordingly, they rejected as too radical the front-running candidate, New York Senator William H. Seward, in favor of Illinois's favorite son, Abraham Lincoln (1809–1865). The platform called for federal support of a transcontinental railroad and for the containment of slavery. On Election Day, the voting went along strictly sectional lines. Although Lincoln led in popular votes, he was short of a majority. He did have, however, the needed majority of Electoral College votes and was elected president.

The Secession

On December 20, 1860, South Carolina, by vote of a special convention, seceded from the Union. By February 1, 1861, six more states (Alabama, Georgia, Florida, Mississippi, Louisiana, and Texas) had followed suit. Representatives of the seceded states met in Montgomery, Alabama, in February 1861 and declared themselves to be the Confederate States of America. They elected former secretary of war and United States senator Jefferson Davis (1808–1889) of Mississippi as president and Alexander Stephens (1812–1883) of Georgia as vice president.

Beginnings of the Civil War

In his inaugural address, Lincoln urged Southerners to reconsider their actions but warned that the Union was perpetual, that states could not secede, and that he would therefore hold the federal forts and installations in the South. Only two remained in federal hands: Fort Pickens, off Pensacola, Florida; and Fort Sumter, in the harbor of Charleston, South Carolina.

From Major Robert Anderson, commander of the small garrison at Fort Sumter, Lincoln soon received word that supplies were running low. Desiring to send in the needed supplies, Lincoln informed the governor of South Carolina of his intentions but promised that no attempt would be made to send arms, ammunition, or reinforcements unless Southerners initiated hostilities. Confederate General P. G. T. Beauregard, acting on orders from President Davis, demanded Anderson's surrender. Anderson said he would surrender if not resupplied. Knowing supplies were on the way, the Confederates opened fire at 4:30 a.m. on April 12, 1861. The next day, the fort surrendered. The day following Sumter's surrender, Lincoln declared an insurrection and called for the states to provide 75,000 volunteers to put it down. In response, Virginia, Tennessee, North Carolina, and Arkansas declared their secession. The remaining slave states—Delaware, Kentucky, Maryland, and Missouri—wavered but stayed with the Union.

The North enjoyed many advantages over the South. It had the majority of wealth and was vastly superior in industry. The North also had an advantage of almost three to one in manpower; over one-third of the South's population was slaves, whom Southerners would not use as soldiers. Unlike the South, the North received large numbers of immigrants during the war. The North retained control of the U.S. Navy; it could command the sea and blockade the South. Finally, the North enjoyed a much superior system of railroads. The South did, however, have some advantages. It was vast in size and difficult to conquer. In addition, its troops would be fighting on their own ground, a fact that would give them the advantage of familiarity with the terrain and the added motivation of defending their homes and families.

The Homestead Act and the Morrill Land Grant Act

In 1862, Congress passed two highly important acts dealing with domestic affairs in the North. The Homestead Act granted 160 acres of government land free of charge to any person who would farm it for at least five years. Many of the settlers of the West used the provisions of this act. The Morrill Land Grant Act offered large amounts of federal land to states that would establish "agricultural and mechanical" colleges. The founding of many of the nation's large state universities was under the provisions of this act.

The Emancipation Proclamation

By mid-1862, Lincoln, under pressure from radical elements of his own party and hoping to create a favorable impression on foreign public opinion, determined to issue the Emancipation Proclamation, which declared free all slaves in areas still in rebellion as of January 1, 1863. At Seward's recommendation, Lincoln waited to announce the proclamation until the North won some sort of victory. The Battle of Antietam (September 17, 1862) provided this victory.

Northern Victory

In September 1864, word came that Union General William Sherman (1820–1891) had taken Atlanta. The capture of this vital southern rail and manufacturing center brought an enormous boost to northern morale. Along with other northern victories that summer and fall, it ensured a resounding election victory for Lincoln and the continuation of the war on highly favorable terms for the North.

Confederate General Robert E. Lee (1807–1870) abandoned Richmond on April 3, 1865, and attempted to escape with what was left of his army. Pursued by Union General Ulysses S. Grant (1822–1885), Northern forces cornered Lee's troops and forced his surrender at Appomattox, Virginia, on April 9, 1865. Other Confederate troops still holding out in various parts of the South surrendered over the next few weeks. Lincoln did not live to receive news of the final surrenders. On April 14, 1865, John Wilkes Booth shot Lincoln in the back of the head while the president was watching a play in Ford's Theater in Washington, D.C.

Reconstruction

In 1865, Congress created the Freedmen's Bureau to provide food, clothing, and education to former slaves and to look after their interests. To restore legal governments in the seceded states, Lincoln developed a policy that made it relatively easy for southern states to enter the collateral process.

Congress passed a Civil Rights Act in 1866, declaring that all citizens born in the United States are, regardless of race, equal citizens under the law. This act became the model of the Fourteenth Amendment to the Constitution.

President Andrew Johnson obeyed the letter but not the spirit of the Reconstruction acts. Congress, angry at his refusal to cooperate, sought in vain for grounds to impeach him. In August 1867, Johnson violated the Tenure of Office Act, which forbade the president from removing from office officials who had been approved by the Senate. This test of the act's constitutionality took place not in the courts but in Congress. The House of Representatives impeached Johnson, and he came within one vote of being removed from office by the Senate.

The Fifteenth Amendment

In 1868, the Republicans nominated Ulysses S. Grant for president. His narrow victory prompted Republican leaders to decide that it would be politically expedient to give the vote to black men, northern as well as southern. The vote was extended only to black men because as of 1868 no women were allowed to vote. (Woman suffrage would not come for another half-century.) For this purpose, leaders of the North drew up and submitted to the states the Fifteenth Amendment. Ironically, the idea was so unpopular in the North that it won the necessary three-fourths approval only because Congress required the southern states to ratify it.

Industrialism

In the late nineteenth and early twentieth centuries, captains of industry—such as John D. Rockefeller in oil, J. P. Morgan in banking, Gustavus Swift in meat processing, Andrew Carnegie in steel, and E. H. Harriman in railroads—created major industrial empires. In 1886, Samuel Gompers and Adolph Strasser put together a combination of national craft unions, the American Federation of Labor (AFL), to represent labor's concerns about wages, hours, and safety conditions. Although militant in its use of the strike and in its demand for collective bargaining in labor contracts with large corporations, the AFL did not promote violence or radicalism.

The Spanish-American War

The Cuban revolt against Spain in 1895 threatened American business interests in Cuba. Sensational "yellow" journalism and nationalistic statements from officials such as Assistant Secretary of the Navy Theodore Roosevelt (1858–1919) encouraged popular support for direct American military intervention on behalf of Cuban independence.

On March 27, 1897, President William McKinley (1843–1901) asked Spain to call an armistice, accept American mediation to end the war, and stop using concentration camps in Cuba. Spain refused to comply. On April 21, Congress declared war on Spain with the objective of establishing Cuban independence (Teller Amendment). The first U.S. forces landed in Cuba on June 22, 1898, and by July 17 had defeated the Spanish forces. Spain ceded the Philippines, Puerto Rico, and Guam to the United States in return for a payment of $20 million to Spain for the Philippines.

Progressive Reforms and Social Change

On September 6, 1901, while attending the Pan American Exposition in Buffalo, New York, President McKinley was shot by Leon Czolgosz, an anarchist. The president died on September 14. Theodore Roosevelt, at age 42, became the nation's twenty-fifth president and its youngest president to date.

In accordance with the Antitrust Policy (1902), Roosevelt ordered the Justice Department to prosecute corporations pursuing monopolistic practices. Attorney General P. C. Knox first brought suit against the Northern Securities Company, a railroad holding corporation put together by J. P. Morgan, and then moved against Rockefeller's Standard Oil Company. By the time he left office in 1909, Roosevelt had indictments against 25 monopolies.

Roosevelt engineered the separation of Panama from Colombia and the recognition of Panama as an independent country. The Hay-Bunau-Varilla Treaty of 1903 granted the United States control of the Canal Zone in Panama for $10 million and an annual fee of $250,000; the control would begin nine years after ratification of the treaty by both parties. Construction of the Panama Canal began in 1904 and was completed in 1914.

In 1905, the African American intellectual and militant W. E. B. DuBois founded the Niagara Movement, which called for federal legislation to protect racial equality and to grant full citizenship rights. Formed in 1909, the National Association for the Advancement of Colored People (NAACP) pressed actively for the rights of the African Americans. A third organization of the time, the radical labor organization called the Industrial Workers of the World (IWW, or Wobblies; 1905–1924), promoted violence and revolution. The IWW organized effective strikes in the textile industry in 1912 and among a few western miners' groups, but it had little appeal to the average American worker. After the Red Scare (fear of the rise of Communism) of 1919, the government worked to smash the IWW and deported many of its immigrant leaders and members.

The nation elected Democratic candidate Woodrow Wilson (1856–1924) as president in 1912. Before the outbreak of World War I in 1914, Wilson, working with cooperative majorities in both houses of Congress, achieved much of the remaining progressive agenda, including lower tariff reform (Underwood-Simmons Act, 1913); the Sixteenth Amendment (graduated income tax, 1913); the Seventeenth Amendment (direct election of senators, 1913); the Federal Reserve banking system (which provided regulation and flexibility to monetary policy, 1913); the Federal Trade Commission (to investigate unfair business practices, 1914); and the Clayton Antitrust Act (improving the old Sherman Act and protecting labor unions and farm cooperatives from prosecution,1914).

Prior to World War I, delicate alliances in Europe maintained the balance of power. World War I shattered that tenuous balance and was declared the "War to End All Wars" because of the use of mustard and chlorine gases and other new technologies of destruction. When America entered World War I in 1917, President Wilson maintained that the war would make the world safe for democracy. In an address to Congress on January 8, 1918, he presented his specific peace plan in the form of the Fourteen Points. The first five points called for open rather than secret peace treaties, freedom of the seas, free trade, arms reduction, and a fair adjustment of colonial claims. The next eight points addressed national aspirations of various European peoples and the adjustment of boundaries. The fourteenth point, which he considered the most important and which he had espoused as early as 1916. Called for a "general association of nations" to preserve the peace. This point served as the conceptual basis for the United Nations.

Discrimination

Although many Americans had called for immigration restriction since the late nineteenth century: the only major restriction imposed on immigration by 1920 had been the Chinese Exclusion Act of 1882. Labor leaders believed that immigrants depressed wages and impeded unionization. Some progressives believed that they created social problems. In June 1917, Congress, over Wilson's veto, imposed a literacy test for immigrants and excluded many Asian nationalities.

In 1921, Congress passed the Emergency Quota Act. In practice, the law admitted almost as many immigrants as the nation wanted from such nations as Britain, Ireland, and Germany but severely restricted Italians, Greeks, Poles, and eastern European Jews hoping to enter the country. The law became effective in 1922 and reduced the number of immigrants annually to about 40 percent of the1921 total. Congress then passed the National Origins Act of 1924, which further reduced the number of southern and eastern European immigrants and cut the annual immigration total to 20 percent of the 1921 figure. In 1927, the nation set the annual maximum number of immigrants allowed into the United States at 150,000.

On Thanksgiving Day in 1915, William J. Simmons founded the Knights of the Ku Klux Klan. (A predecessor 19th-century Klan had been founded in 1866.) Its main purpose was to intimidate African Americans, who were experiencing an apparent rise in status during World War I. The Klan's methods of repression included cross burning, tar and feathering, kidnapping, lynching, and burning. The Klan was not a political party, but it endorsed and opposed candidates and exerted considerable control over elections and politicians in at least nine states.

Fundamentalist Protestants, under the leadership of William Jennings Bryan, began a campaign in 1921 to prohibit the teaching of evolution in the schools and protect the belief in the literal Biblical account of creation. The South especially received the idea well.

The Great Depression

Signs of recession were apparent before the market crash in 1929. The farm economy, which involved almost 25 percent of the population, as well as the coal, railroad, and New England textile industries, had not been prosperous during the1920s.

After 1927, new construction declined and auto sales began to sag. Many workers lost their jobs before the crash of 1929. Stock prices increased throughout the decade. The boom in prices and volume of sales was especially active after 1925 and was intensive from 1928 to 1929. Careful investors recognized that the overpricing of stocks was occurring and began to sell to take their profits.

During October 1929, prices declined as more people began to sell their stock. "Black Thursday," October 24, 1929, saw the trading of almost 13 million shares; this was a large number for that time, and prices fell precipitously. Investment banks tried to boost the market by buying, but on October 29, "Black Tuesday," the market fell about 40 points, with 16.5 million shares traded. The effects of the Great Depression were widespread, as many people suffered economic loss.

The Hawley-Smoot Tariff of June 1930 raised duties on both agricultural and manufactured imports. Chartered by Congress in 1932, the Reconstruction Finance Corporation loaned money to railroads, banks, and other financial institutions. It prevented the failure of basic firms, on which many other elements of the economy depended, but many people criticized it as relief for the rich. The Federal Home Loan Bank Act, passed in July 1932, created home loan banks, which made loans to building and loan associations, savings banks, and insurance companies. Its purpose was to help avoid foreclosures on homes.

The First New Deal

Franklin D. Roosevelt (1882–1945), governor of New York, easily defeated Herbert Hoover in the election of 1932. At his inauguration on March 4, 1933, the American economic system seemed to be on the verge of collapse. Roosevelt, assuring the nation that "the only thing we have to fear is fear itself," called for a special session of Congress to convene on March 9 and asked for "broad executive powers to wage war against the emergency." Two days later, he closed all banks for a brief time and forbade the export of gold or the redemption of currency in gold. A special session of Congress, from March 9 to June 16, 1933 ("The Hundred Days"), passed a great body of legislation that has left a lasting mark on the nation. Historians have divided Roosevelt's legislation into the First

New Deal (1933–1935) and a new wave of programs beginning in 1935 called the Second New Deal.

Following are some of the achievements of the First New Deal:

- The *Emergency Banking Relief Act*, passed on March 9, 1933, the first day of the special congressional session, provided additional funds for banks from the Reconstruction Finance Corporation and the Federal Reserve, allowed the Treasury to open sound banks after 10 days and to merge or liquidate unsound ones, and forbade the hoarding or exporting of gold. On March 12, Roosevelt assured the public of the soundness of the banks in the first of many "fireside chats" or radio addresses. People believed him, and most banks were soon open, with deposits outnumbering withdrawals.

- The *Banking Act of 1933*, or the *Glass-Steagall Act*, established the Federal Deposit Insurance Corporation (FDIC) to insure individual deposits in commercial banks and to separate commercial banking from the more speculative activity of investment banking. The Federal Emergency Relief Act appropriated $500 million for state and local governments to distribute to aid the poor. The act also established the Federal Emergency Relief Administration under Harry Hopkins (1890 1946).

- The *Civilian Conservation Corps* enrolled 250,000 young men aged 18 to 24 from families on relief to go to camps where they worked on flood control, soil conservation, and forest projects under the direction of the War Department.

- The *Public Works Administration* distributed $3.3 billion to state and local governments for building projects such as schools, highways, and hospitals.

- The *Agricultural Adjustment Act of 1933* created the Agricultural Adjustment Administration. Farmers agreed to reduce production of principal farm commodities and received subsidies in return. Farm prices increased when owners took land out of cultivation; however, tenants and sharecroppers suffered. The repeal of the law came in January 1936 on the grounds that the processing tax was not constitutional.

- The *National Industrial Recovery Act (NIRA)* was the cornerstone of the recovery program. In June 1933, Congress passed this act and created the National Recovery Administration (NRA); the goal was the self-regulation of business and the development off air prices, wages, hours, and working conditions. Section 7a of the NIRA permitted collective bargaining for workers; laborers would test the federal support for their bargaining in the days to come. The slogan of the NRA was "We do our part." The economy improved but did not recover.

The Second New Deal

Following are some of the accomplishments of the Second New Deal:

- The *Works Progress Administration (WPA)* began in May 1935, following the passage of the Emergency Relief Appropriations Act of April 1935. The WPA employed people from the relief rolls for 30 hours of work a week at pay double that of the relief payment but less than private employment.

- The *Rural Electrification Administration (REA)*, created in May1935, provided loans and WPA labor to electric cooperatives so they could build lines into rural areas that the private companies did not serve.

- The *Social Security Act*, passed in August 1935, established for persons over age 65 a retirement plan to be funded by a tax on wages paid equally by employee and employer. The government paid the first benefits, ranging from $10 to $85 per month in 1942. Another provision of the act forced states to initiate unemployment insurance programs.

Labor Unions

The 1935 passage of the National Labor Relations Act, or the Wagner Act, resulted in an upsurge in union membership but at the expense of bitter conflict within the labor movement. The American Federation of Labor (AFL), formed in 1886, was composed primarily of craft unions. However, some leaders wanted to unionize the mass-production industries, such as automobiles and rubber, with industrial unions. In November 1935, John L. Lewis formed the Committee for Industrial Organization (CIO) to unionize basic industries, presumably within the AFL. President William Green of the AFL ordered the CIO to disband in January 1936. When the rebels refused, the AFL expelled them. The insurgents then reorganized the CIO as the independent Congress of Industrial Organizations. Labor strikes, particularly in the textile mills, marked the end of the 1930s.

American Response to the War in Europe

In August 1939, Theodore Roosevelt created the War Resources Board to develop a plan for industrial mobilization in the event of war. The next month, he established the Office of Emergency Management in the White House to centralize mobilization activities.

Roosevelt officially proclaimed the neutrality of the United States on September 5, 1939. The Democratic Congress, in a vote that followed party lines, passed a new Neutrality Act in November. It allowed the cash-and-carry sale of arms and short-term loans to belligerents but forbade American ships to trade with belligerents or Americans to travel on belligerent ships. Roosevelt determined that to aid Britain in every way possible was the best way to avoid war with Germany. In September 1940, he signed an agreement to give Britain 50 American destroyers in return for a 99-year lease on air and naval bases in British territories in Newfoundland, Bermuda, and the Caribbean.

American Entry into World War II

In late July 1941, the United States placed an embargo on the export of aviation gasoline, lubricants, and scrap iron and steel to Japan and granted an additional loan to China. In December, additional articles—iron ore and pig iron, some chemicals, machine tools, and other products—fell under the embargo.

In October 1941, a new military cabinet headed by General Hideki Tojo took control of Japan. The Japanese secretly decided to make a final effort to negotiate and to go to war if there was no solution by November 25. A new round of talks followed in Washington, but neither side would make a substantive change in its position. The Japanese made the final decision on December 1 for an attack on the United States. Specifically, the Japanese planned a major offensive to take the Dutch East Indies, Malaya, and the Philippines and to obtain the oil, metals, and other raw materials they needed. At the same time, they intended to attack Pearl Harbor in Hawaii to destroy the American Pacific fleet to keep it from interfering with their plans.

At 7:55 a.m. on Sunday, December 7, 1941, the first wave of Japanese carrier-based planes attacked the American fleet in Pearl Harbor. A second wave followed at 8:50 a.m. The United States suffered two battleships sunk, six damaged and out of action, three cruisers and three destroyers sunk or damaged, several lesser vessels destroyed or damaged, and the destruction of all the150 aircraft on the ground. A total of 2,323 American servicemen were killed and about 1,100 were wounded. The Japanese lost 29 planes, five midget submarines, and one fleet submarine.

On December 8, 1941, Congress declared war on Japan, with one dissenting vote from Representative Jeanette Rankin of Montana. On December 11, Germany and Italy declared war on the United States. Great Britain and the United States then established the Combined Chiefs of Staff, headquartered in Washington, to direct Anglo-American military operations.

On January 1, 1942, representatives of 26 nations met in Washington, D.C., and signed the Declaration of the United Nations, pledged themselves to the principles of the Atlantic Charter, and promised not to make a separate peace with their common enemies. The U.S. geared up for war. Men enlisted in various branches of the military. Women were admitted to the military for the first time. Many companies quickly retooled to create war materials. Women also assumed new roles in industry in the absence of the men who had gone to war.

The End of World War II

The Army Corps of Engineers established the Manhattan Engineering District in August 1942 for the purpose of developing an atomic bomb; the program eventually took the name the Manhattan Project. J. Robert Oppenheimer directed the design and construction of a transportable atomic bomb at Los Alamos, New Mexico. On July 16, 1945, the Manhattan Project exploded the first atomic bomb at Alamogordo, New Mexico.

The Enola Gay dropped an atomic bomb on Hiroshima, Japan, on August 6, 1945. In the short term, the bomb killed about 78,000 persons and injured 100,000 more. Subsequently, there were additional radiation-related casualties. On August 9, the United States dropped a second bomb on Nagasaki, Japan. Japan surrendered on August 14, 1945, and signed the formal surrender on September 2.

The war not only ended, but the world changed. The U.S. emerged as the world superpower in the "Atomic Age." National confidence was high.

The Holocaust

The Holocaust, a systematic ethnic cleansing, began about 1933 and continued to the end of World War II (WWII) in 1945. During this period, Adolf Hitler was the German leader. In addition to Jewish people, the "National Socialist German Workers' Party," or Nazis, also targeted other minority groups such as gypsies, homosexuals, Jehovah's Witnesses, and disabled people. It is estimated that 11 million people were killed during the Holocaust. Six million of these people were Jews. The Nazis killed approximately two-thirds of all Jews living in Europe, and an estimated 1.1 million of these lost lives were children.

The persecution of Jews began on a large scale on April 1, 1933, when the Nazis announced a boycott of all Jewish-run businesses in Germany. In 1935, newly established laws began to exclude Jews from public life. The Nuremberg Laws included a law that stripped German Jews of their citizenship and a law that prohibited marriages between Jews and Germans. These laws set the legal model for more anti-Jewish legislation that the Nazis issued over the next several years. Some of these laws excluded Jews from public places like parks, fired them from civil service jobs, made them register their property, and prevented Jewish doctors from working on anyone other than Jewish patients.

In November 1938, the Nazis engaged in terrifying acts against Jews in Austria and Germany in what has been termed "Kristallnacht." This night of violence resulted in the looting and burning of synagogues, breaking the windows of Jewish-owned businesses, and looting of their stores. Many Jews were physically attacked, and approximately 30,000 Jews were arrested and sent to concentration camps that night.

After World War II started in 1939 and the Nazis began occupying surrounding countries, they ordered the Jews to wear an emblem of "The Star of David" on their clothing so that they could be easily recognized and targeted.

Anne Frank

Anne Frank was one of over one million Jewish children wearing "The Star of David" who died in the Holocaust. She was born on June 12, 1929, in Frankfurt, Germany. During the first years of her life, Anne lived with her parents and sister, Margot, in an apartment on the outskirts of Frankfurt. After the Nazis came into power in 1933, the family moved to Amsterdam, in the Netherlands, where Anne's father, Otto Frank, had business connections.

The Netherlands was occupied in May 1940 by the Germans. In July 1942, German authorities and their Dutch collaborators began to assemble Jewish people from throughout the Netherlands at a place called Westerbork, a transit camp near the Dutch town of Assen, in Friesland, not far from the German border. From Westerbork, German officials deported the Jews to the Polish concentration camps in German-occupied Poland.

During the first half of July 1942, Anne and her family went into hiding in a secret attic apartment. For two years, they lived in this apartment behind the office of the family-owned business at 263 Prinsengracht Street, which Anne referred to in her diary as the Secret Annex. Otto Frank and his friends and colleagues, Johannes Kleiman, Victor Kugler, Jan Gies, and Miep Gies, had previously helped to prepare the hiding place and smuggled food and clothing to the Franks at great risk to their own lives. On August 4, 1944, the Gestapo (German Secret State Police) discovered the hiding place after being tipped off by an anonymous Dutch caller. That same day, the Gestapo sent them to Westerbork, and one month later, in September 1944, the SS and police authorities placed the Franks on a train transport from Westerbork to Auschwitz, a concentration camp complex in German-occupied Poland. Because they had been selected for labor due to their youth, Anne and her sister Margot were transferred to the Bergen-Belsen concentration camp near Celle, in northern Germany, in late October 1944. Both sisters died of typhus in March 1945, just a few weeks before British troops liberated Bergen-Belsen on April 15, 1945. Anne's mother, Edith Frank, died in Auschwitz in early January 1945. Only Anne's father, Otto Frank, survived the war. The Soviet forces liberated Otto at Auschwitz on January 27, 1945.

While in hiding, Anne kept a diary in which she recorded her fears, hopes, and experiences. This diary was found in the secret apartment after the family was arrested. The diary was kept for Anne by Miep Gies, one of the people who had helped hide the Franks.

It was published after the war in many languages and is used in thousands of middle school and high school curricula in Europe and the Americas. Through this diary, Anne Frank has become a symbol of the children who died in the Holocaust and a source of inspiration to many readers.

American Post-War Foreign Policy

In February 1947, Great Britain notified the United States that it could no longer aid the Greek government in its war against Communist insurgents. The next month, President Truman asked Congress for $400 million in military and economic aid for Greece and Turkey. Truman argued in what is now known as the Truman Doctrine that the United States must support free peoples who were resisting Communist domination.

Secretary of State George C. Marshall proposed in June 1947 that the United States provide economic aid to help rebuild Europe. The following March, Congress passed the European Recovery Program; popularly known as the Marshall Plan, the program provided more than $12 billion in aid.

Spread of Communism

On June 25, 1950, Communist North Korea invaded South Korea. President Truman committed U.S. forces under the United Nations (UN) auspices; General Douglas MacArthur would command the troops. By October, UN forces (mostly American) had driven north of the 38th parallel, which divided North and South Korea. Chinese troops attacked MacArthur's forces on November 26, pushing them south of the 38th parallel, but by spring 1951, UN forces had recovered their offensive. The armistice of June 1953 left Korea divided along virtually the same boundary that had existed before the war.

After several years of nationalist war against French occupation, in July 1954 France, Great Britain, the Soviet Union, and China signed the Geneva Accords, which divided Vietnam along the 17th parallel. The north would be under the leadership of Ho Chi Minh and the South under Emperor Bao Dai. The purpose of the scheduled elections was to unify the country, but Ngo Dinh Diem overthrew Bao Dai and prevented the elections from taking place. The United States supplied economic aid to South Vietnam.

In January 1959, Fidel Castro overthrew the dictator of Cuba. Castro criticized the United States, moved closer to the Soviet Union, and signed a trade agreement with the Soviets in February 1960. The United States prohibited the importation of Cuban sugar in October 1960 and broke off diplomatic relations in January 1961. Diplomatic relations did not resume until 2015.

Space Exploration

The launching of the Soviet space satellite *Sputnik* on October 4, 1957, created fear that America was falling behind technologically. Although the United States launched *Explorer I* on January 31, 1958, concerns continued unabated. In 1958, Congress established the National Aeronautics and Space Administration, or NASA, to coordinate research and development and passed the National Defense Education Act to provide grants and loans for education.

Civil Rights

Although the American Civil War freed the slaves, it did not provide African Americans with all of the same rights and opportunities available to other Americans. The Civil Rights Movement sought to achieve equality for African Americans in many areas of American life. Major events in the early years of the Civil Rights Movement included the following:

- President Eisenhower completed the formal integration of the armed forces; desegregated public services in Washington, D.C., naval yards and veterans' hospitals; and appointed a civil rights commission.

- In *Brown vs. Board of Education of Topeka* (1954), Thurgood Marshall, lawyer for the National Association for the Advancement of Colored People, challenged the doctrine of "separate but equal" (*Plessy v. Ferguson*, 1896). The Supreme Court declared that separate educational facilities were inherently unequal. In 1955, the Court ordered states to integrate "with all deliberate speed."

- On December 11, 1955, in Montgomery, Alabama, Rosa Parks, a 42-year-old African American woman, refused to give up her seat on a city bus to a white man and faced arrest, an act of enduring symbolic importance.

- Under the leadership of the Reverend Martin Luther King Jr. (1929–1968), African Americans of Montgomery organized a bus boycott that lasted for a year and influenced similar actions in other cities.

- In February 1960, a segregated lunch counter in Greensboro, North Carolina denied four African American students service; the students staged a sit-in. This inspired sit-ins elsewhere in the South and led to the formation of the Student Nonviolent Coordinating Committee (SNCC), which had a chief aim of ending segregation in public accommodations.

- President Kennedy presented a comprehensive civil rights bill to Congress in 1963. With the bill held up in Congress, 200,000 people marched and demonstrated on its behalf, and Martin Luther King Jr. gave his "I Have a Dream" speech.

The New Frontier

After Democratic Senator John F. Kennedy (1917–1963) won the presidential election of 1960, the Justice Department, under Attorney General Robert F. Kennedy, began to push for civil rights, including desegregation of interstate transportation in the South, integration of schools, and supervision of elections to allow more African Americans to vote freely.

America and Cuba

Under President Dwight Eisenhower, the Central Intelligence Agency (CIA) had begun training some 2,000 men to invade Cuba and to overthrow Fidel Castro. On April 19, 1961, this force invaded at the Bay of Pigs; opposing forces pinned them down, demanded their surrender, and captured some 1,200 men.

On October 14, 1962, a U-2 reconnaissance plane brought photographic evidence of the construction of missile sites in Cuba. President Kennedy, on October 22, announced a blockade of Cuba and called on the Soviet premier, Nikita Khrushchev (1894–1971), to dismantle the missile bases and remove all weapons capable of attacking the United States from Cuba. Six days later, Khrushchev backed down and withdrew the missiles. Kennedy lifted the blockade.

Civil Rights and Social Unrest

Following the assassination of John F. Kennedy and the succession of Lyndon B. Johnson to the presidency, the 1964 Civil Rights Act outlawed racial discrimination by employers and unions, created the Equal Employment Opportunity Commission (EEOC) to enforce the law, and eliminated the remaining restrictions on black voting.

In 1965, Martin Luther King Jr. announced a voter registration drive. With help from the federal courts, he dramatized his effort by leading a march from Selma, Alabama, to Montgomery, Alabama, between March 21 and 25. The Voting Rights Act of 1965 authorized the attorney general to appoint officials to register voters.

Seventy percent of African Americans lived in city ghettos at this time. In 1966, New York and Chicago experienced riots, and the following year there were riots in Newark and Detroit. The Kerner Commission, appointed to investigate the riots, concluded that the focus of the riots was a social system that prevented African Americans from getting good jobs and crowded them into ghettos. On April 4, 1968, James Earl Ray assassinated Martin Luther King Jr. in Memphis, Tennessee. Ray was an escaped convict; he pled guilty to the murder and received a sentence of 99 years in prison. Riots in more than 100 cities followed.

Beginnings of the Vietnam War

After the defeat of the French in Vietnam in 1954, the United States sent military advisors to South Vietnam to aid the government of Ngo Dinh Diem. The pro-Communist Vietcong forces gradually grew in strength because Diem failed to follow through on promised reforms and because of support from North Vietnam, the Soviet Union, and China. Pro-war "Hawks" defended the president's policy and, drawing on the containment theory, said that the nation had the responsibility to resist aggression. The claim was if Vietnam should fall to the Communists, all Southeast Asia would eventually go (domino theory). Anti-war "Doves" argued that the war was a civil war in which the United States should not meddle.

On January 31, 1968, the first day of the Vietnamese New Year (Tet), the Vietcong attacked numerous cities and towns, American bases, and even Saigon. Although they suffered large losses, the Vietcong won a psychological victory as American opinion quickly began turning against the war.

The End of the Vietnam War

President Richard M. Nixon (1913–1994) initiated "Vietnamization," the effort to build up South Vietnamese forces while withdrawing American troops. In 1969, Nixon reduced American troop strength by 60,000 but at the same time ordered the bombing of Cambodia, a neutral country. In the summer of 1972, negotiations between the United States and North Vietnam began in Paris. A few days before the 1972 presidential election, Henry Kissinger, the president's national security advisor, announced that "peace was at hand."

Nixon resumed the bombing of North Vietnam in December 1972; he claimed that the North Vietnamese were not bargaining in good faith. In January 1973, the two sides reached a settlement in which the North Vietnamese retained control over large areas of the South and agreed to release American prisoners of war within 60 days. Nearly 60,000 Americans had been killed and 300,000 more wounded, and the war had cost American taxpayers $109 billion. On March 29, 1973, the last American combat troops left South Vietnam. The North Vietnamese forces continued to push back the South Vietnamese, and in April 1975, Saigon fell to the North.

Watergate

What became known as Watergate emerged during the 1972 Presidential campaign in which Nixon was re-elected. Early on the morning of June 17, a security officer for the Committee for the Reelection of the President, along with four other men, broke into Democratic headquarters at the Watergate office building in Washington, D.C. The authorities caught the men going through files and installing electronic eavesdropping devices. In March 1974, a grand jury indicted some of Nixon's top aides and named Nixon an unindicted coconspirator. Meanwhile, the House Judiciary Committee televised its debate over impeachment. The committee charged the president with obstructing justice, misusing presidential power, and failing to obey the committee's subpoenas. Before the House voted on impeachment, Nixon announced his resignation on August 8, 1974, to take effect at noon the following day. Gerald Ford (1913–2006) then became president and almost immediately encountered controversy when in September 1974 he offered to pardon Nixon. Nixon accepted the offer although he admitted no wrongdoing and had not yet been charged with any crime.

The Carter Administration

Having won the 1976 presidential election, Jimmy Carter offered amnesty to Americans who had fled the draft and gone to other countries during the Vietnam War. He established the Departments of Energy and Education and placed the civil service on a merit basis. He created a "superfund" for cleanup of chemical waste dumps, established controls over strip mining, and protected 100 million acres of Alaskan wilderness from development.

With respect to foreign policy, Carter negotiated a controversial treaty with Panama, affirmed by the Senate in 1978, that provided for the transfer of ownership of the canal to Panama in 1999 and guaranteed its neutrality. In 1978, Carter negotiated the Camp David Accords between Israel and Egypt. Israel promised to return occupied land in the Sinai to Egypt in exchange for Egyptian recognition, a process completed in 1982. An agreement to negotiate the Palestinian refugee problem proved ineffective.

In 1978, a revolution forced the Shah of Iran to flee the country and replaced him with a religious leader, Ayatollah Ruhollah Khomeini (ca. 1900–1989). Because the United States had supported the Shah with arms and money, the revolutionaries were strongly anti-American, calling the United States the "Great Satan." After Carter allowed the exiled Shah to come to the United States for medical treatment in October 1979, some 400 Iranians broke into the American embassy in Tehran on November 4 and took the occupants captive. They demanded the return of the Shah to Iran for trial, the confiscation of his wealth, and the presentation of his wealth to Iran. Carter rejected these demands; instead, he froze Iranian assets in the United States and established a trade embargo against Iran. After extensive negotiations with Iran, in which Algeria acted as an intermediary, the Iranians freed the American hostages on January 20, 1981.

Attacking Big Government

After election to the presidency in 1980, Ronald Reagan placed priority on cutting taxes. He based his approach on supply-side economics, the idea that if government left more money in the hands of the people, they would invest rather than spend the excess on consumer goods. The results would be greater production, more jobs, and greater prosperity, resulting in more income for the government despite lower tax rates. However, from a deficit of $59 billion in1980, the federal budget deficit increased to $195 billion by 1983. Reagan ended ongoing antitrust suits against IBM and AT&T and fulfilled his promise to reduce government interference with business.

Iran-Contra

In 1985 and 1986, several Reagan officials sold arms to the Iranians in hopes of encouraging them to use their influence in obtaining the release of American hostages being held in Lebanon. Profits from these sales went to the Nicaraguan contras—a militant group opposed to the left-leaning elected government—in an attempt to get around congressional restrictions on funding the contras. The attorney general appointed a special prosecutor, and Congress held hearings on the affair in May 1987.

Operation Just Cause

Since winning the presidential election in 1988, the Bush administration had been concerned that Panamanian dictator Manuel Noriega was providing an important link in the drug traffic between South America and the United States. After economic sanctions, diplomatic efforts, and an October 1989 coup failed to oust Noriega, Bush ordered 12,000 troops into Panama on December 20 for what became known as Operation Just Cause. On January 3, 1990, Noriega surrendered to the Americans and faced drug trafficking charges in the United States. Found guilty in 1992, his sentence was 40 years.

Persian Gulf Crisis

On August 2, 1990, Iraq invaded Kuwait, an act that President George H. W. Bush denounced as "naked aggression." The United States quickly banned most trade with Iraq, froze Iraq's and Kuwait's assets in the United States, and sent aircraft carriers to the Persian Gulf. On August 6, after the UN Security Council condemned the invasion, Bush ordered the deployment of air, sea, and land forces to Saudi Arabia and dubbed the operation Desert Shield.

On February 23, 1991, the allied air assault began. Four days later, Bush announced the liberation of Kuwait and ordered offensive operations to cease. The United Nations established the terms for the ceasefire, which Iraq accepted on April 6.

Health Care

In October 1993, the Clinton administration proposed legislation to reform the health care system, which included universal coverage with a guaranteed benefits package, managed competition through health care alliances that would bargain with insurance companies, and employer mandates to provide health insurance for employees. With most Republicans and small business, insurance, and medical business interests opposed to the legislation, the Democrats dropped their attempt at a compromise package in September 1994.

Presidential Impeachment and Acquittal

President William Jefferson Clinton received criticism for alleged wrongdoing in connection with a real estate development called Whitewater. While governor of Arkansas, Clinton had invested in Whitewater, along with James B. and Susan McDougal, owners of a failed savings and loan institution. After Congress renewed the independent counsel law, a three-judge panel appointed Kenneth W. Starr to the new role of independent prosecutor. The Starr investigation yielded massive findings in late 1998, roughly midway into Clinton's second term, including information on an adulterous affair that Clinton had had with Monica Lewinsky while she was an intern at the White House. It was on charges stemming from this report that the House of Representatives impeached Clinton in December 1998 for perjury and obstruction of justice. The Senate acquitted him of all charges in February 1999.

Continuing Crisis in the Balkans

During President Clinton's second term, continued political unrest abroad and civil war in the Balkans continued to be a major foreign policy challenge. In 1999, the Serbian government attacked ethnic Albanians in Kosovo, a province of Serbia. In response, North Atlantic Treaty Organization (NATO) forces, led by the United States, bombed Serbia. Several weeks of bombing forced Serbian forces to withdraw from Kosovo.

The Election of 2000

The outcome of the 2000 presidential election was unclear for several weeks after the election. Al Gore won the popular vote, but the Electoral College vote was very close, and Florida was pivotal in deciding the election. George W. Bush (1946-), son of former President George H. W. Bush, appeared to win Florida, but by a very small margin. Controversy over how to conduct the recount of the Florida votes led to a series of court challenges, with the matter ultimately decided by the U.S. Supreme Court in favor of Bush.

Terrorism

On the morning of September 11, 2001, hijackers deliberately crashed U.S. commercial jetliners into the World Trade Center in New York—toppling its 110-story twin towers—and the Pentagon just outside Washington, D.C. Thousands died in the deadliest act of terrorism in American history.

Though the person or persons behind the attacks were not immediately known, President Bush cast prime suspicion on the Saudi exile Osama bin Laden, the alleged mastermind of the bombings of two U.S. embassies in 1998 and of a U.S. naval destroyer in 2000. Bin Laden, who was found to have orchestrated the 9/11 attacks, was captured and killed in a raid, authorized by President Barack Obama, on his Pakistan compound in May 2011. The United States had earlier seen terrorism on its home soil carried out by Islamic militants in the 1993 bombing of the World Trade Center and by a member of the American militia movement in the bombing of the Oklahoma City federal building in 1995. The dispute with Iraq continued, and President Bush declared war (a disputed option) with Iraq. The outcome of sending troops to Iraq remains to be seen.

Barack Obama

On January 20, 2009, Barack H. Obama became the 44th President of the United States and the first African American President. President Obama was born in Hawaii on August 4, 1961, to a middle-class family; his father was from Kenya and his mother was from Kansas. President Obama was raised by his mother with help from his grandfather, who had served in General Patton's army during World War II, and his grandmother, who was a successful bank employee. As a law student, President Obama was the first African American president of the Harvard Law Review. In the Illinois State Senate, he helped pass the first major ethics reform in 25 years, cut taxes for working families, and expanded health care for children and their parents. As a United States Senator, he helped pass an innovative lobbying reform and to make information about federal spending accessible online.

Skill 2.8: Analyze Immigration and Settlement Patterns that Have Shaped the History of the United States

"The United States is a nation of immigrants" is a frequently quoted remark, although the Europeans who founded the nation came to a country already peopled by those we call Native Americans, and, as discussed in earlier sections, many people who subsequently came to America did not immigrate willingly.

The Earliest Americans

The New World that Columbus and other explorers discovered in the late fifteenth and early sixteenth centuries was neither recently formed nor recently settled. It had actually been settled between 15,000 and 35,000 years before. As in other areas of the world, the native peoples of the "New World" formed communities but did not immediately develop written languages. The lack of any kind of written record makes interpreting the prehistoric past more difficult. Archaeologists and anthropologists working in North and South America have unearthed the remains of these early communities, and it is on this evidence that anthropologists base the theories about the earliest origins, movements, and lifestyles of native peoples. It is known, for example, that by the time Europeans came into contact with the indigenous peoples of the Americas, more than 2,000 distinct cultures and hundreds of distinct languages existed.

Fundamental Immigration Questions

Some of the specific patterns of immigration and governmental response are discussed in earlier sections. Since the recording of the first arrivals in 1820, the United States has accepted 66 million legal immigrants, with 11 percent arriving from Germany and 10 percent from Mexico. However, two centuries of immigration and integration have not yielded consensus on the three major immigration questions:

1. How many immigrants should be permitted?

2. From where should immigrants be permitted?

3. Under what status should immigrants enter the country?

National Immigration Trends

As pointed out by a former director of the U.S. Census Bureau, Kenneth Prewitt, America is the first country in history in which peoples from every part of the world are represented. During the early twenty-first century, it has been calculated that each year the U.S. immigration system recognizes 800,000 to 900,000 foreigners as legal immigrants, admits 35 million nonimmigrant tourist and business visitors, and is aware of another 300,000 to 400,000 unauthorized foreigners who settle in the country. Martin (2002) predicts that these immigration trends are likely to continue at current levels. Recent decades have witnessed contentious debates over the place of immigrants and their children in the educational, welfare, and political systems of the U.S. or, more broadly, whether the immigration system serves U.S. national interests.

Florida Demographics

The population of Florida is characterized by considerable ethnic and racial diversity, as indicated by the 2010 Census. The population of Florida (18,801,310) comprises 6.08 percent of the population of the United States (308,745,538). It has grown 17.6 percent from Census 2000, resulting in two new seats in the U.S. House of Representatives for a total of 27 representatives. Flagler County (named after Henry Flagler, the railroad and hotel magnate) in particular doubled its population since 2000 and became the fastest-growing county in Florida.

The following chart, derived from U.S. Census categories, illustrates the ethnic and racial diversity of Florida residents and highlights its multiculturalism:

Race	Percentage
White persons of non-Hispanic origin	57.9
Hispanic or Latino origin	22.5
Black	16.0
Asian	2.4
American Indian and Alaska Native	.4
Native Hawaiian or other Pacific Islander	.1
Persons reporting 2 or more races	2.5

According to 2010 census data, 25.8 percent of the Florida population speaks a language other than English at home. This statistic underscores the importance of maintaining programs to help the English Language Learner (ELL).

Census data also reveal that 15 percent of Florida's population falls below the poverty line. Children of low-income families face serious obstacles to academic success, including insufficient access to food, unsafe and/or uncomfortable living conditions, and challenges to physical and emotional health. These are challenges to the educational system in Florida that teachers must recognize and deal with.

Skill 2.9: Identify How Various Cultures Contributed to the Unique Social, Cultural, Economic, and Political Features of Florida

During the 1930s, the Works Progress Administration collected folklore from Florida. The collection documented African American, Arabic, Bahamian, British American, Cuban, Greek, Italian, Minorcan, Seminole, and Slavic cultures throughout Florida. The Library of Congress presents these documents as part of the record of the past and a distinctive cultural contribution of Florida.

The many cultural backgrounds of a population that originated from many countries make Florida unique. Native Americans, descendants of the pioneering settlers, Cubans, Puerto Ricans, Greeks, Asians, African Americans, Caucasians, and dozens of other ethnic groups, old and young, are featured throughout the Florida boundaries. This varied background began with the exploration and settlement of the state.

Early History

About 12,000 years ago, hunters and gatherers reached Florida and settled in areas with a water supply, stones for tools, and firewood. These Floridians created complex cultures. Before the arrival of Europeans, these native peoples developed cultivated agriculture, traded with groups in the southeastern United States, and expanded their social organization. Their temple mounds and villages reflect their complex social organization.

The First European Explorers

The Spanish explorer and adventurer Juan Ponce de Leon arrived near what is now St. Augustine in 1513. The written record of Florida began with his arrival. He called the land *la Florida*, in honor of the Feast of the Flowers, an Easter celebration in Spain. No evidence exists of other Europeans arriving before him, but it is a possibility. Eight years later, Ponce de Leon, 200 people, 50 horses, and other beasts of burden returned to Florida's southwest coast. With attacks from the natives there, however, the colonization attempt failed. Still, Ponce de Leon described the area as a suitable place for missionaries, explorers, and treasure seekers.

Hernando de Soto began another treasure-hunting expedition in 1539. His travels through Florida and the southeastern United States took his group to what is now Tallahassee; they camped there for five months. Although de Soto died in 1542 near the Mississippi, some of his expedition reached as far as Mexico.

The First European Settlements

Stories from Ponce de Leon's and de Soto's parties gradually circulated through Europe and influenced the development of exploration in what is now Florida and other areas. Spain regularly shipped silver, gold, and other products from Cuba, Mexico, Central America, and South America; accounts of these activities also spread rapidly to others interested in exploration. In 1559, Tristan de Luna y Arellano led another group that attempted to settle in Florida. After a series of misfortunes over a two-year period, however, they had to abandon the settlement. The French also arrived in Florida. In 1562, Jean Ribault explored the area near what is now Jacksonville, and in 1564, Rene Goulaine de Laudonniere established a colony there.

At around this time, Spain began to accelerate its colonization plans. In 1565, Pedro Menendez de Aviles settled near St. Augustine. This was the first permanent European settlement in what is now America. Pedro Menendez de Aviles worked to remove all the French and to kill all French settlers except those who were Roman Catholic or noncombatants. Menendez captured the Spanish Fort Caroline and renamed it San Mateo. Two years later, the Frenchman Dominique de Gourgues captured San Mateo and killed the Spanish there. The Spanish, however, continued to explore, construct forts, and establish Roman Catholic missions among the Floridians. The English also continued to explore. Conflict frequently arose between the Spanish and the English. Sir Francis Drake and his crew burned the Spanish settlement of St. Augustine in 1586.

Spain's power in the southeastern part of the New World was unassailable in the 1600s. The English did establish colonies at that time, but these were primarily in Jamestown, Virginia (1607); Plymouth, Massachusetts (1620); and Georgia (1733). French explorers continued to move down the Mississippi and along the Gulf Coast during that time.

The Eighteenth Century

Feuds between Spain and England—particularly in Florida—continued into the eighteenth century. The Englishman Colonel James Moore, along with the Carolinians and their Creek Indian allies, attacked Spanish Florida in 1702 and destroyed the town of St. Augustine. The fort Castillo de San Marcos was not captured, however. In 1704, the English moved between Tallahassee and St. Augustine and destroyed the Spanish missions they encountered. The French harassed the Spanish on the western side and captured Pensacola in 1719. Then Georgians attacked in 1740, but, like the English, they were unable to take the Castillo de San Marcos at St. Augustine.

In exchange for Havana (which the British had taken from Spain during the Seven Years' War of 1756–1763), the British took control of Florida. Spain evacuated Florida after the exchange, and British surveyors tried to establish relations with the Native

Americans, Seminoles of Creek Indian descent who were moving into the area. To attract other settlers, Britain offered land for settling and help if settlers produced exportable items. The plan lasted only 20 years. Spain captured Pensacola from the British in 1781 and retained it as part of the peace treaty that ended the American Revolution.

American Possession

Other Spanish colonists came pouring into Florida after the British evacuation. Some came because of the favorable terms for obtaining property (i.e., land grants) that the Spanish offered to immigrants; some were escaped slaves trying to find freedom. Spain then ceded Florida to the United States in 1821. Andrew Jackson had already been in Florida battling the Seminoles in 1818, during the First Seminole War. Returning in 1821 to establish a new territorial government, he found a combination of Native Americans, African Americans, and Spaniards. In 1845, Florida became the twenty-seventh state.

Many Southerners now began moving to Florida. A divided state became more unified, with Tallahassee as capital. As the population increased through immigration, the residents began to pressure the federal government to remove the Creeks, the Miccosukees, and the African American refugees, in order to make desirable land more available.

Origins of Reservations

As the federal government began to press Native Americans to leave their homeland, Osceola, a Seminole war leader, refused to relocate his people. While waging the Seminole War of 1835–1842, President Andrew Jackson allocated $20 million and many U.S. soldiers to enforce the movement of the Seminoles to Oklahoma. The war ended, but not as the government had planned. Many Seminoles, private citizens, and soldiers lost their lives. Soldiers captured some of the Seminoles and sent them West under guard, others "volunteered" to go, but some fled into the Everglades and made a life for themselves there. The government eventually established reservations, and forced or encouraged Native Americans to relocate to these areas.

Slavery

By 1840, the population of Florida had reached 54,477; about half of the population consisted of slaves. At this time, the state consisted of three parts: east, middle, and west. The middle area had many plantations, whose owners set the political tone for the state until the time of the Civil War.

Florida residents were concerned about the North's objections to slavery. Most Floridians at the time did not oppose slavery, and Abraham Lincoln did not win the state in the presidential election.

The Civil War and Reconstruction

On January 10, 1861, Florida seceded from the Union. No decisive battles occurred in Florida, but the state provided 15,000 soldiers and many supplies; in addition, 2,000 African Americans and whites from Florida joined the Union army.

The state and the lives of many of its residents changed after the Civil War. Although Tallahassee was the only southern capital east of the Mississippi River to avoid capture during the war, federal troops occupied Tallahassee on May 10, 1865. The ports of Jacksonville and Pensacola subsequently began to thrive. Slaves became free, and plantations did not regain their prewar levels; instead, tenant farmers and sharecroppers—white and African American—began to develop the farming sector.

Beginning in 1868, the federal government began Reconstruction in Florida. Investors in industries brought more people to the state through the increased construction of roads and railroads. Citrus fruit cultivation, sponge harvesting, steamboat tours, and the tourist industry in general flourished. From this time through the beginning of World War I, Florida's offer of free or cheap public land to investors brought diverse cultures into the state. Draining large tracts of land made it more usable, and businessmen such as Henry Flagler and Henry B. Plant built lavish hotels for tourists near their railroad lines. Florida also became the staging area for American troops bound for the war in Cuba during the Spanish-American War, and this too brought many people through the state and permanently changed it.

Early Twentieth Century

By the beginning of the twentieth century, per capita income and population were rising in Florida. After World War I, increasing numbers of tourists and land developers came into the state, and inflation became a problem. Hurricanes in 1926 and in 1928 helped hasten the bursting of Florida's economic bubble. Money and credit began to dry up, and the "paper" millionaires lost their credibility. By the time the rest of the nation felt the Great Depression, Florida was already accustomed to economic hard times. Adding to Florida's troubles was the invasion of the Mediterranean fruit fly in 1929 that caused citrus production to fall by 60 percent.

The face of Florida's voting population changed after developments such as women winning the right to vote in 1920, the repeal of the poll tax (a tax of a uniform, fixed amount per individual) in 1937, and the U.S. Supreme Court's decision to outlaw a system of all-white primary elections in 1944. In addition, more newcomers entered the state when World War II began. With its mild climate, the state became a major training center for the military, and it continues to attract both U.S. and international citizens as a desirable location for vacations and for retirement.

Postwar Immigration and Migration

With the influx of large numbers of people from places within the United States and from countries within the Western Hemisphere (primarily Cuba and Haiti), Florida has experienced a surge in population in recent years. It is now the third most populous state in the nation, and the diverse population has worked to make the Sunshine State a place where all citizens have equal rights under the law.

Many changes have occurred in Florida since the 1950s. Schools and other institutions are integrated. The economy has diversified. Electronics, plastics, construction, real estate, and international banking have recently joined tourism, citrus fruit cultivation, and phosphate production as major elements in Florida's economy. The state's community colleges, technical colleges, and universities draw large numbers of students to Florida each year, and the tourist industry continues to flourish.

U.S. Space Program

The U.S. Space Program, an integral element of Florida's history since the late 1950s, has generated substantial tourism, media attention, and employment.

The National Aeronautics and Space Administration (NASA) had its beginnings under President Dwight D. Eisenhower in July 1958 with the signing of Public Law 85–568.The Launch Operations Center was established in 1962 on Florida's east coast and was renamed the John F. Kennedy Space Center in 1963 to honor the president who initiated the prospect of exploring the moon.

Cape Canaveral was chosen as the primary site of many space missions, for several reasons. Since the Cape was undeveloped, it became the ideal location for testing missiles without affecting nearby communities. The Florida climate permitted year-round operations and being on the coast allowed launches over water instead of populated areas. As a consequence, Florida has been the hub of numerous missions, from the early days of Project Mercury to the Space Shuttles, the International Space Station, the Hubble Space Telescope, and the Mars Exploration Rovers.

As of August 14, 2011, NASA's Kennedy Space Center established the Ground Processing Directorate (GPD). This organization will focus on future launch processing, overseeing operations for the International Space Station, maintaining a new customer center, and integration of launch complex operations.

Of utmost importance to educators is the Kennedy *Educate to Innovate* program that connects NASA employees with teachers, students, and the general public. Virtual Lab, one of the associated projects, consists of software that provides virtual access to sophisticated scientific instruments. Students are entertained with hands-on experiences relevant to class material. A variety of virtual tours allows students to be part of teams that work on the space shuttle and other missions. Of deep interest to educators is the Kennedy Launch Academy Simulation System (KLASS). The software and curriculum materials bring a launch countdown into the classroom. Lessons are interactive and inquiry-based.

 ## Skill 2.10: Identify the Significant Contributions of the Early and Classical Civilizations

Although the Greek and Roman civilizations often are described and studied as classical civilizations, other classical civilizations developed in China, India, and other parts of the world.

Several elements characterize what is considered to be a classical civilization. The development of agriculture that would produce food surpluses contributed to the rise of urban centers of densely populations areas in permanent habitats that featured safety in numbers and the development of public services such as water and roads. Family structures became more defined because a family had a permanent place to live. Most family structures were patriarchal. The urban centers permitted the development of specialized occupational groups or professions that focused on work activities (craft work or art) or trade rather than food production. This produced an economy. The separation of social groups led to the rise of a ruling elite class (e.g., nobles, priests, or warriors) that was above individuals in either agricultural or occupational groups. Since the elites did not "work," they created a political structure or government and public wealth based on taxes and/or tributes. The public wealth was often used for public architecture or work such as city walls, temples, theaters, baths, and aqueducts that contributed to safety and a higher standard of living. Literacy (a system of reading and writing) allowed civilizations to create records, literature, and government documents and to communicate a greater world view, religion, philosophy, or other aspects of culture.

Competency 3: Knowledge of People, Places, and Environment

In acquainting students with geography, teachers focus on not only space and place, the physical dimensions of geography, but also the human dimension consisting of the study of people, places, and environments (termed human geography). Students quickly become aware that as a people, we do not live in isolation. We are all interconnected and must, therefore, concern ourselves with our connections to the environment and to each other. Teachers guide students to become young geographers through observation, questioning, investigation, and evaluation. Competency 3 focuses on geography.

Skill 3.1: Identify and Apply the Six Essential Elements of Geography Including the Specific Terms for Each Element

The six essential elements of geography are closely interrelated. According to various scholars, these elements can be described as follows:

1. *Understanding the world in spatial terms.* This element encompasses the characteristics of spatial features and layouts. It enables the student to have a spatial perspective and to be familiar with associated geographic tools used to organize and interpret information about people, places, and environments. These tools include maps, globes, graphs and charts, and databases. Students also develop the ability to construct models depicting Earth-sun relationships, planets, landforms, and other geographic phenomena.

2. *Understanding the world in terms of places and regions.* This element encompasses knowledge of continents, regions, countries, cities, and so on. Both teachers and students must update their knowledge regularly as boundaries and place-names change. In addition, the element of place encompasses knowledge of how places are associated with physical characteristics such as latitude, altitude, climate, landforms, and physical environment (e.g., plants and animals), as well as human characteristics such as language, religion, architecture, music, politics, and other aspects of culture.

3. *Understanding the world in terms of physical systems.* This element encompasses knowledge of the physical features of the world such as mountains, deserts, and oceans, as well as the understanding that that these features are constantly changing as a result of tectonic activity, glaciation process, meteorological events, and human activity. Students learn to identify and understand individual physical features of the environment as well as the functioning of entire ecosystems.

4. *Understanding the world in terms of human systems.* This element encompasses knowledge of human characteristics and groups. Movements of people, materials, and ideas, the evolution of human societies, the establishment of cultural and political institutions, and the development of social and economic interrelationships between groups of humans are among the topics students learn to analyze and discuss.

5. *Understanding the world in terms of environment and society.* This element encompasses knowledge of interactions between humans and their environments and how these ongoing interactions constantly change the nature of society as well as the physical features of the environment such as the quality of the air, water, and soil and the characteristics of flora and fauna. Students learn how society is shaped by both positive and negative environmental

influences and how social practices in turn have beneficial or harmful influences on the environment.

6. *Understanding the uses of geography*. This element encompasses the understanding of how geography can be used. Students learn that with geographical tools and knowledge one can examine the past, interpret the present, and plan for the future. Students learn that the knowledge obtained through geography influences our understanding of the physical and social worlds and allows us to make informed, useful, and ultimately critical decisions about how to best relate to the physical world and to each other.

Skill 3.2: Analyze and Interpret Maps and Other Graphic Representations of Physical and Human Systems

The study of maps begins with a study of the globe—a model of the Earth with a map on its surface. Regular use of the globe helps students understand the Earth's shape and structure. Some of the features on the globe that students should be able to locate and name include the following:

- The Continents
- The United States and Major Countries
- The Equator
- The North and South Poles
- The Antarctic and Arctic Circles
- Key Meridians and Parallels
- The International Date Line and Time Zones

Maps can be political or physical. Political maps show governmental boundaries for countries, states and counties. They can also show locations of major cities and large bodies of water. Physical maps show topographic features of landforms such as deserts, mountains, and plains in addition to political features. The use of maps requires students to identify four main types of map projections:

- Conic
- Cylindrical
- Interrupted
- Plane

Additional graphics that students use in geography include charts, graphs, and picture maps. Internet resources as well as commercially available software programs provide many geographic tools for students, including interactive maps that allow for deeper exploration of physical geography. The goals for the teacher of geography are to help students understand how to obtain information from these graphic tools and to interpret and analyze their findings. Students will thus need to learn the conventions of each type of graphic representation including the use of legends on a map or the representation of lines of latitude and longitude on a globe.

Skill 3.3: Identify and Evaluate Tools and Technologies (e.g., Maps, Globe, GPS, Satellite Imagery) Used to Acquire, Process, and Report Information from a Spatial Perspective

The National Geographic Society provides educators with tools and content for teaching and learning at *My Wonderful World* (*http://test.mywonderfulworld.org/index.html*) including the *Geographic Perspective Content Guide for Educators* (Brown & LaVasseur, 2006). The guide defines geographic perspective as a "lens used to analyze virtually any topic that has a spatial distribution, that is, anything that can be mapped." Brown and LaVasseur (2006) state that geography is a "unique way to understand anything that is distributed across space, including the ever-changing relationship between humans and the environment, and thus make predictions and even propose solutions to current problems." Thus, the geographic perspective uses what is known about spatial distributions to understand spatial processes in order to apply that understanding to the world today. This interdisciplinary approach advocates the use of all available and relevant resources, tools, and technologies including maps and globes as well as Geographic Information Systems (GIS) and Global Positioning Systems (GPS). GIS produces maps as the result of integrating hardware, software, and data. This facilitates layering of maps so that relationships among the data within the layers can be identified. GPS consists of a network of 24 satellites that orbit the earth. This provides time and location identification for any place in the world.

While a geographic perspective allows students to see the "big picture" of the world, this perspective might be too big and abstract for young students. Rather, teachers might help students develop a geographic perspective by encouraging them to think about their own physical place in the world in terms of the location of their homes, school, and other local landmarks. Satellite imagery (e.g., *Google Earth*) allows students to see their locales and zoom in on relevant details. Using "home" as a starting point, students can see how their geographic locales fit into larger and larger geographic regions as they apply the six elements of geography.

Skill 3.4: Interpret Statistics that Show How Places Differ in Their Human and Physical Characteristics

Cultural geography focuses on the relationship between humans and the living and nonliving features of their environments. We know, for example, that the physical environment in which people reside affects their diet, shelter, clothing, tools, and products. Physical characteristics include climate, resources, terrain, and location. For example, National Geographic's *Earth Pulse* provides statistics about that state of the world in terms of population trends, household consumption, deforestation, water usage and other data. In terms of the geographic perspective (Brown & LaVasseur, 2006), interpretation of such statistics permits students to answer geographic questions such as the following:

- Who or what spatial region is being observed and analyzed?

- What human and natural systems and interrelationships exist and how did they come to be?

- What should be done to maintain or change the distributions and relationships? Why?

Skill 3.5: Analyze Ways in Which People Adapt to an Environment through the Production and Use of Clothing, Food, and Shelter

Humans change their environments to better suit their wants and needs. At the same time, humans adapt to their environments in order to survive. These adaptations can be observed in the choice of clothing, food, and modes of shelter. For example, humans live on all continents with the exception of Antarctica and on most inhabitable islands. Traditionally, humans in colder Arctic climates often used animal fur, hides, and hair (e.g., wool) in clothing and creating shelters. As a result, they were hunters who moved with animal migrations and ate the meat of the animals such as seal and walrus or cold water fish. Oil and fat were also important to eat because it kept early humans warm. Humans living in hotter tropic or sub-tropic regions often could use native plants for food as well as clothing (e.g., cotton) and shelter (e.g., wood, bamboo, woven grasses).

Skill 3.6: Determine the Ways Tools and Technological Advances Affect the Environment

Tools and technology are developed to improve people's lives. Both are created by humans to help achieve goals. Technology describes the skills or processes used to create goods or services and technology includes tool creation and use. The use of tools allowed humans to do things that they couldn't otherwise accomplish. Early tools were made of stone and included simple carving knives which allowed them to make other tools from bones or other natural items. Tool use developed to include ways to join items together for shelter (hammers, pegs), make clothing to protect against the elements (needles), catch fish and animals (spears, bows, arrows, hooks), and create culture (wall art or carvings). The use of tools as simple machines (wheels, axles, inclined planes) fostered greater movement and development.

Until the Industrial Revolution, tools were used by hand. The Industrial Revolution and later development of the assembly line mechanized the use of tools to create more goods or services. Technology today includes information technology, which allows humans to create, share, and communicate knowledge using computers and the Internet.

Along with their benefits, tools and technologies can have negative influences on people as well as the environments. Pollution of the air, water, and soil, which accelerated following the Industrial Revolution, is a critical example of these negative influences. Global warming is another example of a negative effect on environments and the people who live within them. Sustainable technologies such as solar energy or wind power are ways to decrease negative effects of production on the environment.

■ Skill 3.7: Identify and Analyze Physical, Cultural, Economic, and Political Reasons for the Movement of People in the World, Nation, or State

When the characteristics of their environments become unpalatable to residents, they may consider relocation. In such cases, people are, so to speak, driven away from their place of residence. In other cases, people may relocate to an area that appears to be highly desirable. In these cases, people are drawn to a new place of residence.

One or more of several kinds of forces, detailed below, are responsible for driving people away from or drawing them to particular areas.

Economic Forces

Economic reasons for relocation are related to the financial conditions and aspirations of residents. Some residents wish to move to more expensive areas, while others wish to move to less expensive ones. In some cases, a change in the financial situation of individuals and individual families is responsible for the relocation, as when a person loses a job and must move to a less expensive area. In other cases, physical or social events are responsible for economic change. Following are some examples:

1. An entire industry in a region begins to flourish or fail (e.g., the demise of the textile industry in nineteenth-century New England).

2. Regional or national economic changes impact the financial conditions of individuals in a specific area (e.g., the Great Depression of the 1930s).

3. Discoveries or natural disasters impact the economy of an area (e.g., the discovery of oil in the Gulf of Mexico; the destruction and redevelopment of New Orleans following Hurricane Katrina).

Cultural Forces

Cultural reasons for relocation include a desire to live with people who are more similar to oneself or to find an area with greater diversity (or at least greater tolerance for diversity). The goal of relocation may be essential to a person's cultural identity or simply a matter of finding a more interesting cultural environment. Some of the dimensions of similarity or dissimilarity that motivate people to move for cultural reasons include the following:

- Race
- Ethnicity
- Religion
- Lifestyle

Physical Forces

The purely physical features of an area can influence people's interest in relocation. Following are some of the many examples:

1. The climate of an area seems especially desirable or undesirable.

2. A natural disaster (e.g., a hurricane), or the prospect of natural disasters (e.g., forest fires), makes an area undesirable.

3. The physical geography of an area contains especially attractive features (e.g., mountains and lakes) or especially unattractive ones (e.g., insects).

4. The physical location of an area relative to cities or key geographic features seems especially desirable or undesirable.

Political Forces

Political changes, as well as the more enduring qualities of political systems, motivate people to relocate. In some cases, people are legally forced to move, while in others, relocation is simply motivated by the desire for a better life. Following are some examples of political changes that stimulate the movement of peoples:

1. Immigration law changes, such that people must leave an area, or, for the first time, they are permitted to reside in an area.

2. Laws governing freedom of expression, freedom of worship, and other important freedoms become more or less restrictive.

3. The dominant political affiliation of an area shifts in a direction that is considered desirable or undesirable.

4. Political practices in an area begin to strongly encourage or discourage certain kinds of business development.

Movement Patterns and Changes in the U.S.

The United States is a country of immigrants. Some scientists even theorize that prehistoric Native Americans migrated to the Americas in the Ice Age. A great influx of immigrants came in the nineteenth century as the result of famines and other natural disasters in other parts of the world. In 1891, the Immigration and Naturalization Service (INS) was created. Its purpose was twofold: to oversee the admission process of applicants, as well as the exclusion and deportation of aliens, and to oversee the naturalization of aliens lawfully residing in the United States. Due to the influx of European immigrants at the turn of the century, an immigration screening station was established at Ellis Island, New York, in 1892, and over the next 30 years more than 30 million immigrants became naturalized citizens.

One consequence of the diversity of immigrants was the creation of the public school system in the late nineteenth and early twentieth centuries. Part of the mandate of public schools was to provide a common language and set of social standards for students from the various cultural backgrounds. The term "melting pot" was used to describe how the immigrants would assimilate into the American culture. A common assumption was that immigrants would let go of their native language, learn English, and conform to the American way of life. In short, creating a homogenous culture was a common value at this time.

Over time, however, the assimilationist model was gradually replaced by a model that can be described as cultural pluralism. Some of the legal decisions that contributed to cultural pluralism in the twentieth century are as follows:

Brown v. Board of Education (1954) laid the groundwork for desegregation.

*Pierce v. Society of Sisters (*1925) established the legitimacy of parochial schools and other private schools.

The Civil Rights Act (1964) prohibits discrimination on the basis of race, color, or national origin.

The Bilingual Education Act (1968) provides funding for bilingual programs and acknowledged the importance of language and culture heritage.

Serrano v. Priest (1971) brought about significant changes in the formula used for funding students in low income districts.

*Title IX of the Education Amendment*s (1972) prohibits discrimination on the basis of sex.

Lau v. Nichol (1974) established steps to be taken by a school district if a student was found to have a language deficiency.

The Individuals with Disabilities Education Act (1976/1990) ensures that children receive free assessment for disabilities as well as free and appropriate education in the least restrictive environment.

Understanding the various sources of diversity, such as race, ethnicity, language, religion, gender, and socioeconomic status have promoted a pluralistic model where differences among people are valued and appreciated. Rather than a melting pot, the analogy often used now is that of a salad bowl in which all ingredients are mixed, but retain distinct flavors that work together to create a healthy society.

Skill 3.8: Evaluate the Impact of Transportation and Communication Networks on the Economic Development in Different Regions

The ability to move from one place to another has always affected economic development. For example, the trade routes known as the Silk Road originated around 139 BCE and continued to be used for over 1,500 years. This route from Asia and Africa to regions of Europe introduced new products that created a demand. As a result, as bigger and better ships were eventually developed that could travel the high seas, Europeans set out for quicker and more efficient ways to get to the sources of those products. This resulted in the colonization of the Americas.

Today, advances in communication—through satellite technologies—make it possible for people all over the world to connect with each other, and to learn about each other's situations, in real time. The economic impact of this virtually instantaneous interconnectivity is vast. The food supplier on the West Coast can observe the progress of a hurricane on the East Coast and anticipate changes in consumer needs. Investors in Tokyo and New York can monitor each other's financial markets and make significant decisions rapidly. The joint producers of a new technology who reside in the U.S. and China can collaborate in real time. These are just a few examples of the direct economic impact of new communication technologies on the way people conduct business. At the same time, the communications industry itself is a major economic force. Technologies for communication such as computers and cell phones are among the world's leading industries, and a great deal of revenue is generated through personal and business use of these technologies.

In the same way, developments in transportation technology have had a major and enduring economic impact. In the U.S., the development of railroads and roads, as well as improvements in shipping, significantly altered the economic landscape of the eighteenth and nineteenth centuries. In the twentieth century, the economic effects of automobiles, trucks, and airplanes were also profound.

Development of these transportation technologies facilitates business, as raw materials and products can be moved more quickly and efficiently. The new modes of transportation also allow people to relocate more readily for work-related reasons and have been responsible for numerous mass migrations of people toward areas that offer plentiful opportunities for employment. At the same time, the convenience of modern transportation has supported the development of increasingly profitable tourist industries.

Skill 3.9: Compare and Contrast Major Regions of the World, Nation, or State

Although geography can be viewed from a physical perspective (e.g., landforms, hydrosphere, atmosphere and ecosystems) or human perspective (e.g., culture, languages, politics, conflicts, products), the interrelationships among the elements of these perspectives result in similarities and differences as well as causes and effects. Following are some examples of the many ways of comparing and contrasting regions of the world.

1. The equator can be used as the dividing line between the Northern and Southern Hemispheres.

2. A meridian or longitudinal line circles the earth through the North and South Poles divide the Eastern Hemisphere from the Western Hemisphere.

3. Continental land masses can be used to divide the Earth into Africa, Asia, Australia, Europe, North America, and South America. (Some geographers include Antarctica as a separate continent.)

4. Political, cultural, and/or ethnic distinctions can be used to divide the world, as can elements of physical geography such as biomes.

Comparing and contrasting are higher-order thinking skills that teachers encourage among their students. Thinking about dividing the world into major regions is an ideal way to deploy these skills. Students can be presented with an existing system for classifying major regions and can then use their comparing and contrasting skills to understand the similarities within a region as well as the differences across regions. Alternatively, students can be presented with information about the world and encouraged to use their comparing and contrasting skills to create regions based on systematic analysis of similarities and differences. Teachers can provide more or less scaffolding for this kind of activity.

Competency 4: Knowledge of Government and the Citizen

Government is an agency that regulates the activities of people. It is the system that carries out the rules and decisions of the political system and its leader or leaders. Civics is study of the rights and obligations of citizens. The focus of Competency 4 is on the nature of government and its interrelationship with citizens.

Skill 4.1: Distinguish Between the Structure, Functions, and Purposes of Federal, State, and Local Government

Government in the United States exists on several levels starting with the overarching federal government that affects all of the people, state government which provides leadership and laws for citizens within each state, and local governments of cities and counties.

Structure of Government

The distribution and separation of powers within the various structures of government is important in understanding governments and comparing different types. Following are some different types of governmental structures:

Government Structure	Description	Examples
Confederation	Weak central government that delegates principal authority to smaller units, such as states	U.S. under the Articles of Confederation before the Constitution was ratified
Federal	Sovereignty divided between a central government and a group of states	United States Brazil India
Unitary	Centralized authority in which power is concentrated	France Japan
Authoritarian	Power resides with one or a few individuals with little input from legislative and judicial bodies	People's Republic of China Former Soviet Union Nazi Germany
Parliamentary	Combined legislative and executive branches with a prime minister and cabinet selected from within the legislative body	Great Britain

Structure of American Government

America has a federal system of government; it divides sovereignty between the central government and the states. It also represents a presidential form of government, in that the executive branch is clear separated from the legislative and judicial branches. Powers are divided across the three branches of government, and a system of checks and balances is in place to prevent any one branch from political dominance.

According to the Constitution, all governmental powers ultimately stem from the people. Local governments generally handle local matters, those issues that affect all state residents are handled by states, and issues that affect all citizens of the country are the responsibility of the federal government. Such a system is a natural outgrowth of the colonial relationship between the Americans and the mother country of England.

The following powers are reserved for the federal government:

1. Regulate foreign commerce

2. Regulate interstate commerce

3. Mint money

4. Regulate naturalization and immigration

5.   Grant copyrights and patents

6.   Declare and wage war and declare peace

7.   Admit new states

8.   Fix standards for weights and measures

9.   Raise and maintain an army and a navy

10. Govern Washington, D.C.

11. Conduct relations with foreign powers

12. Universalize bankruptcy laws

Each state government has the following powers:

1.   Conduct and monitor elections

2.   Establish voter qualifications within the guidelines established by the Constitution

3.   Provide for local governments

4.   Ratify proposed amendments to the Constitution

5.   Regulate contracts and wills

6.   Regulate intrastate commerce

7.   Provide for education for its citizens

8.   Levy direct taxes

Functions of Government

The functions of a government include the following:

- Maintaining domestic order

- Protecting its borders

- Enabling a productive economy

- Promoting the well-being of the society and its citizens

Although most or all citizens may agree that this list encompasses the functions of government, not everyone would agree on the details of each function or how it should be implemented. For example, most American citizens would agree that the government has at least some responsibility in protecting our borders, but there are ongoing disagreements about the extent of protection needed as well as the methods of protection.

Purposes of Government

Since the time of Plato in ancient Greece, there has been substantial debate about the purposes of government. For example many people believe that the government should play at least some role in the education of citizens, but there no consensus on the appropriate nature or extent of governmental participation in the educational process, and some would hold that educating citizens is not among the government's fundamental purposes.

Differing ideologies, such as communism, socialism, capitalism, and so on, differ in part through their assumptions about what constitutes the fundamental purposes of government. The points of disagreement are both practical and philosophical and reflect important ethical considerations.

Skill 4.2: Compare and Contrast the Rights and Responsibilities of a Citizen in the World, Nation, State, and Community

Each citizen has both rights and responsibilities. Every citizen is entitled to all rights. While most responsibilities are mandatory, a couple of the responsibilities are voluntary. Examples of legal rights guaranteed to citizens and responsibilities of citizenship include the following:

Citizen Rights	Citizen Responsibilities
• The right to freedom of speech, religion, press, and petition • The right to keep and bear arms • The right to due process • The right to a fair and speedy trial • The right to be free from unlawful search and seizure • The right to avoid self-incrimination	• Obey laws (mandatory) • Pay taxes (mandatory) • Serve on juries (mandatory) • Serve as a witness (mandatory) • Support and defend the Constitution. (mandatory) • Stay informed of the issues affecting local community (voluntary) • Participate in the democratic process by voting (voluntary)

It is essential for students to not only be aware of these and other rights, but also to understand where they originate. Students need to know the basis of their rights and responsibilities as citizens, so that they can familiarize themselves with them as needed, and so they can understand and critically evaluate them. Doing so is part of being an active citizen in a democratic society.

 ## Skill 4.3: Identify and Interpret Major Concepts of the U.S. Constitution and Other Historical Documents

Declaration of Independence

The Declaration of Independence was a practical and legal document that set forth the reasons why Britain's thirteen colonies in North America wanted independence from Great Britain. It enumerated what was viewed as King George's abuses and, more importantly, promoted equality as a human right. It identified the purpose of government as securing the people's rights and deriving its powers from the consent of the governed. This concept provided the foundation of the thinking for the U.S. Constitution.

Articles of Confederation

The Articles of Confederation, adopted in 1777, provided for a unicameral Congress, in which each state would have one vote, as had been the case in the Continental Congress. Executive authority under the Articles was to be vested in committee of 13, with one member from each state. Amending the Articles required the unanimous consent of all the states. Under the Articles of Confederation, the government could declare war, make treaties, determine the number of troops and amount of money each state should contribute to a war effort, settle disputes between states, admit new states to the Union, and borrow money. It could not levy taxes, raise troops, or regulate commerce.

Origins of the U.S. Constitution

As time went on, the inadequacy of the Articles of Confederation became increasingly apparent. In 1787, there was a call for a convention of all the states in Philadelphia for the purpose of revising the Articles and creating what would eventually be the U.S. Constitution. The assembly unanimously elected George Washington to preside, and the enormous respect that he commanded helped hold the convention together through difficult times.

The 55 delegates who met in Philadelphia in 1787 to draft the Constitution drew on a variety of sources to shape the government that would be outlined in the document. Three British documents in particular were important to the delegates' work: the Magna Carta (1215), the Petition of Right (1628), and the Bill of Rights (1689). These three documents promoted the concept of limited government and were influential in shaping the fundamental principles embodied in the Constitution. The collection of essays called *Politics* by the Greek philosopher Aristotle provided a basis for the concept of constitutions including a "right" constitution based on "the common good," a "wrong" constitution based on personal self-interest, and a middle "ideal" constitution. The British philosopher John Locke, who wrote about the social contract concept of government and the right of people to alter or abolish a government that did not protect their interests, was another guiding force in the drafting of the Constitution.

Compromise in Establishing the Constitution

One of the most significant principles embodied in the Constitution is the concept of a federal system that divides the powers of government between the states and the national government. The federal government and those of the separate states have powers that may in practice overlap, but in cases where they conflict, the federal government is supreme.

The relationship between the national government and the states is one that reflects a compromise between delegates on how power should be distributed, with some delegates favoring a stronger central government than others.

A specific problem that the delegates faced in determining state participation in national politics involved how to specify the number of state representatives. In some respects, each state should be equal to the others, but in other respects, states with larger populations should have more influence than states with smaller ones. With George Washington presiding over the discussions, the delegates finally adopted a proposal known as the Great Compromise, which provided for a president, two senators per state, and representatives elected to the House according to their states' populations.

Another major crisis in the discussions involved disagreement between the North and the South over slavery. To reach a compromise on this point, the delegates decided that each slave was to count as three-fifths of a person for purposes of apportioning representation and direct taxation on the states. This practice was known as the Three-Fifths Compromise.

Finally, the delegates had to compromise on the nature and power of the presidency. The result was a strong presidency with control over foreign policy and the power to veto congressional legislation. Should the president commit a crime, Congress would have the power of impeachment. Otherwise, the president would serve for a term of four years and was eligible for reelection without limit. As a check to the possible excesses of democracy, an Electoral College elected the president; each state would have the same number of electors as it did senators and representatives combined.

The Content of the U.S. Constitution

The content of the U.S. Constitution consists of a preamble, seven articles, and 27 amendments.

Preamble

The Preamble introduces the Constitution and identifies its purposes: to specify that the Constitution is the act of all of the people ("We the people") and to detail the objectives of the document and the government it establishes. This reflects the philosophy that government derives its powers from the consent of the governed and that people organized a government to serve their common welfare.

The Constitution sets forth 6 basic principles:

1. Equality of states

2. Three branches of government (legislative, executive, judicial)

3. Each person (rich or poor) equal before the law

4. No person above the law

5. Ability to change the government by altering the Constitution

6. Constitution as the highest law of the land

Articles I, II, and III of the U.S. Constitution are concerned with defining and delineating the legislative, executive, and judicial powers. Article IV guarantees citizens of each state the privileges and immunities of the other states and provides protection to the states. Articles V and VII are concerned with amending and ratifying the Constitution, and Article VI concerns federal power. The first 10 amendments to the Constitution are known as the Bill of Rights, and to these have been added 17 additional amendments.

The Bill of Rights

A point of concern among some delegates to the Constitutional Convention was that the emerging document contained no bill of rights. The first Congress met in 1789. On the agenda was the consideration of 12 amendments to the Constitution written by James Madison. The states approved 10 of the 12 amendments on December 15, 1791, and these make up what is known as the Bill of Rights, which can be briefly summarized as follows:

1. First Amendment: Guarantees freedom of worship, speech, press, assembly, and petition.

2. Second Amendment: Forbids infringement on the right to bear arms.

3. Third Amendment: Forbids use of private homes for quartering of troops.

4. Fourth Amendment: Forbids unreasonable arrest, search, and seizure.

5. Fifth Amendment: Guarantees various legal protections, including due process and provisions that people not testify against themselves.

6. Sixth Amendment: Guarantees various legal protections, including access to counsel for those accused of a crime.

7. Seventh Amendment: Guarantees a trial by jury in civil cases.

8. Eighth Amendment: Forbids excessive penalties, including cruel and unusual punishment.

9. Ninth Amendment: Indicates that citizens possess rights over and above those named in the Articles and Bill of Rights.

10. Tenth Amendment: Grants to states and citizens those rights not granted to the federal government.

Additional Constitutional Amendments

Making amendments (i.e., additions or revisions) to the Constitution is no small feat. Since 1787, more than 9,000 amendments have been proposed, but only 27 have been approved. Following is a brief summary of those following the Bill of Rights:

11. Eleventh Amendment: A citizen of one state may sue a citizen of another state only if that person has the state's permission.

12. Twelfth Amendment: Election of the president.

13. Thirteenth Amendment: Abolishment of slavery.

14. Fourteenth Amendment: Definition and protection of citizens.

15. Fifteenth Amendment: Universal male suffrage.

16. Sixteenth Amendment: Income tax.

17. Seventeenth Amendment: Election of Senators by popular vote.

18. Eighteenth Amendment: Prohibition of intoxicating substances.

19. Nineteenth Amendment: Women's suffrage.

20. Twentieth Amendment: Beginning and ending terms of elected officials.

21. Twenty-first Amendment: Repeal of Eighteenth Amendment.

22. Twenty-second Amendment: Limitation of presidency to two terms.

23. Twenty-third Amendment: District of Columbia given presidential vote.

24. Twenty-fourth Amendment: Repeal of poll tax in federal elections.

25. Twenty-fifth Amendment: Procedures for unexpected presidential or vice-presidential vacancy.

26. Twenty-sixth Amendment: Establishment of 18 as voting age.

27. Twenty-seventh Amendment: Limits on change in congressional compensation.

Skill 4.4 Compare and Contrast the Ways the Legislative, Executive, and Judicial Branches Share Powers and Responsibility

A key principle of the U.S. Constitution is separation of powers. The national government is divided into three branches—legislative, executive, and judicial—with separate functions, but they are not entirely independent, nor can they operate without constraints imposed by the others. Articles I, II, and III of the main body of the Constitution outline these functions.

The Legislative Branch

Article I of the Constitution deals with the legislative branch. Through this Article, legislative power is vested in a bicameral congress (i.e., one composed of two houses). Each state gets two Senators. The number of House of Representative members from each state is determined by the population of the state. Some states have two representatives while others have as many as forty representatives. The expressed or delegated powers of Congress are set forth in Section 8 of the Article and can be divided into several broad categories:

1. Economic powers include the following:

   • Set and collect taxes

   • Borrow money

   • Regulate foreign and interstate commerce

   • Coin money and regulate its value

- Establish rules concerning bankruptcy

2. Judicial powers include the following:

- Establish courts inferior to the Supreme Court

- Provide punishment for counterfeiting

- Define and punish piracies and felonies committed on the high seas

3. War powers include the following:

- Declare war

- Raise and support armies

- Provide and maintain a navy

- Provide for organizing, arming, and calling forth the militia

4. Other general peace powers include the following:

- Establish uniform rules on naturalization

- Establish post offices and post roads

- Promote science and the arts by issuing patents and copyrights

- Exercise jurisdiction over the seat of the federal government (District of Columbia)

The Constitution also grants Congress the power to discipline federal officials through impeachment and removal from office. The House of Representatives has the power to charge officials (impeach), and the Senate has the power to conduct the trials.

Significant also is the Senate's power to confirm presidential appointments (to the cabinet, federal judiciary, and major bureaucracies) and to ratify treaties. Both houses are involved in choosing a president and vice president if there is no majority in the Electoral College. The House of Representatives votes for the president from among the top three electoral candidates, with each state delegation casting one vote. The Senate votes for the vice president. The Senate has exercised this power only twice, in the disputed elections of 1800 and 1824.

The Executive Branch

Article II of the Constitution identifies the powers and duties of the president. The chief executive's constitutional responsibilities include the following:

1. Serve as commander-in-chief

2. Negotiate treaties (with the approval of two-thirds of the Senate)

3. Appoint ambassadors, judges, and other high officials (with the consent of the Senate)

4. Grant pardons and reprieves for those convicted of federal crimes (except in impeachment cases)

5. Seek counsel of department heads (cabinet secretaries)

6. Recommend legislation

7. Meet with representatives of foreign states

8. See that federal laws are "faithfully executed"

The president's powers with respect to foreign policy are paramount. Civilian control of the military is a fundamental concept embodied in the naming of the president as commander in chief. In essence, the president is the nation's leading general. As such, the president can make battlefield decisions and shape military policy.

The president also has broad powers in domestic policy. The most significant domestic policy tool is the President's budget, which he/she must submit to Congress. Though Congress must approve all spending, the president has a great deal of power in budget negotiations. The president can use considerable resources in persuading Congress to enact legislation, and the president also has opportunities, such as in the "State of the Union" address, to reach out directly to the American people to convince them to support presidential policies.

The Judicial Branch

Article III of the Constitution pertains to the judicial branch. This article provides for the creation and operation of the Supreme Court, as well as those inferior courts (i.e., lower in authority than the Supreme Court) that Congress is authorized to establish.

Skill 4.5 Analyze the U.S. Electoral System and the Election Process

To become president, a candidate must meet the following criteria:

- He/she must be a natural-born United States citizen.

- He/she must be a resident of the United States for at least 14 years.

- He/she must be at least 35 years old.

Each political party selects a candidate as its representative in an upcoming election. At the end of the primaries and caucuses, each party holds a national convention and finalizes its selection of its presidential nominee. Each presidential candidate chooses a vice presidential candidate.

The candidates usually begin their campaign tours once they have received the nomination of their parties. In November, U.S. citizens cast their votes, but they are not actually voting directly for the presidential candidate of their choice. Instead, voters cast their votes for electors, who are part of the Electoral College and who are expected to vote for the candidate that their state prefers.

The Electoral College

The 55 delegates who met in Philadelphia in 1787 to draft a constitution established the Electoral College originally as a compromise between presidential election by popular vote and by Congressional election. At first the legislators in some states chose their electors, while in other states voters elected the electors.

In 1796, separate political parties began to operate. At this time each state had the same number of electors as the state had senators and representatives, and each elector voted for two candidates. The person receiving the highest number of votes became the president, and the person receiving the second highest number of votes became the vice president (as specified in Article II).

The Twelfth Amendment to the U.S. Constitution specifies that the electors must meet in their respective states and cast their votes for president and vice president. The slates of electors pledge to vote for the candidates of the parties that the people select. Each elector must have his/her vote signed and certified. The electors send the votes to the president of the Senate for counting in front of Congress. The person having the majority (two-thirds of the votes cast) is declared president. The House chooses the president from the top three if there is no majority. The Twentieth Amendment dictates the process that must take place if no president has qualified by the third day of January.

The president and vice president are the only two nationally elected officials. (The states elect their senators and representatives on a state-by-state basis.) Both houses of Congress are involved in choosing a president and vice president if no majority is achieved in the Electoral College. The House of Representatives votes for the president from among the top three electoral candidates, with each state delegation casting one vote. The Senate votes for the vice president.

Skill 4.6: Identify and Analyze the Relationships Between Social, Economic, and Political Rights and the Historical Documents that Secure These Rights in the United States

The relationships between the rights of citizens and the documents that guarantee those rights can be complicated. In the U.S., for example, citizens' rights are ultimately grounded in the Constitution, but the Constitution does not specify the details of every specific situation in which a person's rights are in question. The Constitution must be interpreted, and there are disagreements about interpretation. Moreover, some of the rights of citizens, although not in conflict with the guidelines of the Constitution, have been established through social or legal practice and are only locally normative. For this reason, people who move to a new city may experience differences in some of their specific rights.

 ## Skill 4.7: Identify and Analyze the Processes of the U.S. Legal System

The contemporary judicial branch consists of thousands of courts and is, in essence, a dual system, with each state having its own judicial structure functioning simultaneously with a complete set of federal courts.

The Supreme Court

The most significant piece of legislation with reference to establishing a federal court network was the Judiciary Act of 1789. That law organized the Supreme Court and set up the 13 federal district courts and 3 circuit (appeal) courts.

The Supreme Court today is made up of one chief justice and eight associate justices. The president, with the approval of the Senate, appoints the justices for life. The justices often come from the ranks of the federal judiciary. In recent years, the public has examined the appointment of Supreme Court justices with intense scrutiny and, in some cases, heated political controversy has accompanied the choices for appointment.

Judicial Principles and the Constitution

Understanding the role of law in a democratic society results from knowledge of the nature of civil, criminal, and constitutional law and how the organization of the judicial system serves to interpret and apply such laws. Essential judicial principles include comprehension of rights, such as the right of due process, the right to a fair and speedy trial, and the right to a hearing before a jury of one's peers. Additional judicial principles include an understanding of the protections granted in the Constitution, which include protection from self-incrimination and unlawful searches and seizures.

The U.S. Constitution makes two references to trial by jury (Article III and the Sixth Amendment). The accused seems to benefit by the provision because a jury consists of 12 persons; the accused cannot be convicted unless all 12 agree that the defendant is guilty. There is mention of a speedy trial to prevent incarceration indefinitely unless the jury finds the accused guilty and the person receives such a sentence. The public trial statement ensures that the defendant receives just treatment. In 1968, the Supreme Court ruled that jury trials in criminal courts extended to the state courts as well as the federal courts. The Sixth Amendment uses the phrase "compulsory process for obtaining witnesses." This means that it is compulsory for witnesses for the defendant to appear in court, although there is some flexibility in the nature of the appearance.

Women on the Supreme Court

In its 220-year history, only four women justices have served on the Supreme Court: Sandra Day O'Connor (1981–2005); Ruth Bader Ginsburg (1993–present); Sonia Sotomayor (2009–present), and former U.S. Solicitor General Elena Kagan (2010–present). The latter two, nominated by President Barack Obama, each earned a distinct footnote in history. Confirmed by the U.S. Senate on August 6, 2009, Sotomayor became the first Hispanic on the Supreme Court. When Kagan was confirmed on August 5, 2010, the Supreme Court became one-third female for the first time in its history.

Sandra Day O'Connor was nominated by President Reagan in 1981 and was regarded as a conservative. She served for 24 years on the Supreme Court until resigning in 2005 in order to care for her ailing husband. The second female justice, Ruth Bader Ginsburg, was nominated by President Clinton in 1993 and is viewed as liberal. O'Connor and Ginsburg served together until O'Connor's retirement in 2005. Ginsburg remained as the lone female justice on the Supreme Court until Sonia Sotomayor was nominated by President Obama and took the bench in the fall of 2009. Sotomayor brought more federal judicial experience to the Supreme Court than any other justice in the past century. Finally, Elena Kagan was nominated to the Supreme Court by President Obama and confirmed by the U.S. Senate in 2010.

Competency 5: Knowledge of Production, Distribution, and Consumption

Economics is a broad field of study. As economists, teachers ensure that their students obtain basic knowledge of production, distribution, and consumption. Students learn how resources have a powerful impact on political functioning and individual decision-making as the importance of interconnectedness is emphasized and global awareness is explored. By introducing students to basic economic concepts such as scarcity, opportunity, cost, and capital, the teacher as economist helps students think locally, nationally, and internationally. The focus of Competency 5 is on knowledge of some of the most fundamental economic concepts.

Skill 5.1: Determine Ways that Scarcity Affects the Choices Made by Governments and Individuals

A basic understanding in economics is that wants are unlimited while resources are limited. When resources are scarce, the impact is observed in prices (the amounts of money needed to buy goods, services, or resources). Productivity impacts scarcity. The more of an item or service that is produced, the more it becomes available and prices decrease. While this might seem like a positive effect, overproduction results in a market in which there are more goods available than needs or wants. As a result, production declines and jobs may be lost.

Ideally, there should be equilibrium between availability and need. Individuals, institutions and governments must, therefore, make choices when budgeting for expenditures, making purchases and impacting production. These seemingly local decisions may affect other people and even other nations and vice versa. For example, at an individual level, the quantity and quality of education attained by a person affects—to some degree—the occupations that are available. Occupational choice affects the amount of money a person makes and has available to spend and pay in terms of taxes to the state. At an institutional level, a school makes curricular decisions based on student needs and abilities and governmental budgetary support. Whether or not a school provides a quality "product" in the form of education can affect the options available to the individuals who attend the school. For example, students in an ineffective school will not have the knowledge and abilities that will enable them to get good jobs. These individuals make less money and pay fewer dollars in taxes. At the state level, the government budgets funding based on what revenues and expenses are anticipated over the next year. If revenues are higher and expenses lower, the state can afford to fund education and other agencies at a higher level, whereas if revenues are lower and expenses are higher, the state must either borrow money or cut budgets.

A true sense of global interdependence results from an understanding of the relationship between local decisions and global issues. For example, individual or community actions regarding waste disposal or recycling can affect the availability of resources worldwide. A country's fuel standards can affect air pollution, oil supplies, and gas prices. The government can provide the legal structure and support needed to maintain competition, redistribute income, reallocate resources, and promote stability.

Combining resources may result in entrepreneurship. As a human resource that also takes advantage of economic resources to create a product, entrepreneurship is characterized by non-routine decisions, innovation, and the willingness to take risks. An economic boom occurs when the economy grows quickly, people are employed, and production is high. A slump occurs when the economy slows. If the slump continues and unemployment increases, the economy enters a recession. Recovery occurs when the economy returns to stability or a boom.

Skill 5.2: Compare and Contrast the Characteristics and Importance of Currency

Currency refers to money as a medium of exchange and as the system of monetary units in common use in a nation. A currency, therefore, is defined and backed by the government that issues it. Examples of currency include the U.S. dollar, British pound, and European euro. These have absolute values within a country or region and relative global values, which are traded, among nations in foreign exchange markets.

Currency also includes other ways in which money is gained or spent. Credit is based on trust that payment will later be made; the payment usually includes interest on what is owed. Companies offer "credit cards" that allow buyers to purchase items. The amount that the individual can spend is usually limited by a credit limit. Loans are also ways to buy without funds. Secured loans (e.g., home loans, car loans) use the item that is purchased as collateral. If the person fails to make payments, the lender can take the house or car. Unsecured loans (e.g., personal loans, student loans, credit) allow a borrower to purchase goods or services without the lender having the security of collateral. The interest rates for secured loans are less than that of unsecured loans.

It is important for students to understand the importance of budgeting and credit. Many people think of credit as "free money" and buy items on credit that they really don't need or can't afford. As a result, they often make minimum payments and the resulting interest often outweighs the cost of the original item. And, if borrowers can't make payments, they damage their credit ratings. Poor credit ratings impact the ability to get loans for cars, houses, and other large purchases. In some cases, employers check credit ratings of prospective employees. A poor credit rating can affect a person's ability to get a job.

Currency facilitates the trade of goods and services and is regulated by a country's economic institutions.

Following are the main economic institutions of the United States:

1. Banks serve the general public. They are owned by small groups of investors who expect a certain return on their investments. Only the investors have vot-

ing privileges; customers do not have voting rights, cannot be elected board members, and do not participate in governing the institution. The Federal Deposit Insurance Corporation (FDIC) insures the banks. Typically, banks do not share information, ideas, or resources. Bank accounts can be savings accounts or checking accounts. Checks or debit cards draw available funds from accounts and are used like cash.

2. Credit unions are owned by members. Each person who deposits money is a member, not a customer. Surplus earnings go to the members in higher dividends, low-cost or free services, and lower loan rates. The National Credit Union Share Insurance Fund insures credit unions. All credit unions share ideas, information, and resources.

3. The Federal Reserve System is the central banking system of the United States. It has a central board of governors in Washington, D.C. There are 12 Federal Reserve Bank districts in major cities throughout the nation. The district banks issue bank notes, lend money to member banks, maintain reserves, supervise member banks, and help set the national monetary policy. In 2014, Janet Yellen became the first woman chair of the Fed in its 100-year history.

4. The stock market is an abstract concept. It is the mechanism that enables the trading of company stocks. It is different from the stock exchange, which is a corporation in the business of bringing together stock buyers and sellers.

Skill 5.3: Identify and Analyze the Role of Markets From Production through Distribution to Consumption

A market is the interaction between potential buyers and sellers of goods and services. Money is the usual medium of exchange. Market economies have no central authority, and custom plays a very small role. Every consumer makes buying decisions based on his or her own needs, desires, and income. In short, individual self-interest rules.

In a market economy, every producer decides personally what goods or services to produce, what price to charge, what resources to employ, and what production methods to use. Profits motivate the producers. There is vigorous competition in a market economy. Supply and demand may affect the availability of resources needed for production, distribution, and consumption. Distribution, in terms of the economy, refers to the apportionment of resources, income or wealth as well as to the factors of production (e.g., land, labor, capital). In the United States, there is a large and active government sector, but greater emphasis emanates from the market economy.

Types of Economies

Following are the major types of economies in the world today:

1. *Command economies* rely on a central authority to make decisions. The central authority may be a dictator or a democratically constituted government. For example, the Russian economy relies mainly on the government to direct economic activity; there is a small market sector as well.

2. *Traditional economies* rely mainly on custom to determine production and distribution practices. While not static, traditional economies are slow to change and are not well equipped to propel a society into sustained growth. Many of the poorer countries of the developing world have traditional economies.

3. *Mixed economies* contain elements of both command and traditional economies. All real-world economies are mixed economies, but the proportions of the mixture can vary greatly.

4. Capitalist economies produce resources owned by individuals.

5. *Socialist economies* produce resources owned collectively by society. In other words, resources are under the control of the government.

Efficiency occurs when a society produces the types and quantities of goods and services that most satisfy its people. Failure to do so wastes resources. Technical efficiency occurs when a society produces the greatest types and quantities of goods and services from its resources. Again, failure to do so wastes resources. Equity occurs when the distribution of goods and services conforms to a society's notions of "fairness." These goals often determine the type of economic system that a country has.

Skill 5.4: Identify and Analyze Factors to Consider When Making Consumer Decisions

Adam Smith (1723–1790) was a Scottish economist whose work helped inaugurate the modern era of economic analysis. Published in 1776, "The Wealth of Nations" is Smith's analysis of a market economy.

Smith believed that a market economy was a superior form of organization from the standpoint of both economic progress and human liberty. Smith acknowledged that self-interest was a dominant motivating force in a market economy; this self-interest, he said, was ultimately consistent with the public interest. An "invisible hand" guided market participants to act in ways that promoted the public interest. Profits may be the main concern of firms, but only firms that satisfy consumer demand and offer suitable prices earn profits.

Supply and Demand

Goods and services refer to things that satisfy human needs or desires. Goods are tangible items, such as food, cars, and clothing; services are intangible items, such as education and health care. A market is the interaction between potential buyers and sellers of goods and services. Money is usually the medium of exchange. The supply of a good is the quantity of that good that producers offer at a certain price. The collection of all such points for every price is the supply curve. Demand for a good is the quantity of a good that consumers are willing and able to purchase at a certain price. The demand curve is the combination of quantity and price, at all price levels. The Law of Supply states that the quantity supplied is directly proportional to the price. The Law of Demand states that the quantity that is offered is directly proportional to the price.

Skill 5.5: Analyze the Economic Interdependence Between Nations

Economic interdependence among nations is studied primarily from the perspective of macroeconomics. Macroeconomics is the study of entire economies, including national and international economies. Some of the topics considered include trade, economic growth, and unemployment.

Microeconomics, in contrast, focuses on problems specific to a household, firm, or industry, rather than national or global issues. Microeconomics gives particular emphasis to how these smaller units make decisions as well as the consequences of those decisions.

Interdependence of trade among peoples and societies has almost always existed in one form or another. Trade can be traced back to bartering for resources or goods among people of the Stone Age. Trade among countries was the engine that fueled early discovery and colonization of "new lands." Financial trading began in the 1600s with the Amsterdam Market in the Netherlands. Financial trading promotes minimizes risk by diversification for governments and multinational corporations.

Multinational companies promote distribution of labor as well as resources. Today's companies may sell items that are produced in one part of the world, sold in another part of the world, and serviced (by phone or on the Internet) in a different part of the world.

Skill 5.6: Identify Human, Natural, and Capital Resources and Evaluate How These Resources are Used in the Production of Goods and Services

There are three main types of resources:

1. *Economic resources* include the labor, capital, productive agents, and entrepreneurial ability used in the production of goods and services.

2. *Human resources* include the physical and mental talents and efforts of people that are necessary to produce goods and services.

3. *Natural resources* include the materials that are available in a natural state and have economic value, such as water, timber, and mineral deposits. Natural resources also include renewable resources such as solar power, wind power, or geothermal power.

Traditionally, the term "capital" referred to profit. Currently, it refers to how much real, usable money is in the possession of a person, group, or company.

Review Questions

1. Mr. Carson is planning a unit on the U.S. Constitution. He has analyzed the content in terms of quantitative features, qualitative features, and matching reader to text. This analysis focuses on

   (A) the Constitution as a primary source.

   (B) complex informational text.

   (C) components of narrative text.

   (D) Constitutional law.

2. Ms. Lopez is teaching American history from World War II. She invites Mrs. Brandt to come talk to the class about her experiences as a WAVE in the Navy during the war. Use of Mrs. Brandt exemplifies

   (A) realia.

   (B) a primary source.

   (C) a human resource.

   (D) a secondary source.

3. The era when machines began to displace human and animal power in the production and distribution of goods is known as the

   (A) Classical age.

   (B) Industrial Revolution.

   (C) Roman Empire.

   (D) Renaissance.

4. In which country did Anne Frank live and write her story, later known as *The Diary of Anne Frank*?

   (A) Italy

   (B) England

   (C) Netherlands

   (D) Germany

5. Ms. Brown is looking for some materials for her geography class. She finds several types of something to use. The types are conic, cylindrical, interrupted, and plane. What is Ms. Brown examining?

   (A) map projections

   (B) GIS

   (C) GPS

   (D) satellite imagery

6. Which of the following legal decisions laid the groundwork for school desegregation?

   (A) *Brown v. Board of Education of Topeka*

   (B) *Pierce v. Society of Sisters*

   (C) *Serrano v. Priest*

   (D) *Lau v. Nichol*

7. Mr. Jackson's class is learning about different kinds of government. Today they are learning about a weak central government that delegates principal authority to smaller units such as states. What is the focus of the lesson?

    (A) Federal Government

    (B) Parliamentary Government

    (C) Confederation Government

    (D) Authoritarian Government

8. Who was the first woman to serve on the Supreme Court?

    (A) Sandra Day O'Connor

    (B) Elena Kagan

    (C) Sonia Sotomayor

    (D) Ruth Bader Ginsburg

9. A country's economy slowed and then continued with increased unemployment. This exemplifies

    (A) entrepreneurship.

    (B) slump.

    (C) recession.

    (D) recovery.

10. Which of the following terms best describes the study of economic issues specific to a household, firm, or industry?

    (A) macroeconomics

    (B) microeconomics

    (C) global interdependence

    (D) command economy

Answer Key and Explanations

1. **(B)**

   A *primary source* is an original document. The Constitution exemplifies expository text, not narrative text. *Constitutional law* is the interpretation of the Constitution. *For more information, see Competency 1.*

2. **(C)**

   Realia is use of real items. A *primary source* is an original document. A *secondary source* is an interpretation of an original document. *For more information, see Competency 1.*

3. **(B)**

   The *Classical Age* was the high point of Greek Civilization. The *Roman Empire* was an ancient civilization of Rome, which controlled a large part of the world at that time. The Renaissance was a rebirth of art, music and architecture during the Middle Ages. *For more information, see Competency 2.*

4. **(C)**

   For more information, see Competency 2.

5. **(A)**

   GPS is a network of 24 satellites around the Earth. Satellite imagery (*GIS*) refers to maps created as the result of integrating hardware, software, and data. *Satellite imagery* (e.g., *Google Earth*) describes pictures taken from satellites of various regions that allow viewers to see a locale and zoom in on relevant details. *For more information, see Competency 3.*

6. **(A)**

   Pierce v. Society of Sisters (1925) established the legitimacy of parochial schools and other private schools. *Serrano v. Priest* (1971) brought about significant changes in the formula used for funding students in low-income districts. *Lau v. Nichol* (1974) established steps to be taken by a school district if a student was found to have a language deficiency. *For more information, see Competency 3.*

7.   **(C)**

A *federal government* is defined as sovereignty divided between a central government and a group of states. In an *authoritarian government* power resides with one or a few individuals with little input from legislative and judicial bodies. A *parliamentary government* combines legislative and executive branches with a prime minister and cabinet selected from within the legislative body. *For more information, see Competency 4.*

8.   **(A)**

Sandra Day O'Connor was the first woman to serve on the U.S. Supreme Court. She was appointed by Ronald Reagan in 1981 and retired in 2006. *For more information, see Competency 4.*

9.   **(C)**

Entrepreneurship is characterized by non-routine decisions, innovation, and the willingness to take risks. A *slump* occurs when the economy slows. *Recovery* occurs when the economy returns to stability or a boom. *For more information, see Competency 5.*

10.   **(B)**

Macroeconomics refers to national or international economics. *Global interdependence* is the connections among countries in terms of trade, finance, and other areas of the economy. *Command economy* is a type of economy in which governments or other authorities control the economy. *For more information, see Competency 5.*

Science

Science is the study of the physical or material world. Scientists observe, identify, describe, investigate, and explain. Teaching science involves providing students with background knowledge and experiences for learning about the world. The National Academy of Science (1996) identifies six competencies for teachers of science at any grade level:

(1) planning inquiry-based science programs;

(2) guiding and facilitating student learning;

(3) assessing teaching and student learning;

(4) developing environments that enable students to learn science;

(5) creating communities of science learners; and

(6) contributing to the planning and development of the school science program.

Competency 1 addresses what teachers need to know for effective science instruction.

Skill 1.1: Analyze and Apply Developmentally Appropriate Research-Based Strategies for Teaching Science Practices

Science is based on universal principles and procedures in the physical world. Science advances from the concrete to the abstract, and students should learn to observe and measure before they are asked to hypothesize and analyze. Developmentally appropriate practice identifies students' current levels of knowledge, abilities, and maturity to provide them with experiences that relate to their level of understanding, challenge them, and take them to the next step. Best practice is based on understanding the predictable levels of cognitive development (for example, the Piagetian levels) and providing the right material at the right time to motivate and engage learners.

Research-based teaching strategies in science focus on student-centered learning and inquiry in the context of social interaction. Educational theorist Lev Vygotsky suggested zone of proximal development (ZPD) in which children assimilate new patterns of thinking by learning with and from individuals who are more proficient. Scaffolding provides the structured support for facilitating these interactions and moving to the next level. Thus, teachers must identify a student's level and then create and facilitate experiences that move thinking and learning a step at a time.

Many of the same teaching strategies used in other subjects apply to science teaching and learning; however, the basic goals of science instruction are scientific literacy and application of the scientific method to everyday situations and daily life. In some ways, this is a very natural process for children. Gòpnik (2012) and her colleagues created a series of experiments that demonstrated "children, in their play and interactions with their surroundings, learn from statistics, experiments, and from the actions of others in much the same way that scientists do." However, Klahr, Zimmerman, and Jirout (2011) point out that instructional strategies need to match cognitive capacity and that teachers need to strike a balance between unstructured activities that fail to provide enough scaffolding for learning and highly structured content that can be boring.

Skill 1.2: Select and Apply Safe and Effective Instructional Strategies to Utilize Manipulatives, Models, Scientific Equipment, Real-World Examples, and Print and Digital Representations to Support and Enhance Science Instruction

While much of the world is safe and cognitively accessible for scientists of any age, many aspects of the physical world are dangerous and/or complex. Manipulatives, models, scientific examples, and print and digital images provide safe, hands-on opportunities to do what scientists do: observe, identify, describe, analyze, hypothesize, investigate, and explain. Real-life contexts provide opportunities for students to explore science concepts in concrete ways that relate to their level of understanding and background knowledge.

Selection of the right material depends on purpose as supported by the selected science standard. For example, an astronomy lesson (*SC.3.E.5.2: Identify the Sun as a star that emits energy; some of it in the form of light*) would probably use models, simulations, and representations. A physical science lesson (*SC.3.P.10.4 Demonstrate that light can be reflected, refracted, and absorbed*) would be better suited to hands-on exploration with different kinds of lights, lenses, and other materials to demonstrate absorption, reflection, and refraction.

Observation and curiosity about daily life events, newspapers, and online content can provide background for authentic questions and investigations. For example, in 2013, a 15-year-old Maryland student, Jake Andraka, won an Intel award for his work in identifying a potentially effective and low-cost way to screen for pancreatic cancer. Jake wondered why there wasn't a better way to screen for that type of cancer and used the Internet and other available information to research the question after a family friend died of pancreatic cancer.

Some examples of manipulatives for science centers and labs include:

- Animals and their food and housing (if available and no allergies are present) or an aquarium
- Plant and/or seeds for growing (may be seasonal)
- Balance scales with items to weigh
- Magnifying lenses
- Telescope
- Magnets and assorted objects
- Feely bags
- Microscope
- Containers of assorted objects to sort, classify, measure
- Books related to science topics
- Thermometer
- Filled containers with contents to smell
- Examples of simple machines
- Toy gear-sets
- Blocks
- Recyclable and nonrecyclable items

- Pictures of living and nonliving things
- Rocks, fossils, shells, and other natural objects
- Modeling clay

Skill 1.3: Identify and Analyze Strategies for Formal and Informal Learning Experiences to Provide Science Curriculum that Promotes Students' Innate Curiosity and Active Inquiry

Scientific inquiry, as defined by the National Science Education Standards (National Academy of Science, 1996) involves "the diverse ways in which scientists study the natural world and propose explanations based on the evidence derived from their work." Although the standards advocate direct student applications of scientific inquiry in hands-on and authentic contexts, the standards also note that there is no single approach to science instruction and that "conducting hands-on science activities does not guarantee inquiry, nor is reading about science incompatible with inquiry."

The National Science Teachers Association Position Statement on Elementary School Science (NSTA Board of Directors, 2002) advocates inquiry-based science as part of the daily curriculum at every grade as a means of developing problem-solving skills and scientific literacy. The goal is for students to develop positive attitudes and to value science. The statement reports that elementary school students value science best when:

- A variety of presentation modes are used to accommodate different learning preferences, and students are given opportunities to interact and share ideas with their peers.

- The scientific contributions of individuals from all ethnic origins are recognized and valued.

- Other subject areas are infused into science.

- Inquiry skills and positive attitudes are modeled by the teacher and others involved in the education process.

Formal learning activities are traditionally thought of as structured, school-based, and curriculum-driven. Standards and assessments also comprise components of formal learning activities. Informal learning activities occur outside traditional classroom settings and can include science museums, zoos, homes, and businesses. Informal learning can also occur in clubs or organizations. Informal experiences involve authentic, collaborative, and real-life situations. For example, a zoo may use animal care as a way to focus on environmental issues around the world. This might encourage a student to think, "How do I affect the environment?" A company might use energy-saving measures. The student might wonder, "How could those measures be applied at my school?" Informal learning gives students more "ownership" of the purpose and direction for what they learn. As a result, learning is often reported as more enjoyable and permanent, and often leads to continued interest in science, technology, engineering, and math (STEM) fields. The key is developing a mind-set and attitude that views education—whether formal or informal—through the lens of science inquiry. With informal learning, the teacher provides information and enthusiasm. For example, a teacher might announce that the local science center is hosting a special exhibit on mummies or let students know that a lunar eclipse occurs on a particular evening. A teacher could encourage students to track space launches on the NASA website. Once the event is over, the teacher might discuss the experience and inquire about what the student liked or learned from the experience and then connect that learning to curriculum content or other resources. The National Science Teachers Association (*http://ngss.nsta.org*) provides a variety of resources for science instruction.

Skill 1.4: Select and Analyze Collaborative Strategies to Help Students Explain Concepts, to Introduce and Clarify Formal Science Terms, and to Identify Misconceptions

The same collaborative strategies used in other content areas also apply to science learning. Communicating and working together are important life and job skills. These include the following:

- *Cooperative learning:* structured groups that combine positive interdependence (i.e., each person has an important contribution to the success of the entire group) with individual accountability to develop social skills as well as content knowledge through group interactions and processing.

- *Collaborative learning:* loosely structured groups that allow students to learn from and with each other.

- *Peer tutoring:* one student helps another student master a concept.

- *Google Docs (or other interactive word processors):* students writing and editing documents together in real time.

- *Problem-based learning:* working together to solve complex, open-ended problems (i.e., determining how much paper is thrown away at a school to provide a rationale for recycling).

- *Simulations:* Depicting and modeling real-life situations (i.e., amusement park physics, frog dissection).

- *Instructional games:* rule-guided competition for practicing and refining concepts (i.e., anatomy arcade, drill-and-practice software or online apps)

- *Contextual learning:* authentic real-life situations (i.e., learning about science in a garden project or seeing examples of simple machines—inclined plane, screw, lever, axle, and wheel—on vehicles)

Skill 1.5: Identify and Apply Appropriate Reading Strategies, Mathematical Practices, and Science-Content Materials to Enhance Science Instruction for Learners at All Levels

All reading strategies contribute to the understanding of science. Teachers can use science content to help students develop and apply reading skills and strategies. Common Core math practices describe ways of thinking that apply to science, math, and other subjects.

Reading Skills and Strategies

- Find main ideas and relevant details.

- Analyze and evaluate information.

- Interpret findings and draw conclusions.

- Identify and use content-specific vocabulary.

- Identify causes and effects.

- Ask and answer questions.

- Use structural analysis or other decoding strategies.

- Assimilate content from digital and print sources.

- Use metacognitive reasoning to recognize when comprehension fails and use "fix-up" strategies to repair understanding.

Mathematical Practices

- Make sense of problems and persevere in solving them.
- Reason abstractly and quantitatively.
- Construct viable arguments and critique the reasoning of others.
- Model with mathematics.
- Use appropriate tools strategically.
- Attend to precision.
- Look for and make use of structure.
- Look for and express regularity in repeated reasoning.

Choosing and Using Science Reading Materials

Science reading materials serve two purposes: instruction and leisure. Instructional materials should support the standard and content of the lesson by providing additional perspectives, different details, and/or new ways to view the content (i.e., graphics, photographs). As with any reading material, information should be related to student background and at an appropriate reading level. Reading materials outside standard textbooks should be engaging. Teachers should preview content to know and connect new information to what students already know and make sure that students understand clearly the connection between the materials. When needed, teachers should identify and pre-teach key content and academic vocabulary to create scaffolding for the content. Science reading materials for leisure or recreational reading should capture students' interest and motivate them to learn more about science. Science teachers might provide a collection of grade-level appropriate books, magazines, and articles on science topics for students to peruse. These can be narrative or expository at a variety of reading levels.

Skill 1.6: Apply Differentiated Strategies in Science Instruction and Assessments Based on Student Needs

The typical K–6 classroom is diverse in many ways. Students come with various levels of background knowledge, skills, and needs. One-size-fits-all teaching is obsolete because there is no one approach that meets the needs of all students. Rather, teachers need to know their students on an individual basis and plan accordingly.

Thus, differentiation of instruction is not an intervention strategy. It is the way teachers teach on a daily basis. Differentiating instruction is inherently student-centered and uses groups and discussion to process concepts. It results in increased participation and student engagement. While differentiation of instruction should be grounded in standards, it should include choice for how information is delivered and assessed. Differentiation of instruction can be accomplished in different ways by presenting form of content, processing or assimilating content, and demonstrating or understanding content.

For example, in terms of instruction, all students typically read the same content to learn the information. To differentiate, a teacher could use a jigsaw strategy in which one group reads and learns content from traditional text content, a second group uses videos and graphics to learn the content, and a third group focuses on terms and meanings. In the jigsaw, a member from each source group would come together in learning triads to discuss what was read, viewed, and learned about key concepts and vocabulary. Then each group would deliver a presentation based on their understanding. Follow-up formative assessments would identify gaps in understanding for subsequent lesson content and reinforcement or to extend learning.

Authentic contexts and problems in science form natural environments for differentiating instruction because each student can bring different knowledge and expertise to the solution. This is also authentic because teams of individuals representing diverse interests, and with varied backgrounds, can solve many real-world problems. Rather than using an objective multiple-choice exam, the assessment might focus on identifying a problem, finding resources from research, and presenting possible solutions. Differentiation of instruction accommodates students with disabilities and also exemplifies a universal design that benefits everyone.

Skill 1.7: Identify and Apply Ways to Organize and Manage a Classroom for Safe, Effective Science Teaching that Reflect State Safety Procedures and Restrictions

In April 2015, the Florida Department of Education published *A Summary of Safety Statutes, Rules and Recommendations for Science*. The report provides a sample K–5 "Contract for Student Safety" that addresses safety procedures in science as follows:

- I know that being safe is important, and I agree to follow these rules.

- I will follow all written precautions and verbal instructions.

- I will do the experimental procedure as directed.

- I will not taste, eat, smell, or touch substances unless specifically told to do so by my instructor.

- I will handle all equipment and materials carefully and use as directed.

- I will wear safety goggles to protect my eyes when appropriate or as directed by the teacher.

- I will notify the teacher if any hazard is present.

- I will clean up my work area after each experiment.

- I will inform my teacher of any health problems or difficulties I might encounter while doing a given experiment.

- I will make sure I do not remove any substances or equipment from the lab or classroom unless my teacher tells me to do so.

- I will not eat or drink anything in the laboratory or classroom without my teacher's permission.

- I will report any accident or mishap to my teacher immediately no matter how trivial it might appear.

- I will not pick up broken glass with bare hands.

- I will make sure an adult is present when I am working in the lab or classroom.

- I will wear gloves when handling animals.

- I will not run or participate in horseplay in the lab or classroom.

Handling Living Organisms

In the *Summary of Safety Statutes, Rules and Recommendations for Science,* the care and safe handling of live animals in a science classroom are also addressed. Some animals represent a high level of safety concern because their behavior is often unpredictable. In addition, many animals carry pathogens or allergens that may affect student health. These issues must be resolved before allowing animals in the student areas by requiring written permission from parents, guardians, and the principal. Animals in a classroom should be directly connected to the school curriculum. While it is important for all animals to be certified by a veterinarian for safety, it is especially important that reptiles have a veterinary certificate because they can carry salmonella. Stray animals (i.e., birds, frogs, turtles, and snakes) should not be allowed unless proper veterinary documentation is obtained. Pets should not be brought to school for show-and-tell that could result in dangerous animal interactions. Additionally, the summary designates that the teacher is responsible for all animals kept in the classroom. The teacher must provide detailed procedures for caring and interacting with animals and supervise contact to ensure safety of both the animal and the students.

An elementary classroom that contains hazardous chemicals or equipment must have:

- a dousing shower, a floor drain, and an eye-washing facility;

- emergency exhaust systems, fume hoods, and fume hood supply fans that shut down when emergency exhaust fans are operating; and

- lockable cabinets for hazardous materials or hazardous chemicals.

Monitoring Guide for Chemical Storage

- Secure chemical storage areas with lock and key and limit student access.

- Clearly post signs prohibiting student access.

- Chemical storage areas must be well lighted to avoid mix-ups.

- The floor space must not be cluttered.

- Inventory the area at least once a year. The chemical labels and the inventory list must have the name, supplier, date of purchase of mix, the concentration, and the amount available.

- Chemicals must be purged at least once a year.

- Chemical storage must use recognized storage patterns and chemicals should be in compatible groups—not in alphabetical order.

- There must be materials to dilute and absorb a large volume (one-gallon) chemical spill.

- Certain chemicals that present a potential for explosion are not permitted in science classrooms or storage areas. These chemicals include benzoylperoxide, phosphorus, carbon disulfide, ethyl ether, isopropyl ether, picric acid, perchloric acid, potassium chlorate, and potassium metal.

- Some chemicals present a danger as a human carcinogen and are not allowed in science classrooms or chemical storage areas. These include arsenic compounds, benzene, chloroform, nickel powder, asbestos, acrylonitrile, benzidine, chromium compound, ortho-toluidine, cadmium compounds, and and ethylene oxide.

Teachers can use the following checklists to ensure that their classrooms are safe for students to learn science.

Checklist for Chemical Storage in Schools According to Florida Law

Ventilation	
Temperature	
Heat detector	
Secured	
Well illuminated	
Uncluttered floor	
Chemical inventory	
Chemicals purged annually	
Chemicals grouped correctly	
Labels on chemical containers	
Flammables cabinet	
Spill protection	
No explosives	
No carcinogens	

Checklist for Science Classrooms According to Florida Law

Fire extinguisher	
Fire blanket	
Gas cutoff (present and labeled)	
Water cutoff (present and labeled)	
Electrical cutoff (present and labeled)	
Dousing shower	
Floor drain	
Eye-washing facility	
Room ventilation adequate	
Fume hood	
Grounded receptacles	
Ground fault circuit interrupters within 2 inches of water	
No flammable storage	
Face protection that meets standards	
Face protection in sufficient numbers	

Additional resources for safety in science can be obtained from the Council of State Science Supervisors (*http://www.csss-science.org/safety.shtml*).

Through active, hands-on activities, science instruction is richer and more meaningful. From simple observations and activities at early grades to detailed controlled experiments at higher grades, students use science to learn science and understand science better. While students are engaged in the process of discovery and exploration, the teacher must be engaged in protecting students' health and safety. The hazards vary with the discipline, but thoughtful planning and management of the activities will significantly reduce the risks to students. In all cases, students must follow personal hygiene procedures (hand washing) and wear personal protective equipment (goggles, gloves) while engaged in laboratory or field activities.

Science teachers should substitute less hazardous materials whenever possible. For example, in the physical sciences, teachers can (1) replace mercury thermometers with alcohol or electronic thermometers; (2) replace glass beakers and graduated cylinders with durable polyethylene containers; and (3) eliminate or reduce the use of hazardous chemicals. In the Earth sciences, (1) rocks and minerals used in class should not contain inherently hazardous materials; (2) students should not taste the minerals; and (3) teachers should dispense reagents like hydrochloric acid, used for identification of carbonate minerals, from spill-proof plastic containers. In the life sciences, teachers should give special care to (1) safe practices with sharp objects; (2) the safe handling of living organisms; and (3) the care and use of microscopes. For example, teachers should discourage experiments or activities involving the collection or culture of human cells or fluids and make sure to use proper sterilization procedures to prevent the growth or spread of disease agents.

Field activities, such as visiting nature centers or other facilities or museums, enrich the science curriculum in all disciplines. The teacher must assume responsibility for planning and implementing activities that not only increase students' learning but also maintain their health and safety.

Skill 1.8: Select and Apply Appropriate Technology, Science Tools, and Measurement Units for Students' Use in Data Collection and the Pursuit of Science

Science teachers should use technology effectively to plan, organize, deliver, and evaluate instruction for all students. From the pencil-and-field notebook to modern instruments in the laboratory, science uses tools for observation, measurement, and computational analysis. Compared to the goose quill, the modern mechanical pencil is a dramatic advancement in the technology for written communication, but neither the quill nor the pencil replaces the critical, analytical, and creative act of authorship. Many technological tools support observation, the collection of data, analysis, and presentation of scientific information, yet none replace the role of the investigator who must formulate meaningful questions afforded by the application of technology. Technology gives students the opportunity to participate firsthand in the process of inquiry and discovery. Technology should facilitate student learning and remove barriers to understanding, but it should not create new barriers to delay and obscure the scientific concepts being taught.

Data is synonymous with facts and information. Thus, K–6 students need to realize that scientific inquiry involves collection of data—the facts and information about their physical or material world. Science is the perfect place for students to apply reading and math development by selecting and using technology, science tools, and units of measurement. Many tools have digital counterparts (i.e., timers) that can be demonstrated with a smartboard. Some scientific tools (i.e., microscopes) can be connected to computers and projected on a large screen for discussion.

Basic Science Tools

Tool	Function
Thermometer	Measures heat in Fahrenheit or Centigrade
Scale	Measures weight in ounces or grams
Microscope or magnifying glass	Magnifies or enlarges
Telescope	Makes distant items seem closer
Ruler	Measures size in metric or standard units
Weather vane	Indicates wind direction
Anemometer	Measures wind speed
Measures of capacity (measuring spoons or cups, graduated cylinders or beakers)	Measures volume
Calculator	Computes results
Timer or stopwatch	Measures elapsed time

As scientific tools are introduced, teachers can ask students to differentiate the tools by use. For example, if a student wants to know how hot it is in a car at the end of the day, what science tool should the student use? How is that tool used?

Thus, scientific process skills, including the proper and accurate use of laboratory equipment, are an important component of science education. Instruction is necessary to guide the effective use of each measurement or observational tool (i.e., rulers, microscopes, balances, and laboratory glassware). As students develop these skills, they move from simple observations and confirmatory activities to applying these tools for discovering answers to their questions. Through active, hands-on activities, science instruction becomes a richer and more meaningful experience. From simple observations and activities in the early grades through detailed controlled experiments at higher grade levels, students who do science to learn science understand science better.

Collection of Data

Students should be taught how to collect data as they use various tools to observe physical phenomena. Students can start by keeping an online or physical science journal and sketchbook for what they observe. They can describe or draw what they see under a microscope or magnifying glass or create simple tables of data (i.e., date and temperature). In lower grades, teachers can provide worksheets to help students collect data. For example, a teacher might create a monthly wall chart for temperatures at 9 a.m., noon, and 2 p.m. Data would be collected at the various times to identify and write about trends. Students in upper grades might use a spreadsheet to record data and create graphs by week, day, or time of day.

In general, the goal is for students to realize that data can be found everywhere; by using the right tool to observe systematically and record data accurately, they can identify trends, problems, and possible solutions. Thus, as students collect data, they need to realize that what they collect must be accurate and as precise as possible. This is a good opportunity to apply understanding of decimals and fractions. Students can also describe data in mathematical terms using measures of central tendency (i.e., median and mean) for mathematical comparisons. For example, in measuring temperature over the day, students might note that, in general, temperatures rise during the day. This might be expressed as "the temperature is 10% lower in the morning than later in the afternoon."

Digital Tools

Many twenty-first-century Florida classrooms have become completely digital, with books and other materials available on iPads, tablets, or notebook computers. Software tools for the computer are extremely useful for both teachers and students.

Word-processing programs allow students to write and edit assignments such as term papers and research reports. Most programs include spelling and grammar checkers that enable students to enhance the quality of their written assignments. With most word processors, students can put the text into columns with headlines of varying sizes to produce class newsletters. For example, a class could write a series of reviews of scientific articles and add information about class activities in science. Desktop publishing programs allow students to integrate text and graphics to produce more complex publications, such as a school newspaper or yearbook.

Databases are like electronic file cards. They allow students to input data and then retrieve it in various formats. For example, science students can input data about an experiment on temperature, volume, or time and then manipulate the data to report information in a variety of ways. The most important learning concept about databases is that, when dealing with huge quantities of information, students can learn how to analyze and interpret the data to discover connections among isolated facts and figures and how to eliminate unnecessary information.

Online databases are essential tools for research. Students can access databases related to science and other subject areas. E-mail allows students to communicate over the Internet with scientific associations and scientists from around the world. Massive bibliographic databases help students and teachers find resources. Electronic library systems can significantly increase the materials available to students. Materials can then be borrowed through interlibrary loan agreements.

Spreadsheets are similar to teacher gradebooks. Rows and columns of numbers can be calculated to produce totals and averages. Formulas can connect information in one cell (the intersection of a row and column) to another cell. Students can use spreadsheets to collect and analyze numerical data; sort the data in various orders; and create various types of graphs (bars, columns, scatters, histograms, and pies) to report findings. Students can use the graphics to enhance written reports or multimedia presentations.

Digital cameras also benefit science instruction by collecting data for future reference or to document change over time (i.e., erosion after rain and plant growth). Digital cameras can photograph completed projects to share with others when presenting results.

Computer-Assisted Instruction

Computer-assisted instruction via software and online or mobile applications maximize instructional time. While drill-and-practice programs provide practice of basic facts or skills, tutorials can include explanations and information that go beyond drill and practice. When a student makes a response, the program branches to the most appropriate section based on the student's answer. Tutorials support remedial work but can also be useful for instruction—for instance, the metric system. Improved graphics and sound allow non-English-speaking students to hear the correct pronunciation of words while viewing related pictures. However, tutorials should supplement teacher instruction, not supplant it.

Simulations or problem-solving programs allow students to experience situations that otherwise could not take place in the classroom because of time or cost constraints. For example, students could learn to dissect animals using a simulator rather than performing real dissections. This approach saves time and materials, avoids creating a mess, and helps students who might be reluctant to dissect real animals. Also, simulations can speed up processes (i.e., a flower blooming) or slow them down (i.e., a bumblebee in flight). Other software might explore the effects of weightlessness on plant growth, a situation that would be impossible to set up in a classroom lab. Instructional games and problem-solving software allow students to think through scientific issues and dilemmas. Digital maps and atlases provide opportunities to explore geologic and oceanic formations.

Graphics or drawing programs allow students to produce images of cells viewed under a microscope or plants and animals observed outdoors. Students can use these programs to illustrate displays, individual research projects, or multimedia presentations.

Teachers can use concept mapping templates as advance organizers to help students organize ideas, identify key points, and highlight supporting details. They can be used to compare and contrast processes, identify the sequence in processes, identify cause-effect relationships, and create timelines.

Students may even teach each other through multimedia presentations or Web 2.0 tools. Using an inquiry method, students can take responsibility for their own learning by planning, carrying out, and presenting research.

Selection and Evaluation Criteria

Teachers use criteria to evaluate technological resources. The first thing to look for is alignment with state standards and lesson goals. If the software does not reinforce learning outcomes, the teacher should not use it in the classroom no matter how flashy or well-crafted it is. A checklist for instructional computer software or mobile apps includes: (1) appropriate sequence of instruction; (2) meaningful student interaction; (3) learner control of screens and pacing; (4) motivation; (5) ability to control sound and progress; (6) effective use of color, clarity of text, and appropriate use of graphics; and (7) potential use for individual or group assignments.

In addition to congruence with curriculum goals and state standards, the teacher needs to consider: (1) students' strengths and needs, (2) their learning preferences or modalities, and (3) their interests. Formal and informal assessments can help determine students' needs and preferences. Most standardized tests indicate the objectives that students fail to master. Students can then receive help in mastering these objectives using digital or mobile aids.

 ### Skill 1.9: Select and Analyze Developmentally Appropriate Diagnostic, Formative, and Summative Assessments to Evaluate Prior Knowledge, Guide Instruction, and Evaluate Student Achievement

As in other content areas, assessment is not an end to itself. The type of assessment depends on three purposes: (1) determining prior knowledge and skills (diagnostic), (2) tracking progress and guiding instruction (formative), and (3) evaluating learning (summative). The type of assessment also depends on the content of the assessment: knowledge, skills, or attitude.

The choice of assessment is based on two factors: the standard that supports learning and the specific learning outcomes identified for the lesson. For example, the learning outcome for Florida Science Standard SC.3.E.5.2, "Identify the Sun as a star that emits energy; some of it in the form of light," might be "to identify attributes of the Sun." In this example, a formative assessment might be a classroom assessment technique at the end of the lesson with a summative assessment of a conceptual test or concept map. However, given the Florida Science Standard SC.3.E.5.4, "Explore the Law of Gravity by demonstrating that gravity is a force that can be overcome," the learning outcome might be to "Explain the Law of Gravity as a force to be overcome based on classroom experimentation." In this situation, the assessment is based on what the student observed while carrying out the experiments and the conclusions that the student drew from those observations. This could be assessment by a subjective essay, concept map, or performance.

Assessments can be objective (i.e., multiple choice, matching, etc.), subjective (i.e., concept map, essay, short answer), or performance-based (i.e., how to use a scientific tool, presentation, project). Objective tests have a single right response and are scored as correct or incorrect. While subjective, short-answer responses could be scored similarly, rubrics must be developed for essays or concept maps. They should also be developed for performance assessments. Rubrics identify key criteria for expected outcomes or performance with a scale to show the degree to which the outcome or performance must be demonstrated.

Types of Assessments and Uses

Type	Use
Attitude	Student perceptions of self and experience.
Classroom assessment technique (CAT)	Brief prompts used to gather information about student understanding or perception at the end of a class or lesson.
Conceptual	Comprehension and application of content in written or oral form.
Concept map	Graphic representation of concepts and how they relate to each other.
Performance	Demonstration of ability or knowledge.
Portfolio	Collection of work over time to demonstrate progress of learning.
Project-based learning or problem-based learning	Investigation and response to an engaging, authentic, and complex question, problem, or challenge.
Socratic questioning	Directed discussion focusing on critical thinking as revealed through systematic responses to questions about concepts or problems.

Skill 1.10: Choose Scientifically and Professionally Responsible Content and Activities that Are Socially and Culturally Sensitive

In the mid-twentieth century, reading materials in most schools were dominated by British and American literature. Photographs in books lacked diversity. Later in the twentieth century, literature and textbook art increasingly represented the diverse nature and lives of their readers. The same sort of trend applied to math and science and, with a few exceptions (e.g., Madame Curie, George Washington Carver), mid- to late twentieth-century educational curricula focused on the contributions of males of European descent.

Today's classrooms should reflect and recognize the social and cultural contributions from around the world in science and other subjects to provide equity for learning by all students. They are tomorrow's adult citizens. Science education helps them make informed choices about a variety of life issues, from health and nutrition to actions involving technology or the environment. Recognizing the need for science education for all learners, the National Science Teachers Association (NSTA) addressed diverse perspectives and needs, including information about multicultural science, science for English language learners, international science education, gender equity, students with disabilities, and parent involvement in science learning.

Social and cultural sensitivity goes beyond the inclusion of diverse groups in curriculum materials. Rather, it identifies and illuminates paths for active involvement in science and careers. It also means that teachers observe interactions within a class to determine issues in group dynamics and make sure they notice and encourage all students fairly and consistently. For example, students from more economically stable homes may attend informal science opportunities not available to students without financial resources or transportation. Many students with low socioeconomic status lack consistent access to technology; the gap in access between students of low socioeconomic status and those of high socioeconomic status is sometimes referred to as the digitial divide. English language learners (ELLs) might be interested and knowledgeable, but they may lack the academic language skills to communicate their interest and understanding. The same may be true for students with disabilities: They can be marginalized if accommodations do not support full participation in science activities. Thus, these students may be knowledgeable and interested in science at school as the result of their experiences, communication skills, and participation, but teachers often reinforce differences in behaviors and interests by inadvertently overlooking students who might be more interested if they had the same skills and opportunities. This unintentionally creates a cycle. Students who are more successful in science, for whatever reason, get more encouragement with their science endeavors and future careers. Students who are less successful, for whatever reason, may be encouraged to follow interests and careers in fields other than the sciences.

How do teachers know if they are contributing to the cycle? Teachers should know their students and avoid stereotyping and making assumptions. Teachers should consider the kind of feedback they provide to students. For example, if a teacher reviews comments on a science report, do papers with the same grade get the same kind of comments and feedback, or does the teacher simply write "Excellent" on some and "Very good" on others? In other words, are some students graded more rigorously than others? If so, why? How are students grouped, and why? What are the teacher's responses to students who respond quickly versus those who respond after reflection?

When teaching ELLs, teachers should make sure that information is clear, direct, and provided in multiple formats (i.e., text, auditory, graphics, and video). Teachers can scaffold information in terms of language and group ELLs with native learners to provide language support. Assessments should focus on demonstration of science concepts and skills in practice more than on writing or speaking. This approach is sometimes referred to as sheltered English instruction.

Students with disabilities also benefit from approaches that feature clear and direct instruction, present content in multiple formats, use cooperative or collaborative groups, and are participatory in nature.

In reality, typical approaches used for ELLs and students with disabilities maximize learning for all students through universal design, which is characterized by (1) multiple means of representing or providing content, (2) varied options for expression of learning, and (3) different opportunities for engagement.

As students begin to view their own thinking and lives from the perspective of science, they must be challenged to identify and counteract stereotypical attitudes and perceptions. For example, a teacher could ask students how scientists are typically portrayed on television, in movies, and in other media and why. This would also be a good opportunity for teachers to involve families and members of the community in science education by asking them to talk about their experiences and careers in science and science-related areas.

Florida students are diverse in geographic terms. While many students attend schools in rural or suburban areas, others are schooled in urban settings that are (1) highly diverse in ethnic, cultural, and economic characteristics; (2) dominated by a constructed rather than a natural environment; and (3) located in regional and cultural centers. Inner-city schools may reflect the rest of the environment with few green spaces and natural features. Teachers need to take specific steps to provide these students with nature experiences and to introduce science issues and problems inherent in an urban environment. For example, students could explore examples of simple machines (e.g., inclined planes, pulleys) in the environment and how they benefit the movement of goods. Or students could collect samples of paint from buildings that were erected in different time periods to examine their composition.

Students need to realize that the world is much larger than their neighborhoods and communities and that local decisions involving science can have global effects. Communication tools like Skype could be used to contact individuals around the world to discuss common issues and problems in both urban and rural areas.

Competency 2: Knowledge of the Nature of Science

Knowledge of the nature of science is knowledge of the physical world and how it functions through observation and experimentation. Knowledge of the nature of science depends on thinking scientifically as well as on using math to collect and analyze data, and on language arts to learn and express what is learned. The application of knowledge of the nature of science informs related areas, such as engineering and technology, and forms the basis for continued scientific investigations.

Skill 2.1: Analyze the Dynamic Nature of Science Models, Laws, Mechanisms, and Theories that Explain Natural Phenomena

As stated previously, science is the study of the physical or material world. This brief and seemingly simple statement embodies many of the underlying concepts of the nature of science. For example, the use of the word *study* means that science is something that involves time and attention to gaining knowledge in a detailed, analytical, and organized investigation. *Physical* or *material* means that science is observed through evidence. *World* doesn't mean just Earth; it refers to the universe and everything in and about it. The word *science* traces back to the Latin root *scient,* meaning *to know*. And that is what the nature of science really is. It's not just a body of knowledge such as chemistry, biology, or geology—it's an active and ongoing way to know the world in which we live.

The American Association for the Advancement of Science (AAAS) created *Project 2061,* an initiative to improve science education so that all Americans can become literate in science, mathematics, and technology. One of their resources is *Science for All Americans Online* (1990). It describes the nature of science in terms of a worldview, scientific inquiry, and scientific enterprise.

Worldview	Scientific Inquiry	Scientific Enterprise
• The world is understandable and predictable. • Scientific ideas are subject to change. • Scientific knowledge is durable. • Science cannot answer all questions completely.	• Science demands evidence. • Science is a blend of logic and imagination. • Science explains and predicts. • Scientists try to identify and avoid bias. • Science is not authoritarian.	• Science is a complex social activity. • Science is organized into content disciplines and is conducted in various institutions. • There are generally accepted ethical principles in the conduct of science. • Scientists participate in public affairs both as specialists and as citizens.

Source: Project 2061: Science for All Americans Online (http://www.project2061.org).

So what does this mean? In terms of a worldview and, as far as we know, the world is a consistent place. Scientific laws truthfully and accurately describe—but do not explain—what occurs consistently under certain conditions. This means that what occurs in one part of the universe applies to other parts of the universe. Scientific theories are validated and supported explanations of what occurs in the universe. What has been learned has stood the test of time and experience, is durable, and can be replicated. It also means that we can predict what will occur in the world. Science doesn't explain everything because sometimes we haven't asked the right questions, tried enough options, or used the right tools. In those cases, results and findings may be tentative. As such, laws and theories are subject to change given new evidence. Whereas the Earth was once considered the center of the universe, we now know that we are a tiny part of a tiny solar system at the edge of what we can see. We use both logic and imagination to wonder "What if?" and develop new hypotheses to test. The scientific method tests those hypotheses systematically, carefully avoiding biases (preferences) and, when needed, challenging what have been authoritative answers. Finally, science is an enterprise, an organized social endeavor with many people contributing in different ways and at different places and always ethically. If science is, indeed, something we all do and are part of, it means that we have a responsibility as citizens to make and advocate for scientifically appropriate and ethical solutions.

Skill 2.2: Identify and Apply Science and Engineering Practices Through Integrated Process Skills

The concept of science, technology, engineering, and math (STEM) fields means that these fields do not exist in isolation; they exist in relationship to each other. The scientific method and the processes within it are not just specific steps requiring rigorous adherence whenever a question arises involving the knowledge and techniques of science. Rather, the scientific method is a process of observation and analysis that contributes to a reliable, consistent, and objective representation and understanding of our world in an authentic, relevant, and useful way. Thus, science and math provide ways to help solve engineering, technological, and other problems. The processes that make up the scientific method are: observing and describing, formulating hypotheses, making predictions based on the hypotheses, testing those predictions (experimenting), and deriving conclusions.

The following table outlines the process of scientific investigation and experimentation:

Process	Definition	Key Points
Observing	Sensing some measurable phenomenon.	• Sensory data that can be enhanced through the use of tools (i.e., microscope, telescope, spectroscope) • Can be quantitative or qualitative
Classifying	Comparing and contrasting features for grouping	• Identification of similarities and differences • Can focus on one trait (single state) or several traits (multiple states) • Multistate classification divides groups into increasingly smaller groups based on finer distinctions • Can also result in a serial continuum of related items in terms of one trait
Measuring	Determining quantity	• Use of metric units • Base units include meter (length), liter (volume), gram (mass), Celsius (temperature) • Unit prefix indicates increases (i.e., kilo-) or decreases (i.e., milli-) in size
Inferencing	Drawing conclusions based on observation data	• Used to examine past or present conditions • Looking for patterns or trends based on available data • Additional data may change inference • Multiple conclusions may result from same data set

(continued)

Process	Definition	Key Points
Predicting	Guessing the outcome of an event in advance of it occurring	• Using data and inference about trends and patterns to make informed guesses about future events • Additional data may change prediction • Multiple predictions may result from same data set
Hypothesizing	Creating a testable question for experimentation	• Based on prior knowledge and data • Tentative explanation of relationship between independent and dependent variables • Should be testable in that there must be a way to observe and measure the results
Experimenting	Using integrated process skills in an experiment	• Testing a hypothesis by manipulating the independent variable to observe the effect on the dependent variable and holding other variables constant (control), accurately and precisely collecting data, interpreting data, and formulating models
Collecting and organizing data	Using observation and tools to gather information or investigate a problem	• Using a structure (notebook, data table, spreadsheet, photographs, sketches) to save and organize data for later analysis and interpretation • Data tables show results for the independent and dependent variable
Interpreting data	Transforming raw data into meaningful results and drawing conclusions	• Graphing ordered pairs to identify a best-fit line that illustrates a pattern • Identifying measures of central tendency and deviation to summarize data • Identifying patterns in results and stating the observed relationship between the independent and dependent variable
Sharing results	Sharing outcomes	• Using graphics, verbal presentations, or writing to describe the investigation precisely and accurately • Asking for feedback about communication of results

Skill 2.3: Differentiate Between the Characteristics of Experiments and Other Types of Scientific Investigations

Investigation differs from experimentation because investigation involves fact finding and data collection. Scientific research does both—investigation often precedes experimentation. In some cases, experimentation is not possible or feasible. Both, however, start with questions.

For example, a student might wonder about the effect of light on plant growth. That would be a testable question because the student could plant several seeds in the same type of soil, provide the same amount of water, and vary the amount of sunlight each plant receives: One plant could be in a sunny window, one could be out of the sun on a table, and one could be in the room in a box. This would exemplify an experiment. The independent variable would be amount of sun. The dependent variable would be the amount of sunlight. The experiment could be repeated over multiple trials to determine if the outcome occurred consistently. This would exemplify a controlled investigation because the plants are in the same environment. A field experiment occurs in real-world settings, however, such as in a garden. Extraneous variables in field experiments are harder to control.

Because of time or other constraints, experimentation is sometimes impossible. In such cases, investigation is another way to gather information. For example, perhaps children have been taught guidelines for handwashing and how handwashing affects transmission of germs and disease. The students might observe people at home or in school restrooms washing their hands to determine if their actions demonstrate good handwashing procedures (i.e., time spent washing hands, use of soap). From their data, students could draw conclusions and then create a handwashing campaign to inform other students about correct handwashing procedures.

In planning experiments, the scientist or student is generally attempting to test a hypothesis (prediction). A hypothesis is an educated guess about the relationship between two variables; the hypothesis is subject to testing and verification. The outcome of the test in a well-designed experiment answers questions suggested by the hypothesis in a clear and unambiguous way.

In planning and conducting an experiment, the scientist or student must:

1. Identify relevant variables.

2. Identify necessary equipment and apparatus for measuring and recording the variables.

3. Eliminate or suppress any other factors that could influence measured variables.

4. Decide on a means of analyzing the data obtained.

When conducting experiments, questions raised by the hypotheses must be testable and the data recorded must be sufficiently accurate and repeatable. An example of a testable question might be, "Does mass have an influence on acceleration for bodies subjected to unbalanced forces?" This question is testable because it identifies specific variables (force, mass, and acceleration) that can be measured and controlled in an experiment that seeks to establish a connection. Thus, testable questions must specify variables that are subject to both measurement and control.

Experimental and Other Forms of Investigation

The science fair project is a common tool for instruction in the scientific method. Many formal and informal sources, often Web-based, provide lists of suggested science fair topics, but not all the topics are experiments. For the youngest students, it is appropriate and useful for the focus to be on models and demonstrations—for example, a model of the solar system or a volcano. The next step in development might be to collect data through observation or survey (questionnaire) and summarize and draw conclusions for presentation. Older students should move to true experiments that focus on identifying a testable hypothesis and controlling all experimental variables but the one of interest.

It is possible to elevate many projects that begin as models or demonstrations to experiments. One can develop a demonstration on how windmills work into an experiment when the student adds quantitative measurements of one variable against variations in another variable; the student must hold all other variables constant. For example, using an electric fan, the student could measure the number of rotations per minute as a function of the fan setting (low, medium, or high). Then, while keeping the fan setting constant, the student could conduct multiple trials that vary the number of fans, power of fans, sizes of fans, or shapes of fans and measure the rotational speed at each variation.

Skill 2.4: Identify and Analyze Attitudes and Dispositions Underlying Scientific Thinking

While there may not be a stereotypical scientist in terms of looks or interests, scientists generally share certain attitudes and characteristics. Scientists are generally curious and passionate about learning more about the world. They ask questions and seek answers. They are imaginative and creative; however, they are also critical thinkers who look at problems and data objectively. Scientists are observant and know how to use tools to collect data that is both accurate and precise. They are organized and know how to set goals and make plans. They can suspend judgment when needed and are open to new information or ideas. They are objective and honest even when results don't turn out as hypothesized. They learn from mistakes and failures and persist in their efforts. Careful records help them avoid making the same mistake twice. They know how to work independently as well as with others to accomplish tasks. They know how to communicate in writing, speaking, and through graphics and they know how to gain information from reading, listening, and visuals. Scientists have confidence in themselves and their skills; however, they also know when to ask for help. They advocate for change based on what they find.

While these characteristics apply to scientific thinking, they actually apply to thinking about life. Each characteristic—passion for learning, objectivity, persistence, ability to overcome failure, communication skills, confidence, and more—apply to all endeavors.

Skill 2.5: Identify and Select Appropriate Tools, Including Digital Technologies, and Units of Measurement for Various Science Tasks

Scientific experimentation uses a variety of tools or instruments, including microscopes, graduated cylinders, scales, voltmeters, ammeters, meter sticks, and micrometers. In general, these devices measure mass, volume, length, and voltage. Digital technologies include spreadsheets, databases, word processors, presentation applications, and online or graphic calculators.

Inherent to the proper use of measuring devices is recognition of their limitations in accuracy and precision. Precision concerns the number of places that can be read reliably from any measurement device. For example, a meter stick is generally good to three-place precision, the first two places being determined by scale markings and the third place determined by the estimated position between scale markings.

Scientific process skills, including the proper and accurate use of laboratory equipment, are an important component of science education. Instruction is necessary to guide the effective use of each measurement or observational tool: rulers, microscopes, balances, laboratory glassware, spreadsheets, databases, graphing calculators, and so forth. As students develop their measuring skills, they move from simple observations and teacher-directed activities to using these tools to find answers to questions that they develop themselves.

Measurement skills include:

1. Estimating and converting measurements within customary and metric systems.

2. Applying procedures for using measurement to describe and compare phenomena.

3. Identifying appropriate measurement instruments, units, and procedures for problems involving length, area, angles, volume, mass, time, money, and temperature.

4. Using a variety of materials, models, and methods to explore concepts and solve problems involving measurement.

Skill 2.6: Evaluate and Interpret Pictorial Representations, Charts, Tables, and Graphs of Authentic Data from Scientific Investigations to Make Predictions, Construct Explanations, and Support Conclusions

One way of representing data is in graphical form, which shows the plotting of raw data. The independent (controlled) variable is usually shown on the x-axis of a graph (horizontal), and the dependent variable is usually shown on the y-axis (vertical). Graphs can either be linear (a straight line) or nonlinear. Graphs can display equations and can aid in finer analyses. Use of a graphing calculator and specialized software can facilitate both the data collection and data representation in graphical form. The x- and y-graphs are not the only ways to represent data, however; charts, diagrams, and tables can display results, too.

Sometimes experimental work involves measurements that do not directly yield the desired value, but interpretation or reduction can provide the desired value. The experimental approach in that case is indirect.

An example is the measurement of the acceleration of gravity, or g, a fundamental gravitational constant. One common method is to measure displacement over time for a falling body. Reducing (interpreting) the resulting graph yields a plot of velocity versus time. In turn, reducing (interpreting) this plot yields a plot of acceleration versus time; one can read the acceleration of gravity, g, from the plot. Inherent in each of the reductions is finding the slope (the rise divided by the run) at various points, which is a mathematical technique that enables interpretation of the results.

From a science perspective, the key is interpreting the results of representations from either personal research or research from others. It's not enough to know that there is a correlation between two sets of data or that one variable causes another to change. What's important is what that means in the context of life. For example, a student might wonder how much paper is discarded in a classroom. The student might collect data by weighing the amount of trash each day. The results could be summarized and graphed. For example, perhaps there's always more paper discarded on Friday than on any other day. Why would that be? After computing the total amount of trash per day, per week, and per month, the student could predict the average amount of trash that is discarded by the entire school over the course of year. But the real question is: So what? What might be concluded is that discarded paper could be recycled. How would that affect resources in the community? Thus, the meaning of the data should be in real-life and authentic applications.

◼ Skill 2.7: Identify and Analyze Ways in Which Science Is an Interdisciplinary Process and Interconnected to STEM Disciplines

STEM is an acronym for the academic disciplines of science, technology, engineering, mathematics, and more recently computer science. It is often used in the context of supporting education policy, funding opportunities, and curriculum choices in schools for improving competitiveness in technology development. Beginning in elementary school, STEM programs apply principles and methodologies within each of the other subjects that mirror the reality of professional engineering through:

- practical real-life problems that require research-relevant knowledge.

- solutions that require application of new knowledge.

- evaluation that leads to improved solutions.

Engineering contexts and challenges support the integrated teaching of science, technology, and mathematics through investigation, observation, reflection, and development of testing concepts in new situations. The interdisciplinary approach of teaching should enable "learning how to learn" by ensuring reflection on strategies for problem solving; explanations by learners of their intentions, processes, and solutions; constructive feedback; self- and peer assessment; learners managing their own problem-solving processes; and space for learning. The STEM schools deliver enrichment activities (such as holding a science week or sponsoring a technology club) and adapt strategies for overlapping subjects to transfer skills for communication, teamwork, and problem solving.

At the core, science involves the scientific method applied to the natural world. Engineering combines science with creativity and innovation, which can be harder to quantify and teach. Teachers need to understand and nurture creative processes, and they also need to create a classroom climate for creativity.

The interactions between science and engineering with the remaining STEM topics (math and technology) are also fairly clear. Math skills are essential tools for both scientists and engineers, and technology, especially computer technology, allows students to capture, analyze, and evaluate data to create models and simulations. Technology is loosely defined as the application of science for the benefit of humankind. By the same token, advances in science and engineering can stimulate the development of new technology.

Integration of disciplines is the hallmark of the STEM classroom. Each subject naturally blends into the others. Knowledge and skills in one area supports application to the solution of authentic, real-world problems. While not specifically indicated as part of the STEM subjects, language arts also plays a role because students must use language effectively to gather information from text, listen to others, discuss findings, and report results.

Just as scientific thinking is a way of thinking about life, thinking from a STEM perspective takes that thinking a step further. STEM thinking is, by definition, the application and integration of thinking. The same traits that characterize scientific thinking—passion for learning, objectivity, persistence, ability to overcome failure, communication skills, confidence, and more—also apply to STEM endeavors. Together, the skills—and the students—exemplify collaboration and teamwork. Subjects are not in silos of information, and students are not just working independently. Rather, they are learning that life and work are interrelated processes.

Skill 2.8: Analyze the Interactions of Science and Technology with Society, Including Cultural, Ethical, Economic, Political, and Global Factors

From science and technology, our society now has the knowledge and tools to understand some of nature's principles and to apply that knowledge for some useful purpose. Few would debate the benefits of the wheel and axle, the electric light, the polio vaccine, and plastic. The benefits of science and technology become more complicated to evaluate, however, when discussing the applications of gene splicing for genetically modified foods, of cloning, of nuclear energy to replace fossil fuels, or of atomic energy to weapons of mass destruction. Science can tell us how to do something, not whether we should do it.

Scientific literacy helps us participate in the decision-making process of our society as well-informed and contributing members. Real-world decisions have social, political, and economic dimensions, and scientific information is often used both to support and to refute those decisions. While some of these could be actualized in the classroom, other concepts can also be the subject of discussion based on current or historical events. For example, how do decisions to vaccinate or not to vaccinate affect society? What is the relationship between food that is wasted and hunger in different countries? In terms of ethics and global connections, if the discovery of a new product from an endangered plant in the Amazon rainforest saves lives, should we harvest those plants? In terms of political interactions, how does the platform of a candidate reflect and support science? How do elected officials support scientific issues through their initiatives, funding support, and views? In terms of economic decisions, money is always a limitation. How are decisions made in terms of what to fund?

Understanding that the inherent nature of scientific information is unbiased and is based on experimental evidence that can be reproduced by any laboratory under the same conditions can help us all make better decisions, recognize false arguments, and participate fully as active and responsible citizens.

Competency 3: Knowledge of Physical Sciences

The physical sciences focus on a variety of areas concerning inanimate objects, natural objects in terms of content and form, and the ways in which they change and affect other objects.

Skill 3.1: Identify and Differentiate Among the Physical Properties of Matter

Substances (that is, matter) can be analyzed and classified by their physical properties through observations, descriptions, or measurements. Students' ability to observe, describe, or measure physical properties may depend on their age and cognitive ability. For example, absorption or electrical properties might be appropriate for upper grades; abstract concepts of photosynthesis or electron particles may not be as comprehensible for kindergarten students.

An object's mass and volume are perhaps the most basic components for measuring an object (i.e., how much there is of an object, or mass, and how much space it occupies, or volume). For example, the volume of a rectangular object is length times width times height ($L \times W \times H$). According to Newton's second law of motion, mass relates to force and acceleration: Force equals mass times acceleration ($F = M \times A$).

Pressure (amount of force) applied to matter affects volume. For example, imagine a shoebox filled with cotton. The volume ($L \times W \times H$) can be measured. When applying force, the cotton can be pressed into a smaller box. The greater the force, the greater the pressure. Applying the same amount of force to a smaller area also increases pressure. For example, standing on two feet (larger area) feels different than standing on one foot (smaller area) because of increased pressure. Pressure is also affected by temperature. Cold air has a higher pressure than warm air. Thus, when a cold front approaches warm air, it pushes the warm air out of the way and temperatures drop.

Although often confused with mass, weight measures the force of gravity on an object. Thus, a scale may show an object's mass in grams, but the function of the scale depends on gravity. Although an object orbiting the Earth in space appears weightless, it still has mass and gravitational forces from both the Earth and the Sun that hold the object in orbit. The force of gravity for objects is proportional to the product of the masses divided by the square of the distance between them. For example, Earth is larger and more massive than Mars; thus, it has proportionally higher gravitational forces.

Density is the ratio of mass to volume ($D = M/V$). An intrinsic property, density depends on the type of matter, not on the amount of matter. Thus, the density of a 5-ton cube of pure copper is the same as that of a small copper penny. However, the modern penny is a thin shell of copper over a zinc plug, and the density of the coin may be significantly lower than that of the older, pure copper coin.

Density relates to buoyancy. Objects sink in liquids or gases if they are denser than the material that surrounds them. Also related to density, Archimedes' principle states that an object is buoyed up by a force equal to the mass of the material the object displaces. Thus, a 160-pound concrete canoe will float in water if the volume of the submerged portion of the canoe is equal to the volume of 20 gallons of water. Why? The weight of water is approximately 8 pounds per gallon; therefore, 8 lbs/gal × 20 gal = 160 lbs.

Viscosity, a measure of thickness or ability to flow, is not the same as density. The strength of forces between molecules determines viscosity. For example, the flow of molasses in the winter months is slow because cold temperatures bring the molecules closer together. Hydrogen bromide is a gas in any season because the molecules are far apart. The boiling point occurs when a liquid material becomes a vapor. The freezing point occurs when a liquid material becomes a solid. Other physical properties include electrical (i.e., charge, conductivity, field), magnetism, absorption, frequency, and momentum.

Skill 3.2: Identify and Differentiate Between Physical and Chemical Changes

Matter can change chemically or physically. A physical change (i.e., melting, bending, cracking) affects the size, form, or appearance of a material. Physical changes do not alter the molecular structure of a material. For example, water that is frozen to form ice or boiled to release steam changes in form, but it is still water molecules. Also, tearing a cloth doesn't change the physical properties of the cloth. However, chemical changes (i.e., burning, rusting, and digestion) do alter the molecular structure of matter. For example, as cloth burns, carbon dioxide is released and the ashes can no longer remain as a piece of cloth. When iron is exposed to air and water, it combines with oxygen to form rust. After food is digested, it is converted into energy. Thus, under the right conditions, a chemical reaction can break apart, combine, or recombine properties to form new compounds. Those chemical reactions can be described using chemical equations. For instance, sodium hydroxide and hydrochloride combine to form sodium chloride and water. The chemical equation for that reaction is:

$$NaOH + HCl \rightarrow NaCl + H_2O$$

The materials to the left of the arrow are reactants, and the materials to the right of the arrow are products. Just because something changes in appearance, it doesn't necessarily mean that a chemical change has occurred. If you crush rock, it's still rock. If you whip egg whites, they are still egg. If you cut a tree for firewood, it remains as wood until it is burned.

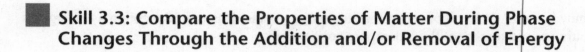
■ Skill 3.3: Compare the Properties of Matter During Phase Changes Through the Addition and/or Removal of Energy

Matter commonly exists in four states: solid, liquid, gas, and plasma. Each state of matter has its own characteristics and properties. Molecules in certain types of matter bond differently or not at all, and move differently. Thus, H_2O molecules in liquid, solid (frozen), or gaseous states are still H_2O molecules. As a solid, the molecules are packed tightly in rows to provide size and shape. As a liquid, the molecules can roll over each other to create a flow. As a gas, the water molecules move freely. Regardless of the form (solid, liquid, or gas) the molecules themselves are constantly vibrating as a form of kinetic energy. Faster vibrations create warmth by releasing energy (exothermic). Slower vibrations result in cooling when energy is absorbed (endothermic). Thus, when heating an ice cube, it becomes water. Adding more heat results in steam. Molecules that are heated past the gaseous state form plasma. Removing the source of heat (energy) reverses the process.

State	Definition	Example
Solid	Definite volume and shape, with strong bonds among molecules.	Ice
Liquid	Definite volume without definite shape, and weak bonds among molecules; can be contained or flow.	Water
Gas	No definite volume or shape, and no bonds among molecules; can be contained or flow freely.	Steam
Plasma	No definite volume or shape; high-energy gas-like fluid of charged particles; occurs when matter is heated beyond its gaseous state to become ionized; predominant state of matter in the universe (i.e., stars, atmosphere, comets, and so on).	Gas inside neon signs and fluorescent lights

Matter can be classified by the phase changes it undergoes when energy is either added or removed. During a phase change, energy is absorbed by the change and the temperature remains the same. For example, once water reaches its boiling point, it stays at that temperature as the liquid evaporates into a gas as steam.

Phase	Change
Freezing	Liquid changes to solid through subtraction of heat.
Condensation	Gas changes to liquid through subtraction of heat.
Evaporation	Liquid becomes a gas through addition of heat.
Sublimation	Solid changes to gas through addition of heat.
Melting	Solid changes to liquid through addition of heat.

Skill 3.4: Differentiate Between the Properties of Homogeneous Mixtures and Heterogeneous Mixtures

A mixture has one or more types of molecules that are not chemically combined and are without any definite weight proportions. Mixtures can be heterogeneous or homogeneous. The difference between heterogeneous and homogeneous mixtures is the degree at which the materials are mixed together and the uniformity of their composition. For example, milk is a mixture of water and butterfat particles. Mixtures can be separated by either physical or chemical means. A physical process would be straining the butterfat from milk to make skim milk.

Solutions are homogeneous mixtures in which the individual components are uniformly distributed throughout the mixture. In other words, the composition of the mixture is the same throughout. The components of a homogeneous mixture can't be separated by simple mechanical means into individual chemicals or ingredients.

A heterogeneous mixture contains liquid(s), solid(s), and/or gas(es) in which the components are not uniform or have localized regions with different properties. For example, vegetable soup is a mixture because different samples from the mixture are not identical to each other. Heterogeneous mixtures always contain two or more phases where you can identify a region with properties that are distinct from those of another region, even with the same state of matter (i.e., liquid, solid). Individual components of a heterogeneous mixture can be physically separated. For example, you can remove ice cubes from soda or cereal from milk.

Examples of Homogeneous and Heterogeneous Mixtures

Homogeneous	Heterogeneous
Air	Cereal in milk
Water	Pizza
Vinegar	Blood
Dishwashing detergent	Gravel
Steel	Ice in soda
Cup of coffee	Salad dressing
Plain chocolate	Mixed nuts
Sugar water	Soil
Olive oil	Paint in an aerosol can

Types of Heterogeneous Mixtures

Type	Composition	Example
Emulsion	Liquid and liquid	Oil and vinegar salad dressing
Suspension	Liquid and solid	Vegetable soup
Aerosol	Gas and liquid	Spray paint
Gas and solid	Smoke	Burning leaves

Skill 3.5: Identify Examples of and Relationships Among Atoms, Elements, Molecules, and Compounds

An element (i.e., iron, carbon, copper) consists of only one type of atom. An atom is the smallest particle of an element that retains the characteristics of that element. Atoms of the same element have the same number of protons in their nuclei. Each element has an atomic number, which is equal to the number of protons in an atom of that element and represented by one or two letters (i.e., *Fe* for iron and *C* for carbon). The periodic table organizes the elements according to their atomic number and gives their atomic structure, mass, and reactive tendencies. They are grouped vertically according to their chemical properties. The periodic table includes 90 elements that occur naturally, and many other created elements that have radioactive properties, are unstable, and have limited lifespans.

Two or more atoms may combine chemically to form **molecules**. Molecules can be elements with the same kind of atoms or **compounds** with different kinds of atoms. Compounds have atoms that are chemically combined in specific weight proportions. For example, water has oxygen and hydrogen elements combined in the ratio of two hydrogen atoms to one oxygen atom, which is represented as a molecule of H_2O. The chemical bonds in molecules can be covalent (atoms held together by the mutual attraction of two or more electrons) or ionic (atoms with opposite charges are held together by electrical force).

Everything is comprised of atoms that form the basic chemical building blocks of matter. Atoms can have three types of subatomic particles: protons, neutrons, and electrons. Protons and neutrons are in the nucleus, or center, of an atom. Electrons exist in the outer portion of an atom. While atoms have been commonly pictured with electrons orbiting a large nucleus, newer models depict an atom with a large cloud of electrons with wave-like and particle-like properties around a very small nucleus.

Under normal conditions, atoms remain intact; however, during atomic reactions, atoms may split or combine to form new atoms. Atomic reactions occur inside the Sun, nuclear reactors, and nuclear bombs, and during radioactive decay.

Skill 3.6: Identify and Compare Potential and Kinetic Energy

Energy is the ability of matter to move other matter or produce a chemical change through transformation or transference. Scientists also define energy as the ability to do work. *Work* is defined as the application of force (push or pull) over distance. The law of conservation of energy states that energy cannot be created or destroyed. All energy is potential or kinetic. Potential energy is stored through chemical structure, position, or physical configuration (i.e., batteries), whereas kinetic energy is energy in motion (i.e., light, sound, heat, a moving car).

Skill 3.7: Differentiate Among Forms of Energy, Transformations of Energy, and Their Real-World Applications

There are many types of energy, including thermal, mechanical, electrical, light, chemical, sound, and nuclear. Transformations of energy are all around and even within us. For example, plants and trees use a process called photosynthesis to transform the Sun's energy into food and oxygen. When we eat plants, the energy is transformed into mechanical, chemical, or thermal energy. When energy transforms, it becomes less orderly and more disorganized in a process called entropy. For example, potential (gravitational) energy in a dam is released when the higher water falls. The water moves turbines to form mechanical energy. The mechanical action can then be converted into electrical energy.

Type	Definition	Examples	Potential or Kinetic
Thermal (heat)	Energy caused by or related to heat created by increased kinetic movement in molecules that is transferred by conduction, convection, or radiation	Stove burner, fire	Kinetic
Mechanical	Energy of objects based on position (potential energy) or motion (kinetic energy)	Movement of the physical body, simple machines	Kinetic or potential
Electrical	Energy produced by moving electrons	Electrical current, lightning	Kinetic
Radient	Energy produced by electromagnetic waves, energy traveling in transverse waves	Visible light and colors, X rays, gamma rays, ultraviolet light, radio waves, and microwaves	Kinetic
Chemical	Energy resulting from the bonds of atoms and molecules	Coal, oil, natural gas, batteries, food, wood	Potential
Sound	Energy produced by movement of longitudinal waves	Music, voices	Kinetic

(continued)

(continued)

Type	Definition	Examples	Potential or Kinetic
Nuclear	Energy that results when the nucleus of an atom splits in two (fission) or when the nuclei of atoms become fused together (fusion)	Uranium	Potential
Gravity	Energy stored in an object's height, with higher and heavier objects storing more energy	Hydropower, grandfather clocks, water wheels	Potential

Skill 3.8: Distinguish Among Temperature, Heat, and Forms of Heat Transfer

Heat is the energy of moving molecules. Temperature has nothing to do with the amount of heat a material has; it only has to do with the degree of hotness or coldness of the material. Temperature depends on the speed that the molecules in a material are moving. The faster the molecules are moving, the hotter the temperature becomes.

A thermometer measures temperature. There are several types of thermometers, but the most common ones are glass tubes containing mercury or a liquid, such as colored alcohol. Thermometers typically display temperatures using the Fahrenheit, Kelvin, or Celsius scale.

Heat can be transferred in several ways. Conduction occurs when energy transfers between objects that are in physical contact. For example, if you put a metal spoon in a cup of hot coffee, the spoon becomes warm through conduction. Convection occurs when energy transfers between an object and its environment as the result of motion. Boiling water shows conduction when water from the bottom rises and the cooler water moves down to replace it, causing a circular motion. You've probably heard that heat rises. Rooms on an upper floor of a home are generally warmer than rooms on lower floors. This is another example of convection. Radiation occurs when energy transfers from movement of charged particles within atoms. Radiation can be ionizing when the ions of an atom change (i.e., X-rays and nuclear weapons), whereas non-ionizing radiation is typically released as heat (i.e., campfire and visible light).

Skill 3.9: Analyze the Functionality of an Electrical Circuit Based on its Conductors, Insulators, and Components

A neutral atom has an equal number of protons and electrons; therefore, the charges of protons and electrons cancel each other, so the atom has no charge. This characterizes most objects in our environment. When an atom has more electrons than protons, the atom has a negative charge. If an atom has fewer electrons than protons, the atom has a positive charge.

Although electrons can flow through certain materials, the principle of conservation of change states that electrons cannot be destroyed. They can only be transferred from one atom to another. For example, when two objects are rubbed together, electrons move from one object to the other, leaving both objects charged. The flow of electrons produces an electric current. Insulators are materials that prevent electrons from flowing freely (i.e., glass, rubber, and air). Most metals allow electric current to flow easily. Copper is a good conductor of electricity, so electrical wire is often made of copper, which has a covering of rubber (insulator) to help prevent electric shock if someone touches the wire.

Circuits are closed paths through which electric current flows; they are usually created by linking electrical components together with wire. For example, a flashlight is a simple circuit formed from a switch, a lamp, and a battery connected by wire. Circuits can be in series or parallel. Series circuits are made of a single path through which all current must flow. If any part of a series circuit breaks, the circuit is opened, and the flow of the current stops. For example, some strings of Christmas tree lights use series circuits. If one bulb in the string of lights burns out, none of the lights in the string work because the current stops. However, parallel circuits provide more than one path for current to flow. When current stops in one path, it continues to move through other paths. Homes use parallel circuits for electrical wiring so burned-out light bulbs and turned-off devices do not disrupt the flow of electricity used in other parts of the house.

Skill 3.10: Identify and Apply the Characteristics of Contact Forces, At-a-Distance Forces, and Their Effects on Matter

A force is a push (forward movement) or a pull (backward movement) to operate machines. If the force is unbalanced, the object accelerates. A good example of an unbalanced force is the push of a rocket engine moving upward at ever-increasing speeds from a launch pad. If there is a balanced force on an object, however, it will not accelerate. It either remains still or continues to move at a constant speed. Newton's laws of motion describe interactions of force, motion, and energy.

Newton's Laws of Motion

First law of motion (also called the law of inertia)	An object at rest tends to stay at rest; an object in motion tends to stay in motion at a constant speed in a straight line or path.	Imagine that you are in a car at a stoplight. You are at rest. When the light turns green and the car accelerates, your body is pushed back because of the movement of the car. But imagine again that you have something on the seat of your car, and you must make a sudden stop. The item is thrown forward. This shows the second part of the law.
Second law of motion	When a net force acts on an object, the object accelerates. The acceleration is directly proportional to the net force and inversely proportional to the mass.	The larger the size of an item, the more force is needed to move it. For example, a large heavy truck would need more force to get moving than would a small car.
Third law of motion	For every action, there is an equal and opposite reaction.	If the air is let out of a balloon, the balloon moves in the opposite direction of the released air.

There are two main types of force: contact and at-a-distance. Contact force occurs when objects physically touch. For example, a person pushing a large box across the floor is an example of applied force because force is required to move the object. Another contact force, friction, occurs when one surface resists moving over another surface (i.e., rubbing your hands together). Friction also generates heat. For example, rubbing two sticks together can help start a fire. With mechanical force, machines multiply or change the direction of force. Other types of contact force include normal force, tension, applied force, frictional force, air resistance force, and spring force.

At-a-distance forces do not physically touch. For example, magnets can move objects without touching them. Gravity attracts, or pulls, objects. For example, the gravitational effects of the Moon and the Sun pull the ocean to form tides. Like magnets, electrostatic forces can repel or push each other. The law of electrostatic repulsion applies when the same type of charge (positive or negative) repel objects; the law of electrostatic attraction applies when opposite charges attract each other. For example, rubbing a balloon on a blanket or sweater creates static electricity charges, which cause the balloon to stick to the surface of an object with an opposite charge until the charges are released or discharged.

Competency 4: Knowledge of Earth and Space

Understanding the universe involves several related areas of Earth science: geology, meteorology, oceanography, and astronomy.

Skill 4.1: Identify Characteristics of Geologic Formations and the Mechanisms by Which They Are Changed

Geology is the study of the structure and composition of the Earth. The Earth is composed of three layers: core, mantle, and crust. The core has two layers separated by a region called the Bullen discontinuity.

Earth's Core	Position	Composition	Size
Crust Mantle Outer Core Inner Core	Crust: Outer Layer	Bedrock overlaid with mineral and/or organic sediment (soil)	5–40 kilometers thick
	Mantle: Middle Layer	Magma—semi-molten rock	3,000 kilometers thick
	Outer Core	Mostly liquid nickel, iron, and sulfur	2,200 kilometers thick
	Inner Core	Mostly iron; although above iron's melting point, the plasma form behaves as a solid because of pressure and density	1,200 kilometers

Geologic Activity: Plates

Large sections of the Earth's crust called lithospheric plates change position over time. At one time, the continents were, if not touching, very close to each other to form a supercontinent called Pangaea. Continental drift explains how the continents moved across the Earth's surface. Seafloor spreading explains the creation of new oceanic crust at mid-ocean ridges and movement of the crust away from the mid-ocean ridges. Combining these processes into what is now referred to as plate tectonics revolutionized the way geologists thought about the Earth. The edges of the plates, where they move against each other, are sites of intense geologic activity such as earthquakes, volcanoes, and mountain formation.

The following shows support for continental drift and the underlying plate tectonics:

- The shapes of many continents look like pieces of a jigsaw puzzle. For example, the east coasts of North America and South America and the west coasts of Africa and Europe appear to fit together.

- Many fossil comparisons along the edges of continents that look like they fit together suggest species similarities that would only make sense if the two continents were joined at some point in the past.

- Seismic, volcanic, and geothermal activity occurs more frequently along plate boundaries than in sites far from boundaries.

- Ridges, such as the Mid-Atlantic Ridge, occur where plates are separating because of lava welling up between the plates as they pull apart. Mountain ranges form where plates are pushing against each other (i.e., the Himalayas, which are still growing).

Plate Tectonics

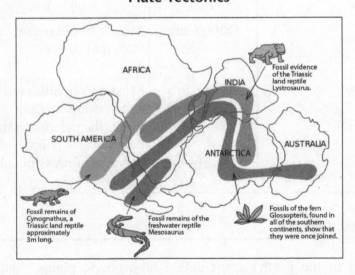

Faults are cracks in the crust and are the results of the movements of plates. Volcanoes form when two plates separate enough for magma (molten rock) to release through the crust, usually in a violent explosion. As the magma cools, it becomes lava and releases ash. Sometimes the erupting volcano forms rivers of lava that, over long periods of time, become islands or mountain ranges (i.e., the Hawaiian Islands and the southeastern border of Asia). Volcanic activity causes the crust of the Earth to buckle upward and form mountains. Earthquakes occur when volcanoes erupt or plates slide past one another quickly and suddenly release energy. A seismograph measures earthquakes using the Richter scale.

Geological Formations

The diverse geology of the Earth consists of plains, mountains, and plateaus. Mountains can be found on land and under the oceans.

Plains are relatively level areas that cover about one-third of the Earth's surface. They occur on every continent with the exception of Antarctica and vary in the kinds of vegetation they support. Plateaus are similar to plains, but have high plains of relatively flat terrain above the surrounding area. They can be formed by an upwelling of volcanic magma or by glacial erosion.

Mountains form when tectonic plates push rock through the crust. There are four types of mountains: folded, fault-block, domes, and volcanic. Folded mountains have a wavy appearance caused by sideward pressures from the Earth (i.e., the Alps, Rockies, and Appalachian Mountains). Fault-block mountains occur when a fault forms and layers on one side are pressured and become higher and sharper than the other sides (i.e., Alaska Range on the Denali fault line). Dome mounts result from the flow of magma between two layers of rock; however, the magma does not push through the crust. Rather, the rock is pushed up into a dome-like shape. Dome mountains are not as high or sharp as folded or fault-block mountains. Volcanic mountains form around cracks in the Earth where the plates separate. Repeated eruptions cause the gradual accumulation of layers of lava.

Other Geologic Activity

Earth's tectonic plates are not the only process that changes the surface of the Earth. Erosion occurs when water washes, glaciers push, or wind blows soil or rock away and deposits it in another area (deposition). Rivers that cut through rock and erode it over time or heavy rains that create mudslides form canyons. Avalanches of snow can move rock and other matter down a hillside. Soil in areas with no plants can be blown away. Even a light rain shower can cause small amounts of soil to shift to another location.

Glaciers have dramatically reshaped the surface of the Earth by forming rivers of ice in the fields of mountains and valleys. The glaciers slowly move downward in large U-shaped paths. As they move, they smooth some mountains and carve others. Small pieces of rock are carried along and deposited as the glacier reaches warmer climates and begins to melt.

Similar to erosion, weathering can break down rock into small pieces that change the Earth's surface. Weathering can be broken into three broad categories of mechanisms: chemical, physical, and biological:

- **Chemical weathering** changes the atomic structure of matter through hydrolysis, oxidation, reduction, hydration, carbonation, and solution. Changes in climatic conditions (moisture and temperature) affect the rate of chemical weathering.

- **Physical weathering** occurs when minerals and rocks are broken down by mechanical methods such as abrasion, crystallization, wetting and drying, or pressure release. These can originate from internal or external forces.

- **Biological weathering** occurs when an organism's (bacteria, plant, animal) physical or chemical agents disintegrate rocks or minerals. These processes can be physical or biological. For example, pressure from roots or organisms that dig can break rocks apart. Areas shaded by trees often weather differently than those in the open.

Sinkholes

Sinkholes are openings in the Earth that occur suddenly. If the rock beneath the land is limestone or other carbonate rock, it can be dissolved by acid rain (atmospherically polluted rain water with high levels of hydrogen ions) that seeps through the soil. This creates underground spaces or caverns. If the layer above the pocket gets too thin because of erosion or weathering, the top layer suddenly collapses and whatever is above ground falls into the space. In some cases, changes to layers of permeable rock that store water in a kind of natural holding system called aquifers form sinkholes. If there is a drought or if the aquifers are depleted for other reasons (i.e., irrigation, human consumption), the rock becomes fragile without the support of the water and collapses. The Florida Aquifer is one of the most productive in the world and covers an area over 100,000 square miles. This provides water for various purposes; as a result of that use, however, Florida is one of seven states with sinkhole activity.

Skill 4.2: Identify and Distinguish Among Major Groups and Properties of Rocks and Minerals, and the Processes of Their Formations

Rocks are naturally occurring solids found on or below the Earth's surface. According to their method of formation, there are three types of rocks: igneous, sedimentary, and metamorphic. Individual pieces of rock are called grains. A grain of sand is actually a grain of rock. A mineral is a single inorganic compound with a unique chemical structure and physical properties. However, they can be formed organically or inorganically. For example, calcite is found in rock (inorganic) and in shells (organic). Examples of minerals include clay, copper, gold, iron, uranium, and zinc. Rocks are aggregates; that is, they are typically composed of one or more minerals.

The formation of rock follows a cycle. Larger rocks are formed and broken down into smaller rocks and eventually become sediment that undergoes a repeated process of heating, pressing, and melting.

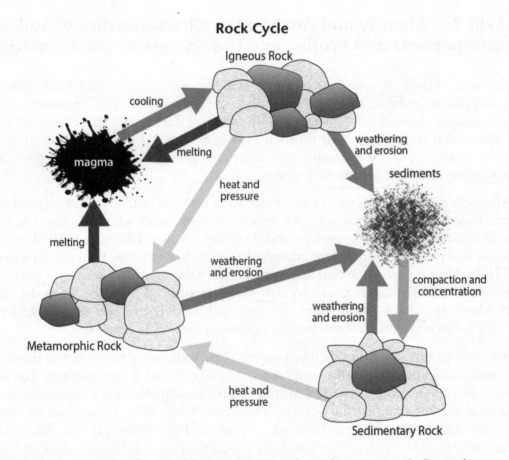

Rock Cycle

Igneous rocks can be found either underground or above ground. Sometimes melted rock, called magma, becomes trapped in small pockets deep within the Earth. As these pockets of magma slowly cool underground, the magma becomes igneous rock. When volcanoes erupt and the magma rises above the Earth's surface, it is called lava. Igneous rocks (i.e., granite and obsidian) are the result of the lava cooling above ground.

Sedimentary rocks result from wind or water breaking or wearing down small pieces of Earth that often settle to the bottom of rivers, lakes, and oceans. Rock forms over thousands or even millions of years as layer after layer of eroded dirt, silt, or rock fragments compact at high pressure (i.e., shale and limestone).

Metamorphic rocks change or "morph" into other kinds of rocks. Igneous or sedimentary rocks heated under tons of pressure change into metamorphic rocks. Geologists examining metamorphic rock samples (i.e., marble and slate) found that some of the grains in the rocks are flattened.

Skill 4.3: Identify and Analyze the Characteristics of Soil, Its Components and Profile, and the Process of Soil Formation

Soil is a mixture of water, air, mineral, and organic materials that have various textures, structures, amount of organic material, and chemistry. The characteristics of a specific sample depend on the matter from which it forms and the effects of climate, topography, and weathering. Soil forms from weathering during the rock cycle in layers called horizons. Topsoil is the uppermost layer and generally contains rock particles and organic (decaying plant and animal) matter.

Although the content of soil varies by location and is constantly changing, three main mineral-based components of soil give soil its texture: sand, silt, and clay. The components of soil affect its absorption or ability to hold water. Therefore, soil that is more porous or has more clay or organic materials absorbs water better than soil that is dense. Sand is the largest particle in soil and does not contain many nutrients. Silt particles are smaller than sand but larger than clay. Silt feels smooth and powdery when dry, and not sticky when wet. Clay is the smallest of particles. It is smooth when dry and sticky when wet. Clay holds nutrients well and usually contains more water than sand.

Water from precipitation or other sources (i.e., watering a plant) seeps through layers of soil (called the water table) until it reaches a layer called groundwater. The amount of water in groundwater depends on rainfall and absorption of the materials above it. Groundwater can be tapped for wells or other uses. Watersheds form when all the water drains into a river, river system, large lake, or ocean. For example, the St. Johns River in northeastern Florida has two watersheds in which the river's tributaries flow. A reservoir stores large amounts of water for human use and can be natural or artificial. Water that falls and is not easily stored or diverted to a reservoir is called runoff.

Skill 4.4: Identify and Analyze Processes by Which Energy From the Sun Is Transferred Through Earth's Systems

A system is defined as a complex whole formed from a set of connected items or parts. Several systems (air, water, land, and life) exist on Earth. The Sun's radiant energy forms the main source of heat, which interacts with the various Earth systems in many different ways.

Biosphere	The word part *bio* means "life," so the Earth's biosphere consists of the Earth's surface, atmosphere, and hydrosphere that support life. Without heat, living organisms could not exist. The Sun's energy warms the planet, and plants absorb the energy through photosynthesis. Plants, in turn, supply herbivorous animals with energy.
Hydrosphere	The word part *hydro* means "water," so the Earth's hydrosphere consists of all water on the surface (i.e., rivers, lakes, oceans, seas) and sometimes water above the Earth in the form of clouds. The hydrosphere forms about 70% of the Earth's surface. The Sun's radiant energy affects the hydrosphere when creating weather.
Geosphere	The word part *geo* means "earth," so the word *geosphere* refers to the Earth itself and the three components that comprise it: core, mantle, and crust. The surface of the Earth absorbs and reflects heat energy from the Sun.
Atmosphere	The word part *atmos* means "vapors," so the word *atmosphere* refers to the gases that envelop the Earth. Radiant energy from the Sun passes through the atmosphere, and part of that energy is reflected back from Earth into the atmosphere.
Cryosphere	The word part *cryo* means "cold," so the word *cryosphere* refers to the frozen parts of the Earth's surface (i.e., polar regions, glaciers). Interactions between the Sun and atmosphere affect the size of the cryosphere.

Energy from the Sun

Electromagnetic radiant energy from the Sun moving through space and the Earth's atmosphere forms the main source of heat energy on Earth. This heat energy is transferred throughout the planet's systems by radiation, conduction, and convection.

Heat travels by conduction and radiation in solids and by convection in fluids like air and water. As convection heat, radiant energy travels from the Sun in the form of invisible waves into the layers of the Earth's hydrosphere and atmosphere. The oceans absorb more energy in the tropics around the equator where currents (i.e., the Gulf Stream) moderate the oceans' temperatures as they redistribute heat. When the Earth's land, plants, and bodies of water absorb the radiant waves, the energy becomes heat. Because the Earth is cooler than the Sun, about one-third of this heat transfers back into the Earth's atmosphere as water vapor and carbon dioxide. That energy is re-radiated back to the Earth, where it increases the Earth's temperature. The greenhouse effect occurs when radiation becomes trapped in the Earth's lower atmosphere.

Layers of Earth's Atmosphere

EARTH'S SURFACE	
Exosphere Thermosphere Mesosphere Stratosphere Troposphere	**EXOSPHERE** Farthest layer; very little air; 400–40,000 miles above Earth
	THERMOSPHERE Temperature rises as thin air absorbs solar radiation; can be as hot as 230°C; contains the ionosphere (electrically charged particles) and the magnetosphere (charged particles affected by Earth's magnetism that create the Northern and Southern lights; 50–400 miles above Earth
	MESOSPHERE Space debris burns up at this level to create shooting stars; temperature as low as −90°C; 31–50 miles above Earth
	STRATOSPHERE Layer of protective ozone that protects Earth; contains about 20% of the atmosphere's molecules and warms as distance from Earth increases; 10–31 miles above Earth
	TROPOSPHERE Layer where Earth's weather occurs; contains about 75% of the atmosphere; up to 10 miles above Earth's surface

Conduction transfers heat between substances that are in direct contact with each other. Heating Earth's surface occurs through the air; however, air conducts heat poorly and is only significant within a few millimeters of the surface. The Earth's absorption of energy from the Sun is uneven across its surface because of its curved shape. Convection transfers heat through the movement of molecules in water or air and forms cool and warm currents of winds due to differences in heat absorption. The Earth has six convection currents that occur as belts of wind, with three on each side of the equator: polar easterlies, westerlies, and trade winds. When warm air expands and becomes less dense, thermals form, which rise and transfer the heat back to the atmosphere. Thermals contribute to the formation of clouds.

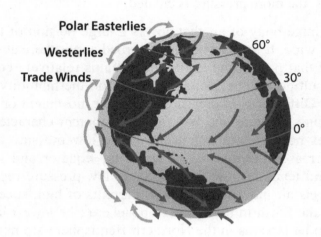

Skill 4.5: Identify and Analyze the Causes and Effects of Atmospheric Processes and Conditions

The distance between the Sun and the Earth is stable throughout the year. The atmospheric changes in seasons, climate, and weather result, in part, from changes in the tilt of the Earth. The Sun's heat affects Earth's weather and climate. Weather is the day-to-day state of the atmosphere in terms of temperature, precipitation, and wind. Climate refers to long-term weather patterns in a particular region. Climates are determined by a variety of factors, including patterns in maximum and minimum temperatures, distribution of precipitation, ocean currents, prevailing winds, distance from the equator, surface features, and El Niño and La Niña weather patterns resulting from variations in ocean temperatures in the equatorial Pacific. For example, the climates closer to the equator are warmer, wetter, and more consistent year-round because as the Earth tilts, the effect on the center is minor. Earth is divided into six climate zones:

- **Polar**—very cold and dry year-round

- **Temperate**—cold winters and mild summers

- **Arid**—hot and dry year-round

- **Tropical**—hot and wet year-round

- **Mediterranean**—mild winters and dry, hot summers

- **Mountain (tundra)**—very cold year-round

Unless it is polluted, air is a colorless, odorless, and tasteless gas comprised of 78% nitrogen, 21% oxygen, and 1% other gases. Air has weight and volume, and exerts pressure. In the form of wind, moving air exerts more pressure than still air. The faster and harder the wind blows, the more pressure is created.

An air mass is a huge body of air that covers a large portion of the Earth's surface and may be high and wide. It forms when undisturbed atmosphere absorbs the temperature and humidity of that part of the Earth and remains relatively constant throughout the air mass. The resulting weather depends mostly on the humidity and the temperature of that air mass. Differences in pressure govern air movement or wind in the atmosphere. In general, high pressure and low moisture content characterize air masses at the poles. Air masses near the equator usually have low pressure and high moisture content. Heating decreases the density of air at the equator and increases it at the poles. Therefore, wind tends to flow from high- to low-pressure regions. The rotation of the Earth also affects air movement. Narrow currents of high-speed winds called jet streams flow around the Earth in the upper troposphere (the lowest layer of the Earth's atmosphere). The two jet streams in the Northern Hemisphere are near the pole and the middle latitudes; similar ones exist in the Southern Hemisphere. When two air masses meet, the boundary between them is called a warm or cold front. Most stormy weather occurs at these fronts.

Weather

Weather is the local, short-term condition of the atmosphere. The factors that affect weather most are the amounts of energy and water present. Clouds help predict the weather. The main types of clouds are stratus, cumulus, cirrus, and cumulonimbus (also called nimbus).

Type	Appearance		Weather
Stratus	Flat	Light	Stable weather
		Dark	Rain expected soon
Cumulus	Fluffy	Solid, light	Good weather
Cirrus	Thin	Wispy	Changes in weather expected
Cumulonimbus (also called nimbus)	Tall and thick	Dark	Heavy rain, perhaps a thunderstorm

Storms

Students are most familiar with three main types of storms: hurricanes, tornadoes, and thunderstorms. Hurricanes (intense lows) form over the oceans in the tropics—usually between June and November. The large amounts of heat energy created during these months evaporate ocean water and form warm moist air as clouds. When cooler air pushes on the warm air, a violent storm with rain often results.

A hurricane has no front, but it does have a center, often referred to as the eye, which is a calm area surrounded by the highest winds within the hurricane called the eyewall. The winds in a hurricane move swiftly, and the speed of the winds—rated on a scale of 1 to 5—determines the hurricane's strength. A hurricane can be hundreds of miles in diameter and usually moves slowly. The waves produced by the hurricane on the surface of the ocean usually cause most of the damage. Hurricanes are called typhoons in the western Pacific Ocean, cyclones in the Indian Ocean, willy-willies in Australia, and baguios in the Philippines.

Tornadoes are violent, short-lived storms that form when cold, heavy air moves under warm, moist air and pushes it upward. They occur almost exclusively in the North American continent. The tornado cloud is very thick, black, and funnel-shaped. Like hurricanes, a tornado's strength is rated by the wind speed that ranges from 1 (72 mph) to 5 (over 260 mph). A tornado can travel quickly and is accompanied by a deafening roar that is often compared to a train engine. If the tornado passes over a body of water, it is called a waterspout.

Cumulonimbus (nimbus) clouds are often a predictor of strong thunderstorms. Lightning, heavy rain, gusts of wind, thunder, and sometimes hail accompany hot air-mass thunderstorms. A thunderstorm rarely lasts more than 2 hours; however, it is possible to have more than one thunderstorm a day in a particular area. A frontal thunderstorm forms when a cold front pushes warm air ahead of it and quickly rising moist air condenses to form clouds. As the droplets in the cloud grow, they begin to fall. This results in both upward and downward air currents. As the cloud reduces in size, the currents begin to move downward.

Water Cycle

Water is continually recycled in Earth's water cycle (also called the hydrological cycle) through a series of movements of water above, on, and below the surface of the Earth. Thus, the water you drink today could have been water consumed by dinosaurs millions of years ago. This means that water is a limited resource. About 97% of the Earth's water is ocean (salty) water, leaving only 3% as freshwater for human consumption. Less than 1% of freshwater is found on the surface of the Earth: 2% flows in rivers, 11% exists in swamps, and 87% is found in lakes. About a third of the Earth's freshwater exists as groundwater, and the rest exists in polar icecaps and glaciers. The water cycle consists of four stages: evaporation, condensation, precipitation, and collection.

Water Cycle

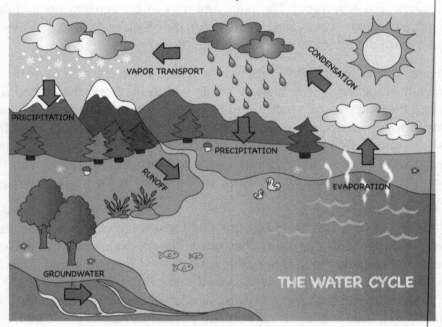

The Sun's heat energy evaporates water to form a vapor. Water vapor in the Earth's atmosphere causes humidity, fog, clouds, dew, and precipitation. When rising air cools, water vapor condenses to form clouds that sometimes cause precipitation. If the surrounding air is above freezing (32° Fahrenheit), precipitation occurs as raindrops. When the air is below freezing, sleet, hail, or snow may form. Collection occurs when water returns to the oceans, lakes, rivers, or land. When water falls on land, some soaks into the Earth and becomes part of the groundwater; the rest flows into the rivers, lakes, or oceans.

Skill 4.6: Identify and Analyze Various Conservation Methods and Their Effectiveness in Relation to Renewable and Nonrenewable Natural Resources

Conservation is the practice of using natural areas without affecting their ecosystems (communities of interacting organisms and their physical environment). This definition suggests interdependence among people, the world, and practices or actions to improve or maintain the world. These practices support both renewable and nonrenewable resources. Renewable resources (i.e., soil, vegetation, animals, and freshwater) can endure indefinitely when good practices are followed. However, it is possible to deplete nonrenewable natural resources (fossil fuels such as coal and oil, and minerals such as gold, sulfur, and iron).

Nonrenewable Natural Resources

Nonrenewable natural resources are generally found beneath the top layers of soil and are obtained through mining or drilling. Strip mining and open-pit mining are used when resources are just below the surface; both can cause severe damage to ecosystems through toxic pollution and erosion, and the ecosystems often never recover. The United States has depleted its resources of over 15 minerals and now imports them. In addition, the demand for these resources has increased worldwide. To conserve nonrenewable resources, laws that manage the mining and drilling of natural resources and the use and recycling of natural resources are necessary. Conservation relies on education to convey the importance of managing nonrenewable natural resources.

Fossil fuels come from plants, animals, and other organisms that died millions of years ago. Time, heat, and pressure transformed these into hydrocarbons in the form of oil, natural gas, and coal. Their energy is released by burning that contributes to air pollution and global warming. As inexpensive and effective energy sources, they are quickly being depleted. Oil is used in the production of many products, including plastics, which do not easily decompose. Use of other renewable sources of energy (i.e., solar, wind, water) helps conserve fossil fuels and prevents pollution. Recycling and reuse help prevent plastics from getting into the environment.

Renewable Resources

Renewable resources are interdependent. Crops cannot grow in the soil without water. Bees play a part in the life cycle of many plants, and animals help provide carbon dioxide for photosynthesis. Enforced laws governing hunting and fishing can ensure that wildlife can renew themselves and continue their role in the web of life.

Biotics

Biotics (living organisms) are important renewable resources. For example, forests provide products, including medications, not available from other sources. They are producers needed in the energy pyramid. The roots of trees protect and hold soil together. Forests contribute oxygen to the environment and remove greenhouse gases; however, forests are often cut to provide pulp for paper and other products. Paper production contributes to water pollution. Cutting forests destroys ecosystems and has a negative impact on the environment. Recycling paper is less costly than making new paper and saves trees. Selective cutting rather than clear cutting supports sustainable forest management that ensures a supply of wood, a steady flow of water, and protection of the soil against wind and water damage.

A fishery supports an aquatic population in salt or freshwater. Fish provide over half of the protein consumed by humans. As human populations and the demand for fish increase, overfishing threatens some species. Fishing limits for some species and aquaculture (farming fish in artificial ponds and bays) help sustain fish populations and protect their role in ecosystems.

Solar and Wind Energy

Solar energy from our Sun is plentiful and does not cause pollution. The lifespan of the Sun should continue for several billion years. Solar energy must be captured during the day when the Sun is not obstructed by clouds. Solar energy must be concentrated to be effective. Solar cells and solar heating produce energy from the Sun.

Because the surface of the Earth is uneven, the Sun's energy is not evenly dispersed. This causes variations in air pressure and temperature that cause wind. Wind energy is an indirect form of solar energy. Wind can turn large turbines on wind farms to generate energy. However, the size of the turbines requires a lot of space and steady winds to turn them. As a result, they are not practical in many locations. While wind farms do not pollute the air, water, or land, they do sometimes result in noise pollution because of the sound they make. In addition, they can affect ecosystems by altering migratory paths of some birds or changing the physical landscape of the areas in which they are placed.

Freshwater

Three-quarters of the Earth is covered by water; however, 97% of the water is saltwater in the oceans and seas. About 99% of freshwater is frozen in polar ice caps and glaciers. The remaining freshwater is either surface water (i.e., ponds and streams) or groundwater. Water is recycled through evaporation and precipitation; therefore, it should be a renewable resource; however, freshwater resources are misused and often polluted, making them unavailable for use by humans.

According to the World Health Organization, almost 2 billion people live in environments without clean water. Waterborne disease is the leading cause of illness and death worldwide. Water resources are unevenly distributed; for example, much of the western half of the United States does not have sufficient water supply. Climate change and pollution also affects freshwater. If drought reduces oxygen in lakes and reservoirs, algae overwhelm the water wildlife. Overpopulation of aquatic wildlife or increases in water temperature can cause localized deaths (fishkill) in an ecosystem. The process of water percolating through the surface of the Earth and creating groundwater takes about 100 years. As development and population increase in Florida, freshwater is depleted from groundwater faster than it can be replenished. Reducing our use of water and eliminating pollutants can help protect our freshwater resources.

Water as Energy

Water can be used to create hydroelectric power. Dams block the flow of rivers and, when the gates open, water flows through tunnels to turbines that turn to produce electricity. Once dams are built, hydroelectric energy is inexpensive to produce and does not pollute. However, the building of the dams alters ecosystems, which may affect nearby populations and aquatic wildlife. Also, hydroelectric power plants may not operate during droughts.

Conservation: Reduce, Reuse, Recycle

Students should understand, analyze, and evaluate conservation efforts. For example, a lesson about the water cycle might show ways to reduce water usage (i.e., turning off water while brushing teeth or washing hands) or to keep waterways clean (i.e., avoid littering, support recycling), and track the progress of these measures. Inquiry projects could address energy-saving issues, such as comparing vehicles in terms of power (electric, gasoline, diesel, hybrid) or types of lightbulbs in terms of cost and energy saved. Math lessons could focus on real-world applications. For example, "If one family recycles 5 pounds of aluminum per month, how much would they recycle in a year? If 25 families recycled the same amount, how much would be recycled? What if the entire city recycled? How much would be saved?" Education is critical for conveying the lesson that the effect of conservation by one individual might be small, but the effect of many conserving is large.

Skill 4.7: Analyze the Sun-Earth-Moon System in Order to Explain Repeated Patterns Such as Day and Night, Phases of the Moon, Tides, and Seasons

The Earth is one of the nine planets* that revolve around the Sun; the Earth's revolution takes approximately 365 days. The Earth rotates on its axis every 24 hours. Whatever part of the Earth faces the Sun experiences daylight. As the Earth rotates, the day passes into night as another part of the Earth begins its day.

As a satellite, the Moon orbits the Earth once every 29½ days. The Moon exerts a gravitational pull on Earth that causes tides, or regular changes in the ocean depths. When

---

* Following Pluto's demotion several years ago to dwarf-planet status, evidence of "Planet Nine" was unveiled in 2016.

facing the Moon, high tide occurs; the side opposite the Moon also experiences a high tide from inertia. Each lunar day has two high tides and two low tides.

An eclipse occurs when the Earth or Moon obstructs the light from the Sun. When Earth blocks sunlight from reaching the Moon, it creates a shadow on the Moon's surface known as a lunar eclipse. When the Moon blocks sunlight from reaching the Earth, a solar eclipse occurs.

Moon Phases

The Moon reflects light from the Sun. The amount of lighted Moon that we see on Earth are called phases. When the Moon is between the Earth and the Sun, the dark side of the Moon is turned toward Earth. It is difficult to see the Moon from Earth and is called a new Moon. As the Moon revolves around Earth (west to east), a little more of the lighted side is visible from Earth. When the visible part of the Moon is crescent-shaped and getting larger, it is called a waxing crescent Moon, followed by the first quarter and then the waxing gibbous Moon, which has about three-quarters of the Moon visible. A full Moon occurs when the entire side of Moon facing the Earth is visible. As the Moon becomes less bright, it is called waning. As the lighted side becomes less visible, the phases are called waning gibbous, last quarter, and waning crescent.

Phases of the Moon

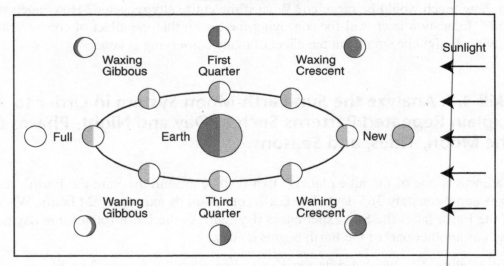

Seasons

Earth revolves around the Sun. Earth's axis is tilted at a 23½-degree angle that always points toward the North Star (Polaris). The tilt and revolution of the Earth around the

Sun—not Earth's distance from the Sun—causes the seasons. In fact, the Northern Hemisphere is closer to the Sun in the winter—not the summer. When it is summer in the Northern Hemisphere, it is winter in the Southern Hemisphere. When it is winter in the Northern Hemisphere, it is summer in the Southern Hemisphere.

Summer begins in the Northern Hemisphere on or about June 21 when the Northern Hemisphere tilts toward the Sun. In the summer, the energy from the Sun is stronger, but it covers a smaller part of the surface. Because of the tilt of the Earth's axis, the Northern Hemisphere surface has higher temperatures and more hours of sunlight than darkness; therefore, the longer direct rays of the Sun last longer in the summer.

When the Northern Hemisphere tilts away from the Sun beginning with the winter solstice on December 21 or 22, the Northern Hemisphere experiences winter. During the winter season, the days are shorter; fewer direct rays from the Sun reach the Northern Hemisphere, which experiences more hours of night than during the summer.

In the fall and spring, Earth is not tilted toward or away from the Sun and the days and nights have an almost equal number of hours. In the Northern Hemisphere, spring begins at the vernal equinox (March 19, 20, or 21) and fall begins at the autumnal equinox (September 22, 23, or 24).

Earth Rotation

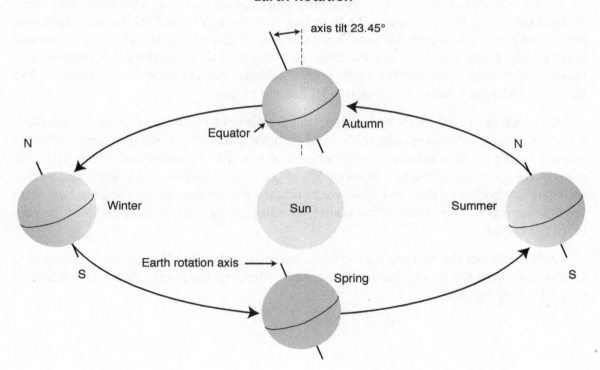

Skill 4.8: Compare and Differentiate the Composition and Various Relationships Among the Objects of Our Solar System

With the reclassification of Pluto as a dwarf planet, the solar system includes the Sun, eight visible planets (with a ninth recently detected), and many other bodies. Composed mostly of hydrogen, our Sun is a medium-sized star that contains about 99% of the mass of the entire solar system. It releases energy from nuclear reactions. The temperature at the core of the Sun is 27 million degrees Fahrenheit and the temperature at its surface is 11,000 degrees Fahrenheit. Rays from the Sun extend about 3 billion miles into space.

Beginning with the closest to the Sun, the visible planets include Mercury, Venus, Earth, Mars, Jupiter, Saturn, Uranus, and Neptune. The innermost planets (Mercury, Venus, Earth, and Mars) are composed of rocky and metallic materials. The outermost planets (Jupiter, Saturn, Uranus, and Neptune) are composed of hydrogen, helium, and ices of ammonia and methane. Jupiter, a giant, half-formed sun (it didn't grow big enough to ignite), is composed largely of hydrogen gas (and has a giant red spot) and is an exception among the planets. Many of the planets have satellite moons, including Earth (1), Mars (2), Jupiter (8), and Pluto (2). The moons are held in place by the respective planet's gravity. Saturn has the distinguishing feature of rings around its equator. Both Earth and Venus have significant atmospheres.

Planets revolve around the Sun in slightly elliptical counterclockwise orbits and rotate on their own axis. Planets vary in the time they take to revolve around the Sun. This time period for the Earth is called a year. For example, an Earth year is 365¼ days. Neptune requires 164 Earth years to orbit the Sun. The length of time for planetary rotation also varies. For example, the Earth rotates every 24 hours, but the rotation for Venus is 243 Earth days and the rotation for Saturn is 10.2 Earth hours.

Asteroids are small rocky bodies sometimes referred to as dwarf planets, minor planets, or planetoids. Although asteroids exist in other parts of our solar system, most are located within an area (asteroid belt) between the orbits of Jupiter and Mars. The total mass of the asteroids in the belt is about 4% of our Moon. Unlike rocky asteroids, comets are small icy bodies of dust and small rock. When a comet approaches the Sun, heat from the Sun vaporizes the surface of the comet, forming a long tail that streams from the center of the comet.

Distances from the Sun are measured in astronomical units (AUs), with 1 AU equal to the distance from the Sun to Earth. For example, Mercury, the planet closest to the Sun, is 0.39 AU from the Sun.

Skill 4.9: Identify Major Events in the History of Space Exploration and Their Effects on Society

During and after World War II, scientists began to study rockets and made great advances. They sent rockets containing instruments and cameras into space for extended periods of time. The launching of the Soviet space satellite *Sputnik* on October 4, 1957, created fear that the United States was falling behind technologically. *Sputnik* was the first satellite to orbit the Earth. Although the United States launched *Explorer I* on January 31, 1958, the concern continued. In 1958, Congress established the National Aeronautics and Space Administration (NASA) to coordinate space research and development. In another important action, Congress passed the National Defense Education Act to provide grants and loans for education. The failure of the early Pioneer rockets heightened concern among Americans. In 1959, *Pioneer 4* finally escaped Earth's gravity and reached orbit.

Both the Union of Soviet Socialist Republics (USSR; now the Commonwealth of Independent States) and the United States continued with their space exploration programs. The United States launched *Ranger 7* on July 31, 1964, to send back pictures from the Moon. In January 1966, the USSR's *Luna 9* managed to achieve a soft landing on the Moon and send pictures from the surface. The United States followed that lead the following April with the soft landing of *Surveyor 1* on the lunar surface. Four months later, America's *Lunar Orbiter 1* orbited the Moon, photographed the far side, and landed on command.

The USSR and the United States continued to compete in space exploration, focusing on the Moon and Venus. The *Mariner 5* flew by Venus's surface (June 14 to November 1967), studied the Venusian magnetic field, and discovered that the atmosphere was 85% to 99% carbon dioxide.

On December 24, 1967, Frank Borman, James A. Lovell, Jr., and William Anders made 10 orbits of the Moon. They became the first people to fly around the Moon and return. Their success was followed by explorations of Mars (*Mariner 6* and *Mariner 7*) and manned lunar orbits. Then on July 20, 1969, two men (Neil A. Armstrong and Edwin E. Aldrin, Jr.) left their spaceship, *Apollo 11*, which had launched from the Kennedy Space Center four days earlier, to walk on the Moon and gather samples.

Apollo 12 was another successful manned lunar landing for the United States in November 1969. However, the nation held its breath in April of the following year when an explosion destroyed the power and the propulsion systems of the command service module of *Apollo 13*. James A. Lovell, Jr., Fred W. Haise, Jr., and John L. Swigert, Jr., used the lunar module as a "lifeboat" and safely returned to Earth. Other successful manned lunar landings for the United States followed in early 1971 (*Apollo 14*), the summer of 1971 (*Apollo 15*), and April 1972 (*Apollo 16*). However, the USSR landed the first spacecraft on another planet when the *Venera 7* landed on Venus on December 15, 1970.

Japan, the USSR, and the United States continued their flybys and orbits of the planets and even explored comets and the Sun.

Space exploration has not been without tragedy and setback. Many launches failed. The astronauts of *Apollo 1*, Gus Grissom, Ed White, and Roger Chaffee, died during a prelaunch test. In 1986, the Space Shuttle *Challenger* broke apart 73 seconds into its flight, causing the deaths of its seven crew members. In 2003, the Space Shuttle *Columbia* disintegrated as it reentered Earth's atmosphere. All seven crew members perished.

On May 26, 1973, America launched its first space station (*Skylab*) and manned it for 171 days. In 1990, the Hubble Space Telescope (HST) was launched into low Earth orbit and remains in operation. Hubble's orbit outside the distortion of Earth's atmosphere allows it to take extremely high-resolution images with negligible background light. Hubble has recorded some of the most detailed visible-light images ever seen, allowing a deep view into space and time. Many Hubble observations have led to breakthroughs in astrophysics, such as accurately determining the rate of expansion of the universe. In 1998, the first component for the *International Space Station* (ISS), a habitable artificial satellite in low Earth orbit, was launched. The ISS is now the largest artificial body in orbit and consists of pressurized modules, external trusses, solar arrays, and many other components. The ISS is a true international space effort in which over 200 crew members from 15 countries have conducted experiments in biology, physics, chemistry, astronomy, and other fields. Another major achievement was the first space weather satellite (*IMAGE*) launched by the United States to study global response to changes in the solar wind by Earth's magnetosphere. In January 2006, the return capsule from the rendezvous with comet P/Wild 2 returned to Earth with samples.

For budgetary reasons, NASA has curtailed many of its programs, but NASA scientists still believe much exploration of our solar system remains to be done and will yield valuable information about it.

While space exploration may seem far removed from everyday life, it has an impact on technology, science, and society in many ways. For example, the multitude of television channels available and the GPS systems that direct our routes depend on satellites for access. The memory foam in beds was originally developed for astronaut use. Other innovations in fields including health, waste management, and engineering have affected society. Space exploration affects cultural perceptions of our place in the world and inspires humans to find new ways to solve life's problems.

Competency 5: Knowledge of Life Science

Biology is the study of life from single-celled microorganisms, such as bacteria and viruses, to the largest plants and animals in terms of their defining characteristics and classification, cellular structures, and interactions with other organisms and the environment.

Skill 5.1: Identify and Compare the Characteristics of Living and Nonliving Things

A specific set of life activities differentiates living things from nonliving things.

Elementary-age students often have trouble distinguishing between living and non-living things. Many children think the primary criteria for life are simply the abilities to move and to grow. As a result, they may believe nonliving objects or phenomena, like clouds and fire, are alive and that nonmoving organisms, such as sea sponges, barnacles, and even trees, are not alive. Although the ability to move is not a defining characteristic of life, the ability to grow is an essential characteristic of all living things. Given the great diversity of organisms on Earth, what other characteristics do all living things have in common?

From the smallest microscopic single-celled bacterium to the blue whale, the largest creature on the planet, all species share six life-defining activities.

Required Activities of Living Things

Activity	Description
Cellular organization	All living organisms consist of cells: the smallest unit of life that carries on all life processes. Some organisms (bacteria, viruses, and protists) exist as a single-celled organism (unicellular). Most organisms are multicellular, with differentiated cells within the organism (i.e., blood cells differ from skin cells).
Metabolism	Metabolism is the organism's way of getting and using chemical energy (food) to sustain life; it occurs though eating, absorption, or photosynthesis.

(continued)

(continued)

Activity	Description
Homeostasis	An organism has processes that, based on feedback, regulate and maintain internal conditions within limits (i.e., temperature, water content, metabolism) despite environmental conditions. For example, sweating on a hot day is a way of cooling the body to maintain the correct temperature.
Growth and development	Organisms increase in size or change over part or all of a lifespan as the result of their use of energy to power cell division and/or enlargement of cells. In multicellular organisms, development results in greater complexity of the organism (i.e., the development of a fetus during pregnancy and continued growth after birth) or change (i.e., the metamorphosis of a caterpillar into a butterfly).
Irritability or sensitivity	An organism must be able to respond or react to physical or chemical stimuli either internally or in the environment. This function allows the organism to adjust to its environment in order to stay alive. Some reactions (i.e., pupil dilation) are immediate; others occur over time (i.e., a plant bending toward sunlight).
Reproduction	Organisms recreate versions of themselves by making new living things similar to the parent. While reproduction is not essential for the individual organism, it does ensure the perpetuation of the species. In this process, the parent transfers genetic materials to offspring in the form of a genetic blueprint consisting of deoxyribonucleic acid (DNA). DNA provides the information that the new organism needs to grow, develop, and function. Less complex organisms (bacteria, some plants and fungi) reproduce asexually, in which the offspring are identical to the parent organism. However, most organisms (plants and animals) reproduce sexually, with two different parents contributing to the creation of an offspring, that contains DNA from both parents. Some organisms (i.e., sponges, starfish, some plants) can reproduce asexually or sexually.

■ Skill 5.2: Analyze the Cell Theory as It Relates to the Functional and Structural Hierarchy of all Living Things

Seventeenth-century Englishman Robert Hooke had a passion for science and was a keen observer. After placing a slice of cork (a bark that comes from cork oak trees) under a microscope, he observed that the cork consisted of small boxlike structures. Hooke described them as looking like the cells in which monks lived. This was the basis of what later became known as cell theory—the understanding that all cells are alive and that cells come from other cells and form the basic building blocks of life.

Principles of Cell Theory

The following principles apply to living organisms. All cells contain the same basic structures, although the shapes, sizes, and functions of the cells may vary.

- Cells are the building blocks of all living organisms.

- Cell division is the process by which new cells are formed from pre-existing cells.

- Cells contain DNA, the hereditary blueprint that is passed to daughter cells.

- The chemical composition of all cells is similar.

- Metabolic processes of life occur at the cellular level.

Skill 5.3: Identify and Compare the Structures and Functions of Plant and Animal Cells

Plant cells and animal cells, though generally similar, are distinctly different because of the unique plant structures: cell walls and chloroplasts. The following figures illustrate the structures of animal and plant cells.

Cell Structures

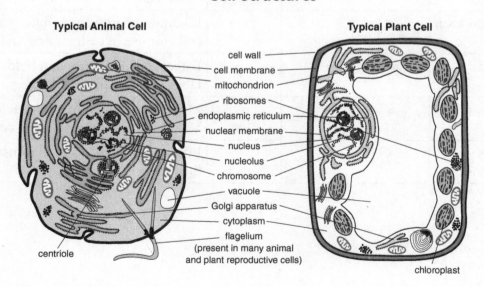

Typical Animal Cell

Typical Plant Cell

cell wall
cell membrane
mitochondrion
ribosomes
endoplasmic reticulum
nuclear membrane
nucleus
nucleolus
chromosome
vacuole
Golgi apparatus
cytoplasm
flagelium
(present in many animal
and plant reproductive cells)

centriole

chloroplast

Several smaller structures, called **organelles**, make up cells. Cell fluid, or cytoplasm, surrounds organelles. The following table lists the functions of several cell structures.

Cell Structures and Their Functions

Organelle	Plants and Animals	Animals Only	Plants Only	Function
Cell membrane	●			Controls movement of materials into and out of cells
Cell wall			●	Cellulose structure that gives rigidity to plant cells
Central vacuole			●	Reservoirs that contain water or other materials. For example, plants with full reservoirs are upright; they wilt when the reservoirs are empty.
Chloroplast (plastids)			●	Contains chlorophyll, which enables green plants to make their own food
Cytoplasm	●			Comprises the cytosol and organelles but not the nucleus (a jellylike substance within a cell)
Endoplasmic reticulum	●			System of tubes and sacs that transport molecules from one part of the cell to another
Golgi apparatus	●			Directs molecules to different parts of the cell
Mitochondrion	●			Liberates energy from glucose in cells for use in cellular activities
Nucleus	●			Directs cell activities and holds DNA (genetic material)
Ribosome	●			Makes proteins from amino acids; Vacuole stores materials in a cell
Vesicles	●			Encase materials taken in or used by the cells

Skill 5.4: Classify Living Things into Major Groups and Compare According to Characteristics

Taxonomy is the theory and practice of describing, naming, and classifying organisms. Classification of organisms is a way to create order. Early Latin naming systems were cumbersome and complex. Eighteenth-century Swedish physician Carolus Linnaeus created a two-word naming system (the Linnaean system), which is still in use today for identifying a species. Following the 1859 publication of Charles Darwin's *On the Origin of Species*, classifications reflected the phylogeny of organisms, their descent by evolution.

Classification is not always clearly evident. The first systems of organization placed organisms in one of two kingdoms: plant or animal. Beginning in the 1960s, organisms were classified into five kingdoms (Monera, Protista, Fungi, Plantae, and Animalia) based on the Linnaean system. New methods, such as genetic sequencing, now allow scientists to think about and classify organisms in new and different ways. As a result, the current system classifies organisms into three domains based on ribosomal RNA structure: Archaea, Bacteria, and Eukarya. Both the Archaea and Bacteria domains contain organisms without membrane-bound nuclei. The Eukarya domain contains organisms that have membrane-bound nuclei (Protista, Fungi, Plantae, and Animalia). The three domains are subdivided into six kingdoms based on cell type (simple or complex), the ability to make food; and the number of cells in their bodies.

Kingdom	Description/ Examples	Complex Cells	Multicellular	Food Source
Archaebacteria	Single-celled organisms that can live in extreme environments (boiling water, no oxygen, or highly acidic)	No	No	Cannot make their own food (heterotrophs)
Eubacteria	Bacteria	No	No	Cannot make their own food (heterotrophs)
Protista	Microorganisms that don't fit into other categories (i.e., not bacteria, animals, plants, or fungi)	Yes	Some are multicellular; others are unicellular	Some make their own food; others do not
Fungi	Mushrooms, mold, mildew	Yes	Mostly	Cannot make their own food

(continued)

(continued)

Kingdom	Description/Examples	Complex Cells	Multicellular	Food Source
Plantae	Second largest kingdom; includes flowering plants, mosses, and ferns	Yes	Yes	Make their own food (autotrophs)
Animalia	Largest kingdom; includes all animals	Yes	Yes	Cannot make their own food (heterotrophs)

In turn, each kingdom subdivides into classes, orders, families, genera (singular: genus), and species (singular: species), with an additional rank lower than species.

Each level in the taxonomy provides more detail about an organism's features, behavior, and development. For example, the defining feature of the Eukarya domain is a membrane-bound nucleus. In the following example of the taxonomy for the red fox, the organism is an animal (kingdom) with a spinal cord (phylum); is a live-bearing, air-breathing mammal (class) that eats meat (order); and is part of the same family as dogs and wolves but is differentiated by its smaller size and flatter skull (genus).

Taxonomy for Red Fox

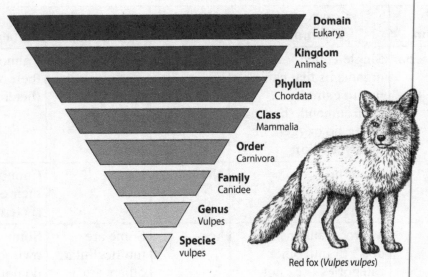

Domain Eukarya
Kingdom Animals
Phylum Chordata
Class Mammalia
Order Carnivora
Family Canidee
Genus Vulpes
Species vulpes

Red fox (*Vulpes vulpes*)

Skill 5.5: Compare and Contrast the Structures, Functions, and Interactions of Human and Other Animal Organ Systems

A group of the same kind of cells is a tissue. A group of the same kind of tissues working together is an organ. Examples of animal organs are the brain, stomach, heart, liver, and kidneys. A group of organs that works together to accomplish a special activity is a system. The complex organism of the human body is made up of eleven organ systems.

Skeletal System

The skeletal system provides a structural framework for the body and the rest of the systems and protects internal organs. It includes bones, cartilage, and ligaments. The human skeleton consists of more than 200 bones. The area where two or more bones come together is called a joint. To reduce friction, cartilage covers bone surfaces in a joint. Ligaments are connective tissues that hold the bones together.

Muscular System

The muscular system controls movement of the skeleton and movement within organs by contracting and relaxing muscles. There are three types of muscle: striated (voluntary), smooth (involuntary), and cardiac (heart). Tendons attach muscles to bone. Skeletal muscles work in pairs to create movements. The alternating contractions of muscles within a pair cause movement in joints.

Nervous System

The central nervous system controls both thinking and movement. It consists of the brain and spinal cord, and connects mental and physical activities. The peripheral nervous system consists of the sensory nerves (i.e., eyes, ears, skin) and motor nerves that carry information to and from the central nervous system. All nerve cells are neurons. The nervous system has two divisions: the somatic, allowing voluntary control over skeletal muscle, and the autonomic, or involuntary, controlling cardiac and glandular functions. Nerve impulses arising in the brain and carried by cranial or spinal cord nerves connecting to skeletal muscles enable voluntary movement such as walking, talking, and writing. Involuntary movements include breathing, the heartbeat, and temperature control, and provide direct response to outside stimulus. Various nerve terminals have receptors that constantly send impulses to the central nervous system. There are three types of receptors:

- Exteroceptors—pain, temperature, touch, and pressure
- Interoceptors—internal environment
- Proprioceptors—feedback of movement, position, and tension

Endocrine System

The endocrine system controls a network of glands that send chemical messages to cells. It includes the pancreas, hypothalamus, pituitary gland, thyroid, adrenal glands, and the ovaries and testes. Glands produce and release various hormones into the blood or other bodily fluids. Some hormones affect processes such as growth, development, reproduction, or behavior. Other hormones control metabolism and react to the environment.

Integumentary System

The integumentary system is the largest organ in the human body. It includes your skin, hair, and nails; it protects the rest of the body from harmful materials, retains fluids within the body, helps regulate body temperature, and aids in eliminating waste products from the body. The skin has two layers. The outer layer (epidermis) has mostly dead cells that protect the body from the outside world. These cells are continually shedding when the skin is rubbed or washed. Much of what we perceive as household dust is really dead skin cells. The inner layer (dermis) contains sweat glands that release water and salt to cool the body when it overheats and sebaceous (oil) glands that prevent the skin from drying out. The inner dermis also contains hair follicles, blood vessels, nerve endings, and muscle fibers.

Digestive System

The digestive system receives and processes food to supply the energy to sustain the body. The digestive system includes the mouth (including the tongue and oral cavity), pharynx, esophagus, stomach, large intestine (colon), small intestine, rectum, and anus. Digestion is both a physical and chemical process. It begins when mastication, or chewing, breaks down the food physically and mixes it with saliva from the salivary glands. The food is then swallowed by the pharynx and moves into the esophagus. Peristalsis— contraction of the muscles—moves it into the stomach and throughout the system. The stomach breaks down food chemically with gastric and intestinal juices. The mixture of food and secretions exit the stomach through the alimentary canal into the small intestine, which absorbs nutrients from the mixture and passes waste into the large intestine (colon), which in turn absorbs water before excreting waste (feces) from the body.

Excretory System

The excretory system eliminates wastes from the body. Excretory organs include the lungs, kidneys, bladder, large intestine, rectum, and skin. The lungs excrete some of the gaseous waste. Nitrogen-based waste from proteins must be dissolved in water before they can be excreted, which occurs in the liver to form urea. The urea and other waste products are released into the bloodstream and are then filtered by the kidneys. The bladder holds liquid wastes until their elimination through the urethra; the rectum stores solid waste until its elimination. The skin excretes waste through perspiration.

Cardiovascular System

Circulation is the internal transportation system of the body. The cardiovascular system is a circulatory system that includes the heart, veins, arteries, and blood. The heart is a muscular four-chambered pump. The upper chambers are the atria and the lower chambers are the ventricles. The heart pumps blood through the right chambers of the heart and through the lungs, where the blood acquires oxygen. From there, the blood is pumped back into the left chambers of the heart. Next, it is pumped into the main artery, the aorta, which branches into increasingly smaller arteries. Beyond that, blood passes through tiny, thin-walled structures called capillaries. In the capillaries, the blood provides oxygen and nutrients to tissues and absorbs a metabolic waste product containing carbon dioxide. Blood returns through small veins that join increasingly larger vessels until the blood reaches the largest veins on the right side of the heart, where the blood is pumped into the lungs to release carbon dioxide and absorb oxygen before repeating the process.

Lymphatic System

The lymphatic system is a circulatory system that includes lymph nodes, lymph vessels, and lymph (a clear, yellowish liquid). Unlike the cardiovascular system, the lymphatic system has no pump and must rely on the contraction of skeletal muscles. This system works with the blood to maintain fluid levels within the body, absorbs digested fats from the small intestine, and removes disease-causing microorganisms and other waste materials. Lymph nodes produce specialized cells called lymphocytes that attack infections throughout the body.

Respiratory System

The respiratory system supports breathing. It exchanges carbon dioxide for oxygen in the circulatory system and includes the lungs, trachea, bronchi, and the diaphragm.

In humans, respiration involves the muscular expansion and contraction of the diaphragm to move and inflate the lungs. During the process of external respiration, inhaling draws air higher in oxygen and lower in carbon dioxide into the lungs; exhaling forces air from the lungs that is high in carbon dioxide and low in oxygen.

Internal respiration occurs in the alveoli of the lungs, where carbon dioxide is released and fresh oxygen is absorbed and transferred into tiny capillaries. In the capillaries, oxygen combines with hemoglobin in the red blood cells to nourish tissues throughout the body.

Reproductive System

The reproductive system produces offspring in living plant or animal organisms. In almost all animal organisms, reproduction is enabled after the period of maximum growth. Reproduction in animals is either asexual or sexual.

Asexual animal propagation occurs primarily in single-celled organisms. Through the process of fission, the parent organism splits into two or more daughter organisms, thereby losing its original identity. In some instances, cell division results in the production of buds that arise from the body of the parent and then later separate to develop into a new organism identical to the parent. A reproductive process in which only one parent gives rise to the offspring is asexual reproduction. The offspring produced are identical to the parent.

Sexual animal propagation results from sperm uniting with ova for fertilization. The primary means of this kind of reproduction are insemination (copulation between a male and female vertebrate) and cross-fertilization (the depositing of ova and sperm in water at some distance from each other, most commonly by fish).

In humans, the male reproductive system includes the testes (which are part of the endocrine system) and the penis. The testes produce both hormones and male reproductive cells called sperm. The human female reproductive system contains special glands that produce hormones and reproductive cells called eggs. The ovaries release eggs into the fallopian tubes, which carry the eggs to the uterus. If the egg is fertilized by a sperm cell, it implants into the wall of the uterus and develops into a fetus. After a gestation period of nine months, the fetus becomes an infant with delivery through the vagina.

■ Skill 5.6: Distinguish Among Infectious Agents, Their Transmission, and Their Effects on the Human Body

An infection occurs when one organism lives inside another organism (the host) from which it gets its nourishment. Infectious agents include viruses, bacteria, fungi, and parasites. An infectious agent may start as a single cell; however, it colonizes and reproduces within the host. It is only an infection if the colonization harms the host by using the host to feed on and multiply to such an extent that the health of the host is affected. An organism that colonizes and harms a host's health is often called a pathogen (i.e., parasites, fungi, bacteria, and viroids). Single-celled pathogens can be eukaryotes (cells with a defined nucleus), like parasites, or prokaryotes (genetic material floating inside a cell), like bacteria.

Comparison of Prokaryote and Eukaryote Cell Structure

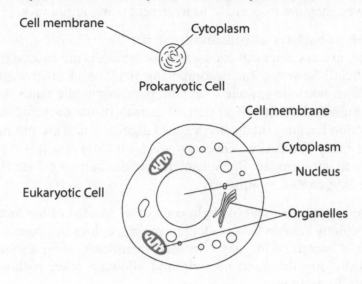

Cell membrane

Cytoplasm

Prokaryotic Cell

Cell membrane

Cytoplasm

Nucleus

Eukaryotic Cell

Organelles

Transmission of Pathogens

Pathogens are transmitted in different ways. Some are airborne (i.e., when someone coughs or sneezes), and some are transmitted through physical contact (i.e., dirty counter-tops, toys, doorknobs, or other surfaces). They can be transmitted through food or water that are poorly handled (i.e., not kept at the correct temperature, contamination). They can also be spread through vectors (i.e., arthropods, such as ticks, fleas, and mosquitoes that transmit pathogenic microbes to humans or animals). Good hygiene (i.e., washing hands, keeping surfaces clean, using insect repellent when outdoors) decreases the transmission of pathogens.

Most humans develop a wide range of infections, but fight them off rapidly. Some require medication or other treatments to overcome the infection. Very young children, elderly individuals, or people with compromised immune systems are in most danger from an infectious agent. Some people develop persistent, long-term (chronic) infections. The majority of chronic infections are caused by viruses, such as hepatitis or herpes. Chronic bacterial infections are more likely to affect patients with diabetes or those with weakened immune systems.

Bacteria

Bacteria are single-cell prokaryotes with various shapes, including rod, round, and spiral. They do not have a defined nucleus, are microscopic, and do not depend on hosts for survival. Most have adapted to a variety of environments, from freezing cold to boiling hot, that are often inhospitable to other organisms. Bacteria reproduce themselves by duplicating; however, they are responsive to treatment using antibiotics.

We often think of bacteria as bad, and some are (i.e., *E. coli, salmonella*). Illnesses such as strep throat, urinary tract infections, and tuberculosis are caused by bacteria. Most bacteria are beneficial, however, for decomposing plants and other organisms that die. They also break down waste in sewage treatment plants or septic tanks. Bacteria serve an important role in human digestion. The normal growth of the bacterial flora in the intestine is not an infection because the bacteria aid in digestion and are not harming the host. The production of many foods (i.e., cheese, yogurt, pickles) depends on bacteria. Plants depend on bacteria to get nitrogen. Some bacteria create their own food from the environment and produce oxygen as a by-product.

Sometimes two organisms in a host fight each other instead of the human body. When the levels of each colony remain balanced, their presence does not pose a problem for the host (i.e., some skin bacteria and yeast). In fact, treatments using antibiotics may upset the balance by destroying the good bacteria and allowing other pathogens to multiply faster and cause health problems.

Parasites

Parasites are organisms that benefit at the expense of their host. Some parasites are visible, but others are microscopic. Parasites do not invade individual cells within the host; rather, they live in or on the host (i.e., tapeworms, mistletoe, lice, ticks, and fleas). Some parasites may not harm the host in which they live. For example, microscopic mites called demodicids live in the eyelashes. Dust mites live in most homes and feed on dead skin cells from animals. Although they are technically harmless, they can cause allergic reactions or asthma in some people.

Protozoans are one-celled parasites that can live inside or outside a cell. When even one protozoa enters a human, it can multiply quickly to create an infection. Some live in the intestine and are transmitted through the fecal-oral route, which is a good reason to always wash hands when leaving a restroom. Protozoa that live in blood or tissue can be transmitted through mosquito bites. Examples of protozoans that cause infections and illness include amoebia, Giardia, toxoplasmia, and malaria. Although most antibiotics are not effective against protozoans, some protozoans are susceptible to antibiotics.

Viruses

A virus is a microorganism that is smaller than a cell. It lives and multiplies within a host cell (animal, plants, and other microorganisms including bacteria) for survival; therefore, a virus is intracellular and not a living thing. Viruses are very hardy and live in almost every ecosystem on Earth. Viruses cause many infections. Respiratory infections of the upper airways, nose, and throat are the most common forms of viral infections.

Before viruses infect a cell, they exist as independent particles called virions that carry genetic material and protein with capabilities to evolve. A virus invades its host and attaches to a cell. After entering the cell, it releases genetic material (DNA or RNA) to help the virus multiply by taking control of cell reproduction to replicate the virus. Viruses can target specific cells in the body (i.e., upper respiratory tract or digestive system) or certain age groups (i.e., croup in babies or young children.). However, some viral infections can be systemic and affect many different parts of the body (i.e., runny nose, sinus congestion, cough, and body aches).

Most cells with viral genetic material inserted into them cannot function properly and soon die. When a cell dies, it releases new viruses that infect other cells and continue the process. Sometimes the genetic material lies dormant in a cell; when the cell and the virus are triggered, they begin multiplying and make the host ill. Not all viruses destroy their host cell. Some just alter what the cell does. Experts suspect some cells become cancerous as a result of a virus interfering with its functions.

Viral particles vary in shape and are very small: about 1/100th of the size of the average bacterium. They contain most but not all of the required elements for life. Viruses exist in a range of host cells and sometimes affect only a few species. In humans, a virus provokes an immune response that tries to destroy the virus by releasing antibodies. The only way to protect a person against viruses is through vaccines that help the body build up antibodies against specific viruses. Vaccines do not cure viruses and are not available for every virus.

Unlike bacteria, viruses are not affected by antibiotics; however, several antiviral medications have been developed that either undermine the virus's ability to reproduce or boost the patient's immune system to produce antibodies. In most cases, the best way to treat a person with a virus is to provide supportive therapy that helps the patient's immune system fight the virus.

Fungal Infections

Fungi are not plants, animals, or bacteria, and they can live in air, water, soil, plants, or the human body. They have their own classification because their cell walls differ from those of plants and animals, and they have other characteristics that distinguish them from plants and animals. A mushroom is an example of a large fungus; however, many fungi are microscopic. For example, yeast fungus has over 1,000 varieties, including some used to make bread rise and others that cause skin infections. Ringworm and athlete's foot are common fungal infections. Some fungi are used in developing antibiotics, and fungal infections are treated with antifungal medications.

Protists

Any organism that cannot be clearly classified as a plant, animal, or fungi is classified as a protist. Protists can be unicellular (i.e., amoeba and paramecium), with a defined nuclei, and also multicellular, with characteristics of plants or animals that reproduce sexually or asexually.

Skill 5.7: Identify and Analyze the Processes of Heredity and Natural Selection and the Scientific Theory of Evolution

Gregor Mendel was an Austrian monk who identified the basic principles of heredity through experiments with pea plants in his monastery's garden. He discovered that predictable variations resulted from combinations of genes from the parent plants. The passing of these traits through genes from one generation to another is known as heredity. The study of how traits pass from generation to generation is called genetics. Traits or genes are carried in a cell's DNA, a kind of blueprint for the cells of an organism. A DNA molecule has the appearance of a twisted ladder, with the rungs carrying a sequence of chemicals that form the code for traits of a specific member of a species.

Early twentieth-century zoologist Reginald C. Punnett developed a diagram, known as the Punnett square, to determine the probability of an offspring having a particular genotype or set of genes. For example, perhaps two parents each carry one gene for a genetic abnormality (A) and one gene that would not cause the abnormality (a). For every child of the parents, the following possibilities exist: (1) a 1-in-4 chance that the child will not have the disease or carry the gene (aa), (2) a 2-in-4 chance that the child will only be a carrier of the disease (Aa), or (3) a 1-in-4 chance that the child will be affected by the disease (AA). The odds from these two parents are the same for each offspring. If the parents have a child affected by the disease (AA), it does not guarantee that the next three children will not be affected. The probability is the same for each generation.

Punnett Square

	A	a
A	AA	Aa
a	Aa	aa

The scientific theory of evolution relates to heredity because it states that advantageous inherited traits of biological populations develop over successive generations.

Nineteenth-century scientist Charles Darwin originated and described this theory in his book, *On the Origin of Species*, in 1859. He said biological evolution or development resulted from natural selection; that is, greater reproductive success among members of a species resulted from inherited characteristics that are advantageous in a specific environment. This occurs through adaptation or changes in an organism that help it survive in a particular environment and transmit genetic material to offspring within the species. This is sometimes called survival of the fittest, which means that the survivability of individual members of a species that live long enough to reproduce are more likely to continue. Fitness refers to the proportion of subsequent generations of offspring that continue to have a genetic trait that contributes to their survival. Through heredity, advantageous variations exhibited by individuals within the population can cause a species to change and survive. Fossil records provide evidence of evolution through the similarities and diversity of life.

For example, with environmental changes that occur as a result of global warming, species may adjust by migrating to more hospitable locations, adapting to the climate change, or developing new traits. Species that cannot move or adapt are less likely to survive and more likely to become extinct.

Skill 5.8: Analyze the Interdependence of Living Things with Each Other and with Their Environment

Life depends on other life and environmental factors for survival. Our surroundings form a complex, interconnected system in which living organisms (biotic factors) exist in relationship with the soil, water, and air (abiotic factors). Earth's inhabitants are in states of continual change or dynamic equilibrium in environments that range from cold to hot and from wet to dry.

Types of Environments

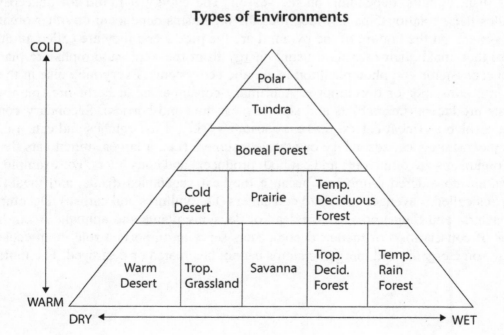

Ecosystems

An ecosystem includes all the living and nonliving things in a given environment and how they interact in terms of cooperation, competition, and/or conflict. A population within an ecosystem is the total of organisms in the species that could interbreed. Each population lives in a particular area and serves a special role in the community. This combination of defined role and living areas is the concept of niche. The niche of a pond snail, for example, is to decompose materials in ponds. The niche of a field mouse is to eat seeds in fields. When two populations try to fill the same niche, competition occurs. If one population replaces another in a niche, succession occurs. Natural succession is the orderly and predictable change of communities as a result of population replacement in niches. A community is a group of populations that interact with one another. A pond community, for example, consists of all the plants and animals in the pond. Thus, an ecosystem is a group of populations that shares a common pool of resources in a specific physical or geographical area. Over time, ecosystems change from natural processes and the activities of humans. Changes can be short-term (i.e., a fire or freeze) or long-term (cutting a forest for urban development or using pesticides).

Energy Transformations within Ecosystems

Energy transformations are the driving force within an ecosystem. Many organisms obtain energy from light. For example, light activates photosynthesis in green plants. Solar energy also provides heat for cold-blooded animals. Another source of energy for organisms is from other organisms, including plants and animals.

When one source of energy is depleted in an ecosystem, many organisms must shift their attention to other sources of energy. For example, a bear gets energy primarily from berries, fish, or nuts, depending on the season. The energy pyramid for an ecosystem illustrates these relationships and identifies the organisms dependent on other organisms in the system. At the bottom of the pyramid are the producers; they are called autotrophs because they make their own food using energy from the Sun. Autotrophs are plant life in land ecosystems and photoplankton in aquatic ecosystems. Everything else in the food chain is a consumer or decomposer. A primary consumer is an herbivore (plant eater) that eats producers (i.e., rabbits and squirrels eat nuts and berries). Secondary consumers are carnivores (meat eaters) that eat consumers (i.e., a fox catches and eats a rabbit). Tertiary consumers eat secondary or other consumers (i.e., a larger animal eats the fox). Some organisms are omnivores and eat both producers and consumers. For example, most humans are considered omnivores because they eat vegetables, fruits, and meat. Some organisms called scavengers eat dead consumers (i.e., vultures and catfish). Decomposers (i.e., bacteria and fungi) break down dead or decaying plants and animals. According to the law of conservation of matter, decomposers serve an important role in an ecosystem because some organic and inorganic atoms cannot be created or destroyed. The molecules are broken down and recycled by the decomposers to form new organisms. A food web is a system of interconnected food chains. The availability of adequate food within an ecosystem helps explain the system's functioning, the size of an animal's territory, or the effects of a single species preying too heavily on organisms above it in the food chain. Higher-order organisms cannot survive for long without the other organisms beneath them in the energy pyramid.

The energy pyramid demonstrates how energy is distributed within an ecosystem by specifying calories. The word *calorie* is used for two different units of energy. A "cal" is a small calorie and describes the amount of energy required to raise the temperature of 1 gram of water by 1 degree Celsius. The second unit is a "Cal" or "kcal" (large calorie). This is how much energy is needed to raise a kilogram of water by 1 degree Celsius. So, 1 kcal = 1,000 cal. Energy in the pyramid is measured in kcal.

In the pyramid, about 90% of the energy within a level is used to maintain the life of the organism within the same level. Therefore, only 10% is transferred to the next level. Each consumer in the chain is larger and gets less of the original energy from the producer. For example, let's say that plants in an ecosystem get 10,000 kcal from the Sun, but 90% of that total is used to sustain the plants, and they store 1,000 cal. Bugs that eat the 1,000 kcal use 90% to exist and store the remaining 10% (100 kcal) in their bodies. A frog eats the insect and now has 10 kcal to release to the fox. As a result, food chains cannot sustain more than about three levels. This is why the organisms at different levels are interdependent. It is also why scientists believe that Earth could support a larger population of humans if they used more plants than animals as food sources.

Energy Pyramid: Producer, Consumers, Decomposers

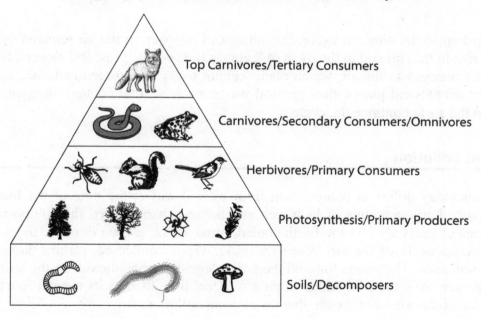

269

Energy Pyramid: Distribution and Use

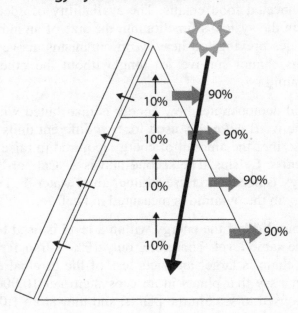

Carbon Dioxide, Oxygen, and Nitrogen Cycles

According to the carbon dioxide–oxygen cycle, the amount of oxygen and carbon dioxide in the air remains the same. To make food, green plants take in carbon dioxide from the air. The waste product that plants give off in the process is oxygen. When animals breathe in oxygen to digest their food, they give off carbon dioxide as a waste product.

According to the nitrogen cycle, the amount of nitrogen in the air remains constant. Bacteria live in the soil and in the roots of legumes (i.e., beans, peas, and clover). Bacteria change the nitrogen in the air, which plants cannot use, into nitrogen materials they can use. After animals eat plants, they give off waste materials that contain nitrogen, which returns to the air to continue the cycle.

Effects of Pollution

The air today differs in composition from what it was at the time of the formation of the Earth. Large amounts of hydrogen and helium characterized the composition of air millions of years ago. As the Earth cooled, water vapor, carbon dioxide, and nitrogen became components of the air. When the water vapor condensed, carbon dioxide and nitrogen remained. The plants lowered the percentage of carbon dioxide in the air by giving off oxygen. Any material added to an ecosystem that disrupts its normal functioning changes the composition of the air, thereby causing pollution.

Typical pollutants are excess fertilizers or other waste materials that factories and manufacturing plants dump into the water or onto the ground, and industrial emissions that are released into the air. Emissions from smokestacks, chimneys, and car exhaust pipes contribute to air pollutants. Some pollutants are simply annoying; others are dangerous to the health of living organisms. Continuous exposure to polluting materials discharged into the air can cause lung diseases or aggravate existing health conditions in humans.

If weather conditions prevent the distribution of polluting materials, air pollution can become increasingly severe. When cold air is next to the ground with warm air above, polluting materials remain concentrated in one area. The warm air acts as a blanket, forcing the cold air to remain stationary. This situation is referred to as a temperature inversion.

Acid rain, a form of precipitation that contains high levels of sulfuric or nitric acid, can pollute drinking water, damage plant and animal life, and even erode monuments and buildings. Among the primary causes of acid rain are forest fires, volcanic eruptions, and the burning of certain fuels, including the gasoline that powers most automobiles.

Skill 5.9: Identify and Analyze Plant Structures and the Processes of Photosynthesis, Transpiration, and Reproduction

Plants are one of the six kingdoms, Plantae. Because they convert energy from the Sun, they are the producers upon which most other life depends. Like organisms in other kingdoms, plants come in diverse forms and live on land and in fresh- or saltwater. Three characteristics distinguish plant life: (1) they have a green pigment called chlorophyll that is required for photosynthesis, (2) their cell walls are formed from cellulose, and (3) they are anchored in place and do not move.

Plants can be classified by how they circulate fluids. Nonvascular plants do not have an internal system to circulate water. They absorb water directly from the environment that surrounds it. Nonvascular plants are generally small and very simple (i.e., mosses and liverwort). Vascular plants, such as flowers and trees, have a structural system to absorb water and transport it to other parts of the plant. Vascular plants divide into two groups that either reproduce from spores or seeds.

Roots and Shoots

The key structures of plants are roots and shoots. Roots are generally below ground and consist of a primary root, lateral roots, and root hairs. The roots hold the plant in the soil and keep it from blowing away in the wind. Roots absorb water and nutrients from the soil. They also prevent soil erosion because plant roots hold soil in place. Some plants have flowers, fruit, and roots (i.e., carrots and beets) that are edible.

The shoot system above ground includes the stem or trunk, leaves, and vascular tissues. The shoot system is responsible for the photosynthesis, reproduction, and dispersal of seeds, and food and water transport. Xylem is found in the stem of a plant or trunk of a tree. Xylem is a support structure that holds up a plant and circulates water and nutrients through a system of tubes and transport cells. The rings of a tree trunk show the remains of xylem that lived and died as the tree grew additional structure. From the Sun's energy, photosynthesis creates sugars in the leaves and transports them through a cellular structure, called phloem, that exists throughout the plant. Similar to the circulatory system of a human, when the phloem dies, the plant dies.

Plant Metabolism

In plants, cells perform several chemical processes to maintain essential life activities that contribute to metabolism—the biochemical processes that convert food into energy for sustaining life. The following table lists the processes and organelles for metabolism in plants.

Processes of Cell Metabolism

Process	Organelle	Life Activity
Diffusion	Cell membrane	Obtaining food, respiration, excretion
Osmosis	Cell membrane	Obtaining food, excretion
Phagocytosis	Cell membrane	Obtaining food
Photosynthesis	Chloroplasts	Obtaining food
Respiration (aerobic)	Mitochondrion	Providing energy
Fermentation	Mitochondrion	Providing energy

Cells transport materials into their structures to get energy for growing. The cell membrane allows certain small molecules (chemicals) to flow freely. This flow of chemicals from areas of high concentration to areas of low concentration is called diffusion. Osmosis is diffusion of water across a semipermeable membrane. The cell membrane may engulf and store particles too large to pass through the cell membranes in vacuoles until the digestion of the particles. This engulfing process is called phagocytosis.

All cells need energy to survive. Photosynthesis converts the Sun's energy to chemical energy, to support biological life. Photosynthesis occurs in the chloroplasts of a plant's green cells within leaves. Chlorophyll, the pigment found in chloroplasts, catalyzes (causes or accelerates) the photosynthetic reaction that turns carbon dioxide and water into glucose (sugar) and oxygen. Sunlight and chlorophyll are necessary for the reaction to occur. Because chlorophyll is only a catalyst for the chemical reaction, it remains available for repeated use.

The term *respiration* has two distinct meanings in the field of biology. As a life activity, respiration is the exchange of gases in living things. As a metabolic process, respiration is the release of energy from sugars for use in life activities. All living things get their energy from the digestion (respiration) of glucose (sugar). Respiration may occur with oxygen (aerobic respiration) or without oxygen (anaerobic respiration, or fermentation). Most often the term *respiration* refers to aerobic respiration, which occurs in most plant and animal cells.

Reproduction

Reproduction is the process of producing offspring. In plants, reproduction may be either sexual or asexual.

Asexual plant propagation, also known as vegetative reproduction, is the method by which plants reproduce without the union of cells or nuclei of cells. The product of asexual plant propagation is genetically identical to the parent. Asexual propagation takes place either by fragmentation or by special asexual structures. An example of fragmentation is growing new plants from cuttings.

Sexual plant propagation almost always involves seeds produced by two individual plants: male and female. Most plant propagation is from seed, including all annual and biennial plants. Seed germination begins when a sufficient amount of water is absorbed by the seed, precipitating biochemical changes that initiate cell division.

The diagram on the next page depicts the process of sexual plant propagation. Flowering plants have male and female reproductive structures. The male structure, the stamen tipped by the anther, surrounds the female structures, the pistil, pollen tube, and ovary. These are surrounded and protected by the flower's petals. The anther produces pollen. Insects pick up pollen as they gather nectar. When the insect goes to another flower, some of the pollen is deposited on the pistil. The pollen goes through the pollen tube to the ovary, where the ovule is fertilized to produce seeds.

Plant Propagation

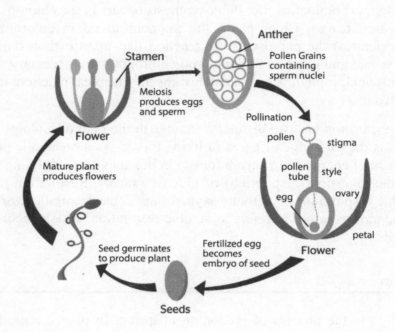

Skill 5.10: Predict the Responses of Plants to Various Stimuli

Because plants require the energy from the Sun for photosynthesis, the stems of plants grow toward the light (phototropism). Plants generally grow upward because the Sun is in the sky, but if the source of the light differs (i.e., a houseplant near a window) the plants can remain bent toward the light source. This occurs because hormones in the plant increase the number of stem cells on the side opposite from the light, causing the stem to bend toward the light.

Gravity allows rainwater to move downward through the soil and reach a plant's roots. Gravity also helps roots grow downward to hold the plant in the soil. In addition, gravity contributes to the downward movement of phloem in a plant's vascular system.

Temperature affects both seed germination and plant growth. Frozen seeds cannot sprout. If seasonal temperatures warm too early, seeds may germinate and begin to grow but slow to a halt if the weather gets cold again. Some plants grow well in hot and warm climates, while others need cold or cool climates (i.e., some fruit trees). Although cold supports the formation of fruit with some plants, freezing does not.

Skill 5.11: Identify and Compare the Life Cycles and Predictable Ways Plants and Animals Change as They Grow, Develop, and Age

A life cycle consists of the changes in the growth and development of an organism. The cycle begins as the organism functions as an independent life form. When the organism becomes mature, it can reproduce to create new offspring. Eventually the organism ages and dies. This cycle is repeated in every living organism in all of life's six kingdoms; however, the stages in the cycle vary in duration because of the size of the organism. For example, in the right conditions, the life cycle of bacteria can be as short as 30 minutes. The life cycle of a fruit fly from egg to death is 14 days. Larger animals, including humans, have a much longer life cycle. A variety of issues, including loss of habitat or food sources, predators, disease, and environmental factors, can interrupt an organism's life cycle and prevent it from reaching adulthood. Life cycles differ in other ways. For example, some organisms, such as humans, dogs, and birds, need parental care after birth, whereas others (i.e., sea turtles, frogs) do not. Some species reproduce only once, while others reproduce many times.

Animal Life Cycle Example

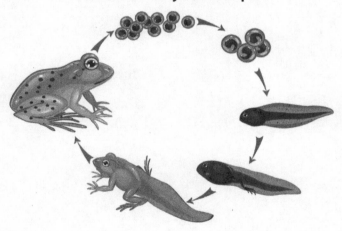

Plant Life Cycle Example

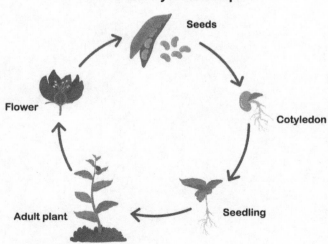

References

Science Laboratory Safety. (2007). Retrieved September 9, 2011, from *http://www. Sunshineconnections.org/strategies/Strategies Paperwork Reduction/Lab Safety Prep.doc*

Gopnik, A. (2012). Scientific thinking in young children: Theoretical advances, empirical research, and policy implications. *Science, 337*(6102): 1623–1627.

Klahr, D., Zimmerman, C., & Jirout, J.. (2011). Educational interventions to advance children's scientific thinking. *Science, 333*(6045): 971. doi:10.1126/science.1204528

NSTA Board of Directors (2002). Position paper on science in elementary education. Retrieved from *http://www.nsta.org/about/positions/elementary.aspx.*

National Governors' Association & Council of Chief State School Officers. (2010). *Common Core state standards for mathematics*. Washington, D.C.: National Governors Association Center for Best Practices (NGA Center).

Review Questions

1. Which of the following best exemplifies research-based teaching strategies in science?

    (A) Mr. Smith has divided his third-grade class into groups. Each group has been given an egg and some simple building materials (e.g., craft sticks, hot glue, three paper towels, two rubber bands, and five drinking straws). Each group needs to research, create, and test structures to protect the egg to see which egg can survive the greatest drop. After completing all the drops, students will explain which structure worked best and why.

    (B) Ms. Van Allen's fifth-grade class is going on a field trip to the local zoo. Each student is told to sketch one animal while she or he is at the zoo. In addition, each student should write a three-page research report describing the animal.

    (C) Ms. Toll's second-grade class is learning about magnets. Ms. Toll has found three books about magnets. She has assigned groups of students to read one of the books about magnets based on their reading levels. After the students read the books, they will take a test on what they learned.

    (D) Ms. Camp has examined the Florida Standards for science and is creating a lesson on the Sun for her third-grade class based on the following standard: *S.3.E.5.2 Identify the Sun as a star that emits energy; some of it in the form of light.* Ms. Camp will show the class a 3-minute video about the Sun and then let them draw a picture of the Sun.

2. Ms. Colson is reviewing policies for safety in teaching her students fifth-grade science. Which policy needs to be changed?

    (A) Replace glass beakers with polyethylene containers.

    (B) Replace mercury thermometers with alcohol thermometers.

    (C) Include the use of human cells (e.g., nail clippings, skin or blood samples) for microscopic observation.

    (D) Prevent students from tasting mineral samples.

3. Mr. Light's fifth-grade class is doing an experiment with plant growth. He divided students into groups. Each group got two daisy seeds from the same package of seeds. The groups all had the same kind of soil and planted them at the same time on the same day. The plants were in the same classroom. Each plant got the same amount of liquids each day. However, each plant got a different type of liquid (i.e., tap water, bottled water, carbonated water, orange juice, milk, and so on). The students measured the plants each week for six weeks. Which statement is correct?

    (A) The experiment is a field experiment because it uses plants.

    (B) The experiment includes multiple trials.

    (C) The extraneous variable is plant growth.

    (D) The independent variable is type of liquid.

4. Mr. Hirumi is using a STEM-based approach with his third-grade class. What would you expect to see students doing in his classroom?

    (A) Observing fish in the classroom's aquarium to see how they interact with each other.

    (B) Researching and identifying new ways to reuse waste products at the school.

    (C) Using the Internet to learn more about magnets and making a poster about magnetism.

    (D) Participating in a science quiz bowl via Skype with students in another school.

5. Which physical science property term is correctly defined?

    (A) *Mass* is defined as the space occupied by an object.

    (B) *Weight* is defined as how much there is of an object.

    (C) *Density* is defined as the ratio of mass to volume.

    (D) *Viscosity* is defined as a measure of density.

6. Which phase change of matter is incorrectly matched to its definition?

    (A) Sublimation occurs when a solid changes to gas through addition of heat.

    (B) Melting occurs when a gas changes to liquid through subtraction of heat.

    (C) Evaporation occurs when a liquid becomes a gas through addition of heat.

    (D) Freezing occurs when a liquid changes to a solid through subtraction of heat.

7. Mr. Plante is showing his students a readout from a seismograph, which is used to measure

    (A) earthquakes.

    (B) the content of magma.

    (C) glacial movement.

    (D) erosion.

8. Ms. Linden is describing the *cryosphere* of the Earth. What information should Ms. Linden include in her lesson?

    (A) A description of the components of soil

    (B) How igneous rock and metamorphic rock are formed

    (C) Why glaciers and polar ice caps are important

    (D) The purpose of Earth's core, mantle, and crust

9. Ms. Caprio's class is learning about the integumentary system. What does Ms. Caprio most likely teach?

    (A) Geology

    (B) Chemistry

    (C) Physics

    (D) Biology

10. What is an example of an *autotroph*?

    (A) An apple tree

    (B) A goldfish

    (C) A dog

    (D) A mushroom

Answer Key and Explanations

1. **(A)**

Research-based teaching strategies in science focus on student-centered learning and inquiry in the context of social interaction. Mr. Camp's class focuses on inquiry in terms of observation, experimentation, explanation, and social interaction. The lessons in the other classes are content-driven rather than student-centered. They do not involve meaningful inquiry or group interaction. *For more information, see Competency 1.*

2. **(C)**

Teachers should discourage the use of human cells in elementary classrooms. All of the other statements are correct. *For more information, see Competency 1.*

3. **(D)**

Response (A) is incorrect because field experiments occur in natural and authentic environments. Response (B) is incorrect because multiple trials would involve conducting the same experiment multiple times. Response (C) is incorrect because plant growth is the dependent variable. *For more information, see Competency 2.*

4. **(B)**

STEM-based classrooms focus on solving real-life problems and improved solutions. The other responses do not focus on integrating subjects in authentic problem-solving contexts. *For more information, see Competency 2.*

5. **(C)**

Response (A) is incorrect because volume is the amount of space an object occupies. Response (B) is incorrect because weight is defined as the force of gravity on an object. Response (D) is incorrect because viscosity is a measure of a substance's ability to flow. *For more information, see Competency 3.*

6. **(B)**

Melting occurs when a solid changes to liquid through addition of heat. *For more information, see Competency 3.*

7. **(A)**

A seismograph measures earthquakes on a Richter scale. *For more information, see Competency 4.*

8.   **(C)**

The cryosphere is the frozen part of the Earth, which includes glaciers and polar ice caps. *For more information, see Competency 4.*

9.   **(D)**

The integumentary system is the largest organ in the human body and includes skin, hair, and fingernails. Therefore, it is most likely to be included in a biology class. *For more information, see Competency 5.*

10.   **(A)**

Autotrophs are producers (plants) and make their own food. Goldfish and dogs are consumers. A mushroom is a decomposer. *For more information, see Competency 5.*

Mathematics

Competency 1: Knowledge of Student Thinking and Instructional Practices

While the processes of math have not changed, the focus of teaching and learning math over the years has changed. At one point, the focus appeared to be on rote memorization and seemingly mindless application of mathematical concepts out of context. Math teaching and learning now place a greater emphasis on mathematical thinking as indicated by the use of words like *make sense of, reason, construct viable arguments, critique the reasoning of others,* and *use tools strategically* in Florida's K–12 math standards. This shift requires that teachers also think differently about math as contextual and authentic processes in terms of instruction. Competency 1 focuses on knowledge of student thinking and instructional practices.

Skill 1.1: Analyze and Apply Appropriate Mathematical Concepts, Procedures, and Professional Vocabulary to Evaluate Student Solutions

One of the most important roles for teachers is that of providing feedback on student work. The feedback process is where students make connections and gain insights from their mistakes. Thus, it is important for teachers to understand math concepts and procedures, use the vocabulary of the subject to illuminate these concepts and processes for students, and possess an array of alternative teaching strategies from concrete manipulatives to abstract problem-solving.

To design and deliver effective math instruction, teachers need to understand the developmental processes common to all learners and how the varied and diverse environmental features and learning styles affect learning. Although there may be some intuitive aspects to teaching (and it seems that some people were born to teach), teaching consists of skills gleaned through processes of discussion, introspection, observation, direct instruction, self-evaluation, and experimentation. This is especially true for elementary teachers because some K–6 teachers admit that math is not their favorite or best subject. That realization is important because teachers in elementary self-contained classrooms must be role models for each subject and teach each one, including math, as if it is a personal favorite in order to build student enthusiasm and interest.

How teachers teach should be directly related to how learners learn. Theories of cognitive development describe how learners learn new information and acquire new skills. At the most basic level, learning starts with real objects, followed by representations of the objects and concluding with symbolic and conceptual understandings.

	Concrete	**Pictorial**	**Abstract**
Characteristics	Hands on exploration	Transition from concrete to abstract	Use of written or spoken words and symbols
Examples	Use of real objects Manipulatives Hands-on exploration	Drawings Pictures	Numbers, expressions, vocabulary, formulas

Understanding this process is important in the teaching of mathematics in that early learners process best through hands-on activities which allow them to manipulate objects in order to practice problem-solving skills and developing conceptual understanding.

Learner-centered instruction is informed by constructivist theories in which children are actively involved in exploring and learning. While many examples of learner-centered instruction are hands-on in nature, some can also be delivered through the use of classroom technologies (e.g., interactive whiteboards, tablets, apps). Learner-centered instruction in math includes variations in grouping, as well as content focus, such as the following:

- **Cooperative Learning:** structured groups which combine positive interdependence (e.g., each person has an important contribution to the success of the entire group) with individual accountability to develop social skills as well as content knowledge through group interactions and processing

- **Collaborative Learning:** loosely structured groups that allow students to learn from and with each other

- **Peer Tutoring:** one student helps another student master a concept

- **Problem-Based Learning:** working together to solve complex, open-ended problems (e.g., creating a menu for Thanksgiving dinner for a given number of people which includes serving sizes/amounts and then using grocery ads to determine the cost per person for the dinner)

- **Simulations:** Depicting and modeling real-life situations (e.g., stock market game; getting "paid" for classroom tasks and then using the "money" to purchase goods or services)

- **Instructional Games:** Rule-guided competition for practicing and refining concepts (e.g., math bingo; drill and practice software or online apps)

- **Contextual Learning:** authentic real-life situations (e.g., learning math and science by having a class garden project)

Experiential learning often involves the use of manipulatives that enhance students' understanding of a concept. They can be physical or virtual. Particularly in mathematics and science classes, manipulatives give students concrete ways to assimilate concepts, but tangible materials are appropriate and helpful in all subject areas. For example, manipulatives help children develop the skill to subitize or instantly see or estimate how many items (up to about 7) are present and then perform iterations (successive estimations) as a problem solving approach for larger groups of items. The National Library of Virtual Manipulatives (*http://nlvm.usu.edu/en/nav/vlibrary.html*) provides a wealth of resources for numbers and operations, algebra, geometry, measurement, and data analysis and probability at different grade levels. Common mathematical manipulatives include the following:

Manipulative	Definition/Description	Concepts
Tiles	One-inch colored squares (usually red, green, yellow, blue)	Color, shape, patterns, estimation, counting, number concepts, equality, inequality, operations on whole numbers & fractions, probability, measurement, area, perimeter, surface area, even & odd numbers, prime & composite numbers, ratio, proportion, percent, integers, square & cubic numbers, numbers, spatial visualization

(continued)

(continued)

Manipulative	Definition/Description	Concepts
Capacity containers	Objects used to measure liquid or other pourable substances	Measurement, capacity, volume, estimation
Centimeter cubes	One cm cubes in various colors with sides that connect with each other	Number concepts, counting, place value, fact strategies, classification, sorting, colors, patterns, square and cubic numbers, equality, inequalities, averages, ratio, proportion, percent, symmetry, spatial visualization, area, perimeter, volume, surface area, transformation geometry, operation on whole numbers & fractions, even & odd numbers, prime & composite numbers, probability
Cuisenaire rods	A set of ten different colored, rectangular pieces ranging in lengths from 1 cm to 10 cm.	Classification, sorting, ordering, counting, number concepts, comparisons, fractions, ratios, proportions, place value, patterns, even & odd numbers, prime & composite numbers, logical reasoning, estimation, operations on whole numbers
Fraction tiles and circles	An assortment of objects in different sizes, shapes, and colors that can be combined to form larger shapes.	Fractions-meaning, recognition, classification, sorting, comparing, ordering, number concepts, equivalence, operations, perimeter, area, percent.
2-D and 3-D shapes	Objects with length, width, and depth including cylindrical or cone-shaped surfaces.	Measurement, sorting, classifying, investigation of size, shape, color, logical reasoning, sequencing, patterns, symmetry, similarity, congruence, geometry
Attribute materials	A set of objects with different shapes, colors, and sizes to develop higher-level thinking	Sorting, classifying, investigation of size, shape, color, logical reasoning, sequencing, patterns, symmetry, similarity, congruence, thinking skills, geometry, organization of data
Counting Frame/ Abacus	An oblong frame with rows of wires or grooves along which beads are moved for calculating	Counting, sorting, classifying, investigation of size, shape, color, logical reasoning, sequencing, patterns, symmetry, operations on whole numbers, patterns, spatial visualization

Manipulative	Definition/Description	Concepts
Balance scale	A device for comparing the weight of two objects placed in pans hanging from each end of a suspended rod on a pedestal	Weight, mass, equality, inequality, equations, operations on whole numbers, estimation, measurement
Clocks	A device for measuring time, in hours, minutes, and, typically by rotating pointers to points, numbers, or Roman numerals	Measurement, estimation, whole numbers & fractions, counting, spatial visualization, order
Dominoes	A set of rectangular tiles with a line dividing its face into two square ends marked with a pattern of spots or left blank.	Counting, number concepts, facts, classification, sorting, patterns, logical reasoning, equality, inequality, percent, perimeter area
Geoboards	A board that uses rubber bands to form shapes around a lattice of protruding nails	Size, shape, counting, area, perimeter, circumference, symmetry, fractions, coordinate geometry, slopes, angles, Pythagorean theorem, estimation, percent, similarity, congruence, rotations, reflections, translations, classification, sorting, square numbers, polygons, spatial visualization, logical reasoning
Geometrical solids	Any object that has height, length, and depth.	Shape, size, relationships between area & volume. Volume, classification, sorting, measurement, spatial visualization
Money	Currency that is printed on paper or stamped into coins for buying things or services	Money, change, comparisons, counting, classifications, sorting equality, inequality, operations on whole numbers, decimals, fractions, probability, fact strategies, number concepts
Number cubes	A set of one-inch numbered cubes in various colors	Counting, number concepts, fact strategies, mental math, operations on whole numbers, fractions, decimals, probability, generation of problems, logical reasoning

(continued)

(continued)

Manipulative	Definition/Description	Concepts
Number cards	A set of cards that vary by number, symbols, shading and color	Counting, classification, sorting, comparisons, equality, inequality, order, fact strategies, number concepts, operations on whole numbers, fractions, decimals, logical reasoning, patterns, odd & even numbers, prime & composite numbers
Rulers and tape measures	A strip or cylinder of plastic, wood, metal, or other rigid material marked at regular intervals to draw straight lines or measure distances	Measurement, area, perimeter, constructions, estimation, operations on whole numbers, volume
Tangrams	A dissection puzzle consisting of seven flat shapes, called *tans*, which are put together to form shapes	Geometric concepts, spatial visualization, logical reasoning, fractions, similarity, congruence, area, perimeter, ratio, proportion, angles, classification, sorting, patterns, symmetry, reflections, translations, rotations

Among the many theories of cognitive development, one of the most influential is Piaget's Theory (and neo-Piagetian). The theory describes learning in discrete and predictable cognitive stages. Therefore, teachers who understand this theory can provide students with developmentally appropriate instruction. This theory also describes learners moving from simpler and concrete ways of thinking to more complex and abstract ways of thinking and problem solving. This is especially relevant for the teaching of mathematical concepts and practices. Although there are age ranges for each stage, these are estimates. Some children may reach a given stage earlier or later than their chronological age. K–6 students are typically at the pre-operational level in early grades and move through concrete operations and, in most cases, to formal operations by middle school.

Piaget's Theory of Cognitive Development

Stage	Age	Description	Cognitive Skill Development	Examples
Sensorimotor	Birth–2	Inability to think about or imagine things not immediately in sight	Trial and error experimentation with physical objects; intentional behaviors to achieve simple goals; recognition that objects not seen still exist; ability to symbolically represent physical objects as thought	Playing Peek-a-boo amuses infants because when the person "hides" behind hands or other object, the child perceives the person as "gone;" thus, when the person reappears (Peek a boo!), it's like a magic trick. Eventually the child realizes the person still exists behind the object and the game ceases to be amusing.
Pre-Operational	2–7	Development of symbolic thought in that the child can think about or imagine something that is not physically present; Inability to think in logical, adult-like ways	Rapid language development; imaginative play or role play; beginning logical (intuitive) thought; lacks a complete understanding of the concept of time	Use of manipulatives; Match a numeral (symbol) to the number of shapes it represents; Hands-on, make-believe activities like having a "store" in which students can pretend to be the buyer or seller with play money; sort objects by 1 dimension (e.g., all red beads in a box; all square beads in a box)
Concrete Operations	7–11	Development of reasoning skills in concrete and real-life situations	Ability to distinguish perspectives; ability to classify objects as belonging to two or more categories simultaneously; realization that an amount remains the same if transferred to different sized containers if nothing is taken away from the original amount	Use of manipulatives; classify items; sort by more than one dimension (e.g. all red, square beads in a box); order objects and numerals in terms of size or amount; place value; basic numerical problem-solving
Formal Operations	11 and older	Development of reasoning applied to abstract ideas as well as concrete objects and situations including math and science	Ability to apply logical reasoning to abstract ideas and hypothetical situations as well as to concrete objects and situations; development of reasoning in science and mathematics; can separate and control variables; proportional reasoning; conceptual understanding of fractions, percentages, decimals, and ratios	Use of variables and algebraic concepts; generating and testing hypotheses; identifying cause and effects; consequences of actions

For teachers, this theoretical perspective has many important implications. For example, teachers must create enriched environments that present learners with multiple opportunities to encounter new and unfamiliar stimuli—be they objects or ideas. Teachers must also provide learners with opportunities to engage in extended dialogue with adults; according to Piaget's Theory, conversational interactions with adults are a key component of learning in the classroom. In math, this would be reflected in the teacher's ability to communicate mathematical concepts in a way that makes sense to children while also focusing on the language of math.

Using educational scaffolding in math provides guidance and support to students in the learning process. Ideally, educational scaffolding

- provides direction,

- uses think-alouds to model thought processes,

- clarifies purpose,

- keeps students on task,

- provides the assessment (rubric) to clarify expectations,

- supplies some suggestions for additional sources, and

- fosters thinking at a variety of levels in Bloom's Taxonomy.

Some teachers do not encourage students to question them or class content. However, to become critical thinkers, students need to learn positive ways to question authority. This means that teachers model critical thinking skills in the classroom by modeling, think-alouds, direct instruction or other means. For example, teachers can show students how to question authority by examining and evaluating readings—whether from textbooks or other sources. Teachers can also demonstrate how to question authority by exposing advertising claims and gimmicks—particularly those that seem to manipulate numbers.

Moreover, by allowing students to question them, teachers acknowledge that everyone is a learner. Everyone should participate in a lifelong process of continuous learning. It is no shame or disgrace for a teacher to admit that sometimes he or she doesn't know the answer to every question. This gives the teacher the opportunity to show students how adults think, how they have a level of awareness (metacognition) even when they do not know something, and how they go about finding answers to their questions. A teacher who admits to not having all the answers has the opportunity to work with students to find answers and/or to help students realize that some of life's most difficult questions do not have easy answers.

Effective teachers express their respect for students as learners by being open to questioning and encouraging investigation. Teachers' affirmations include smiles and nods of approval, positive comments (such as, *That's a good answer.*), and encouraging prompts (such as, *That may seem like a reasonable answer, but can you think of a different answer?* or *Can you explain what you mean by that answer?*). Acknowledging students also means supporting students' voices and giving them ample opportunities to express their ideas, share their opinions, and contribute to class discussions. These opportunities can include times of oral or online discussions as well as written assignments.

Regardless of which theoretical perspective teachers adopt—and even if at times they find themselves taking a rather eclectic approach and borrowing elements from several theoretical bases—it is helpful for teachers to consider whether they are structuring their classrooms to satisfy learners' needs or merely their own needs as teachers. Furthermore, if a teacher's goal is to become a more effective instructor by facilitating learners' knowledge and skill acquisition, then that teacher will engage continuously in a process of self-examination and self-evaluation.

Skill 1.2: Analyze and Discriminate Among Various Problem Structures with Unknowns in all Positions in Order to Develop Student Understanding of Operations

Life is full of unknowns. Can I get to my destination without filling up with gas? If I eat 3 servings of something, how will that affect my diet? If it takes twenty minutes to get to work, what time should I leave? Teachers need to present the concept of unknowns, or variables, in natural, authentic, and varied contexts. In early grades, an unknown is often represented as a line or box (e.g., $6 + \underline{\quad} = 9$; $6 + \square = 9$). For example, in the operation of addition, the unknown could be one of the addends or it could be the sum. Students should be taught that phrases such as *put-together*, *joined with*, and *added to*, *total* and *sum* indicate the operation of addition. Phrases such as *take-apart*, *subtract*, *without*, *from* and *minus* indicate the operation of subtraction, or separating one part from another part. Multiplication is a form of repeated addition ($a \times b = c$) in which a number (a) is added (b) times to form a new number called the product (c). Thus, 3×4 and $3 + 3 + 3 + 3$ both equal 12. Division is the operation of determining how many times one quantity is contained in another ($\frac{a}{b} = c$). Thus, division is repeated subtraction. For example, $\frac{12}{3}$ is really asking how many 3s are in 12 ($12 - 3 = 9$; $9 - 3 = 6$; $6 - 3 = 3$; $3 - 3 = 0$). Thus, the 3 was subtracted 4 times. Division has the same inverse relationship to multiplication that subtraction has to addition. What multiplication does, division undoes. Arrays (ordered arrangements of items) can help students understand this process visually.

Example of an Array 3 × 4

Skill 1.3: Analyze and Evaluate the Validity of a Student's Mathematical Model or Argument Used for Problem Solving

Although students often view "getting the correct answer" as the goal of problem-solving, the real goal is to use a process—either by standard algorithms (traditional processes or sets of rules used in calculations or problem-solving) or inventive strategies (processes other than algorithms or simple counting which result in correct answers)—to solve the problem. This is sometimes termed as teaching math through problem-solving in which there may be more than one way to solve a problem (Van De Walle, Karp, Lovin, and Bay-Williams, 2014). These focus student attention on making sense in context and emphasize math as a process for solving problems, while building student engagement and confidence. The following table shows how solving a simple math problem (41 + 52) could be approached through standard algorithm or invented strategy:

Standard Algorithm   41
                            +52
                            Solution:
                            Add the ones column = 3
                            Add the tens column = 9
                            Correct answer is 93

Invented Strategy   41
                            +52
                            Solution:
                            Add 40 + 50 = 90
                            Add 1 + 2 = 3
                            Correct answer is 93

Problems can be categorized as process, translation, application, and puzzles and the focus can be conceptual or procedural. The teacher's ability to analyze and evaluate the logic of a student's solution is more important than grading an answer as "correct" or "incorrect." In other words, it's not enough for the student to get the correct answer. The student should be able to explain or demonstrate the way in which the correct answer was determined. Aspects of analysis and evaluation include the following:

- Understanding what the problem is asking

- Creating a strategy for solving the problem

- Solving the problem

- Reflecting on the outcome

Types of Problems

Type	Definition	Example
Process	Higher-order situations in which innovation and creativity are used	An artist created performance art using 9 people. Each person was connected to each of the other individuals using a different color of ribbon. How many pieces of ribbon did the artist use?
Translation	Situations which require one- or two-step computational understanding or algorithms	Maria can solve 2 math problems per minute. How many math problems can she solve in 10 minutes?
Application	Use of data and computation to solve real-world problems	A family of four spends $90 per week on food. What is the average cost of meals per day for each person?
Puzzle	Situations that require ingenuity for solution	Daisy, Rose, and Violet decided to buy flowers. One girl bought roses, the second girl purchased daisies, and the third girl got violets. None of the girls bought flowers matching her name. What kind of flowers did each girl get?

Skill 1.4: Interpret Individual Student Mathematics Assessment Data to Guide Instructional Decisions and Differentiate Instruction

While many people might think of assessment as a measure of student learning, it is also a measure of a teacher's instruction. Effective teachers continually view assessment as a vital and integral part of the teaching and learning process. Used daily as part of a sound instructional program, assessment can provide information about the effectiveness of the lesson, the method of delivery, the curriculum (in terms of meeting district goals and expectations), and information on how students are learning. As such, a student's individual score on an assessment is less important that determining the kind of errors a student made and why those errors occurred. This gives the teacher instructional control in that the teacher can use the data to make decisions about future instruction to meet a student's needs. A teacher should use a variety of methods to assess mathematical understanding and reasoning such as the following:

- Teacher-made tests

- Feedback on homework or in-class practice

- Quizzes

- Exit tickets or other end of class feedback

- Pre-tests

- Paper and pencil tests

- Projects, papers, and portfolios

- Machine scored tests

- Authentic assessments

- Observations and anecdotal records of student effort and performance

- Self- and peer assessments

- Criterion-referenced tests

- Norm-referenced tests

- Performance-based assessments

- Online tests

- Checklists and rubrics

- Portfolios

- Games and competitions

How assessments are constructed and administered can skew results. If a student doesn't understand the directions of the test or the vocabulary in a word problem, the student's ability to solve the problem is compromised. Additionally, students who have had previous negative math experiences may have anxiety issues that affect performance. An acceptable testing environment requires that mathematics teachers prepare students by emphasizing the critical knowledge they need to learn. This is accomplished by establishing a setting with clear instructions and fair tests for students to complete and giving feedback that praises correct responses and corrects errors and misunderstandings without making students feel inept.

As teachers review a student's work, they should be looking at incorrect responses as insights into a student's thinking. A single missed item may not provide much information; however, a pattern of errors can provide some of the following insights:

- did not read/follow instructions

- conceptual errors

- computational errors

- can use the correct formula but not apply it to real-world situations

- cannot explain logic of process

- does not understand math or academic vocabulary

- did not remember formula or process

- used incorrect formula to solve a problem

Additionally, individual conversations with a student might identify other issues (e.g., anxiety, tiredness, did not study for assessment, rushed through assessment) which might affect results.

Examples of Initial Math Assessments	
Screening	Given before students start a course or grade; generally administered individually or in small groups; purpose is to accurately place a student or identify if the student needs follow-up diagnostic testing
Diagnostic	Standardized tests, given individually, that identify a student's specific strengths or weaknesses; usually administered based on teacher observation or following screening test; used to determine if additional support or remediation is required.
Pre-Test	An informal, ungraded assessment that occurs immediately before an instructional unit or lesson; provides the teacher with insights about students' background knowledge in terms of the lesson content

(continued)

(continued)

Examples of Formative Math Assessments	
In-Class Practice, Exit Tickets, Homework	Immediate identification of misunderstandings of concepts and processes
Criterion-Referenced	Goal is to determine if a student has demonstrated mastery as determined by the criterion of the learning objective
Progress-Monitoring	A systematic and scientifically-based process in which students are assessed at regular intervals to determine how the level of performance following instruction compares to the expected level of performance in order to determine if students are moving toward mastery at a satisfactory pace.
Authentic (Performance)	Application and demonstration of skill outside of traditional testing through completion of a complex task such as a math project or contextual (real-life) example
Portfolio (Alternative)	Collection of individual student work over time that exemplify progress and understanding using formative and summative examples of math performance; useful for family-teacher conferencing.
Behavioral (Naturalistic)	Informal teacher observations of how students work together in groups, how they organize their work, or how they pay attention to details and instructions. Asking students to self-assess their work can provide great insight into the attitudes, work patterns, and ethics the students have.
Examples of Summative Assessments	
Unit Exam	Teacher-made assessment that occurs at the end of a block of instruction which may or may not use textbook problems or supplements as sources of problems and questions
Common Exam	An assessment created by all teachers who teach the same course; allows teachers to determine if instructional methods and student learning are the same from course to course
Standardized	Commercial, norm-referenced assessments that measure overall achievement and permit statistically valid conclusions about group and individual performance in reference to the norming group.

Skill 1.5: Select and Analyze Structured Experiences for Small and Large Groups of Students According to the Cognitive Complexity of the Task

Today's classrooms are diverse with learners at different stages and needs. A teacher's ability to organize students for learning is essential for fostering learning that is both effective and efficient. An organizational strategy should both engage students and differentiate instruction appropriately. This is often determined by the cognitive complexity of the task as well as by the needs of the students.

Cognitive Complexity in Terms of Depth of Knowledge

The complexity of a concept depends on the interaction of content demands (e.g., processing demands, level of abstraction, number of parts or steps, application) and student factors (background knowledge, ability and fluency in math processes). Florida Standards rate cognitive complexity in terms of a variation of Webb's (2002) Depth of Knowledge Levels.

Webb's Levels	Florida Standards Depth of Knowledge Levels	Definition	Examples
Level 1: Recall	Low: Recall	Rote memory (e.g., fact, definition, term) or fluent use of well-defined or simple 1-step procedures, algorithms, or application of formulas.	• Count to 100 by ones or tens. • Fluent use of addition, subtraction, multiplication, and division. • Enter data into a table.
Level 2: Basic Application of Skills & Concepts	Moderate: Basic Application of Skills & Concepts	Active mental engagement beyond a rote response that requires learners to make decisions about how to approach problems and think logically about their solutions.	• Apply properties of operations. • Measure, record and graph data. • Measure and estimate liquid volumes in standard units.
Level 3: Strategic Thinking & Complex Reasoning	High: Strategic Thinking & Complex Reasoning	Ability to reason, plan, and use evidence in abstract and authentic ways as well as the ability to make conjectures based on results and verbally explain one's thinking processes.	• Given a real-world situation, formulate a mathematical problem. • Organize, show, and interpret data based on experiments or observations. • Justify solutions.
Level 4: Extended Thinking & Complex Reasoning			

Deciding How to Structure Learning Experiences

Analysis of cognitive complexity depends on a teacher's understanding of the content as well as knowledge of the specific student strengths and needs in a given class. The BASE model (Hawbaker, B., Balong, M Buckwalter, S., & Bock, S., 2001), originally designed for co-planning among two or more teachers, can also help individual teachers analyze and select experiences according to the cognitive complexity of a task.

BASE Model

Stage	Questions	Geometric Shapes
Big Ideas	What are the essential concepts? What do you want all students to learn (most basic concepts)? What do you want most students to learn (more advanced concepts)? What do you want some students to learn (most advanced concepts)?	All students should identify basic shapes of square, triangle, rectangle, parallelogram, and rhombus. Most students should identify the relationships between degrees and angles. Some students should demonstrate how to find the degree of an unknown angle, given the degrees of other angles.
Analyze areas of difficulty	What is likely to pose difficulties for students in terms of concepts, processes, or prior knowledge requisites?	Students may think of degree as temperature. Students need to understand concepts of parallel and opposite. Students need to demonstrate basic subtraction skills.
Strategies and Supports	What scaffolds are needed in terms of grouping, materials, guides, or technologies?	Clarify difference between degree as measurement of figures and as measurement of temperature. Have students work in pairs to identify shapes. Demonstrate how to use protractors to measure angles.
Evaluate the outcome	Did learning occur as planned? If not, what should be adjusted for future instruction or remediation?	

Grouping Students

The key to differentiating learning is choosing the right experience for the right group of students. This is based on flexible grouping.

Whole group instruction. Whole group instruction is a good way to start a lesson and should focus on core concepts that the teacher wants all students to learn. Whole group instruction should be brief and based on the age group of the students. Attention span is generally about the same as the age of the learners. Thus the attention span of a first grade student might be 5–7 minutes while the attention span of a fifth-grade student might be 10–12 minutes. Keep in mind that these are estimates with individual children exhibiting shorter or longer attention spans. Whole group instruction within that time-frame might be more of a mini-lesson and include the lesson's introduction, activation of prior knowledge, direct instruction and use of media (e.g., video clip).

Small Group Instruction. Small group instruction, generally 5–7 students, should focus on additional or different instruction, guided practice, reinforcement and review. To do small group instruction, the teacher should sit such that the students are clustered around and the teacher can still see the entire class past the small group. Grouping should be flexible in that one individual might be in one group to work on basic math facts but a different group for working on geometric concepts. A teacher doesn't want a student to feel like s/he is always in the "low" group.

Math Workshops. Math workshops build on the writing workshop tradition of instruction. The goal of math workshops is to develop both specific math skills and concepts. As in the writing workshop model, a math workshop begins with a direct instruction mini-lesson (whole or small group) which focuses on a single strategy or skill termed the *teaching point*. This lasts 10–15 minutes depending on student age and attention span. Following direct instruction, students are actively engaged by practicing the skill independently or with partners. The teacher confers with individual students or partners to coach skills and provide feedback on practice.

Math Centers. Classroom centers are specific classroom locations (e.g., designated tables, small rugs, or computer stations) created for the purpose of guided or independent practice. Most classrooms have several centers. The centers can focus on different subject areas (e.g., math center, science center and so on) or they can focus on different areas of math development (manipulation of 2D and 3D shapes; math facts review; math puzzles and games). Centers can be changed throughout the year as new topics are introduced and mastered or as students need additional practice and review. After instruction (e.g., whole group, small group, workshop), students are assigned to a center for a specific time period while the teacher works with a small group. The center should have a variety of ways to practice and refine the skill. Some activities may be for individuals and other for partners or small group practice.

Learning Partners/Math Buddies. Learning partners are usually peers who work together on the development and practice of skills. Math buddies use the same principle but with students from differing grades. For example, a fifth-grade student's buddy might be a first-grade student. Although it might be assumed that older students with better skills are the most logical candidates for being buddies to novice students, less able older students often make great buddies because they have an authentic reason to practice math skills close to their actual levels. For example, a fifth-grade student who needs to practice math facts might be a good buddy for a second grade student who is just learning math facts. Before partnering older and younger students, make sure that the older student wants to participate and that the older student has been given guidelines on how to work with the younger student.

Skill 1.6: Analyze Learning Progressions to Show How Students' Mathematical Knowledge, Skills, and Understanding Develop Over Time

While there is a progression of learning of mathematical knowledge, skills and understanding over time, this progression is complex. The interaction between mathematical concepts (generalizations about abstract ideas) and processes (sequences of steps) can blur. For example, while multiplication is actually a form of repeated addition, students often memorize multiplication tables without understanding the concepts they represent (repeated addition). A learning progression consists of conceptual and procedural steps in math over time. Grade and subject area standards define the expected progression of learning in terms of complexity. The following tables show how learning progresses in math standard domains in kindergarten, third, and sixth grade and an example of progression in geometry in each grade.

Kindergarten	Third Grade	Sixth Grade
• Counting and Cardinality • Mathematical Practice • Number and Operations in Base Ten • Geometry • Measurement and Data • Algebraic Thinking	• Geometry • Measurement and Data • Number and Operations • Number and Operations in Base Ten • Operations and Algebraic Thinking	• Expressions & Equations • Geometry • Ratios & Proportional Relationships • Statistics & Probability • The Number System

Grade	Example of Learning Progression in Geometry
K	Correctly name shapes regardless of their orientations or overall size.
1	Distinguish between defining attributes (e.g., triangles are closed and three-sided) versus non-defining attributes (e.g., color, orientation, overall size); build and draw shapes to possess defining attributes.
2	Recognize and draw shapes having specified attributes, such as a given number of angles or a given number of equal faces. Identify triangles, quadrilaterals, pentagons, hexagons, and cubes.
3	Understand that shapes in different categories (e.g., rhombuses, rectangles, and others) may share attributes (e.g., having four sides), and that the shared attributes can define a larger category (e.g., quadrilaterals). Recognize rhombuses, rectangles, and squares as examples of quadrilaterals, and draw examples of quadrilaterals that do not belong to any of these subcategories.
4	Draw points, lines, line segments, rays, angles (right, acute, obtuse), and perpendicular and parallel lines. Identify these in two-dimensional figures.
5	Use a pair of perpendicular number lines, called axes, to define a coordinate system, with the intersection of the lines (the origin) arranged to coincide with the 0 on each line and a given point in the plane located by using an ordered pair of numbers, called its coordinates. Understand that the first number indicates how far to travel from the origin in the direction of one axis, and the second number indicates how far to travel in the direction of the second axis, with the convention that the names of the two axes and the coordinates correspond (e.g., x-axis and x-coordinate, y-axis and y-coordinate).
6	Find the area of right triangles, other triangles, special quadrilaterals, and polygons by composing into rectangles or decomposing into triangles and other shapes; apply these techniques in the context of solving real-world and mathematical problems.

Skill 1.7: Distinguish Among the Components of Math Fluency

Fluency has the same meaning in math as it does in speaking or reading in that in refers to confident, correct, and accurate flow or use of content. Like fluency in reading, math fluency develops over time and through practice. Thus, teachers need to provide frequent opportunities to review and refine basic math skills.

Fluency allows the student to solve complex problems without losing mental processing to basic recall. For example, if a student is trying to multiply a three-digit number by a three-digit number, the student who is struggling with single digit computation can get lost in the process. However, fluency is not the same as rote memory. Fluency does involve automaticity in terms of quick and accurate usage of math facts, but not at the expense of actively thinking about the mathematical process. For example, a student must first know how to read a word problem or apply the correct formula to a problem in order to apply mathematical fluency skills. Additionally, the student has to analyze results to be sure that the solution is logical. The student who is fluent in math should also be able to flexibly adjust the rate of calculation according to purpose and personal skills. A student may realize that s/he often makes "careless errors" and will slow to check work. Or a student may recognize a problem as a variation of a problem that has already been well-understood and increase the rate of calculations as a result.

Competency 2: Knowledge of Operations, Algebraic Thinking, Counting and Numbers in Base Ten

A number system has infinite elements called numbers which can be represented both verbally in words and symbolically (e.g., 3, $\frac{1}{2}$, .5). Basic operations can be performed within the system and there are generalizations or rules that apply to the number system. Numbers represent an amount or a value. Base ten forms the foundation of our number system. This means that our system uses 10 digits (0–9) for counting with place values (ones, tens, hundreds) used to show values in terms of regrouping. Competency 2 focuses on the use of the system in terms of operations, algebraic thinking, counting and numbers in base ten.

Skill 2.1: Interpret and Extend Multiple Representations of Patterns and Functional Relationships by Using Tables, Graphs, Equations, Expressions, and Verbal Descriptions

Numbers may be represented in many ways. For example, the following chart shows equivalent representations for 2. Although each looks different and range from concrete to abstract, they all have the same value.

Form	Representation
Blocks	pp
Whole number	2
Integer	+2 or 2
Fraction	2/1
Decimal	2.0
Percent	200%
Exponential Notation	2^1
Scientific Notation	2×10^0

After students understand a basic representation of a value, the next step is to identify patterns (e.g., grouping and regrouping, expanded notation, place value, proportions) within a given representative form or with sets of information such as data.

Graphs and Tables

Graphs and tables are visual aids for sets of information. Often, the impact of numbers and statistics written in text is diminished by an overabundance of tedious numbers. A graph or table helps students rapidly identify patterns, organize a myriad of information, and trace long periods of decline or increase. The principal graphic forms are line graphs, bar graphs, pie charts, and tables.

Line Graphs

A **line graph** shows quantitative trends (increase, decrease, static) for one or more items over time. The lines are composed of connected points displayed on the graph through each period (e.g., years, days, seconds). For example, the following line graph depicts numbers of teachers and pupil/teacher ratios from 1960 to 2008.

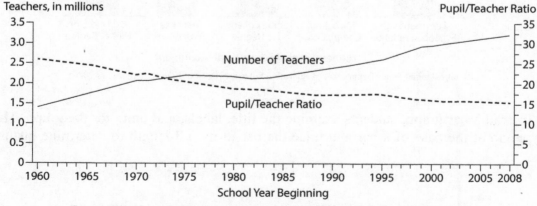

(Source: United States Department of Education Sciences *Digest of Education Statistics 2010*).

To read a line graph, examine (1) the title, heading or captions to identify the general group of items being compared, (2) the labels of headings for each item, and (3) the units used to measure the items. In using a line graph, one looks for trends (changes) or points of change of interest. For example, you might want to see how many teachers taught when you were in school and what the pupil/teacher ratios were during that time period.

Bar Graphs

A bar graph plots one or more dynamic elements of a subject and are used to compare and contrast quantitative values by showing the amount each element possesses. Although the units in which the items are measured must be equal, units can be of any size and start at any value. Sometimes the graph is three-dimensional, and the bars take on the dimension of depth; however, primary-level mathematics normally uses only two-dimensional, single-subject bar graphs. For example, the following bar graph shows unemployment rates of persons 25 years and older, by highest level of educational attainment in 2009. This graph shows that the individuals with more education are more likely to be employed.

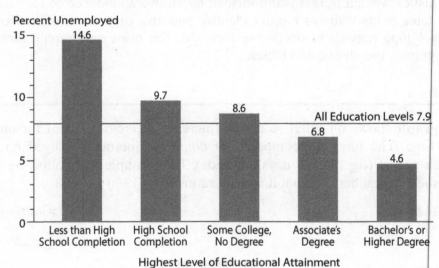

(Source: United States Department of Education Sciences *Digest of Education Statistics 2010*).

To read a bar graph, students examine the title, labels, and units for the graph. Then, they begin at the base of a bar and trace the bar to its full length to determine quantity.

Finally, students cross-reference the other element of information that matches the length of the bar.

Pie (Circle) Charts

A pie (or circle) chart shows how a whole unit is divided into parts. It helps a learner visualize percentages of a particular subject. An entire pie represents 100% of a given quantity. The measurement of the pie slices correspond to their respective shares of the 100. In the following pie chart, the whole is education for individuals 25 years and older. It is divided by level of education attained. This chart shows that, of the total number, the greatest number of individuals completed high school. The smallest group consists of individuals with doctoral degrees.

Highest Level of Education Attained by Individuals 25 Years and Older March 2010

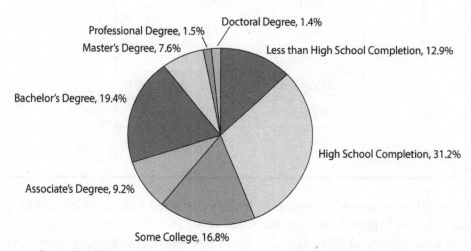

(Source: United States Department of Education Sciences *Digest of Education Statistics 2010*).

To read a pie chart, students choose the element of the subject that interests them and compare its size to those of the other elements. Students must be careful not to assume that elements that are similar in size are equal. The exact percentage of each element will be listed in or near that slice of the chart.

Tables

A table organizes related information into rows and columns. It is useful because it can convey large amounts of information within a confined area. To read a table, students cross-reference the column headings that run horizontally across the top of the table with the row headings that run vertically down the left side of the table. Students can scan the table for the information by reading line by line, as if reading regular text, while referring to the appropriate headings of the table to interpret the information listed. Note that some tables possess horizontal subheadings, which further ease the separation of different areas of information.

The following is an example of a unit conversion table that students might see in an elementary mathematics textbook:

Metric Units	Customary Units
1 meter	39.37 inches
1 meter	1.09 yards
1 kilometer	.62 mile
1 kilogram	2.2 pounds
1 liter	1.057 quarts

Equations

Equations allow learners to express equality between values using equal signs (=). This means that two expressions have the same value $(6 + 3 = 2 + 7)$ or that an expression is equivalent to a numerical value $(6 + 3 = 9)$. While learners often interpret an equal sign as a signal to complete the calculation on one side to get the answer, equal signs actually translate into *is the same as*. Equations that contain only numbers are called number sentences. For example, young children manipulating blocks might say "Two red blocks put together with three red blocks is the same as five red blocks." This would eventually be symbolized and understood as $2 + 3 = 5$.

Symbolic and Verbal Expressions

Expressions and equations are not synonyms although some equations can be expressions or contain expressions. Expressions are symbolic statements and can also show relationships such as greater than (>), less than (<), or values. Expressions can use constants (numbers such as 5, –7 or 0) or variables $(3x)$ and show grouping and operations using parentheses and brackets. Verbal expressions are the language used to express math symbols. These standardized terms facilitate clear communication. For example, instead of describing 2^2 as *the numeral 2 with another two written in a smaller size font to the right and a bit above it,* one can say it is *two squared.*

Algebraic expressions represent relationships among varying numbers (variables). For example, if S represents the number of students in a school and T represents the number of teachers, the total number of students and teachers in the school is $S + T$. If the school has 10 times as many students as teachers, an algebraic expression equating the number of students and teachers in the school is $S = 10T$. (Note that if either the number of students or the number of teachers is known, the other quantity can be found.)

Students should be able to generalize and extend patterns of functional relationships in algebra. This skill involves synthesizing which is at the third level in *Webb's Depth of Knowledge.* Synthesizing involves putting information together in a new, creative way. An example of a synthesis question is:

> *Create a graph to illustrate what you think will be the total number of cars purchased in the year 2015 if purchases continue as they have in the years 2006 through 2014.*

Given the factual knowledge on car purchases from a given chart, students should be able to develop or synthesize the information and generate reasonable numbers.

Skill 2.2: Select the Representation of an Algebraic Expression, Equation, or Inequality that Models a Real-World Situation

Many people tend to dread word problems; however, word problems are really logical real-world problems. Few people are asked to solve 45×25. Computations occur in the context of life. At the elementary level, real-world problems start with simple problems rather than complex ones. That is, a simple problem is a single computation. A complex problem consists of several simple problems combined. For example, a simple real-world problem might be that someone wants to put a fence around a specific area. Given the dimensions of length and width, the problem is actually a simple area problem for a rectangle. The following chart outlines steps for solving simple math problems.

Steps for Solving Math Problems

Problem Statement

A third-grade class is planting a school garden. The garden is 45 feet long and 25 feet wide. A fence is needed around the entire garden. How many feet of fencing is needed?

Steps	Examples
1. Read the whole problem to get the general idea. Visualize the situation and sketch a rough drawing whenever possible. Identify unfamiliar words or phrases and try to interpret them.	The class wants to plant a garden. The garden needs to be fenced so we need to know how much fencing material is needed to enclose the garden. 25 ▭ 45
2. Identify the specific question to be answered. It is usually found in the last sentence or part of the problem.	How much fencing material is needed to enclose a garden?
3. Reread the problem more slowly to identify the facts that are given.	Garden is 45 feet long. Garden is 25 feet wide.
4. Decide which processes are needed to solve the problem. Watch for key words that may imply operation (i.e., *the total number* and *sum*, all indicate addition; *times* and × indicate multiplication).	Figure out the distance (length) around the garden. Adding the length of each side would provide the answer. OR if students know the concept and formula for perimeter (2L + 2W = perimeter) use that.
5. If possible, estimate the answer.	45 could be rounded to 50, so 50 + 50 + 25 + 25 = 150. The answer should be close to 150.
6. Work the problem.	25 + 45 + 25 + 45 = 140 2(25) + 2(45) = 50 + 90 = 140
7. Check your answer against your original estimate.	Is 140 less than 150 (estimate)? Yes.
8. Recheck your answer.	If the answer seems incorrect, go back to Step 1.

There are two keys to solving word problems. The first key is to put the problems in context and think about the logic and the reasonableness of the answer. For example, if you have to determine how much 35 easy payments of $16 will be, you might realize that addition (35 + 16 = 51) doesn't seem to fit because 1 payment would be $16, 2 payments would be $16 + $16 = $32, 3 payments would be $16 + $16 + 16 = $48 and so on. If just 3 payments are $48, 16 payments would be much greater than that so addition is not a logical process. Similarly, subtraction and division will result in a smaller amount. The logical and simpler operation is multiplication.

The second key to converting word problems into numeric equations lies in translating words and phrases into numbers and operations. Look for "key" words in solving problems. The words provide clues as to which operation to use. The following chart provides a list of common key words for each operation as well as examples of their use in word problems. When translating, make sure that the equation accurately matches the information and relationships given in the real world problem.

Operation	Key Words	Examples
Addition	Increased by More than Combined Together Total of Sum Added to	The class size of 25 was increased by 5. How many students are in the class? 25 + 5 = Mr. Smith has 5 more students in his class that Ms. Jones. Ms. Jones has 25 students in her class. How many students does Mr. Smith have? 25 + 5 = If one math exercise has 25 problems and a second exercise has 5 problems, what is the combined number of problems in both exercises? 25 + 5 =
Subtraction	Decreased by Minus Less Difference of Difference between Less than Fewer than Reduced by	Mr. Smith's class was decreased by 5. Mr. Smith had 25 students last year. How many does he have now? 25 − 5 = How much is 25 minus 5? 25 − 5 = What is 25 students less 5 students? 25 − 5 =

(continued)

Operation	Key Words	Examples
Subtraction (cont'd)		There is a difference of 5 students between Mr. Smith's class this year and his class last year. His class last year had 25 students. How many is in his class this year? $25 - 5 =$ The difference between the number of students in Mr. Smith's class last year (25 students) and the number in his class this year is 5. How many students are in his class this year? $25 - 5 =$ Mr. Smith's class this year is 5 less than his class last year. Last year he had 25 students. How many does he now have? $25 - 5 =$ Mr. Smith has 5 fewer students than he had last year. Last year he had 25 students. How many students are in his class this year? $25 - 5 =$ Mr. Smith's class of 25 was reduced by 5. How many students are in the class now? $25 - 5 =$
Multiplication	Times Multiplied by Product of Increased by a factor of	The length of a classroom is two times the width of the classroom. The width is 20 feet. What is the length? $2 \times 20 =$ The length of the classroom is 2 multiplied by the width. The width is 20. What is the length? $2 \times 20 =$ The product of a classroom's width (20 feet) and 2 equals its length. What is the length? $2 \times 20 =$ The width of a classroom was increased by a factor of 2 to determine the length of the classroom. What is the length of the classroom? $2 \times 20 =$

(continued)

Operation	Key Words	Examples
Division	How many to each How many groups Share Separate Equal groups Divide Quotient Per	Mr. Smith has 25 students in his class. If he has five groups of students, how many students are in each group? $\dfrac{25}{5} =$ Mr. Smith has 25 students in his class. If he wants to put exactly 5 students in each group, how many groups will he have? $\dfrac{25}{5} =$ The 25 students in Mr. Smith's class shared 5 computers. How many students share one computer? $\dfrac{25}{5} =$ Mr. Smith separated the 25 students in his class into 5 rooms. How many students were in each room? $\dfrac{25}{5} =$ Mr. Smith has 25 students in his class. If he wants to divide students into equal groups, how many groups will he have? $\dfrac{25}{5} =$ What is the quotient of 25 divided by 5? $\dfrac{25}{5} =$ Mr. Smith has 25 students in his class. He assigned 5 students per computer. How many computers does he have? $\dfrac{25}{5} =$

Mathematical reasoning involves many logical applications including analyzing problem situations, making conjectures, organizing information, and selecting strategies to solve problems. Problem-solvers must rely on both formal and informal reasoning processes and apply logic and reasonableness. Consider this problem:

Center Town Middle School has an enrollment of 640 students. One day, 28 students were absent. What percent of the total number of students were absent?

(A) 28%

(B) 1%

(C) 4%

(D) 25%

Even if someone forgot how to compute percentages, some possible answers could be rejected instantly: 28 is a "small-but-not-tiny" chunk of 640; answers like 1% and 25% are unreasonable.

Simple problems can be categorized into basic operations types depending on what element of the problem is missing.

Type	Real-World Example	Missing Element	Symbolic Translation
Element	Symbolic Translation	Sum (or total)	3 + 2 = SUM
	Tom got 5 books for his birthday. Sam gave him 3 books. Carmen gave him the other books. How many books did Carmen give Tom?	Addend	3 + ADDEND = 5
Subtraction (separating, part-part-to-whole problems, comparison)	Tom had 5 books and he lost 2 of the books. How many does he have left?	Difference	5 − 2 = DIFFERENCE
	Tom lost 2 books; however, he still has 3 books. How many did Tom originally have?	Minuend	MINUEND − 2 = 3
	Tom had 5 books but he lost some. He still has 3 books. How many did he lose?	Subtrahend	5 − SUBTRAHEND = 3

(continued)

Type	Real-World Example	Missing Element	Symbolic Translation
Multiplication (equal groups problems; repeated addition, area, volume and array)	Tom has 3 sets of books. There are 2 books in each set. How many books does Tom have?	Product	$3 \times 2 = \text{PRODUCT}$
	Tom has 6 books in all. There are 3 books to a set. How many sets of books does Tom have?	Factor	$3 \times \text{FACTOR} = 6$
Division Separating groups problems; measurement conversion; partitive)	Tom had 6 books. He wants to make sets of 2 books. How many sets will he have?	Quotient	QUOTIENT
	Tom has 6 books. He made 2 sets. How many books were in a set?	Divisor	$6 \div \text{DIVISOR} = 2$
	Tom has some books. He made 2 sets of 3 books. How many books did Tom have?	Dividend	$\text{DIVIDEND} \div 2 = 3$

▪ Skill 2.3: Analyze and Apply the Properties of Equality and Operations in the Context of Interpreting Solutions

Analyzing and interpreting the solution for errors is an essential component of solving a problem and reflects a child's metacognitive abilities—the ability to think about thinking and determine if it is correct. To do so in math, students need a basic understanding of how math works in terms of logical outcomes for solutions. Estimation and simple algorithms are useful tools that contribute to this kind of thinking. For example, if a student is adding $24 + 52$, the student might round the numbers to tens $20 + 50 = 70$, so the student knows that the answer should be close to 70. At the beginning that might be close enough; however, in time, the student would realize that in both cases, the numbers that were rounded were rounded down. This means that the correct answer will be more than the estimate of 70. Other simple algorithms might include realizing that any number multiplied by another number with a 5 in the ones place will end with 0 or 5 or that multiplying an even number by an even number will result in an even number. Simple fractional to percentage amounts (e.g., $50\% = \frac{1}{2}$ of the total or 25% is $\frac{1}{2}$ of whatever 50% would be) can also be quick and useful tools to determine if operations were accurate.

Skill 2.4: Determine Whether Two Algebraic Expressions Are Equivalent by Applying Properties of Operations or Equality

As students continue to develop cognitively, teachers can introduce properties of the number system. While young children will be able to understand the concepts in verbal terms and with concrete objects or numbers, the abstract nature of the properties themselves (e.g., $a + b = b + a$) are not as easily understood. The bridge from concrete to abstract thinking should occur by scaffolding with the goal of understanding how each property works, rather than simply learning the properties by rote. Properties of whole numbers (and some related terms) include the following:

Property	Meaning	Notation	Example	Notes
Multiplicative identity property of 1	Any number multiplied by 1 (also called the multiplicative identity) remains the same	$a \times 1 = a$	$45 \times 1 = 45$	
Property of reciprocals	Any number (except 0) multiplied by its reciprocal (1) divided by that number equals 1.	$a \times \dfrac{1}{a} = a$	$45 \times \dfrac{1}{45} = 1$	Division by 0 has no meaning. Avoid dividing by 0 when computing or solving equations and inequalities.
Additive identity property of 0	Adding 0 (the additive identity) to any number will not change the number.	$a + 0 = a$	$45 + 0 = 45$	
Commutative property for addition and multiplication	The order of adding addends or multiplying factors does not determine the sum or product.	$a + b = b + a$ $a \times b = b \times a$	$45 + 5 = 5 + 45$ $45 \times 5 = 5 \times 45$	Division and subtraction are not commutative.

(continued)

Property	Meaning	Notation	Example	Notes
Associative property for addition and multiplication	Associating, or grouping, three or more addends or factors in a different way does not change the sum or product.		$(3 + 7) + 5 =$ $3 + (7 + 5)$	Division and subtraction are not associative.
Distributive property of multiplication over addition	A number multiplied by the sum of two other numbers can be handed out, or distributed, to both numbers, multiplied by each of them separately, and the products added together.	$a(b + c) =$ $(a \times b) +$ $(a \times c)$	$6 \times (47) =$ $(6 \times 40) + (6 \times 7)$	The product of a number and a sum can be expressed as a sum of two products

Skill 2.5: Evaluate Expressions with Parentheses, Brackets, and Braces

Some mathematical expressions indicate several operations. Simplifying that type of expression requires following a universally agreed-upon order for performing each operation which can be remembered by the word **PEMDAS**, which stands for the phrase **P**lease **E**xcuse **M**y **D**ear **A**unt **S**ally:

- terms inside **P**arentheses or brackets

- **E**xponents and roots

- **M**ultiplication and **D**ivision *as they appear left to right*

- **A**ddition and **S**ubtraction as they appear left to right

Thus, solving the expression $3 + 7 \times 4 - 2$ requires multiplying 7 by 4 before doing the addition and subtraction to obtain the result of 29. For example, $6 \div (2 \times 1^3) - 2 =$ would be solved in the following way:

$$6 \div (2 \times 1^3) - 2 =$$

$$6 \div (2 \times 1) - 2 =$$

$$6 \div (2) - 2 =$$

$$3 - 2 = 1$$

The rules for performing operations on integers (whole numbers and their negative counterparts) and on fractions and decimal numbers where at least one number is negative are generally the same as the rules for performing operations on nonnegative numbers. The trick is to pay attention to the sign (the positive or negative value) of each answer.

The rules for both multiplication and division when at least one negative number is involved are as follows:

- Two positives OR two negatives give a positive.

- "Mixing" a positive and a negative gives a negative. For example, $-5 \times 3 = -15$ and $-24 \div 3 = -8$.

For adding or subtracting when at least one negative number is involved, it may be useful to think of the values as money, considering adding as "gaining," subtracting as "losing," and positive numbers as "credits," and negative numbers as "debts." Be careful, though: Adding or "gaining" -8 is actually losing 8.

Skill 2.6: Analyze and Apply Strategies to Solve Multistep Word Problems

As stated in a previous section, multistep word problems (complex) are two or more simple problems combined into a single problem. The same strategies, models, estimation, and reasonableness that apply to simple problems also apply to multistep problems. Additionally, students have to realize that one problem involves more than one step or procedure. For example, consider the following problem that takes the previous perimeter fencing problem a step further.

Steps for Solving Math Problems

Problem Statement

A garden is 45 feet long and 25 feet wide. How many fence posts would be required to place one in each corner and additional fence posts every 5 feet?

Steps	Examples
1. Read the whole problem to get the general idea. Visualize the situation in your mind and sketch a rough drawing whenever possible. Identify unfamiliar words or phrases and try to interpret them.	You have a garden and want to know how many fence posts are needed in order to enclose the garden.
2. Identify the specific question to be answered. It is usually found in the last sentence or part of the problem.	How many fence posts would be required to place one in each corner and additional fence posts every 5 feet?
3. Reread the problem more slowly to identify the facts that are given.	Garden is 45 feet long. Garden is 25 feet wide. Need fence posts every 5 feet and at corners.
4. Decide which processes are needed to solve the problem. Watch for key words that may imply operation (i.e., *the total number* and *sum*, all indicate addition; *times* and × indicate multiplication, etc.).	Figure out the perimeter (length around) the garden. Divide the perimeter by 5 because fence posts are 5 feet apart. Subtract the four corner posts.
5. If possible, estimate the answer.	Total perimeter is about $2 \times (50 + 25) = 150$ feet because 45 is close to 50. 150 feet ÷ 5 feet per post = 30 posts approximately. 30 posts − 4 corner posts = 26 (estimated number of posts).
6. Work the problem.	$2 \times (45 + 25) = 140$ $140 \div 5 = 28$ $28 - 4 = 24$
7. Check your answer against your original estimate.	Is 24 less than 26 (estimate)? Yes.
8. Recheck your answer.	If the answer seems incorrect, go back to Step 1.

Skill 2.7: Apply Number Theory Concepts

Number theory examines and categorizes the properties of integers in terms of mathematical relationships. For example, even numbers are always divisible by 2 (separated into two equal groups); however, odd numbers cannot be divided evenly by 2. Parity is the mathematical concept for classifying integers as even or odd.

Factors are any of the numbers or symbols in mathematics that, when multiplied together, form a product. For example, the whole-number factors of 12 are 1, 2, 3, 4, 6, and 12. A number with exactly two whole-number factors—1 and the number itself—is a prime number. The first few primes are 2, 3, 5, 7, 11, 13, and 17. Most other whole numbers are **composite numbers;** that is, they can be expressed as several whole-number factors (e.g., 12 can be expressed by 1×12; 2×6; or 3×4). The number 1 is neither prime nor composite; it has only one whole-number factor.

The multiples of any whole number are the results of multiplying that whole number by the counting numbers. The multiples of 7 are 7, 14, 21, 28, and so on. Every whole number has an infinite number of multiples.

The rules of divisibility are as follows:

- Division by zero is not possible.

- Only whole numbers ending in 0, 2, 4, 6, and 8 are divisible by 2.

- Only whole numbers whose digits add up to a number divisible by 3 are divisible by 3, as the following chart illustrates:

Number	Sum of Digits	Divisible by 3?
12	3	Yes
21	3	Yes
44	8	No
56	11	No
158	14	No

- A number is divisible by 4 if the last two digits are divisible by 4, as the following chart illustrates:

Number	Last Two Digits	Divisible by 4?
28	28	Yes
128	28	Yes
311	11	No
816	16	Yes

- A number is divisible by 5 if the ones place has a 5 or zero.

- A number is divisible by 6 if it is divisible by both 2 and 3. For example, 666 has digits that add to 18, which is divisible by 3; it ends in 6 so it is divisible by 2. Because it is divisible by both 2 and 3, it is also divisible by 6.

- A number is divisible by 8 if the last three digits are divisible by 8. For example, 99816 has 816 as its last digits; 800 can be divided evenly by 8, and 16 is divisible by 8. The number 8 is, therefore, a factor of 99816.

- A number is divisible by 9 if the sum of the digits is divisible by 9. The number 245 has digits that add to 11; 11 is not evenly divisible by 9, so 9 is not a divisor of 245. The number 333 has digits that add to the number 9; because 9 goes evenly into 9,333 is divisible by 9.

- A number that has a 0 in the ones place is divisible by 10.

Skill 2.8: Identify Strategies Based on Place Value to Perform Multidigit Arithmetic

Adding two- and three-digit numbers uses place value to build on the understanding of addition with single numbers. The digits in the ones place are added (see single digit example on the next page). If the resulting sum is more than a single digit, the value in the ones place is written and the number in the tens place is added to the other numbers in the tens place. The process is the same for additional digits that result in two-digit numbers in other positions (e.g., tens place; hundreds place).

Type	Single Digit Example	Two-Digit Example	Three-Digit Example		
Example	6 $+\ 6$ 12	$\begin{array}{c}(1)\\ 26\\ +26\\ \hline 2\end{array}$ $\begin{array}{c}26\\ +26\\ \hline 52\end{array}$	$\begin{array}{c}(1)\\ 266\\ +\ 266\\ \hline 2\end{array}$	$\begin{array}{c}(1)\\ 266\\ +\ 266\\ \hline 32\end{array}$	$\begin{array}{c}(1)\\ 266\\ +\ 266\\ \hline 532\end{array}$
Explanation	6 + 6 is an addition fact resulting in a sum of 12.	6 + 6 is 12 (a two-digit sum) with 1 in the tens place and 2 in the ones place. The 2 is written under the ones place and the 1 (in parentheses) is added to numbers in the tens place (1 + 2 + 2 = 5). The answer is 52: the 5 is in the tens place and the 2 is in the ones place	6 + 6 is 12 (a two-digit sum) with 1 in the tens place and 2 in the ones place. The 2 is written under the ones place and the 1 (in parentheses) is added to numbers in the tens place (1 + 6 + 6 = 13). The 2 is written in the tens place and the 1 is added to the column for the hundreds place. The answer is 532. The 5 is in the hundreds place, the 3 is in the tens place and the 2 is in the ones place.		

Compensation is another addition strategy using place value. In this strategy, students think of two-digit numbers grouped by tens and ones. For example,

$$25 = 2 \text{ tens and } 5 \text{ ones}$$

$$+\ 32 = 3 \text{ tens and } 2 \text{ ones}$$

Therefore: 25 + 32 = 2 tens + 3 tens + 5 ones + 2 ones or 50 + 7 = 57

Competency 3: Knowledge of Fractions, Ratios, and Integers

After students understand basic numerical concepts (e.g., counting and simple operations), the next step is understanding their roles in representing relationships and in negative numbers. The focus of competency 3 is knowledge of fractions, ratios, and integers.

Skill 3.1: Compare Fractions, Integers, and Integers with Integer Exponents and Place Them on a Number Line

Many children start school with some knowledge of the number sequence. Their parents probably taught them in a rote manner to count from 1 to 10. These children have used the **counting numbers** (1, 2, 3, etc.). Early in school, children learn about other sets of numbers. The next set that they encounter is the set of **whole numbers** (0, 1, 2, 3, etc.).

Students discover a new sequence of numbers when they learn about **negative numbers**. Many teachers use a number line, a temperature thermometer, or even a countdown clock, similar to what is used at a satellite launch, to show the integers: . . . . –5, –4, –3, –2, –1, 0, +1, +2, +3, +4 . . . .

Students also encounter **fractions** or **rational numbers**. The sequence of rational numbers varies according to the starting fraction. For example, starting at $\frac{1}{4}$, the sequence of rationals is $\frac{2}{4}$, $\frac{3}{4}$, $\frac{4}{4}$ (1). All these sets of numbers can help children to see sequencing and patterning.

Integers are numbers preceded by either a positive (+) or negative (–) sign. An integer presented without a sign is assumed to be positive (e.g., 4 means +4). On a number line, integers to the left of zero are negative and integers to the right of zero are positive.

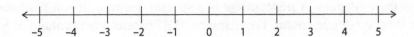

All integers can be written as fractions, but not all fractions can be written as integers.

Common fractions are in the form $\frac{a}{b}$, where a and b are whole numbers. Integers can be expressed as fractions, but not all fractions can be expressed as integers. For example, the number 4 can be expressed as $\frac{4}{1}$. However, the fraction $\frac{1}{4}$ cannot be expressed as an integer. There are more fractions than whole numbers because between every integer is a fraction. Between the fraction and the whole number is another fraction; between the fraction and the other fraction is another fraction, and so on. For example, $\frac{1}{4}$ is between 0 and $\frac{1}{2}$. $\frac{1}{8}$ is between 0 and $\frac{1}{4}$. $\frac{1}{16}$ is between 0 and $\frac{1}{8}$. Negative and positive fractions are not integers (unless they are equivalent to whole numbers or their negative counterparts). Placing fractions on a number line help students visualize size and order of the fractions. For example:

Fraction Number Lines

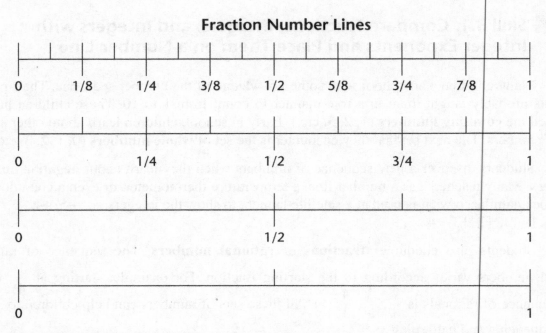

Decimal numbers are fractions written in special notation. For instance, 0.25 is the same as the fraction ¼. Thus, all decimal numbers are actually fractions. When expressed as decimals, some fractions terminate (end) and some do not. For instance, 0.315 is a **terminating decimal**; however, 0.0575757. . . is a **repeating decimal** (nonterminating). Because a decimal is the same as a fraction, there are more decimals than integers, just as there are more fractions than integers. A **percentage** is a special decimal. It is a fraction or ratio with 100 understood as the denominator. For instance, 0.87 equals a percentage of 87.

Decimal Number Lines

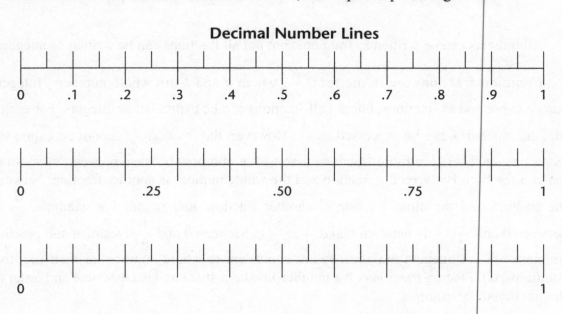

Fractions, decimal numbers, and percentages are different ways of representing values. One form can be converted to the others. For example, the fraction ¼ can be converted to either the decimal .25 or the percentage 25%. Conversions can be done by hand or by using a calculator.

Conversion Tips			
Task	**Process**	**Example**	**Notes**
Convert fraction to a decimal	Divide numerator by denominator	$\frac{1}{4}$ becomes 0.25 when 1 is divided by 4 $$\begin{array}{r} .25 \\ 4\overline{)1.00} \\ -80 \\ \hline 20 \end{array}$$	If the fraction includes a whole number, as in $2\frac{3}{5}$, the whole number is not a part of the division. The decimal number may terminate or repeat. Converting a simple fraction to a decimal number never results in an irrational number.
Convert nonrepeating (terminating) decimal to fraction in lowest terms	Write decimal as a fraction with the denominator a power of 10 and then reduce to lowest terms	0.125 can be written as 125/1,000, which reduces to 1/8.	
Convert decimal to percent	Shift decimal point 2 places to the right and add percent symbol (%)	.145 = 14.5%	If the number preceding the percent symbol is a whole number, there is no need to show the decimal point.
Convert percent to decimal	Shift decimal point 2 places to the left and drop the percent symbol (%)	68.8% = .688	
Convert percent to a fraction	Write percent (without percent symbol) over 100 and reduce to lowest terms	$25\% = \frac{25}{100} = \frac{1}{4}$	

Exponential notation is a way to show repeated multiplication more simply. For example, $2 \times 2 \times 2$ in exponential notation is 2^3 and is equal to 8. (Note that 2^3 does not mean 2×3.) The 2 is called the **base**. The 3 is called the **exponent** or **power**. Thus, a base of 2 with an exponent of 3 is read *2 to the 3rd power* or *2 to the power of 3*. An exponent of 1 is equivalent to the base number. For example 3^1 is equivalent to 3, 5^1 is equivalent to 5, and 9^1 is equivalent to 9. An exponent of 0 for any number is equivalent to 1.

Scientific notation is a special form of exponential notation most useful for very large or very small real numbers in which a number (n) is represented as between 1 and 10 multiplied by a power of 10. In large numbers, the exponent is positive and shows the number of places to the left. For example, 1,000,000,000 can be rewritten as 1×10^9. The exponent ^{9} shows the decimal has moved 9 places to the left to form a number between 1 and 10. In small numbers (e.g., less than 1), the exponent is negative and shows the number of places to the right. For example, 0.0001 can be rewritten as 1.0×10^{-4}. The exponent $^{-4}$ shows the decimal has moved 4 places to the right. An exponent ^{0} is equivalent to the original number. For example, 3.0×10^0 is 3 because the exponent ^{0} shows the decimal hasn't been moved in either direction.

Number	Scientific Notation
1956	1.956×10^3
0.0036	3.6×10^{-3}
59600000	5.96×10^7

Some examples are shown in the following chart:

10^3	$10 \cdot 10 \cdot 10$	1000
10^2	$10 \cdot 10$	100
10^1	10	10
10^0	1	1
10^{-1}	$\dfrac{1}{10}$	0.1
10^{-2}	$\dfrac{1}{10 \cdot 10} = \dfrac{1}{100}$	0.01
10^{-3}	$\dfrac{1}{10 \cdot 10 \cdot 10} = \dfrac{1}{1000}$	0.001

Skill 3.2: Convert Among Standard Measurement Units Within and Between Measurement Systems (e.g., Metric, U.S. Customary) in the Context of Multistep, Real-World Problems

Conversion problems, even simple ones, require some degree of multiple steps. For example, a box weighs 2 pounds. How many kilograms does it weigh? The first step is to remember or look up the formula: 1 pound = 2.2 kilograms. The next step is to compute the results 2 × 2.2 = 4.4 kilograms.

Real-world problems typically involve additional steps. For example: *You have a box and you want to know how much it weighs in metric terms.* Your first step is to weigh the box. You find it weighs 2 pounds. The second step is to identify which metric form is needed: grams, liters, or meters. Remembering that the metric unit of weight is grams, you now have to determine which unit is needed: grams, kilograms, milligrams. Choosing kilograms, you are ready to compute the conversion: 2 × 2.2 = 4.4 kilograms. Generally one would want to know weight for a purpose. Perhaps the problem is now stated as, "*You have a box you want to mail. You look up a packaging site on the internet and the packaging site indicates that the cost of mailing is $5.00 per kilogram. Your scale only provides weight in customary units and the box weighs 2 pounds. How much will it cost to mail the package?*" In this problem you need an additional step. Once you determine the weight (4.4 kilograms), you multiply that by the cost per kilogram ($5.00) to find that answer of $22.00.

Customary units are generally the same as U.S. units. Customary units of length include *inches, feet, yards,* and *miles.* Customary units of weight include *ounces, pounds,* and *tons.* Customary units of capacity (or volume) include *teaspoons, tablespoons, cups, pints, quarts,* and *gallons.*

The **metric system** of measurement relates to base-10 place value. The chart below lists the common metric prefixes:

Prefix	Meaning	Abbreviation
Kilo-	Thousand (1,000)	k
Deci-	Tenth (0.1)	d
Centi-	Hundredth (0.01)	c
Milli-	Thousandth (0.001)	m

The following table provides basic units of measurement in the metric system and their abbreviations by type:

Type	Basic Unit	Abbreviation
Linear (size or distance)	Meter	M
Mass (Weight)	Gram	G
Capacity (Volume)	Liter	L or l

The following table shows relationships among commonly used linear, weight, and volume metric units.

Linear	Weight (Mass)	Volume (Mass)
1 kilometer (km) = 1,000 m 1 meter (m) = 1.0 m 1 decimeter (dm) = 0.1 m 1 centimeter (cm) = 0.01 m 1 millimeter (mm) = 0.001 m	1 kilogram (kg) = 1,000 g gram (g) = 1.0 g 1 milligram (mg) = 0.001 g	1 liter (l) = 1,000 milliliters (ml) 1 deciliter (dl) = 100 ml; 10 cl 1 centiliter (cl) = 10 ml

Metric units of length include *millimeters, centimeters, decimeters, meters,* and *kilometers.* The centimeter is the basic metric unit of length, at least for short distances. About 2.5 centimeters are equal to 1 inch. The kilometer is a metric unit of length used for longer distances. It takes more than 1.5 kilometers to make a mile.

Metric units of weight include grams and kilograms. The gram is the basic metric unit of **mass** (which for many purposes is the same as weight). It takes about 28 grams to make 1 ounce.

Metric units of capacity or **volume** include milliliters and liters. The liter is the basic metric unit of volume (or capacity). A liter is slightly smaller than a quart; it takes more than four liters to make a gallon.

Here are some frequently used customary-to-metric ratios (values are approximate):

1 inch = 2.54 centimeters	
1 yard = 0.91 meter	
1 mile = 1.61 kilometers	
1 ounce = 28.35 grams	
1 pound = 2.2 kilograms	
1 quart = 0.94 liter	

One can determine the metric-to-customary conversions by taking the reciprocals of each of the factors noted above. For instance, 1 kilometer = 0.62 mile (computed by dividing 1 by 1.61).

Skill 3.3: Solve Problems Involving Addition, Subtraction, Multiplication, and Division of Fractions, Including Mixing Whole Numbers and Fractions, Decimals and Percents by Using Visual Models and Equations to Represent the Problems and Their Solutions

Numbers are the basic building blocks of mathematics. Numbers can be shown or represented in different ways. Ways to represent, or show, numbers include the following:

Type of Representation	Examples
Word Names	five, forty-eight, three hundred, five thousand
Standard Numerals	five, 48, 300, 5000
Pictorial models to show number of items (used more often in lower grades).	
Pictorial models to show relationships among items (used more often in upper grades).	

Although one number might seem like any other, there can be some conceptual differences. Basic kinds of numbers include the following:

Kinds of Numbers	Definition	Examples
Counting numbers	Numbers that start with 1 and continue	1, 2, 3, 4, 5, and so on
Whole Numbers	Counting numbers and zero	0, 1, 2, 3, 4, 5 and so on
Integers	Whole numbers preceded by either a + (positive) or − (negative) sign. Integers without signs are assumed to be positive.	−5, 2, +21, −350, 0, +111
Common Fractions	Number in the form $\dfrac{a}{b}$ where a and b are whole numbers. The top number—the dividend—is called the numerator. The bottom number—the divisor—is called the denominator. Zero (0) can never be the denominator because division by 0 is undefined.	½, ¾, 11/100
Decimals	Fractions written in powers of 10 (10, 100, 100 and so on). A relationship exists between the number of digits following the period and the power it represents. 1 digit after the period represent a power of 10; 2 digits after the period represent a power of 100; 3 represent a power of 1000.	0.25 ($\dfrac{25}{100}$ which can be reduced to $\dfrac{1}{4}$), .1 ($\dfrac{1}{10}$); .02 ($\dfrac{2}{100}$ which can be reduced to $\dfrac{1}{50}$)

The ways in which numbers are manipulated or used are called **operations**. There are four basic mathematical operations.

Basic Operations and Symbols	Symbol	Definition	Examples
Addition (+)	+ (plus)	Calculating the sum of two or more numbers	$2 + 2; -7 + -14;$ $\frac{1}{2} + \frac{1}{4}; .22 + .05$
Subtraction (−)	− (minus)	Deducting one number from another	$2 - 2; -7 - -14;$ $\frac{1}{2} - \frac{1}{4}; .22 - .05$
Multiplication	× or · or ( ) (multiplied by)	Repeated addition; adding a number to itself a specified number of times	$2 \times 2; -7 \times -14;$ $\frac{1}{2} \times \frac{1}{4}; .22 \times .05$
Division	÷ or / (divided by)	Repeated subtraction; the number of times one number can be subtracted from another	$2 \div 2; -7 \div -14;$ $\frac{1}{2} \div \frac{1}{4}; .22 \div .05$

Visual models are one way to solve real world problems using whole numbers and fractions. This is especially important for developing concepts in early grades when students are thinking at more concrete levels.

In the following example, representative pictures of the items and grouping can be used to demonstrate the concept of half of an amount.

Bob has 4 pencils and 2 books. Sam has half as many pencils and books as Bob has. How many pencils and books does Sam have?

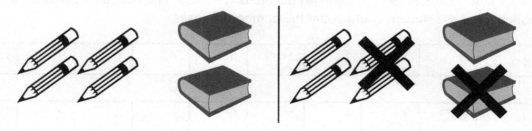

Students can learn to create their own rough sketches for solving problems. The following sketches demonstrate a variation of the previous problem.

Bob has 4 pencils and 2 books. Sam has half as many pencils and books as Bob has. How many pencils and books do both boys have?

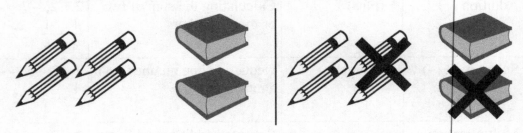

Part to whole fractions can also be depicted visually. For example, the following graphic might be used for the following problem: *Susie had a cookie but she wasn't very hungry. She ate $\frac{1}{3}$ of the cookie. How much cookie is left?* Once students realize that the graphic represents parts of a single unit, the graphic could be used for any part to whole problem. For example: *Susie is reading a book. She has read about $\frac{1}{3}$ of the book. About how much is left for her to read?*

Problems involving percentages and decimals both use specific aspects of the base ten system. Decimals divide whole units into tenths, hundredths and so on. Percentages represent portions of one unit divided into hundredths. For example, the following graphic can be used to use decimals in problem solving.

Chris got scores back on two quizzes. His score on the first quiz was 9.5. His score on the second quiz was 8.3. What is the total of his scores? This is actually addition in two-digits with the inclusion of decimals. However, a student could also think of it as adding two whole numbers (9 + 8) and two decimals (.5 + .3). The decimals could be shown as follows and the student could count the number of boxes.

1.	2.	.3	.4	.5	.6	.7	.8	.9	1.0

1.	2.	.3	.4	.5	.6	.7	.8	.9	1.0

A similar approach could be used with percentages in a two-step problem. For example: *Michelle scored 70% on the first exam. She scored 80% on the second exam. What is the average of her scores?* This could be solved using the following computations $\frac{(70\% + 80\%)}{2} = \frac{150\%}{2} = 75\%$. A student could also shade blocks to show the percentage of each score to get the total and divide by 2. Or the student could notice that there is only 1 box (10%) difference in the scores and that the halfway point between 70% and 80% would be 75%.

10%	20%	30%	40%	50%	60%	70%	80%	90%	100%

10%	20%	30%	40%	50%	60%	70%	80%	90%	100%

 ## Skill 3.4: Select the Representation that Best Represents the Problem and Solution, Given a Word Problem or Equation Involving Fractions

The words in word problems with fractions help students identify which process and which representations fit the situation. Any problem with a single dimension or factor using addition or subtraction is **linear** and can be represented on a number line.

Examples

Carlos is running in the hundred-yard dash. When he was half-way through the race he tripped and fell. How many yards had Carlos completed?

```
  ──────────────────────────────────────────>
  0  10  20  30  40  50  60  70  80  90  100
```

Liz is mailing a package of candy. The most the package can weigh is 2 pounds. Her package weighs $3\frac{1}{3}$ pounds. What is the weight of the candy she needs to remove?

```
              •              X
  ──────────────────────────────────────────>
  1            2            3    X    4            5
  ──────────────────────────────────────────>
                                  $\frac{1}{3}$  $\frac{2}{3}$  $\frac{3}{3}$
```

Area (also called **connected array**) and **set** problems can be used to demonstrate and develop conceptual understandings of multiplication using manipulatives such as Cuisenaire rods, centimeter cubes or tiles. For example, *Jacob has a piece of paper that is 3 inches by 4 inches. How much is half the area?* The student can visually see that the entire area is 12 square inches and that half of the area is 6 square inches.

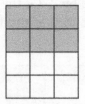

Cubes and tiles can also be used to demonstrate **sets** and multiples. For example, *in how many ways can 12 be represented?* This allows a student to see common relationships among the representations.

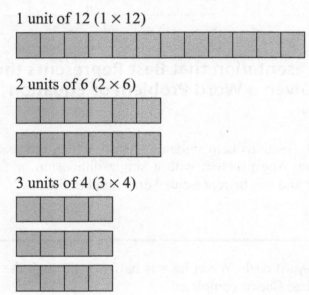

1 unit of 12 (1 × 12)

2 units of 6 (2 × 6)

3 units of 4 (3 × 4)

Skill 3.5: Solve Real-World Problems Involving Ratios and Proportions

Ratio notation is another way to show fractions. For example, $\frac{3}{5}$ can be expressed as *the ratio of 3 to 5*. The use of ratio notation emphasizes the relationship of one number to another. To show ratios, use numbers with a colon between them; therefore *4:5* is the same ratio as *4 to 5* and $\frac{4}{5}$. The relationship between two ratios is one of equality; that is, they are equivalent ratios. An equation of two equivalent ratios is one of proportion.

Examples of Equivalencies and Conversions

Fraction	Decimal	Percent	Ratio
$\frac{17}{20}$	.85	85%	17 to 20 or 17:20
$\frac{1}{2}$	.5	50%	1 to 2 or 1:2
$\frac{99}{100}$	.99	99%	99 to 100 or 99:100

PROBLEM

Pencils cost 2 for 25 cents. How many pencils can Teresa buy for 50 cents?

SOLUTION

Many real world problems involve ratio and proportion, especially those involving purchasing items. For example:

Two pencils for 25 cents suggests the **fixed ratio** of $\frac{2}{25}$:

$$\frac{2 \text{ (pencils)}}{25 \text{ (cents)}}$$

With a fixed ratio, it should be possible to figure out how many pencils Teresa can buy for 50 cents by setting up an equivalent ratio:

$$\frac{x \text{ (number of pencils)}}{50 \text{ (cents)}}$$

There are several ways to solve the equivalent ratio problem with the pencils. One way is to use cross multiplication:

$$\frac{x}{50} \times \frac{2}{25} = \frac{x \times 25}{2 \times 50} = 25x = 100.$$

Solving for x requires dividing 100 by 25 to get 4. Thus, Teresa can buy 4 pencils for 50 cents.

Another way to solve the problem is to set up a chart:

Pencils	Cost
2	25 cents
4	50 cents
x	75 cents

Competency 4: Knowledge of Measurement, Data, and Statistics

As students develop cognitively and understand basic mathematics operations and relationships, they are ready to apply these in other ways. Although measurement is often thought of in basic terms of size or area, Competency 4 focuses on measurement in terms of statistics and mathematical relationships.

Skill 4.1: Calculate and Interpret Statistics of Variability and Central Tendency

Student	Score
Adam	10
Erica	15
Joe	10
Roberto	25
Kim	5
Michelle	10
Kelly	40

Imagine that you have test scores from a group of students. The highest score a student could get is 40. The lowest score would be 0. How would you make sense of it? Luckily, data can be summarized in terms of **central tendency** and **variability**.

Identifying Central Tendency

Measures of central tendency of a set of values are ways to describe data as a single number. These measures consist of the **mean** (mathematical average), **median** (middle score), and **mode** (most frequent score).

To determine the mean of a set of numbers add the values in the set and divide by the total number of elements in the set. For example: If student test scores are 10, 15, 10, 25, 5, 10, and 44, the mean is $(10 + 15 + 10 + 25 + 5 + 10 + 44) \div 7 = 17$. Thus, two students scored above average and five scored below average.

To find the median, order a given set of numbers from smallest to largest; the median is the "middle" number. That is, half the numbers in the set of numbers are below the median and half the numbers in the set are above the median. For example, to find the median of the set of whole numbers 10, 15, 10, 25, 5, 10, 44, the first step is to order the set of numbers sequentially to get 5, 10, 10, 10, 15, 25, 44. Because 10 is the middle number (half of the numbers are below 10, half are above 10), 10 is the median of this set of whole numbers. So in terms of the student scores, the scores of six students were at or above the median. One student had a score below the median score.

If the set has an even number of numbers, the median is the mean of the middle two numbers. For instance, in the set of numbers 2, 4, 6, and 8, the median is the mean of 4 and 6, or 5.

To determine the mode, examine the data to see which value occurs most often. For example, the mode of the set of numbers 10, 15, 10, 25, 5, 10, 44 is the number 10 because it appears most frequently (three times). If two scores have the same frequency, the distribution is termed **bimodal**.

So for this set of the scores, the mean was 17, the median was 10, and the mode was 10. What conclusions can you draw from these measures? No single score tells the whole story of the scores. One conclusion is that one score (the score of 44) had a significant effect on all of the scores and that the number of students who had a score of 10 (3 students) also affected the measures of central tendency. In comparison, if all of the students had the same score (e.g., 7 scores of 25), the mean, the mode, and the median would be the same: 25.

Determining Variability

Where measures of central tendency compute a score to represent the majority of elements in a set, measures of variability look at differences among scores.

One way to think about variability is to identify high and low scores. The difference between these is called the **range.** To determine the range of a set of numbers, subtract the smallest number in the set from the largest number in the set. For example, the range of the set 10, 15, 10, 25, 5, 10, 44 is $44 - 5 = 39$.

A second way to think about variability is to determine the average distance from each data point to the mean—the **absolute standard deviation.** There are three steps to determining the absolute standard deviation using the set $\{10, 15, 10, 25, 5, 10, 44\}$. The absolute standard deviation is 10—how far, on average, the values are from the average of 17.

Steps	Procedure
1	Find the mean (average) of all of the numbers. $(10 + 15 + 10 + 25 + 5 + 10 + 44) = 119$ $119 \div 7 = 17$
2	Find the absolute value differences between each data value and the mean (subtract the smaller from the larger). $17 - 10 = 7$ $17 - 15 = 2$ $17 - 10 = 7$ $25 - 17 = 8$ $17 - 5 = 12$ $17 - 10 = 7$ $44 - 17 = 27$
3	Find the average of the absolute value differences. $(7 + 2 + 7 + 8 + 12 + 7 + 27) \div 7 = 70$ $70 \div 7 = 10$

Skill 4.2: Analyze and Interpret Data Through the Use of Frequency Tables and Graphs

Interpreting—rather than just reading—a table, chart, graph, or plot requires thinking at level 3 of *Webb's Depth of Knowledge Ratings* as used in Florida. Students must not only read the data (numbers and words) on the visual representation, but also understand what the data means. Contextual problems and data are most meaningful in helping students achieve this goal. For example, data could include absences by day of the week, frequency of specific foods on the lunch menu, or daily temperature readings. The important point, however, is determining what the data means. For example, perhaps a class sees that students are more likely to be absent on Mondays. What might account for that? Or perhaps green beans appear on the menu more than any other vegetable. What might be the reason for that? Or what is the relationship between temperature and season?

Frequency refers to how often something happens; therefore, a **frequency table** shows events and how often they occur. For example, perhaps a class wants to plan a field trip to a zoo so it is important for the weather to be good. The class looks at a table showing the number or frequency of rainy days by month. What month would be best to plan the trip?

Rainy Days

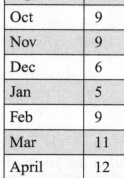

Sept	12
Oct	9
Nov	9
Dec	6
Jan	5
Feb	9
Mar	11
April	12
May	13

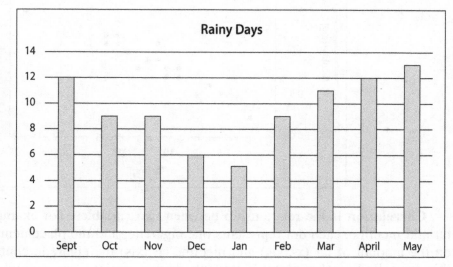

Frequency distributions can also be depicted as bar or line graphs.

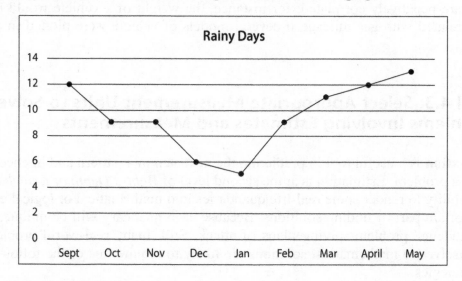

Using data that the students themselves assemble is an important part of their higher-level thinking. For example, after studying the following graph of tar and nicotine in cigarettes, students would display synthesis by anticipating that a new cigarette with 10 mg of tar would have between 0.7 and 0.8 mg of nicotine:

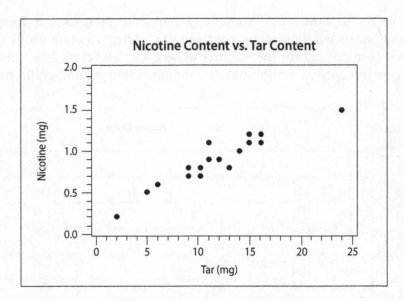

Correlation is the relationship between two variables. For example, in the graph of tar and nicotine, each dot represents one cigarette, and the placement of the dot depends on the amount of tar (*x*-axis) and nicotine (*y*-axis) the cigarette contains. Drawings like this are called **scatter plots**. If students drew a straight line through this scatter plot, it would go up and to the right, because in general the higher amount of tar, the higher amount of nicotine. The amounts of tar and nicotine are thus positively correlated. Some variables are negatively correlated; for instance, the weight of a vehicle would be negatively correlated with gas mileage if several models of vehicle were plotted in a scatter plot.

Skill 4.3: Select Appropriate Measurement Units to Solve Problems Involving Estimates and Measurements

Estimation is a useful tool in predicting the next step in a pattern and in checking the answer to a problem. Estimation is at the second level of *Webb's Depth of Knowledge Rating*. The ability to render some real-life quandaries into mathematical or logical estimates is an important part of finding solutions. Because each quandary will be unique, so, too, will be students' problem-solving plans of attack. Still, many real-world problems that lend themselves to mathematical solutions are likely to require one of the following estimation strategies:

Guess and check. This is not the same as "wild guessing." With this problem-solving strategy, students make their best guess and then check the answer to see whether it is right. Even if the guess does not immediately provide the solution, it may help to get students closer to it so that they can continue to work on it. For example: Three persons' ages add up to 72, and each person is one year older than the last person. What are their ages?

Because the three ages must add up to 72, it is reasonable to take one-third of 72 (24) as the starting point. Of course, even though 24 + 24 + 24 gives a sum of 72, those numbers do not match the information ("each person is one year older"). So, students might guess that the ages are 24, 25, and 26. Checking that guess by addition, students would see that the sum of 75 is too high. Lowering their guesses by one each, they try 23, 24, and 25, which indeed add up to 72, giving students the solution. There are many variations of the guess-and-check method.

Make a sketch or a picture. Being able to visualize a problem can help to clarify it. Consider this problem: Mr. Rosenberg plans to put a 4-foot-wide concrete sidewalk around his backyard pool. The pool is rectangular, with dimensions 12 ft. by 24 ft. The cost of the concrete is $1.28 per square foot. How much concrete is required for the job?

Students with exceptional visualization abilities will not need a sketch. For most, however, a drawing like the one shown here may be helpful in solving this and many other real-life problems.

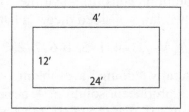

Make a table or a chart. Sometimes organizing the information from a problem makes it easier to find the solution. This is most useful for problems in which data is associated with a specific category. For example, look at the following problem:

PROBLEM

How many hours will a car traveling at 75 miles per hour take to catch up to a car traveling 55 miles per hour if the slower car starts one hour before the faster car?

SOLUTION

A table with 3 rows (hours, slower car distance, faster car distance) organizes the data. The distance of the faster car is greater than the distance of the slower car in hour 4, so the faster car caught up with the slower car in hour 3.

Hour	1	2	3	4
Slower Car	55	110	165	220
Faster Car	0	75	150	225

A table or chart also can be used to organize information provided in the problem by leaving a blank space for information that is not known. For example, information in the following problem could be organized into a table:

PROBLEM

A book has 185 pages in it. John is on page 133. How many more pages does he still need to read?

SOLUTION

Pages Already Read	Pages Still to Read	Total Number of Pages
133	??	185

Make a list. Like a table or chart, a list can help organize information and perhaps provide or at least hint at a solution. Thus, to solve the following: "How many different outcomes are there if you roll two fair six-sided dice?" a list would include:

$$1–1, 1–2, 1–3, 1–4, 1–5, 1–6, 2–2, 2–3, 2–4 \ldots$$

Act it out. Sometimes literally "doing" a problem—with physical objects or even their bodies—can help students produce a solution. A class problem that could be solved in this manner is the following: "If five strangers meet and everyone shakes everyone else's hand once, how many total handshakes will there be?"

Look for patterns. This technique encourages students to ask, "What's happening here?" Spotting a pattern would be helpful in solving a problem such as this: Nevin's weekly savings account balances for 15 weeks are as follows: $125, $135, $148, $72, $85, $96, $105, $50, $64, $74, $87, $42, $51, $60, $70. If the pattern holds, what might Nevin's balance be the next week?

Work a simpler problem. By finding the solution to a different but simpler problem, students might spot a way to solve the harder one. Estimating can be thought of as working a simpler problem. To find the product of 23 times 184 when no calculator or pencil and paper are handy, students could estimate the product by getting the exact answer to the simpler problem, 20×200.

Writing an open math sentence and then solve it. A statement is an equation with one or more variables, or "unknowns." This technique is sometimes called "translating" a problem into mathematics. Here is a sample problem: "Tiana earned grades of 77%, 86%, 90%, and 83% on her first four weekly science quizzes. Assuming all grades are equally weighted, what score will she need on the fifth week's quiz to have an average (or mean) score of 88%?" Using the given information, students could set up and solve the following equation to answer the question:

$$\frac{(77 + 86 + 90 + 83 + x)}{5} = 88$$

Work backward. Consider this problem: "If you add 12 to some number and then multiply the sum by 4, you will get 60. What is the number?" Students could find a solution by starting at the end, with 60. The problem states that the 60 came from multiplying a sum by 4. When 15 is multiplied by 4, the result is 60. The sum must be 15; if 15 is the sum of 12 and something else, the "*something else*" can only be 3.

There are, of course, hybrid approaches to problem solving. Students can mix and match strategies wherever they think they are appropriate. In general, attention to reasonableness may be most crucial to problem-solving success, especially in real-life situations.

Sometimes finding the solution to a simpler problem helps reveal a way to solve a hard one. Estimating is one example of this technique of working a simpler problem. If students need to know the product of 43 times 284 and no calculator or pencil and paper are handy, they could estimate the product by getting the exact answer to the simpler problem: 40×300.

An important step in solving problems involving measurement is to decide what is being measured. Generally, such problems will fall under one of these categories: length, area, angles, volume, mass, time, money, and temperature. Solving measurement problems will likely require knowledge in several other areas of mathematics, especially algebra.

The following is one example of a measurement problem that requires knowledge of several math topics (geometry, multiplication, conversions, estimation, etc.) and steps:

Sophie's Carpet Store charges $19.40 per square yard for the type of carpeting Tony would like in his bedroom (padding and labor included). How much would Tony pay to carpet his 9-by-12-foot room?

One way to find the solution is to convert the room dimensions to yards (3 yards by 4 yards) and then multiply to get 12 square yards. The final step is to multiply 12 by the price of $19.40 per square yard, for a total price of $232.80.

Solving measurement problems requires first determining whether to use customary units or metric units. The next decision is whether the problem involves measurements of length, volume, mass, or temperature. The following chart summarizes the various units used in various types of measurement:

Measure	Metric Units	Customary Units
Length	Meter Centimeter Kilometer	Yard, Inch, Mile
Volume	Liter, Dekaliter, Deciliter	Quart, Gallon, Cup, Teaspoon, Tablespoon
Mass	Kilogram, gram	Ounce, Pound, Ton
Temperature	Kelvin (Kelvin is primarily used in science for extreme temperatures.)	Celsius, Fahrenheit

Using the metric system requires choosing the appropriate prefix. The chart below explains those prefixes.

Metric Prefix	Meaning
kilo-	10^3
hecto-	10^2
deka- (deca-)	10^1
deci-	10^{-1}
centi-	10^{-2}
milli-	10^{-3}

Skill 4.4: Evaluate the Choice of Measures of Center and Variability with Respect to the Shape of the Data Distribution and the Context in Which the Data Were Gathered

While finding the **mean**, **median**, and **mode** of a data set provides the best overall picture of the data, there may be situations in which one measure of central tendency is the best choice.

The mean (arithmetic average) and standard deviation (average distance from each data point to mean) of a distribution are used most often. The mean and standard deviation are best suited to sets for which data are continuous without significant clustering or gaps. If the data is **skewed** (more scores at a specific point) or has significant **outliers** (extreme scores), the median is a better choice. For example, if you wanted to look at average savings, a few people with no savings or just one billionaire in the data set could significantly affect the mean. The mode is least used because while it provides information about score found most often, the mode could be affected by the frequency of that score. For example, in the following data set of quiz scores (1, 1, 1, 1, 1, 9, 10, 15, 15, 16, 17, 18, 20), the mode of 1 doesn't represent the central tendency. Mode is best used for the kind of categorical data found in a frequency chart.

Skill 4.5: Solve Problems Involving Distance, Time, Liquid Volume, Mass, and Money, Which May Include Units Expressed as Fractions or Decimals

Contextual word problems involving distance, time, liquid volume, mass and money use the same principles of problem solving as other one-step and multi-step problems. Since life is not always neatly divided into whole number units, students must learn to work with problems that include fractions and decimals.

	Formulas	Examples
Distance and Time	Speed = Distance ÷ Time Distance = Speed × Time Time = Distance ÷ Speed	A school bus traveled 5 miles in $7\frac{1}{2}$ minutes. What was the speed of the bus? A car drove at a speed of 60 mph for 1.5 hours. How far did the car travel? A car driving at a speed of 50 mph drove 180 miles. How much time did that take?
Volume	Volume of a cube or rectilinear shape = length × width × height	A box is $3\frac{1}{2}$ inches by 18 inches by $5\frac{1}{4}$ inches. What is the volume of the box?
Mass (weight)	Use of other operational formulas	If the mass of 1 car is 1.3 tons, what is the mass of 3 cars?
Money	Use of other operational formulas	Samantha has 13 dollars. She wants to give half of her money to a charity for animals. How much should she give?

Competency 5: Knowledge of Geometric Concepts

The word **geometry** comes from two Greek word parts, *geo* (earth) and *metron* (measurement), and includes **plane geometry** (two dimensions) and **solid geometry** (three dimensions) in terms of attributes, classification, and properties of space such as length, width, depth, mass and volume as well as congruency and similarity. Competency 5 addresses knowledge of geometric concepts.

Skill 5.1: Apply Geometric Properties and Relationships to Solve Problems Involving Perimeter, Area, Surface Area, and Volume

Geometric figures are distinguished by attributes, properties and relationships. **Attributes** are characteristic traits that are used to classify geometric figures. For example, figures can be classified by dimension (two-dimensional, three-dimensional).

Properties are the defining features of a shape or figure. For example, any shape with 4 sides is classified as a quadrilateral; however, size and color are not defining features. A quadrilateral can be any size or color and still be defined as a quadrilateral. The class of quadrilaterals can be subdivided based on the specifics of the 4 sides and angles.

Properties and Examples of Quadrilaterals

Shape	Description	Example
Trapezium	No parallel sides	
Trapezoid	One opposite sides parallel	
Parallelogram	Two opposite sides parallel	
Rhombus	Two opposite sides parallel and equal	
Rectangle	Two opposite sides perpendicular	
Square	Two opposite sides perpendicular and equal	

Polygons may have lines of **symmetry** that can be thought of as imaginary fold lines producing two congruent, mirror-image figures. Squares have four lines of symmetry, and non-square rectangles have two. Circles have an infinite number of lines of symmetry.

Geometric figures are **congruent** if they have the same shape, size, and angles. The following figures are congruent:

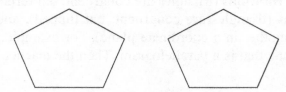

Geometric figures are **similar** if they have exactly the same shape and angles, even if they are not the same size. In the figure that follows, triangles A and B are similar:

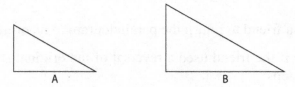

Corresponding angles of similar figures have the same measure, and the lengths of corresponding sides are proportional. In the similar triangles below, $\angle A \cong \angle D$ (meaning "angle A is congruent to angle D"), $\angle B \cong \angle E$, and $\angle C \cong \angle F$. The corresponding sides of the following triangles are **proportional**, meaning that the sides of one triangle are relative to the other as illustrated:

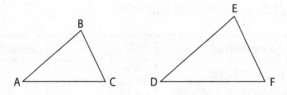

A **tessellation** is a collection of plane figures that fill the plane with no overlaps and no gaps. The following illustrates some examples:

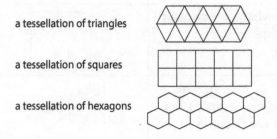

a tessellation of triangles

a tessellation of squares

a tessellation of hexagons

Scaling or **dilation** is a linear transformation that enlarges or reduces an object; the scale factor is the same in all directions. The result of uniform scaling is similar (in the geometric sense) to the original. Scaling may be directional or may have a separate scale factor for each axis direction. This type of scaling may result in a change in shape.

Transformations include a variety of different operations from geometry; these operations can include **rotations** (triangles are congruent, but turned by a specific number of degrees), **reflections** (triangles are congruent, but flipped), and **translations** (moved from one location to another in a coordinate plane). For example, the teacher might ask students to select a shape that is a parallelogram. Then the teacher might ask the students to do the following:

- Describe the original position and size of the parallelogram. Students can use labeled sketches if necessary. Rotate, translate, and reflect the parallelogram several times. Students should list the steps they followed.

- Challenge a friend to return the parallelogram to its original position.

- Determine if the friend used a reversal of the original steps or a different set of steps.

Perimeter of Rectangles, Squares, and Triangles

The word part *peri* means *around*. The word part *meter* means *measure*. Thus, **perimeter** literally refers to the measure or distance around a figure. Perimeter is measured in linear units (e.g., inches, feet, meters). The following table provides formulas for finding the perimeter of rectangles, squares, and triangles.

Figure	Formula	Example	
Rectangle	$P = 2l + 2w$, where l = length and w = width	5 m, 10 m	$P = 2(5\text{m}) + 2(10\text{m})$ $P = 10\text{m} + 20\text{m}$ $P = 30\text{m}$
Square	$P = 4s$, where s = measure of the side length	5 m	$P = 4(5\text{m})$ $P = 20\text{m}$
Triangle	$P = s_1 + s_2 + s_3$, in which s are the measures of the sides of the triangle	3 m, 5 m, 4 m	$P = 3 + 4 + 5$ $P = 12$

Area of Rectangles, Squares, and Triangles

Area refers to the measure of the interior of a figure. The measurement of area is in square units (e.g., square inches, square feet, square meters).

Figure	Formula	Example
Rectangle	$A = l \times w$, where l = length and 2 = width	5m 10m A = 5m × 10m A = 50m²
Square	$A = s^2$, where s is the measure of the side length	5m P = 5² P = 25m²
Triangle	$A = \dfrac{1}{2}bh$, where b is the base of the triangle and h is the height. The height of the triangle is determined by drawing a perpendicular line from one vertex to the opposite side. The opposite side forms the base. 	 $A = \dfrac{1}{2}(11 \text{ cm} \times 7 \text{ cm})$ $A = \dfrac{1}{2}(77 \text{ cm}^2)$ $A = 38.5 \text{ cm}^2$

Circumference and Area of Circles

Just as perimeter is the distance around a square, rectangle, or square, the **circumference** is the distance around a circle. The **radius** (r) of a circle is the distance from the center of the circle to the edge of the circle. The **diameter** (d) of a circle is a line segment that passes through the center of the circle, the end points of which lie on the circle. The measure of the diameter of a circle is twice the measure of the radius; thus, $d = 2r$. The number **pi**, symbolized as π and approximately equal to 3.14, is often used in computations involving circles.

The following table provides the formulas and examples for finding a circle's circumference and area:

Figure	Definition	Formula	Example
Circumference	distance around the circle	$C = \pi \times d$ (diameter) or $C = 2 \times \pi \times r$ (radius)	$d = 8$ cm $C = \pi \times 8$ cm $C = 3.14 \times 8$ cm $C = 25.12$
Area	number of square units within	$A = \pi \times r^2$ or $A = \pi \times (\frac{1}{2}d)^2$	$r = 3$ in $A = \pi \times 3\text{in}^2$ $A = \pi \times 9\text{in}^2$ $A = 3.14 \times 9\text{in}^2$ $A = 28.26$

Volume of Cubes and Rectangular Solids

Volume refers to the measure of the interior of a three-dimensional figure. A rectangular solid is a **rectilinear** (right-angled) figure that has length, width, and height. A **cube** is a rectangular solid with the same measures of length, width, and height on its edges (e).

Figure	Formula	Example
	$V = l \times w \times h$	$V = l \times w \times h$ $V = 4 \times 2 \times 2$ $V = 16$
	$V = e^3$	$V = 3^3$ $V = 9$

While there are formulas for measuring shapes and determining perimeter, area, and volume, geometric thinking and reasoning goes beyond rote application of the formulas. Rather geometric thinking and reasoning encompasses changes in defining properties and relationships when any of the dimensions change. Changing even one number in a formula can affect the final result. Evaluating the effect of that change involves thinking at the highest level of *Webb's Depth of Knowledge Rating*. Having students experiment with geometric numbers, make predictions in terms of patterns or what will occur next, and then evaluate how and why the changes happened takes the work with perimeter, circumference, area, and volume to a level higher than just "plugging in" numbers to a formula. For example, if you have a 2-inch × 2-inch square and you increase the length of 1 set of parallel sides by 1 inch, do you still have a square? Or, what is the relationship between equal increases in length of sides in a square (e.g., 1 inch × 1 inch; 2 inches by 2 inches; 3 inches by 3 inches; 4 inches by 4 inches)? If all of the sides of a triangle are increased by equal units, is the new triangle congruent to the original triangle?

Skill 5.2: Identify and Locate Ordered Pairs in All Four Quadrants of a Rectangular Coordinate System

The **coordinate plane** is useful for graphing individual **ordered pairs** (*x, y*) as points and showing relationships among ordered pairs (e.g., lines, functions). The coordinate plane is divided into four quadrants by an **x-axis** (horizontal) and a **y-axis** (vertical). Each axis represents a number line; however, instead of points on a line, the points exist in a two-dimensional space.

The upper-right quadrant is quadrant I, and the others (moving counterclockwise from quadrant I) are quadrants II, III and IV. Ordered pairs indicate the locations of points on the plane. For instance, the ordered pair (–3, 4) describes a point that is three units left from the center of the plane (the origin) and four units up, as shown in the following diagram:

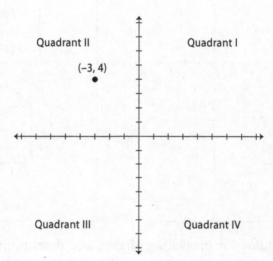

More than one ordered pair form sets of data that one can display in a chart and graph on the coordinate plane. For example, the following set of data demonstrates four ordered pairs:

X	Y
(–4, 3)	
(–2, 2)	
(2, –2)	
(4, 3)	

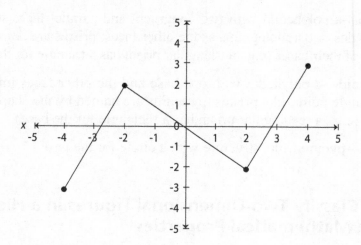

Identifying the quadrant in which a point is placed is determined by the signs of the numbers in the pair as follows:

- If both numbers are positive, the point will be in Quadrant I.

- If the first number is positive and the second number is negative, the point will be in Quadrant IV.

- If both numbers are negative, the point will be in Quadrant III.

- If the first number is negative and the second number is positive, the point will be in Quadrant II.

Skill 5.3: Identify and Analyze Properties of Three-Dimensional Shapes Using Formal Mathematical Terms Such as Volume Faces, Edges, and Vertices

Three-dimensional figures have length, width, and depth (or height), as well as volume and mass, and can be sorted by edges and vertices, faces, and surfaces. Common three-dimensional figures include the following:

- **Sphere**—no edges or vertices; all points on the surface are equidistant from the center

- **Ovoid**—no edges or vertices; egg-shaped

- **Polyhedron**—all faces are polygons

- **Prism**—a polyhedral with two congruent and parallel faces with other rectangles or parallelograms as the other faces; prisms are named by the shape of their bases (e.g., a triangular prism has a triangle for the base)

- **Pyramid**—a polyhedra with one base and the other faces intersecting at a single point; like prisms, pyramids are named by the shape of their bases (e.g., a rectangular prism has a rectangle for the base)

- **Cone**—pyramid-like structure with a circle for the base

Skill 5.4: Classify Two-Dimensional Figures in a Hierarchy Based on Mathematical Properties

Two-dimensional shapes or planes have length, width and area and can be sorted by **curve** (concave, convex, polygon, closed curve), **regularity** (equivalence for all angles and sides), or number of **angles** (e.g., triangle, square, rhombus, hexagon). Common two-dimensional shapes include the following:

- **Polygon**—any shape with any number of sides

- **Triangle**—three sides and three angles which can be further divided by angle (acute, obtuse, right) or sides (scalene, isosceles, equilateral)

- **Quadrilateral**—four sides and four angles

- **Pentagon**—five sides

- **Hexagon**—six sides

- **Octagon**—eight sides

- **Circle**—shape whose boundary (the circumference) consists of points equidistant from a fixed point (the center)

References

Hawbaker, B., Balong, M Buckwalter, S., & Bock, S. (2001). Building a strong base of support for all students through co planning. Teaching Exceptional Children, 33(4), 24–30.

Van, W. J. A., Karp, K., & Bay-Williams, J. M. (2013). *Elementary and middle school mathematics: Teaching developmentally*. Boston: Pearson.

Webb, N.L. (2002) *Depth-of-Knowledge Levels for Four Content Areas*, University of Wisconsin Center for Educational Research.

Review Questions

1. Ms. Ramirez shows a student the following and asks, "Without counting, what do you think is the best answer for the number of items? Two, Five, or Ten?" What is the focus of this question?

    (A) iteration

    (B) prediction

    (C) subitizing

    (D) basic mathematical operations

2. Mr. Hilton will be using Cuisenaire rods with his class today. The content of the lesson is most likely to be

    (A) customary units of mass.

    (B) basic mathematical operations.

    (C) coordinate planes.

    (D) perimeter of triangles.

3. Which of the following key phrases is correctly matched with the operation it signals?

    (A) decreased by; division

    (B) decreased by a factor of; subtraction

    (C) how many to each; addition

    (D) product; division

4. In terms of number theory concepts and properties, which of the following is true?

   (A) The multiplicative identity property of 0 and the additive identity property of 1 are key properties of whole numbers.

   (B) A number is divisible by 6 if it is divisible by both 2 and 3.

   (C) The only factors of a composite number are the number itself and 1.

   (D) The factors of any whole number are the results of multiplying that whole number by the counting numbers.

5. Mr. Foret has written the following on the board: 3.6×10^5. Mr. Foret's lesson is most likely on the subject of

   (A) scientific notation

   (B) exponential notation

   (C) terminating decimals

   (D) ratio notation

6. What is true of systems and units of measurement?

   (A) Customary units are the same as metric units.

   (B) The metric prefix *deci-* means ten.

   (C) Capacity is another name for volume.

   (D) An ounce is smaller than a gram

7. What is true of measures of central tendency?

   (A) The middle number of a set of data in numerical order is called the mean.

   (B) The mode in a set of data is the value that occurs least often.

   (C) To determine the mean, multiply the number of values by the highest and lowest value and divide by 2.

   (D) To determine the range, subtract the smallest number in the set from the highest number.

8. A team of 3 students is working on a science project. They need to compare the distance from the sun to the earth and the earth to the moon in metric units. What unit would be best for them to use?

(A) centigram

(B) dekaliter

(C) Celsius

(D) kilometer

9. What is true of ordered pairs in the four quadrants of a rectangular coordinate system?

(A) An ordered pair with 2 negative values [e.g., (–3, –4)] is in the upper left quadrant.

(B) The *x*-axis is vertical.

(C) The center of the coordinate plane is called the origin.

(D) The ordered pair (2, 3) would be 2 places up from the center and 3 places to the right of the center.

10. Which of the following statements are true regarding the ability to interpret tables, graphs, equations, and verbal descriptions of real world situations?

    I.   A bar graph is used to track one or more subjects, usually over time.

    II.   A line graph depicts percentages of a particular subject.

    III.   All of the slices within a circle graph show the totality of a quantity.

    IV.   A table organizes large amounts of information.

(A) I and II

(B) II and III

(C) III and IV

(D) I and IV

Answer Key and Explanations

1.　**(C)**

Subitize is the skill of instantly seeing or estimating how many items are present. Choice (A) is incorrect because *iteration* involves repetition of *subitizing*. Choice (B) is incorrect because the skill of *prediction* requires that a student identifies what might come next in a pattern or situation. Choice (D) is incorrect because *basic mathematical operations* consist of addition, subtraction, multiplication, and division. *For more information, see Competency 1.*

2.　**(B)**

Cuisenaire rods can be used to teach place value. They cannot be logically used to teach the concept of *customary units, volume,* or *coordinate planes. For more information, see Competency 1.*

3.　**(B)**

Choice (A) is incorrect because *decreased by* signals subtraction. Choice (C) is incorrect because *how many to each* signals division. Choice (D) is incorrect because *product* indicates multiplication. *For more information, see Competency 2.*

4.　**(B)**

Answer (A) is incorrect because key properties of whole numbers include the multiplicative identity property of 1 and the additive identity property of 0. Answer (C) is incorrect because the only factors of a prime number are the number itself and 1. Answer (D) is incorrect because the multiples of any whole number are the results of multiplying that whole number by the counting numbers. *For more information, see Competency 2.*

5.　**(A)**

Choice (B) is incorrect because *exponential notation* shows repeated multiplication more simply (e.g., 3^4). Choice (C) is incorrect because a terminating decimal is one that is nonrepeating and does not involve exponents. Choice (D) is incorrect because ratio notation is an alternative way of showing fractions. *For more information, see Competency 3.*

6.　**(C)**

Choice (A) is incorrect because customary units include measures such as foot, pound, and cup; however, metric units include measures such as liter, gram, and meter.

Choice (B) is incorrect because the metric prefix *deci-* means tenth. Choice (D) is incorrect because an ounce is larger than a gram. *For more information, see Competency 3.*

7. **(D)**

Choice (A) is incorrect because the middle number of a set of data in numerical order is called the median. Choice (B) is incorrect because the mode in a set of data is the value that occurs most often. Choice (C) is incorrect because the mean is determined by adding all of the values and dividing by the number of values. *For more information, see Competency 4.*

8. **(D)**

Choice (A) is incorrect because centigram is a unit of weight. Choice (B) is incorrect because dekaliter is a unit of volume. Choice (C) is incorrect because it is not a metric unit. *For more information, see Competency 4.*

9. **(C)**

Choice (A) is incorrect because an ordered pair with 2 negative values [e.g., $(-3, -4)$] is in the lower left quadrant. Choice (B) is incorrect because the *x*-axis is horizontal. Choice (D) is incorrect because the ordered pair (2, 3) would be 2 places to the right of the center and 3 places up from the center. *For more information, see Competency 5.*

10. **(C)**

Statement I is incorrect because a line graph is used to track one or more subjects, usually over time. Statement II is incorrect because a circle graph depicts percentages of a particular subject. *For more information, see Competency 5.*

PRACTICE TEST 1

FTCE Elementary Education K–6
Subtests 1-4

This practice test and an additional test are available at the online REA Study Center (*www.rea.com/studycenter*).

The FTCE Elementary Education K–6 (060) test is computer-based, so we strongly recommend that you take our online practice tests to simulate test-day conditions and to receive these added benefits:

- **Timed testing conditions**—Gauge how much time you can spend on each question.

- **Automatic scoring**—Find out how you did on the test, instantly.

- **On-screen detailed explanations of answers**—Learn not just the correct answer, but also why the other answers are incorrect.

- **Diagnostic score reports**—Pinpoint where you're strongest and where you need to focus your study.

PRACTICE TEST 1

FTCE Elementary Education K–6 Subtests 1–4

PRACTICE TEST 1

FTCE Elementary Education K-6

Subtest 1:
Language Arts and Reading

This practice test and an additional test are available at the online REA Study Center (*www.rea.com/studycenter*).

The FTCE Elementary Education K–6 (060) test is computer-based, so we strongly recommend that you take our online practice tests to simulate test-day conditions and to receive these added benefits:

- **Timed testing conditions**—Gauge how much time you can spend on each question.

- **Automatic scoring**—Find out how you did on the test, instantly.

- **On-screen detailed explanations of answers**—Learn not just the correct answer, but also why the other answers are incorrect.

- **Diagnostic score reports**—Pinpoint where you're strongest and where you need to focus your study.

Answer Sheet

1. Ⓐ Ⓑ Ⓒ Ⓓ
2. Ⓐ Ⓑ Ⓒ Ⓓ
3. Ⓐ Ⓑ Ⓒ Ⓓ
4. Ⓐ Ⓑ Ⓒ Ⓓ
5. Ⓐ Ⓑ Ⓒ Ⓓ
6. Ⓐ Ⓑ Ⓒ Ⓓ
7. Ⓐ Ⓑ Ⓒ Ⓓ
8. Ⓐ Ⓑ Ⓒ Ⓓ
9. Ⓐ Ⓑ Ⓒ Ⓓ
10. Ⓐ Ⓑ Ⓒ Ⓓ
11. Ⓐ Ⓑ Ⓒ Ⓓ
12. Ⓐ Ⓑ Ⓒ Ⓓ
13. Ⓐ Ⓑ Ⓒ Ⓓ
14. Ⓐ Ⓑ Ⓒ Ⓓ
15. Ⓐ Ⓑ Ⓒ Ⓓ
16. Ⓐ Ⓑ Ⓒ Ⓓ
17. Ⓐ Ⓑ Ⓒ Ⓓ
18. Ⓐ Ⓑ Ⓒ Ⓓ
19. Ⓐ Ⓑ Ⓒ Ⓓ
20. Ⓐ Ⓑ Ⓒ Ⓓ

21. Ⓐ Ⓑ Ⓒ Ⓓ
22. Ⓐ Ⓑ Ⓒ Ⓓ
23. Ⓐ Ⓑ Ⓒ Ⓓ
24. Ⓐ Ⓑ Ⓒ Ⓓ
25. Ⓐ Ⓑ Ⓒ Ⓓ
26. Ⓐ Ⓑ Ⓒ Ⓓ
27. Ⓐ Ⓑ Ⓒ Ⓓ
28. Ⓐ Ⓑ Ⓒ Ⓓ
29. Ⓐ Ⓑ Ⓒ Ⓓ
30. Ⓐ Ⓑ Ⓒ Ⓓ
31. Ⓐ Ⓑ Ⓒ Ⓓ
32. Ⓐ Ⓑ Ⓒ Ⓓ
33. Ⓐ Ⓑ Ⓒ Ⓓ
34. Ⓐ Ⓑ Ⓒ Ⓓ
35. Ⓐ Ⓑ Ⓒ Ⓓ
36. Ⓐ Ⓑ Ⓒ Ⓓ
37. Ⓐ Ⓑ Ⓒ Ⓓ
38. Ⓐ Ⓑ Ⓒ Ⓓ
39. Ⓐ Ⓑ Ⓒ Ⓓ
40. Ⓐ Ⓑ Ⓒ Ⓓ

41. Ⓐ Ⓑ Ⓒ Ⓓ
42. Ⓐ Ⓑ Ⓒ Ⓓ
43. Ⓐ Ⓑ Ⓒ Ⓓ
44. Ⓐ Ⓑ Ⓒ Ⓓ
45. Ⓐ Ⓑ Ⓒ Ⓓ
46. Ⓐ Ⓑ Ⓒ Ⓓ
47. Ⓐ Ⓑ Ⓒ Ⓓ
48. Ⓐ Ⓑ Ⓒ Ⓓ
49. Ⓐ Ⓑ Ⓒ Ⓓ
50. Ⓐ Ⓑ Ⓒ Ⓓ
51. Ⓐ Ⓑ Ⓒ Ⓓ
52. Ⓐ Ⓑ Ⓒ Ⓓ
53. Ⓐ Ⓑ Ⓒ Ⓓ
54. Ⓐ Ⓑ Ⓒ Ⓓ
55. Ⓐ Ⓑ Ⓒ Ⓓ
56. Ⓐ Ⓑ Ⓒ Ⓓ
57. Ⓐ Ⓑ Ⓒ Ⓓ
58. Ⓐ Ⓑ Ⓒ Ⓓ
59. Ⓐ Ⓑ Ⓒ Ⓓ
60. Ⓐ Ⓑ Ⓒ Ⓓ

Subtest 1: Language Arts and Reading

Questions: 60
Time: 1 hour and 5 minutes

Directions: Read each question and select the best response.

1. What is an example of phonemic awareness?

   (A) recognition of the same sound in words

   (B) matching a phoneme to its grapheme

   (C) identifying the meaning of morphemes in a word

   (D) remembering the sound that a letter makes

2. Ms. Wood teaches first grade. She is doing an activity with her class. Ms. Wood said, "If I take the word *mail* and replace the /m/ sound with an /s/ sound, what word would I have?" This activity involves

   (A) three or more types of phoneme manipulation at once.

   (B) phonemic substitution.

   (C) graphemic replacement.

   (D) morphemic identification.

3. Which of the following most clearly reflects structural analysis?

   (A) hearing the difference between "bat," "bad," and "back"

   (B) articulating each syllable of the word "watermelon"

   (C) understanding that the /s/ sound is represented in more than one way

   (D) recognizing that "guarded" consists of the word "guard" plus the suffix "ed"

4. Characteristics of emergent literacy include

   (A) interest in books and printed materials.

   (B) the use of reading as a tool to learn.

   (C) the ability to read from multiple perspectives.

   (D) the understanding of specific words in texts.

5. Which of the following would be used in assessing reading fluency?

   (A) multiple option tests

   (B) story retelling

   (C) sight-word analyses

   (D) running records

6. What is prosody?

   (A) the patterns of recurrent sounds in a language

   (B) the scientific study of reading comprehension

   (C) the rhythm, stress patterns, and intonations of speech

   (D) the sounds in a language that contribute to word meaning

7. Structural analysis involves the ability to

   (A) understand linguistic organization.

   (B) identify missing words in passages.

   (C) apply rules of phonics when decoding.

   (D) break a word into meaningful parts or syllables.

8. Mr. Jackson is asking his students to read a brief essay and identify the theme.

   What level of comprehension is Mr. Jackson requiring of his students?

   (A) analysis

   (B) application

   (C) comprehension

   (D) literal

9. Ms. Darnell is having her class read an expository text that contains many charts, pictures, and other graphics. Which of the following is the best way for her to support her students' comprehension of the text?

   (A) Encourage students to skip the graphics and focus their attention on understanding and reflecting on the text.

   (B) Remind students that the purpose of the graphics is to maintain interest rather than convey essential information.

   (C) Ask students to read the text first and to return to the graphics once they feel they have understood the main ideas.

   (D) Help students understand the specific ways that the graphics support the details presented in the text.

10. After reading her class a story about how one child helped keep his neighborhood clean, the teacher asks the class to brainstorm ways that they can keep their own neighborhood clean. What level in Bloom's Revised Taxonomy is primarily used for this activity?

    (A) applying

    (B) understanding

    (C) analyzing

    (D) remembering

11. Ms. Martinez is discussing the main character of a text with her students. Which of the following activities would best promote her students' thinking at the *evaluation* level of Bloom's Taxonomy?

    (A) Ask students to look at various descriptions of the main character throughout the text and generate a summary description of the character's personality.

    (B) Ask students to make a list of all the pages in which descriptions of the main character occur and note which of the other characters provided each description.

    (C) Ask students to reflect on the author's treatment of the main character and then to write a paper that argues the fairness of the portrayal.

    (D) Ask students to identify people they know whose attitudes and behaviors are similar to those exhibited by the main character.

12. What type of assessment relies on mastery of learning objectives for student achievement?

    (A) performance-based

    (B) norm-referenced

    (C) criterion-referenced

    (D) portfolio

13. The results of what type of assessment are reported in percentile ranks?

    (A) performance-based

    (B) norm-referenced

    (C) criterion-referenced

    (D) portfolio

14. Which of the following is *not* part of emergent literacy?

    (A) showing awareness of the directionality of print

    (B) being able to decode words fluently

    (C) recognizing where the title of a book is located

    (D) understanding that words in books tell stories

15. Your school board is considering a proposal to lengthen the school day. You are encouraging your students to write to the board to express their views either in favor of or against the proposal. You will be encouraging your students to use which mode of writing?

    (A) persuasive

    (B) narrative

    (C) expository

    (D) descriptive

16. A new novel about a fictional Native American girl who lived in the South during the pre-Colonial era represents which of the following genres?

    (A) traditional literature

    (B) fantasy

    (C) science fiction

    (D) historical fiction

17. Mr. Lee is discussing words such as "buzz," "hiss," and "splat" with his students. These words are examples of

    (A) parallelism.

    (B) metaphors.

    (C) onomatopoeia.

    (D) homonyms.

18. *Plot* can be briefly defined as the

    (A) characters and setting of a story.

    (B) fundamental theme of a story.

    (C) main events of a story.

    (D) twist that enlivens a story.

19. Which of the following descriptions contains a simile?

    (A) Patricia is like a bear.

    (B) Jill is practically a parrot.

    (C) Carolyn is more or less of a slug.

    (D) Nancy might be asleep.

20. All of the following would support the use of multicultural literature in the class-room EXCEPT

   (A) guiding students to think about the world from different perspectives.

   (B) informing students about the cultural contributions of different societies.

   (C) encouraging students to celebrate their own distinctive characteristics.

   (D) basing readings on the works of 18th-century European writers.

21. Which of the following is the correct order of stages in process writing?

   (A) prewriting, editing, drafting, revising, publishing

   (B) drafting, prewriting, editing, revising, publishing

   (C) prewriting, drafting, revising, editing, publishing

   (D) drafting, prewriting, editing, publishing, revising

22. When planning an expository essay, which of the following should students consider?

   (A) audience, occasion, and purpose

   (B) means of introducing a main character

   (C) methods of persuasion

   (D) approach to developing plot

23. Which of the following assessments gives a teacher the most specific information about a student's reading strengths and weaknesses?

   (A) screening

   (B) formative assessment

   (C) diagnostic test

   (D) progress monitoring

24. Generally speaking, writing rubrics are helpful in communicating which of the following?

    (A) lesson content

    (B) expectations about the elements of an assignment

    (C) metacognitive strategies

    (D) class goals

25. A student whose scores on a standardized test of reading comprehension are in the 50th percentile is, with respect to reading comprehension,

    (A) far above average.

    (B) slightly above average.

    (C) average.

    (D) failing.

26. Ms. Riker administers a brief test of oral fluency each week and finds that students' scores tend to vary widely from week to week. Which of the following seems like the most plausible explanation for the variability in student scores?

    (A) The students are playing a trick on the teacher.

    (B) The test has poor reliability.

    (C) The test has poor validity.

    (D) The teacher does not know how to score the tests.

27. Which of the following teachers is engaging in active listening during a story retell by one of her students?

    (A) When the student pauses for more than a moment, the teacher asks "What's next?"

    (B) At the outset, the teacher reminds the student to cover the key points.

    (C) At several points, the teacher briefly paraphrases what the student just said or asks a clarifying question.

    (D) As the student finishes, the teacher praises the retell.

28. Which of the following is most similar in meaning to the word *genre*?

    (A) theme of a story

    (B) setting of a story

    (C) response to story

    (D) type of story

29. Which of the following can be a primary source?

    (A) a textbook

    (B) a letter

    (C) a movie review

    (D) a critical summary

30. Which of the following appears to violate the principles of fair use of copyrighted materials?

    (A) posting a photo from a website on the classroom wall

    (B) photocopying a textbook and selling it to students' parents

    (C) integrating several quotations from a book into a slideshow for students

    (D) asking students to write down their favorite passage from a play

31. Kate is learning about the dimensions of language. Which of the following statements is *not* true?

    (A) The dimensions are speaking, thinking, writing, and reading.

    (B) Listening comes before speaking.

    (C) Oral language consists of speaking and listening.

    (D) Oral language provides the foundation for how written language works.

32. Which of the following is defined as the acceptance of the distinctive characteristics of all cultures, including one's own?

    (A) cultural relativism

    (B) cultural appreciation

    (C) cultural assimilation

    (D) cultural pluralism

33. Ms. Carter is teaching her kindergarten students how to write the alphabet. She notices that Erik has problems holding his pencil. What developmental issue might contribute to this problem?

    (A) lack of practice

    (B) small motor development

    (C) cognitive development

    (D) attention deficit

34. Mr. Lassiter has a student whom he thinks could be helped by bibliotherapy. Which of the following students, given their description, is most likely to benefit from this approach?

    (A) Carl because his dog just died.

    (B) Cecil because he is having problems with reading fluency.

    (C) Kara because she is interested in space exploration.

    (D) Mara because she is going with her family on a vacation to Walt Disney World.

35. The focus of Ms. Green's lesson is syntactic understanding. What would you expect to see her students doing?

    (A) answering text-dependent questions on a worksheet

    (B) learning subject-specific vocabulary using flashcards

    (C) using a computer to check for grammar errors

    (D) reading narrative texts

36. Principal Moore is observing Mrs. Kraft's third-grade class. He notes that the focus of the lesson will be conventions of writing. What would Principal Moore expect to see in this lesson?

    (A) Students working together on grammar, spelling and punctuation from a previous writing assignment.

    (B) Mrs. Kraft teaching students how to use a thesaurus to vary word choice.

    (C) Students working in pairs to create realistic dialogue.

    (D) Mrs. Kraft explaining literary devices.

37. After school, Tim showed his mother the very first paragraph he had ever written. What grade would Tim most likely be in?

    (A) kindergarten

    (B) second grade

    (C) fourth grade

    (D) sixth grade

38. Mrs. Jones asked her students to read a folk story and then write their own example of a folk story using a writing process approach. At one point, Zoey makes a bubble map of the characters and ideas she wants to use in her story. Zoey is in which stage of the writing process?

    (A) prewriting

    (B) drafting

    (C) brainstorming

    (D) creating

39. Mr. Wood teaches fifth-grade science. His class completed a short experiment in class. He has given the students a writing assignment about what they observed. This assignment exemplifies which kind of writing?

    (A) narrative

    (B) expository

    (C) personal

    (D) reflective

40. Mr. Nash is teaching his students about parts of speech. He asked the students to identify the preposition in the following sentence: *The carnivorous tiger was running through the forest.* Which student gave the correct answer?

    (A) Jerold said "*carnivorous.*"

    (B) Molly said "*through.*"

    (C) Carmela said "*running.*"

    (D) Mary said "*tiger.*"

41. Mr. Drake often focuses on semantic understanding in his fourth-grade science class. What classroom tool or activity would best exemplify this focus?

    (A) using science fiction as a motivation for learning science concepts

    (B) reading primary sources about scientific concepts

    (C) creating and using a word wall for science vocabulary

    (D) science journals for recording observations and insights

42. Mrs. Lennox's sixth-grade class is comparing dialect and use of language among three sources: A description of love from Shakespeare's *Romeo and Juliet*; lyrics from a pop music song about love; and a humorous Valentine greeting card. What aspect of language is the focus of the comparison?

    (A) vocabulary

    (B) semantic understanding

    (C) syntactic understanding

    (D) pragmatics

43. Mrs. Lee wrote the word *extemporizing* on the board. What is the focus of the lesson?

    (A) speaking

    (B) reading expository text

    (C) readers' theatre

    (D) conventions of writing

44. Eastville Middle School uses a learning management system called *Teaching With Class* for reporting absences, grades, and communication with parents and guardians. This system is an example of which kind of software?

    (A) productivity

    (B) administrative

    (C) instructional

    (D) educational

45. Which of the following best describes the connection between Title IX and choosing books for children?

    (A) avoiding books that are sexist

    (B) avoiding books that could be used for bibliotherapy

    (C) recognizing multicultural perspectives in literature

    (D) including individuals with disabilities in literature

46. Ms. Green's second grade class had a Skype conversation with the author of one of the books they read. After the conversation ended, the class as a whole wrote about the conversation by dictating to Ms. Green. She wrote using a document camera and the students contributed ideas. They edited the document together and they read it aloud. This demonstrates use of

    (A) prewriting.

    (B) language experience.

    (C) literary devices.

    (D) cooperative learning.

47. Ms. Hyatt is teaching a kindergarten class about onset and rime. Which of the following best exemplifies that concept?

    (A) d-og

    (B) tur-tle

    (C) pan-cake

    (D) spo-t

48. Which of the following demonstrates use of a Web 2.0 tool?

    (A) A teacher uses a word processing program to create a writing assignment.

    (B) A teacher researches NASA's online resources for teachers.

    (C) A class creates an online blog on current events.

    (D) A class takes a virtual field trip to an online art exhibit from the Smithsonian.

49. Which of the following is defined as the ability to access, analyze, evaluate, and create media in a variety of forms?

    (A) media literacy

    (B) digital nativism

    (C) technological expertise

    (D) online utilization

50. Ms. Cooper is listening to Kelly read aloud. Kelly reads very slowly because she carefully, but correctly, sounds out every word. In terms of fluency, Kelly's reading best reflects a problem in

    (A) pragmatics.

    (B) prosody.

    (C) accuracy.

    (D) automaticity.

51. The Johnsons have a son who will be entering kindergarten in the fall. The school has scheduled a time for their son to come in to be tested prior to starting school. What kind of testing is their son most likely to be given?

    (A) screening

    (B) diagnostic

    (C) vocabulary

    (D) formative

52. Which of the following is an example of a secondary source?

    (A) a class textbook chapter on space exploration

    (B) a Skype phone call with an astronaut that was on the International Space Station

    (C) a display of authentic moon rocks at Kennedy Space Center

    (D) an autobiography of one of the Mercury astronauts

53. Mrs. Owen showed her students a video clip of Dr. Martin Luther King delivering his "I Have a Dream" speech. She then gave her students 3 minutes to reflect on the content and identify the three most important things they learned from the speech. After that time, she put students into groups of two to compare and contrast what they wrote. This is an example of

   (A) jigsaw.

   (B) think, pair, share.

   (C) RAP.

   (D) use of a listening guide.

54. Third-grade teacher Mr. Giamatti is completing report cards for his students. He is determining grades based on the work students have done this semester. Which of the following should be included in his computations?

   (A) results of a pretest on vocabulary

   (B) results from an informal reading inventory

   (C) results from a summative assessment on reading skills

   (D) results of a feedback prompt: *The muddiest point in today's discussion was . . .*

55. What is true of informal and formal speaking?

   (A) Putting students "on the spot" builds confidence.

   (B) Teacher-created listening guides can help speakers know what to talk about in a speech.

   (C) Pre-teaching vocabulary and incomplete outlines can help students prepare for speaking.

   (D) Informal and formal speaking have little in common.

56. What is the purpose of high-stakes testing?

   (A) accountability

   (B) forming norm-referenced groups for state assessments

   (C) diagnosing individual strengths and weaknesses

   (D) validating the use of state standards and benchmarks

57. Fourth-grade teacher Ms. Cliff gave Joe an individual reading inventory. In terms of oral reading, Joe was 95% accurate at the fourth grade level. His comprehension score on silent reading was 75% and his comprehension score on oral reading was 85%. Which of the following can Ms. Cliff conclude?

    (A) Joe's independent level is fourth grade.

    (B) Joe's instructional level is fourth grade.

    (C) Joe's frustration level is fourth grade.

    (D) Joe's capacity level is fourth grade.

58. Mr. Oakley is learning about reading assessments. The content he is reading includes the abbreviations *WPM* and *WCPM*. Mr. Oakley is reading about which of the following assessments?

    (A) phonemic awareness

    (B) comprehension

    (C) fluency

    (D) screening

59. In terms of testing, which of the following describes how well a test measures what it is supposed to measure?

    (A) norm referencing

    (B) reliability

    (C) percentile ranking

    (D) validity

60. Which of the following instructional examples would specifically help students develop listening and speaking skills?

    (A) Mrs. Johnson assigns her students a chapter to read in preparation for tomorrow's lecture on cell division.

    (B) Mr. Pasley teaches his students how to play charades to practice new vocabulary.

    (C) Ms. Hurst divides her class into groups and gives each group a small plastic ball. She tells the class that whoever has the ball in the group can speak and after that person speaks, s/he should ask a question and then toss the ball to someone else to respond.

    (D) Mr. McDonald shows his students how to use graphic organizers to plan speeches.

Practice Test 1, Subtest 1
Answer Key

1.	(A)	21.	(C)	41.	(C)
2.	(B)	22.	(A)	42.	(D)
3.	(D)	23.	(C)	43.	(A)
4.	(A)	24.	(B)	44.	(B)
5.	(D)	25.	(C)	45.	(A)
6.	(C)	26.	(B)	46.	(B)
7.	(D)	27.	(C)	47.	(A)
8.	(A)	28.	(D)	48.	(C)
9.	(D)	29.	(B)	49.	(A)
10.	(A)	30.	(B)	50.	(D)
11.	(C)	31.	(A)	51.	(A)
12.	(C)	32.	(D)	52.	(A)
13.	(B)	33.	(B)	53.	(B)
14.	(B)	34.	(A)	54.	(C)
15.	(A)	35.	(C)	55.	(C)
16.	(D)	36.	(A)	56.	(A)
17.	(C)	37.	(B)	57.	(B)
18.	(C)	38.	(A)	58.	(C)
19.	(A)	39.	(B)	59.	(D)
20.	(D)	40.	(B)	60.	(C)

Self-Assessment Guide
Language Arts and Reading

Practice-test questions are sorted here by competency. To get an idea of your level of mastery, check the box under the question numbers that you answered correctly.

Competency 1: Knowledge of the Reading Process   __/17

1	2	3	4	6	7	8	9	10	11

14	31	35	41	42	47	50

Competency 2: Knowledge of Literary Analysis and Genres   __/9

16	17	18	19	20	28	32	34	45

Competency 3: Knowledge of Language and the Writing Process   __/10

15	21	22	33	36	37	38	39	40	46

Competency 4: Knowledge of Literacy Instruction and Assessment   __/14

5	12	13	23	24	25	26	27	51	54

56	57	58	59

Competency 5: Knowledge of Communication and Media Literacy   __/10

29	30	43	44	48	49	52	53	55	60

TOTAL   _____/60

Subtest 1: Language Arts and Reading Answer Explanations

1.   (A)

Choice (A) is correct because phonemes and phonemic awareness involve sounds. Graphemes are visual. Morphemes involve meaning. Awareness and memory are not the same.

2.   (B)

Choice (B) is correct because substitution is another name for replacement and because Ms. Wood is manipulating one sound (phoneme) rather than the visual symbol (grapheme), the meaning (morpheme) or multiple phonemes.

3.   (D)

Choice (D) is correct because structural analysis involves breaking a word into meaningful parts. Phonemic awareness involves hearing sound differences in language. The alphabetic principle involves understanding letter-sound relationships. Articulating syllables does not involve the meaningful parts of a word.

4.   (A)

Choice (A) is correct because emergent literacy refers to the aspects of reading that occur before children can read (prereading stage). Thus, an interest in books and print is the best choice. Reading to learn, reading from multiple perspectives, and identifying word meanings in context are more advanced reading skills.

5.   (D)

Choice (D) is correct because running records are defined as informal checks of oral reading accuracy. Multiple option tests are not used for reading fluency. Story retelling is oral, but involves recall and verbal relating of events rather than oral reading. Sight word analysis is not a form of reading fluency.

6.   (C)

Choice (C) is correct because it is the definition of prosody.

7.   (D)

Choice (D) is correct because meaning is the key to structural analysis. It involves deriving meaning from the parts of a word.

8.   (A)

Choice (A) is correct because identification of theme occurs when a reader can break content into parts to determine similarities and differences and draw conclusions about the unifying or dominant idea.

9.   (D)

Choice (D) is correct because graphics in expository (non-narrative) text serve to explain and show meaning in visual ways, rather than stimulate interest. Thus, they play an integral role in understanding rather than a secondary (post-reading) role. Skipping the graphics eliminates a key source of meaning.

10.   (A)

Choice (A) is correct because the teacher is asking the students to use what they have learned (keeping a neighborhood clean) and apply it to a new situation (ways to keep their own neighborhoods clean).

11.   (C)

Choice (C) is correct because evaluation involves judgment in terms of the quality of fairness. Summarization is at the comprehension level. Listing pages of character description is at the knowledge level. Identification of individuals with similar characteristics is at the application level.

12.   (C)

Choice (C) is correct because criterion-referenced tests address mastery of content. Performance-based assessments allow students to show understanding in authentic ways (e.g., project, demonstration) rather than through a pencil-and-paper or online test. Norm-referenced tests compare students to each other rather than to a standard for mastery. A portfolio is a collection of work that demonstrates development of skills and learning over time. Portfolio and performance-based assessments can be criterion-referenced, but that is not necessarily a requirement.

13.   (B)

Choice (B) is correct because norm-referenced tests report student scores in reference to other scores in the norming population.

14.   (B)

Choice (B) is correct because fluency describes a skill belonging to a proficient, rather than an emerging reader. The other options exemplify emergent literacy.

15.   (A)

Choice (A) is correct because students are endeavoring to sway a position through persuasion. Narrative writing tells a story. Expository writing describes writing that is non-fiction and can include persuasive writing, but is not restricted to persuasive writing. Descriptive writing can be narrative or expository, but it does not attempt to sway thinking.

16.   (D)

Choice (D) is correct because Native American girls living in the Southern part of the United States during the pre-Colonial era would be historically accurate. Since the book is new, it is not traditional literature. Since the book describes realistic events and characters in the past it is historical fiction, rather than fantasy (imaginative) or science fiction (future).

17.   (C)

Choice (C) is correct because the examples are words that resemble the sound they make. Parallelism is a type of writing in which grammatical elements are equal. Metaphors are implied comparisons between two things. Homonyms are words that sound the same, but have different spellings and meanings (e.g., *bare* and *bear*).

18.   (C)

Choice (C) is correct because the definition matches the term. Characters and setting are elements of a story. The fundamental theme of a story is the unifying or dominant idea. A twist that enlivens the story can be an aspect of the plot, but is not the only aspect.

19.   (A)

Choice (A) is correct because a simile must use the word *like* or *as* in the comparison.

20.   (D)

Choice (D) is correct because the other choices support multicultural literature through the use of different world perspectives, celebration of the reader's personal and distinctive characteristics, and providing information about cultural contributions of different societies. Focusing specifically on European literature does not demonstrate a multicultural approach.

21.   (C)

Choice (C) is the correct order for the writing process. A writer prewrites by creating an outline, concept map, or other organizational format before beginning. Using that as the foundation, the writer creates a first draft and revises for content and form. The writing is edited and then published (distributed or shared) to form the writer-reader connection.

22.   (A)

Choice (A) is correct because a writer must consider who will be reading the content (audience), what and when the content will be read (occasion) and why the content is being written (purpose).

23.   (C)

Choice (C) is correct because diagnostic tests are designed to identify specific strengths and weaknesses. A screening test would precede a diagnostic test. Formative and progress monitoring assessments provide a teacher with information about ongoing development. While they can be helpful in determining student strengths and weaknesses, they usually focus more narrowly on the target lesson or skill rather than an in-depth examination of skills.

24.   (B)

Choice (B) is correct because rubrics define the way students should complete a complex assignment and how qualitative aspects of the assignment will be converted into quantifiable scores.

25.   (C)

Choice (C) is correct because percentile ranks create a curve of scores from 1 to 100. Thus, a score of 50 is in the middle and represents the average.

26.   (B)

Choice (B) is correct because the test results are not consistent in repeated trials.

27.   (C)

Choice (C) is correct because paraphrasing what was just said shows that the listener was paying attention and can take the thought process to the next step. Asking

"What's next?" or praising the retell can occur even if the listener is not paying attention. Reminders prior to the retelling cannot demonstrate subsequent listening.

28.　(D)

Choice (D) is correct because *genre* is the technical term for story type or category. Theme and setting are derived from the type.

29.　(B)

Choice (B) is correct because a primary source represents the direct view of someone who personally experienced or communicated an event. The other examples are secondary sources because they describe, discuss, evaluate, or otherwise process primary sources.

30.　(B)

Choice (B) is correct because photocopying a textbook is using the whole content rather than a limited selection of it. Fair use allows for limited selections of the original content to be used in teaching and learning. A photo, quotations, or passage are limited parts of a whole.

31.　(A)

Choice (A) is correct (not true) because the dimensions of language are speaking, listening, writing, and reading.

32.　(D)

Choice (D) is correct because smaller groups within a larger group maintain unique cultural identities, values, and practices as long as they are not illegal in the larger group. In cultural relativism, an individual's context provides the understanding for behavior and actions. Cultural assimilation seeks to make a smaller cultural group take on the culture of a larger group. Cultural appreciation is a surface recognition of differences in cultures, but does not mean that those cultures are supported as parts of society.

33.　(B)

Choice (B) is correct because the ability to hold and manipulate a pencil or other item in the hand depends on muscular (motor) skills.

34.　(A)

Choice (A) is correct because bibliotherapy is using the right book at the right time to promote emotional healing. The other examples do not require emotional healing.

35. (C)

Choice (C) is correct because syntactic understanding focuses on understanding the rules involved in language use, which is also called grammar. The other examples focus on understanding content in either general (e.g., reading narrative texts) or specific (vocabulary; answering questions) ways.

36. (A)

Choice (A) is correct because grammar, spelling and punctuation are related to the ways in which language is conventionally and correctly used (syntax).

37. (B)

Choice (B) is correct because students should be able to form and combine sentences by second grade. Kindergarten students focus more on writing words and simple sentences. Fourth-grade and six-grade students should be writing essays, not first attempts at paragraphs.

38. (A)

Choice (A) is correct because a bubble or concept map is used to organize initial thoughts before writing.

39. (B)

Choice (B) is correct because the students are writing informational content about what they observed. Narratives have plots and elements of stories. Personal writing is subjective, rather than objective. Reflective writing involves personal insights or conclusions, rather than observations.

40. (B)

Choice (B) is correct because *through* is a preposition. *Carnivorous* is an adjective. *Running* is a verb and *tiger* is a noun.

41. (C)

Choice (C) is correct because semantic meaning is word meaning and unrelated to motivation, primary sources, or writing in science journals.

42. (D)

Choice (D) is correct because pragmatics focuses on the social or contextual uses of language. Vocabulary and semantic understanding both address word meaning. Syntactic understanding focuses on the grammatical rules of language.

43. (A)

Choice (A) is correct because *extemporizing* refers to a type of speaking without preparation. The other responses involve reading or writing.

44. (B)

Choice (B) is correct because learning management systems focus on the organization and communication of data. Productivity software includes word processing, presentation, and spreadsheets to maximize time and content. Instructional and educational software are used in classroom teaching and learning and include drill-and-practice and simulations.

45. (A)

Choice (A) is correct because Title IX ensures that sex discrimination cannot occur and that both males and females have equal access to educational opportunities.

46. (B)

Choice (B) is correct because the language experience technique is a whole group approach to writing and reading based on a shared event.

47. (A)

Choice (A) is correct because the onset is the beginning sound of a syllable (or 1-syllable word) and the rime is the part of that consists of the vowel and consonant sounds following the vowel.

48. (C)

Choice (C) is correct because online blogs allow users to create and share content that defines Web 2.0 tools. The other options exemplify online web content, but users cannot create and share content.

49. (A)

Choice (A) is correct because the question asks for the definition of media literacy. Digital nativism describes someone who grew up using digital technologies. Technological expertise describes proficiency using technology. Online utilization is the use of Web content.

50. (D)

Choice (D) is correct because *automaticity* describes the ability to read aloud without having to sound out words. Pragmatics involves the social or contextual use of language. Prosody is reading with correct intonation, stress, and rhythm. Accuracy describes correct pronunciation of words.

51. (A)

Choice (A) is correct because screening assessments often occur before students start school in order to filter students who may need additional diagnosis and remediation from those who are ready to proceed.

52. (A)

Choice (A) is correct because textbooks describe, discuss, evaluate, or otherwise process primary sources. A Skype call, a display of authentic moon rocks, and an autobiography are primary sources because they involve personal experience or communication.

53. (B)

Choice (B) is correct because students are asked to reflect and then work with a partner before sharing responses. Jigsaw is also a cooperative learning activity, but students are generally grouped first to learn content and then regrouped so that groups have individuals who are knowledgeable on different aspects of the content. A listening guide helps students identify key points in lectures or other verbal content. RAP (Read, Ask, Put) is a speaking strategy based on reading.

54. (C)

Choice (C) is correct because summative assessments evaluate student learning at the end of an instructional unit by comparing it against some standard or benchmark. Pretests, informal reading inventories, and feedback prompts are formative assessments that do not contribute to grades.

55. (C)

Choice (C) is correct because vocabulary and outlines provide scaffolding for building speaking skills. Putting students on the spot tends to create anxiety rather than building confidence. Listening guides benefit listeners, not speakers. Informal and formal speaking share many features and skills.

56.   (A)

Choice (A) is correct because high-stakes testing is designed to determine if students have met specified benchmarks and, if not, who is accountable for their lack of success. High-stakes tests are criterion-referenced, rather than norm-referenced, tests. They do not identify individual strengths and weaknesses. They do not determine whether or not state standards and benchmarks are valid.

57.   (B)

Choice (B) is correct because instructional level includes word recognition that is 95% or better, while comprehension based on oral reading is 80% or better, and comprehension based on silent reading is 75% or better.

58.   (C)

Choice (C) is correct because the abbreviation WPM stands for words (read) per minute) and WCPM stands for words correct per minute and apply only to oral reading (fluency).

59.   (D)

Choice (D) is correct because assessments that measure what they are supposed to measure are described as valid. Norm-referenced assessments provide scores that compare student scores/skills against a norming group and scores are reported as percentile ranks. Reliability of assessments means that a test has the same or similar results when repeated.

60.   (C)

Choice (C) is correct because the activity involves both speaking (asking questions) and listening (understanding a question in order to respond). Reading a chapter and charades do not involve speaking. Graphic organizers do not involve listening.

PRACTICE TEST 1

FTCE Elementary Education K-6

Subtest 2:
Social Science

This practice test and an additional test are available at the online REA Study Center (www.rea.com/studycenter).

The FTCE Elementary Education K–6 (060) test is computer-based, so we strongly recommend that you take our online practice tests to simulate test-day conditions and to receive these added benefits:

- **Timed testing conditions**—Gauge how much time you can spend on each question.

- **Automatic scoring**—Find out how you did on the test, instantly.

- **On-screen detailed explanations of answers**—Learn not just the correct answer, but also why the other answers are incorrect.

- **Diagnostic score reports**—Pinpoint where you're strongest and where you need to focus your study.

Answer Sheet

1. Ⓐ Ⓑ Ⓒ Ⓓ
2. Ⓐ Ⓑ Ⓒ Ⓓ
3. Ⓐ Ⓑ Ⓒ Ⓓ
4. Ⓐ Ⓑ Ⓒ Ⓓ
5. Ⓐ Ⓑ Ⓒ Ⓓ
6. Ⓐ Ⓑ Ⓒ Ⓓ
7. Ⓐ Ⓑ Ⓒ Ⓓ
8. Ⓐ Ⓑ Ⓒ Ⓓ
9. Ⓐ Ⓑ Ⓒ Ⓓ
10. Ⓐ Ⓑ Ⓒ Ⓓ
11. Ⓐ Ⓑ Ⓒ Ⓓ
12. Ⓐ Ⓑ Ⓒ Ⓓ
13. Ⓐ Ⓑ Ⓒ Ⓓ
14. Ⓐ Ⓑ Ⓒ Ⓓ
15. Ⓐ Ⓑ Ⓒ Ⓓ
16. Ⓐ Ⓑ Ⓒ Ⓓ
17. Ⓐ Ⓑ Ⓒ Ⓓ
18. Ⓐ Ⓑ Ⓒ Ⓓ
19. Ⓐ Ⓑ Ⓒ Ⓓ

20. Ⓐ Ⓑ Ⓒ Ⓓ
21. Ⓐ Ⓑ Ⓒ Ⓓ
22. Ⓐ Ⓑ Ⓒ Ⓓ
23. Ⓐ Ⓑ Ⓒ Ⓓ
24. Ⓐ Ⓑ Ⓒ Ⓓ
25. Ⓐ Ⓑ Ⓒ Ⓓ
26. Ⓐ Ⓑ Ⓒ Ⓓ
27. Ⓐ Ⓑ Ⓒ Ⓓ
28. Ⓐ Ⓑ Ⓒ Ⓓ
29. Ⓐ Ⓑ Ⓒ Ⓓ
30. Ⓐ Ⓑ Ⓒ Ⓓ
31. Ⓐ Ⓑ Ⓒ Ⓓ
32. Ⓐ Ⓑ Ⓒ Ⓓ
33. Ⓐ Ⓑ Ⓒ Ⓓ
34. Ⓐ Ⓑ Ⓒ Ⓓ
35. Ⓐ Ⓑ Ⓒ Ⓓ
36. Ⓐ Ⓑ Ⓒ Ⓓ
37. Ⓐ Ⓑ Ⓒ Ⓓ
38. Ⓐ Ⓑ Ⓒ Ⓓ

39. Ⓐ Ⓑ Ⓒ Ⓓ
40. Ⓐ Ⓑ Ⓒ Ⓓ
41. Ⓐ Ⓑ Ⓒ Ⓓ
42. Ⓐ Ⓑ Ⓒ Ⓓ
43. Ⓐ Ⓑ Ⓒ Ⓓ
44. Ⓐ Ⓑ Ⓒ Ⓓ
45. Ⓐ Ⓑ Ⓒ Ⓓ
46. Ⓐ Ⓑ Ⓒ Ⓓ
47. Ⓐ Ⓑ Ⓒ Ⓓ
48. Ⓐ Ⓑ Ⓒ Ⓓ
49. Ⓐ Ⓑ Ⓒ Ⓓ
50. Ⓐ Ⓑ Ⓒ Ⓓ
51. Ⓐ Ⓑ Ⓒ Ⓓ
52. Ⓐ Ⓑ Ⓒ Ⓓ
53. Ⓐ Ⓑ Ⓒ Ⓓ
54. Ⓐ Ⓑ Ⓒ Ⓓ
55. Ⓐ Ⓑ Ⓒ Ⓓ

Subtest 2: Social Science

Questions: 55
Time: 1 hour and 5 minutes

Directions: Read each question and select the best response.

1. Which of the following is best suited for summarizing historical cause-effect relationships?

   (A) photograph

   (B) drawing

   (C) timeline

   (D) spreadsheet

2. Which of the following list reflects the correct chronological order of events?

   (A) (1) Puritans arrive in New England; (2) Protestant Reformation begins; (3) Columbus sails across the Atlantic; (4) Magna Carta is signed in England

   (B) (1) Magna Carta is signed in England; (2) Protestant Reformation begins; (3) Columbus sails across the Atlantic; (4) Puritans arrive in New England

   (C) (1) Protestant Reformation begins; (2) Magna Carta is signed in England; (3) Columbus sails across the Atlantic; (4) Puritans arrive in New England.

   (D) Columbus sails across the Atlantic; (2) Protestant Reformation begins; (3) Puritans arrive in New England (3) Protestant Reformation begins

3. The intellectual movement that encouraged the use of reason and science and anticipated human progress was called

   (A) the American System.

   (B) the mercantilism.

   (C) the Enlightenment.

   (D) the Age of Belief.

4. In American government, a system of checks and balances was developed to

    (A) regulate the amount of control each branch of government has.

    (B) make each branch of government independent from one another.

    (C) give the president control over political decisions.

    (D) give the Supreme Court control over political decisions.

5. Which of the following prohibited discrimination on the basis of race, color, or national origin?

    (A) *Brown vs. Board of Education of Topeka* (1954)

    (B) The Civil Rights Act (1964)

    (C) *Serrano vs. Priest* (1971)

    (D) Title IX of the Education Amendments (1972)

6. The Bill of Rights

    (A) listed the grievances of the colonists against the British.

    (B) forbade the federal government from encroaching on the rights of citizens.

    (C) gave all white males the right to vote.

    (D) specified the rights of slaves.

7. Studying various economic institutions promotes higher-order thinking skills. In terms of Webb's Depth of Knowledge, these skills are at level

    (A) one.

    (B) two.

    (C) three.

    (D) four.

8. Which of the following is considered the main economic institution in the United States?

    (A) The New Deal

    (B) The Environmental Protection Agency

    (C) The National Education Association

    (D) The Federal Reserve System

9. In what type of economy do individuals own the resources that are produced?

    (A) mixed economy

    (B) socialist economy

    (C) command economy

    (D) capitalist economy

10. The ruling of the Supreme Court in *Brown v. Board of Education of Topeka* (1954) determined that

    (A) separate educational facilities could offer equal educational opportunities to students.

    (B) students could be placed in segregated tracks within desegregated schools.

    (C) segregated schools resulted in unequal opportunities, but caused no psychological effects.

    (D) separate educational facilities were inherently unequal.

11. The written history of Florida begins with the arrival of which explorer?

    (A) Juan Ponce de Leon

    (B) Hernando de Soto

    (C) Pedro Menendez de Aviles

    (D) Tristan de Luna y Arellano

12. The Federal Emergency Relief Act, the Banking Act, and the Civilian Conservation Corps are all associated with which of the following?

    (A) World War II

    (B) The Marshall Plan

    (C) The Truman Doctrine

    (D) The First New Deal

13. Marxist philosophy includes all of the following EXCEPT

    (A) the assumption that economic factors determine history.

    (B) the belief that class struggle occasionally occurs.

    (C) the expectation that socialism is inevitable.

    (D) the theory that the true value of a product is labor.

14. Which of the following best summarizes the Monroe Doctrine?

    (A) The United States and the rest of North and South America will not be subject to future colonization.

    (B) The United States is a politically independent entity.

    (C) The United States has the right to protect its political borders.

    (D) The United States will accept immigration on a limited basis.

15. Leaving a country because of its oppressive, legally-mandated racial segregation policies would be an example of exodus due to

    (A) physical reasons.

    (B) economic reasons.

    (C) cultural reasons.

    (D) political reasons.

16. Which of the following is *not* one of the main types of map projections?

    (A) conic

    (B) cylindrical

    (C) interrupted

    (D) meridial

17. Which of the following is *not* a requirement to become a U.S. president?

    (A) natural-born U.S. citizenship

    (B) resident of the U.S. for at least 14 years

    (C) member of major political party

    (D) at least 35 years of age

18. In terms of complexity of informational text, which of the following is an example of a quantitative variable?

    (A) student motivation

    (B) domain-specific vocabulary

    (C) subject

    (D) readability

19. The most important focus of social studies instruction should be

    (A) causal relationships.

    (B) comparisons and contrast.

    (C) sequential events.

    (D) famous people who influenced history.

20. Mr. Key's class is reading Abraham Lincoln's *Gettysburg Address*. Which of the following is an example of a text-dependent question?

    (A) Where was Gettysburg?

    (B) Lincoln uses the word *dedicate* several times. Does the word have the same meaning each time? Why or why not?

    (C) What is an "address?"

    (D) If you had been a Civil War soldier, what would have been your feelings?

21. Tool creation and use by early humans exemplifies

    (A) technology.

    (B) culture.

    (C) trade.

    (D) cognitive development.

22. What was an outcome of the Industrial Revolution?

    (A) advances in information technology

    (B) mechanization of work

    (C) development of sustainable technologies

    (D) decreases in air, water, and soil pollution

23. Which of the following is *not* a power specifically granted to the federal government?

    (A) minting money

    (B) providing for education

    (C) conducting relations with foreign powers

    (D) regulating naturalization and immigration

24. What was the focus of the Three-Fifths Compromise?

    (A) It mandated that three-fifths of the states must approve an amendment to the U.S. Constitution.

    (B) It determined the fractional proportions for immigration from European countries versus countries from other parts of the world.

    (C) In terms of representation and taxation of states, slaves counted as three-fifths of a person.

    (D) In presidential elections, the winner must receive a minimum of three-fifths of the votes that are cast.

25. Mrs. Fernando's class is studying currencies of the world. Some of her students have brought coins from Brazil, Ireland, Canada, and Mexico. In terms of instruction, these examples are called

    (A) realia.

    (B) regalia.

    (C) models.

    (D) monies.

26. What is true of the legislative branch of the United States?

    (A) It is unicameral.

    (B) A state's population does not determine how many representatives represent that state in the House of Representatives.

    (C) It has the power to veto legislation.

    (D) Article 1 of the Constitution describes the form and function of the legislative branch.

27. The oldest human bones have been discovered in

    (A) Europe.

    (B) Africa.

    (C) North America.

    (D) South America.

28. Anthony is traveling outside of the United States. He is in a country that has a parliamentary form of government. Which country could he be in?

    (A) Great Britain

    (B) North Korea

    (C) France

    (D) India

29. What is true of the Declaration of Independence?

    (A) It established a system of checks and balances.

    (B) It promoted equality as a human right.

    (C) It contained the Bill of Rights.

    (D) It was based on the Articles of Confederation.

30. Mr. Tomlinson's class has been studying the Mayan civilization. He has posed the question, "What did the Mayans believe?" This question focuses on what aspect of the civilization?

    (A) social

    (B) political

    (C) theoretical

    (D) religious

31. The interaction between potential buyers and sellers of goods and services is defined as

    (A) the market.

    (B) the stock market.

    (C) entrepreneurship.

    (D) the federal reserve.

32. Which concept and country are correctly matched?

    (A) *shogun*; China

    (B) *patricians*; France

    (C) *city-state (polis)*; Greece

    (D) *oligarch*; India

33. Which individual and concept are correctly matched?

    (A) William the Conqueror; Domesday Book

    (B) Martin Luther; Crusades

    (C) Charlemagne; Reformation

    (D) Thomas Aquinas; Calvinism

34. What is the purpose of U.S. Citizenship and Immigration Services?

    (A) to increase the number of immigrants coming to the United States

    (B) to oversee the naturalization of aliens lawfully residing in the United States

    (C) to create laws to regulate where immigrants could come from and how many could come

    (D) to develop procedures for protecting U.S. borders

35. In the first week of Mrs. Drake's fourth-grade class, she shared her class vision and instructional expectations for the class and then she had the class help develop five classroom rules that would be followed throughout the year. The class discussed and debated the rules and voted on the ones that best fit the class vision and student interests. What was Mrs. Drake's purpose for this class activity?

   (A) to demonstrate democratic principles

   (B) to allow for multicultural perspectives

   (C) to create educational equity

   (D) to advocate for cultural plurality

36. What was British philosopher John Locke's influence on the development of the U.S. Constitution?

   (A) responsibilities of citizens to uphold the government

   (B) the right of people to alter or abolish a government that did not protect their interests

   (C) development of checks and balances

   (D) inclusion of a federal judicial system

37. Which branch of the government has impeachment power?

   (A) federal

   (B) executive

   (C) judicial

   (D) legislative

38. Who was one of the authors of the Constitution?

   (A) George Washington

   (B) Thomas Jefferson

   (C) James Madison

   (D) Benjamin Franklin

39. Credit unions are owned by

    (A) the Federal Deposit Insurance Corporation

    (B) the people who deposit money in them

    (C) credit companies such as Visa and American Express

    (D) the Federal Reserve

40. Mr. Carson's class has been studying the cultures that contributed to modern-day Florida. What would be the most authentic way for students to demonstrate their understanding?

    (A) writing a research paper on one of Florida's Native American tribes

    (B) taking a criterion-referenced test on Florida history

    (C) creating a project using the most recent census data

    (D) writing a short story from a first-person perspective about living in Florida

41. Which of the following could be defined as a "good" in economic terms?

    (A) a used car

    (B) money in the bank

    (C) a college education

    (D) a school loan

42. Mrs. Clark's class is learning about money and its relationship to their lives. She has divided the students into groups. Each group has a scenario in which a family of varying size and income must decide how to budget and spend available funds. This activity reflects the concept of

    (A) Law of Supply.

    (B) Law of Demand.

    (C) macroeconomics.

    (D) microeconomics.

43. Which of the following terms describes the assimilationist view of immigrants who came to the United States?

    (A) salad bowl

    (B) melting pot

    (C) frying pan

    (D) coffee cup

44. The *Great Awakening* focused on

    (A) religion.

    (B) colonization of the New World by European countries.

    (C) a rebirth of interest in the arts.

    (D) science.

45. Mrs. Silvio's students are working on learning from complex informational texts. Which of the following is a reader variable that Mrs. Silvio should take into consideration?

    (A) student motivation

    (B) readability of the reading materials

    (C) vocabulary in the reading selections

    (D) use of primary versus secondary sources

46. In a market economy, which of the following motivates producers?

    (A) the government

    (B) profit

    (C) labor resources

    (D) natural resources

47. Which of the following is an example of a secured loan?

    (A) a car loan

    (B) a school loan

    (C) money owed on a credit card

    (D) a personal loan

48. In terms of economics, which is true?

    (A) Wants are the same as needs.

    (B) Productivity impacts scarcity.

    (C) An economic boom occurs when natural resources are depleted.

    (D) Currency has absolute values globally and relative values within the country that issues it.

49. Val is a volunteer in another country. The country could be characterized as poor and developing. She observes that production and distribution of goods is determined by custom and economic changes occur very slowly. The country could be described as having what kind of economy?

    (A) traditional

    (B) command

    (C) socialist

    (D) mixed

50. Mrs. Kwan is planning a lesson on the Constitution for her fifth-grade students. She has several video clips in which American citizens describe what the Constitution means to them. The videos exemplify Mrs. Kwan's use of

    (A) educational media.

    (B) expert opinions.

    (C) scaffolding.

    (D) complex informational text.

51. What was the result of the Treaty of Paris of 1783?

    (A) It started the Spanish American War.

    (B) It recognized the United States as an independent nation.

    (C) It started the industrial revolution.

    (D) It ended the French Revolution.

52. A biome is most related to

    (A) physical geography.

    (B) religious differences.

    (C) cultural assimilation.

    (D) immigration and naturalization.

53. Mrs. Kelso's class has learned about using globes. She asked each student to identify one fact about globes. Which student's response is *incorrect*?

    (A) Geoff said, "The equator divides the earth into Northern and Southern Hemispheres."

    (B) Kim said, "The International Date Line is a meridian."

    (C) Rod said, "The equator crosses the poles."

    (D) Ashleigh said, "The prime meridian is on the opposite side of the globe from the International Date Line."

54. Mrs. Griffin's class is reading about the Trail of Tears. What group is the focus of the lesson?

    (A) Cherokee Indians

    (B) Irish immigrants

    (C) Mexican revolutionaries

    (D) Civil War Confederate forces

55. Mrs. Lawton wants her students to understand the meaning of *civilization*. She has given her students paragraphs to read. Each paragraph is about a different ancient civilization. The students have read the paragraphs. They used a comparison/contrast chart to identify similar characteristics and then they grouped the characteristics. Mrs. Lawton's approach could best be described as

    (A) authentic assessment.

    (B) concept development.

    (C) use of primary sources.

    (D) project-based learning.

Practice Test 1, Subtest 2
Answer Key

1.	(C)	20.	(B)	39.	(B)
2.	(B)	21.	(A)	40.	(C)
3.	(C)	22.	(B)	41.	(A)
4.	(A)	23.	(B)	42.	(D)
5.	(B)	24.	(C)	43.	(B)
6.	(B)	25.	(A)	44.	(A)
7.	(D)	26.	(D)	45.	(A)
8.	(D)	27.	(B)	46.	(B)
9.	(D)	28.	(A)	47.	(A)
10.	(D)	29.	(B)	48.	(B)
11.	(A)	30.	(D)	49.	(A)
12.	(D)	31.	(A)	50.	(A)
13.	(B)	32.	(C)	51.	(B)
14.	(A)	33.	(A)	52.	(A)
15.	(D)	34.	(B)	53.	(C)
16.	(D)	35.	(A)	54.	(A)
17.	(C)	36.	(B)	55.	(B)
18.	(D)	37.	(D)		
19.	(A)	38.	(C)		

Self-Assessment Guide
Social Science

Practice-test questions are sorted here by competency. To get an idea of your level of mastery, check the box under the question numbers that you answered correctly.

Competency 1: Knowledge of Effective Instructional Practices and Assessment of the Social Sciences   __/10

1	18	20	25	30	35	40	45	50	55

Competency 2: Knowledge of Time, Continuity, and Change (History)   __/14

2	3	7	11	12	13	14	19	27	32

33	44	51	54

Competency 3: Knowledge of People, Places, and Environments (Geography)   __/10

5	10	15	16	21	22	34	43	52	53

Competency 4: Knowledge of Government and the Citizen   __/11

4	6	17	23	24	26	28	29	36	37

38

Competency 5: Knowledge of Production, Distribution, and Production (Economics)   __/10

8	9	31	39	41	42	46	47	48	49

TOTAL   _____/55

Subtest 2: Social Science
Answer Explanations

1.   (C)

Choice (C) is correct because a timeline orders events sequentially. This allows relationships such as causes and effects to be seen across time. Photographs and drawings show only one point in time. Spreadsheets show if-then relationships.

2.   (B)

Choice (B) is correct because the events occurred in the following order: (1) Magna Carta is signed in England; (2) Protestant Reformation begins; (3) Columbus sails across the Atlantic; (4) Puritans arrive in New England.

3.   (C)

Choice (C) is correct because the Enlightenment followed the scientific revolution that focused more on the use of reason and freedom, rather than on church dogma, as the source of knowledge.

4.   (A)

Choice (A) is correct because the checks and balances system gives each branch of the government a way to check what the other branches are doing and bring the system into balance. Thus, the branches are dependent on each other rather than independent and no branch has full control.

5.   (B)

Choice (B) is correct because the Civil Rights Act did prohibit discrimination on the basis of race, color or national origin. *Brown vs. Board of Education of Topeka* declared that "separate but equal schools" were unconstitutional. *Serrano vs. Priest* sought to overcome disparities in education funding. Title IX prohibits discrimination based on sex in any federally-funded program or activity.

6.   (B)

Choice (B) is correct because the purpose of the Bill of Rights (the first ten amendments) is to specify and guarantee citizen entitlements. The Bill of Rights is not a list of grievances. The right to vote and rights of slaves are not addressed in the first ten amendments.

7.   (D)

Choice (D) is correct because the highest level of thinking occurs at the fourth level of Webb's Depth of Knowledge. Level one addresses recall. Level two addresses concept and skill development. Level three addresses strategic thinking.

8.   (D)

Choice (D) is correct because the Federal Reserve System is the main economic institution in the U.S. The New Deal created domestic programs in the 1930s to bolster the economy following the Great Depression and focused on relief, recovery, and reform. Neither the Environmental Protection Agency nor the National Education Agency is considered to be an economic institution.

9.   (D)

Choice (D) is correct because a capitalist economy is defined as one in which individuals own what they produce. In a command economy, the government controls what is produced, how much is produced, and the value. In a socialist economy, the people as a society (rather than individuals in the society) control the economy. A mixed economy combines features of the three major economic types.

10.   (D)

Choice (D) is correct because *Brown v. Board of Education of Topeka* determined that the concept of "separate but equal" was unconstitutional.

11.   (A)

Choice (A) is correct because Juan Ponce de Leon was the first European explorer in Florida, arriving in 1513. De Soto arrived in 1539. De Luna came to Pensacola Bay in 1559 and Pedro Menendez de Aviles founded St. Augustine in 1565.

12.   (D)

Choice (D) is correct because the New Deal sought to stabilize the economy after the Great Depression by providing opportunities for relief, recovery, and reform. The Marshall Plan is related to World War II and the Truman Doctrine is related to the Cold War, which followed World War II.

13. **(B)**

Choice (B) is correct because Marxist philosophy believes that class struggle is inevitable.

14. **(A)**

Choice (A) is correct because it correctly summarizes the intent of the Monroe Doctrine.

15. **(D)**

Choice (D) is correct because legal mandates imply governmental (political) control.

16. **(D)**

Choice (D) is correct because conic, cylindrical, and interrupted are map types.

17. **(C)**

Choice (C) is correct because there is no requirement that a U.S. president be a member of a political party. A candidate can run on an independent ticket.

18. **(D)**

Choice (D) is correct because readability is determined by a formula based on text characteristics such as word or sentence length and results in a numerical rating. The other variables are qualitative.

19. **(A)**

Choice (A) is correct because the key idea in understanding social studies is understanding why events occurred as they did.

20. **(B)**

Choice (B) is correct because the reader has to consider the word in context to determine meaning and explain the response. The other questions can be answered without reading the *Gettysburg Address*.

21. **(A)**

Choice (A) is correct because *technology* refers to tool development regardless of the time period.

22. (B)

Choice (B) is correct because the production transitioned from mostly home-based and individually-produced goods to goods that were produced by individuals who operated machines that produced goods.

23. (B)

Choice (B) is correct because provision of education is a power granted to the states.

24. (C)

Choice (C) is correct because the Three-Fifths Compromise focused on the representation and taxation of states.

25. (A)

Choice (A) is correct because *realia* describes the use of authentic objects from everyday life that can be used as teaching aids.

26. (D)

Choice (D) is correct. The legislative branch is bicameral. A state's population determines how many representatives a state can have in the House of Representatives. The President has the power to veto legislation.

27. (B)

Choice (B) is correct because the oldest human remains have been found in Ethiopia and other African countries.

28. (A)

Choice (A) is correct. India has a federal form of government. France has a unitary form of government. North Korea has an authoritarian form of government.

29. (B)

Choice (B) is correct because the Declaration of Independence states that "all men are created equal with certain unalienable rights." Checks and balances and the Bill of Rights are part of the Constitution, and the Constitution is based on the Articles of Confederation.

30. **(D)**

Choice (D) is correct because beliefs are based on faith and religion.

31. **(A)**

Choice (A) is correct. The stock market is the market in which the purchase or sale of equity in publicly held companies takes place. Entrepreneurship is the creation of new businesses. The Federal Reserve is the central bank for the United States.

32. **(C)**

Choice (C) is correct because the concept and country are correctly matched. Shogun is associated with Japan. Patricians are associated with ancient Rome. Although the word *oligarch* has Greek roots, it is most often used in connection with Russian governments.

33. **(A)**

Choice (A) is correct because William the Conqueror was responsible for commanding that there be a survey to discover what taxes (based on holdings) had been owed during the reign of King Edward the Confessor. Martin Luther is associated with the Protestant Reformation. Charlemagne is considered to be the Father of Europe. Thomas Aquinas is associated with endeavoring to bridge the gap between religious belief and reason/science.

34. **(B)**

Choice (B) is correct because overseeing the naturalization of aliens lawfully residing in the U.S. is the mission of the U.S. Citizenship and Immigration Services.

35. **(A)**

Choice (A) is correct because debate and voting characterize governance "by the people."

36. **(B)**

Choice (B) is correct because John Locke was known for his social contract theory, which questioned the legitimacy of authority of the state (government) over the people.

37. **(D)**

Choice (D) is correct because the legislative branch best represents the people. *Federal* refers to all branches of national government, rather than a specific branch. Since impeachment refers to removal of the President, the executive branch does not have that power. The judicial branch interprets the law.

38. (C)

Choice (C) is correct. James Madison is widely regarded as the father of the U.S. Constitution. Thomas Jefferson and Benjamin Franklin were two of the authors of the Declaration of Independence. Washington was eventually chosen as the first President of the United States, but did not contribute to the writing of the Constitution.

39. (B)

Choice (B) is correct. The FDIC insures deposits in banks. Credit companies do not own credit unions. The Federal Reserve is the central banking institution in the U.S.

40. (C)

Choice (C) is correct because authenticity involves real-life information such as census data. Research, testing, and creative writing do not focus on real-life information.

41. (A)

Choice (A) is correct because a used car is a tangible item that satisfies human wants or needs.

42. (D)

Choice (D) is correct because using a family to demonstrate how budgeting works occurs on a small (micro) scale.

43. (B)

Choice (B) is correct because assimilationist views of immigrants want the immigrants to blend into society and become indistinguishable from it.

44. (A)

Choice (A) is correct. The Great Awakening referred to revivals of religious interest in the U.S. in the late 1700s and early 1800s.

45. (A)

Choice (A) is correct because the other variables are text variables.

46. (B)

Choice (B) is correct because the more money (profit) that a producer makes, the more the producer is encouraged to continue or increase production.

47. (A)

Choice (A) is correct because a secured loan is based on a tangible item or asset.

48. (B)

Choice (B) is correct because the more of an item or service that is produced, the more it becomes available and prices decrease. Wants are not the same as needs. The depletion of natural resources does not contribute to an economic boom. Currency has relative values globally and absolute values within the country that distributes it.

49. (A)

Choice (A) is correct because traditional economies are characteristic in developing parts of the world which rely more on the way things have customarily been done. A command economy relies on a central authority to make decisions. A socialist economy relies on collective societies or the government to make decisions. Mixed economies have characteristics of more than one economic type.

50. (A)

Choice (A) is correct because video is a type of media.

51. (B)

Choice (B) is correct. The Treaty of Paris did not contribute to the other events.

52. (A)

Choice (A) is correct because a biome is defined as all the plants and animals in a natural habitat, which relates to geography.

53. (C)

Choice (C) is correct because the equator is equidistant from the poles.

54. (A)

Choice (A) is correct because the Trail of Tears was the route taken by Indians who were forcibly moved from lands east of the Mississippi and sent to what is now Oklahoma.

55. (B)

Choice (B) is correct because Mrs. Lawson is using various approaches to help students understand the universal meaning of civilization. Authentic assessment would be one that would require students to apply concepts to everyday life. Primary source usage would involve first-person accounts and records. Project-based learning would focus on the resolution of a complex question or challenge over time.

PRACTICE TEST 1

FTCE Elementary Education K-6

Subtest 3: Science

This practice test and an additional test are available at the online REA Study Center (www.rea.com/studycenter).

The FTCE Elementary Education K–6 (060) test is computer-based, so we strongly recommend that you take our online practice tests to simulate test-day conditions and to receive these added benefits:

- **Timed testing conditions**—Gauge how much time you can spend on each question.

- **Automatic scoring**—Find out how you did on the test, instantly.

- **On-screen detailed explanations of answers**—Learn not just the correct answer, but also why the other answers are incorrect.

- **Diagnostic score reports**—Pinpoint where you're strongest and where you need to focus your study.

Answer Sheet

1. Ⓐ Ⓑ Ⓒ Ⓓ
2. Ⓐ Ⓑ Ⓒ Ⓓ
3. Ⓐ Ⓑ Ⓒ Ⓓ
4. Ⓐ Ⓑ Ⓒ Ⓓ
5. Ⓐ Ⓑ Ⓒ Ⓓ
6. Ⓐ Ⓑ Ⓒ Ⓓ
7. Ⓐ Ⓑ Ⓒ Ⓓ
8. Ⓐ Ⓑ Ⓒ Ⓓ
9. Ⓐ Ⓑ Ⓒ Ⓓ
10. Ⓐ Ⓑ Ⓒ Ⓓ
11. Ⓐ Ⓑ Ⓒ Ⓓ
12. Ⓐ Ⓑ Ⓒ Ⓓ
13. Ⓐ Ⓑ Ⓒ Ⓓ
14. Ⓐ Ⓑ Ⓒ Ⓓ
15. Ⓐ Ⓑ Ⓒ Ⓓ
16. Ⓐ Ⓑ Ⓒ Ⓓ
17. Ⓐ Ⓑ Ⓒ Ⓓ
18. Ⓐ Ⓑ Ⓒ Ⓓ
19. Ⓐ Ⓑ Ⓒ Ⓓ

20. Ⓐ Ⓑ Ⓒ Ⓓ
21. Ⓐ Ⓑ Ⓒ Ⓓ
22. Ⓐ Ⓑ Ⓒ Ⓓ
23. Ⓐ Ⓑ Ⓒ Ⓓ
24. Ⓐ Ⓑ Ⓒ Ⓓ
25. Ⓐ Ⓑ Ⓒ Ⓓ
26. Ⓐ Ⓑ Ⓒ Ⓓ
27. Ⓐ Ⓑ Ⓒ Ⓓ
28. Ⓐ Ⓑ Ⓒ Ⓓ
29. Ⓐ Ⓑ Ⓒ Ⓓ
30. Ⓐ Ⓑ Ⓒ Ⓓ
31. Ⓐ Ⓑ Ⓒ Ⓓ
32. Ⓐ Ⓑ Ⓒ Ⓓ
33. Ⓐ Ⓑ Ⓒ Ⓓ
34. Ⓐ Ⓑ Ⓒ Ⓓ
35. Ⓐ Ⓑ Ⓒ Ⓓ
36. Ⓐ Ⓑ Ⓒ Ⓓ
37. Ⓐ Ⓑ Ⓒ Ⓓ
38. Ⓐ Ⓑ Ⓒ Ⓓ

39. Ⓐ Ⓑ Ⓒ Ⓓ
40. Ⓐ Ⓑ Ⓒ Ⓓ
41. Ⓐ Ⓑ Ⓒ Ⓓ
42. Ⓐ Ⓑ Ⓒ Ⓓ
43. Ⓐ Ⓑ Ⓒ Ⓓ
44. Ⓐ Ⓑ Ⓒ Ⓓ
45. Ⓐ Ⓑ Ⓒ Ⓓ
46. Ⓐ Ⓑ Ⓒ Ⓓ
47. Ⓐ Ⓑ Ⓒ Ⓓ
48. Ⓐ Ⓑ Ⓒ Ⓓ
49. Ⓐ Ⓑ Ⓒ Ⓓ
50. Ⓐ Ⓑ Ⓒ Ⓓ
51. Ⓐ Ⓑ Ⓒ Ⓓ
52. Ⓐ Ⓑ Ⓒ Ⓓ
53. Ⓐ Ⓑ Ⓒ Ⓓ
54. Ⓐ Ⓑ Ⓒ Ⓓ
55. Ⓐ Ⓑ Ⓒ Ⓓ

Subtest 3: Science

Questions: 55
Time: 1 hour and 10 minutes

Directions: Read each question and select the best response.

1. A principal is walking by Mr. Longman's classroom and hears him say, "Today we are going to be learning about the energy of moving molecules." What is the topic of Mr. Longman's lesson?

    (A) parallel circuits

    (B) heat

    (C) magnets

    (D) chemical energy

2. Mrs. Arton wants her students to learn to think scientifically. Which of the following is most likely to result in the deepest scientific understanding?

    (A) Providing drill and practice preparation for the statewide science assessment.

    (B) Teaching students to design and do simple experiments.

    (C) Obtaining classroom subscriptions to science periodicals.

    (D) Asking students to locate examples of real-world science in newspapers.

3. All of the following are examples of fossils EXCEPT

    (A) an insect in a piece of amber found in South America.

    (B) an arrowhead found in North America.

    (C) a dinosaur bone found in Europe.

    (D) a leaf imprint in coal found in China.

4. What was the most immediate, concrete result of the launching of the Soviet space satellite *Sputnik* on October 4, 1957?

(A) Congress established NASA in 1958 to focus on space exploration.

(B) The U.S. feared it was lagging behind in technology and took steps to catch up.

(C) The U.S. and Soviets worked collaboratively to win the space race.

(D) The U.S. had a manned lunar landing the following year.

5. Which of the following would be the correct labels for the water cycle?

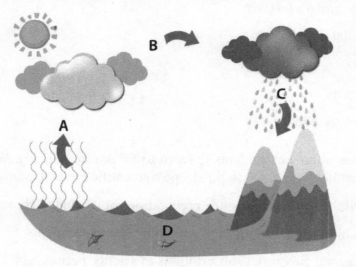

(A) A = evaporation, B = condensation, C = precipitation, D = collection

(B) A = condensation, B = evaporation, C = collection, D = precipitation

(C) A = collection, B = condensation, C = precipitation, D = evaporation

(D) A = precipitation, B = collection, C = evaporation, D = condensation

6. A student has created a Venn diagram to compare and contrast bacteria and viruses. What, if anything, is incorrect?

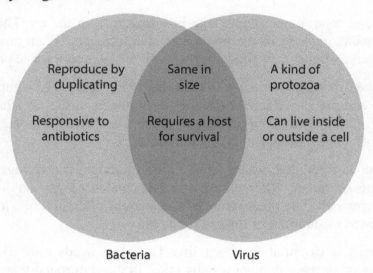

(A) There are no factual mistakes.

(B) The information about bacteria is correct; however, the information about viruses and the information about how viruses and bacteria are alike are incorrect.

(C) The information about bacteria and the information about viruses are correct; however, the information about how viruses and bacteria are alike is incorrect.

(D) The information about how viruses and bacteria are alike is correct; however the information about bacteria and the information about viruses are incorrect.

7. A student dropped a book on his toe and said, "Ouch! That hurt!" This is a result of which aspect of the nervous system?

(A) striated muscles

(B) autonomic responses

(C) exteroceptors

(D) antibody molecules

8. Mrs. Smith had the following short-answer question on an exam: *Describe the nitrogen cycle.* Which response is correct?

(A) To make food, green plants take in nitrogen from the air. The waste product that plants give off in the process is also nitrogen. When animals breathe in nitrogen to digest their food, they give off nitrogen as a waste product.

(B) Nitrogen-fixing bacteria live in the soil and in the roots of legumes (e.g., beans, peas, and clover). Bacteria change the nitrogen in the air (that plants cannot use) into nitrogen materials that plants can use. After animals eat plants, they give off waste materials that contain nitrogen.

(C) As the earth cooled, water vapor, carbon dioxide, and nitrogen became components of the air. When the water vapor condensed, carbon dioxide and nitrogen remained. The plants reduced the amount of carbon dioxide in the air and increased the amount of oxygen in the air.

(D) Nitrogen is essential for plant life. The plant needs nitrogen to make food, among other uses. A plant usually takes in more nitrogen than it needs. To get rid of excess nitrogen, the stomata of the leaves allow the nitrogen to pass out as water vapor. This evaporation of nitrogen from the plant is transpiration.

9. Ms. Lee is teaching her fifth-grade students how to use a microscope. Which of the following microscope activities would *not* be appropriate in meeting this goal?

(A) examining cotton fibers

(B) having students examine a leaf

(C) looking at soil samples

(D) having students prick their fingers and examine a drop of blood

10. Mr. Post is teaching a lesson on force at a distance. Which of the following can he use as an example?

(A) a lever

(B) a screw

(C) a magnet

(D) a pulley

11. Ms. Jackson's fourth-grade students are doing a project on weather. First, she had them look up different kinds of clouds. Then she had them observe the sky at 8 am, noon, and 2 pm, describe the clouds, and predict the weather. She is checking their observations for different dates and sees one that is clearly incorrect. Which one is it?

(A) September 3, 10 am. I see light-colored stratus clouds in a blue sky. I predict the weather will stay the same.

(B) September 8, noon: I see thin, wispy cirrus clouds. I predict a change in the weather.

(C) September 12, 2 pm: I see dark, flat stratus clouds. I predict sunshine for the rest of the day.

(D) September 14, 10 am: I see white fluffy cumulus clouds. I predict good weather.

12. What aspects of a plant cell distinguish it from an animal cell?

(A) nuclear membrane and mitochondria

(B) nucleus and chromosomes

(C) chloroplasts and cell walls

(D) cytoplasm and vesicles

13. In plant cells, what process allows the energy in sunlight to be converted to chemical energy and become biologically available?

(A) photosynthesis

(B) osmosis

(C) fermentation

(D) propagation

14. What is another name for a testable question?

(A) prediction

(B) experiment

(C) observation

(D) hypothesis

15. Which of the following is the application of science for the benefit of mankind?

    (A) technology

    (B) STEM

    (C) experimentation

    (D) investigation

16. Which of the following could be best used to collect data for analysis?

    (A) scale model of the solar system

    (B) survey of a class's food preferences in terms of calories

    (C) demonstration of ways to graph an equation

    (D) creating a testable hypothesis

17. Mr. Kwan wants to apply Vygotsky's theory of the Zone of Proximal Development in his third grade classroom in terms of learning about the human skeleton. Which activity would achieve this goal?

    (A) showing students a video about bone growth and development

    (B) partnering his students with fourth grade students who learned about the human skeleton last year

    (C) asking a nurse to visit the class and answer questions about health and the human body

    (D) playing an online drill-and-practice review of names of bones

18. The principal in Ms. Bridge's school wants the teachers to include more formal learning activities into science instruction. What activity would best achieve this goal?

    (A) a field trip to a local farm to see how crops are grown

    (B) a lecture and test on cell division

    (C) forming an after-school science club to learn to fly drones

    (D) skyping with experts at NASA to learn more about experiments on the International Space Station

19. Mr. Alder wants to know the difference between cooperative and collaborative learning. Which colleague has the answer?

    (A) Mr. Bell: Cooperative learning is another name for collaborative learning.

    (B) Ms. Carter: Cooperative learning includes positive interdependence and structured group interactions whereas collaborative learning is loosely organized small groups.

    (C) Mrs. Skelton: Collaborative learning utilizes scientific inquiry to make sense of authentic problems whereas cooperative learning is really the same as learning partners.

    (D) Mr. Griffith: Collaborative learning is highly structured and everyone has a contribution to the total project and cooperative learning is a kind of peer-tutoring approach.

20. Which of the following exemplifies a chemical change?

    (A) a rusty frying pan

    (B) the evaporation of rainwater

    (C) freezing a popsicle

    (D) heating tomato soup in a microwave oven

21. Mrs. Penny asked her students to name a food that is a homogeneous mixture. Which student has the correct answer?

    (A) Jake: Spaghetti and meatballs

    (B) Austin: apple pie

    (C) Kelsey: vanilla yogurt

    (D) Cody: chicken noodle soup

22. Principal McManus looked in Mr. Kelly's fifth-grade classroom and heard the class discussing Pangaea. What was most likely a topic in Mr. Kelly's lesson?

    (A) continental drift

    (B) photosynthesis

    (C) principles of motion

    (D) differences between viruses and bacteria

23. What is measured by the Richter scale?

    (A) the amount of seafloor spreading

    (B) the magnitude of an earthquake

    (C) the strength of a hurricane

    (D) the speed of viscosity

24. What is the purpose of the *Linnaean system*?

    (A) taxonomy for geological formations

    (B) classification of matter as gas, solid, liquid or plasma

    (C) rating system for the force of a tornado

    (D) naming structure for species

25. Paula has been observing a plant and sees evidence of *phototropism*. What did Paula see?

    (A) parasites on the plant

    (B) wilted leaves due to a lack of water

    (C) the plant bending toward the light

    (D) lack of growth because the plant doesn't get enough sunlight

26. Mr. Carrier wants to teach his second-grade class about the process of observation. He divided his students into groups and gave each group 4 worksheets divided into five sections: *taste, touch, smell, see, listen*. He also included pictures (e.g., eyes for *see*; ears for *listen*) to help cue the words so students will remember what to do. He has given the students a piece of lemon, a piece of apple, a piece of celery, and a small carrot. The groups are to complete the worksheet by recording their observations for each item. This activity exemplifies

    (A) scaffolding.

    (B) problem-solving.

    (C) modeling.

    (D) simulation.

27. Mrs. Thompson is teaching her first-grade students different aspects of the scientific method. She has divided the class into groups and has given each group a box of wooden beads of differing colors, shapes, and sizes. She has asked the students to organize the beads and then explain how the beads were organized. Which aspect of the scientific method does the activity best exemplify?

    (A) classification

    (B) forming a hypothesis

    (C) measuring

    (D) predicting

28. Ms. Catalano is playing a game with her students. She describes a state of matter and then they tell her what exemplifies it. She said, "This matter has molecules that move freely." Which guess is correct?

    (A) a ball rolling down a hill

    (B) air inside a balloon

    (C) cereal and milk in a bowl

    (D) water in a drinking fountain

29. Anna wrote the following paragraph about atoms:

    > Atoms are made of molecules. If the atoms are the same, it forms an element. The atomic number is used to organize the periodic table.

    What sentence, if any, is factually *incorrect*?

    (A) Atoms are made of molecules.

    (B) If the atoms are the same, it forms an element.

    (C) The atomic number is used to organize the periodic table.

    (D) All of the sentences are factually correct.

30. Mr. Carpenter wrote the following words on the board: *folded, fault-block, domes, volcanic*. What geological feature is most likely to be the topic of his lesson?

    (A) plateaus

    (B) plains

    (C) mountains

    (D) canyons

31. Mrs. Donovan asked her students to identify something that has a positive effect on the environment. Which student has the correct answer?

    (A) Gerald: clear cutting a forest

    (B) Logan: aquaculture

    (C) Rachel: using fossil fuels

    (D) Nova: algae bloom

32. What do the following three words have in common? *archaea, bacteria, eukarya*

    (A) domain names

    (B) single-celled organisms

    (C) viruses

    (D) plant species

33. What is *protista*?

    (A) an inorganic substance

    (B) an organism that doesn't fit into other categories

    (C) part of plant metabolism

    (D) a fungal virus

34. How do *scientific laws* differ *from scientific theories*?

    (A) There is no difference; they are synonyms.

    (B) Scientific laws apply to inorganic matter in the universe whereas scientific theories apply to organic materials.

    (C) Scientific laws describe and scientific theories explain.

    (D) Scientific laws are not subject to change; however, scientific theories change continually.

35. What is a goal of *scientific literacy*?

    (A) learning to conduct scientific experimentation

    (B) participation in the decision-making process of our society

    (C) increasing test scores on state assessments

    (D) encouraging students to engage in STEM activities

36. The National Academy of Sciences identified six competencies for teachers of science at any grade level. Which of the following is *not* one of these competencies?

    (A) planning of inquiry-based science programs

    (B) guiding and facilitating student learning

    (C) increasing assessment scores on state exams

    (D) creating communities of science learners

37. Ms. Kendrick is teaching first grade and she wants her students to learn about the scientific method. In terms of developmental skills, what would be the best activity to teach first?

    (A) observation

    (B) classification

    (C) hypothesizing

    (D) analysis

38. Which of the following is defined as the ability of matter to move other matter or produce a chemical change in other matter?

    (A) force at a distance

    (B) energy

    (C) magnetism

    (D) conservation

39. Which of the following exemplifies potential energy?

    (A) music

    (B) an electric heater

    (C) sunlight

    (D) gravity

40. In terms of the composition of Earth, in what layer would you find semi-molten rock?

    (A) crust

    (B) mantle

    (C) outer core

    (D) inner core

41. Marble is which type of rock?

    (A) igneous

    (B) metamorphic

    (C) sedimentary

    (D) volcanic

42. Asexual propagation is most likely to occur in

    (A) reptiles.

    (B) single-celled organisms.

    (C) fish.

    (D) flowering plants.

43. A discussion about Punnett squares is most likely to address an aspect of

    (A) reproduction.

    (B) homeostasis.

    (C) photosynthesis.

    (D) metabolism.

44. Which of the following is true about differentiation of instruction?

    (A) It is in intervention strategy that targets struggling students.

    (B) It is used to help students with disabilities.

    (C) It exemplifies universal design for learning.

    (D) It is a whole group strategy designed to maximize test scores.

45. Mrs. Proctor's fourth-grade students are investigating wind speed. What science tool would be best to use?

    (A) a weather vane

    (B) a barometer

    (C) an anemometer

    (D) a stopwatch

46. Mr. Cohen's second-grade class has been learning about measurement in terms of the scientific method. He is reviewing various measurements that were recorded. Which one is correct?

    (A) increase in weight by 6 kiloliters

    (B) temperature of 43 kcal

    (C) wood chip density of 3 grams

    (D) plant height of 1 meter

47. A class is investigating the relationship between temperature and time of day. What would be the best way to capture that data in order to identify a pattern?

    (A) data table

    (B) photographs

    (C) sketches

    (D) discussion

48. Where would you most likely see Archimedes' Principle in action?

    (A) in a volcanic eruption

    (B) in a bathtub of water

    (C) measuring wind speed

    (D) in an experiment focusing on plant growth

49. As a state of matter, where would plasma most likely be found?

    (A) on the Sun

    (B) under the ocean

    (C) in the Earth's core

    (D) in the winds of a tornado

50. Which of the following statements about atoms is true?

    (A) A neutral atom has an equal number of protons and neutrons.

    (B) If an atom has more electrons than protons, the atom has a negative charge.

    (C) If an atom has fewer electrons than neutrons, the atom has a positive charge.

    (D) Protons and electrons are in the nucleus of an atom.

51. What characterizes the world view of science?

    (A) The world is unpredictable.

    (B) Scientific ideas, laws, and theories, once proven, do not change.

    (C) Scientific knowledge is durable.

    (D) Science completely answers all questions.

52. Mr. Bass is teaching his fifth-grade students how to plot data from an experiment. The students wanted to see how long it would take beans to sprout in terms of differing amounts of water. The beans were placed in a row near a sunny window. What should Mr. Bass tell the class?

    (A) The amount of water is the independent variable and it should be graphed on the x-axis.

    (B) The amount of sunlight represents the control group and those points should be on the y-axis

    (C) The dependent variable is the water and it should be graphed on the y-axis.

    (D) None of these are correct.

53. Ms. Spaulding showed her students a picture that showed a small, rolling hill that recently had the soil plowed in rows. The rows went up one side of the hill and down the other side. She asked the students to examine the picture and predict what might happen after a heavy rain. Which is the correct prediction?

    (A) new plants would sprout

    (B) erosion at the top of the hill and deposition at the bottom

    (C) the Earth's mantle would be exposed

    (D) a plateau would form

54. Mr. Carter's class is learning about cells. He asked his students to identify the most important thing they learned about cells and why it was important. The information some students gave was factually incorrect. Who provided the correct information and rationale?

    (A) William: The cell wall is most important because it make rocks and minerals strong.

    (B) Clarissa: DNA is most important because it is used to help the cell maintain homeostasis

    (C) Tonya: Cell division is important because pre-existing cells are gained through osmosis.

    (D) Phil: The metabolic process of a cell is most important because that's how life is sustained.

55. Jasmine notices that the pupils of her cat's eyes get larger in the dark and smaller in the light. This is an example of

    (A) irritability.

    (B) homeostasis.

    (C) metamorphosis.

    (D) phototropism.

Practice Test 1, Subtest 3
Answer Key

1.	(B)	20.	(A)	39.	(D)
2.	(B)	21.	(C)	40.	(B)
3.	(B)	22.	(A)	41.	(B)
4.	(A)	23.	(B)	42.	(B)
5.	(A)	24.	(D)	43.	(A)
6.	(B)	25.	(C)	44.	(C)
7.	(C)	26.	(A)	45.	(C)
8.	(B)	27.	(A)	46.	(D)
9.	(D)	28.	(B)	47.	(A)
10.	(C)	29.	(A)	48.	(B)
11.	(C)	30.	(C)	49.	(A)
12.	(C)	31.	(B)	50.	(B)
13.	(A)	32.	(A)	51.	(C)
14.	(D)	33.	(B)	52.	(A)
15.	(A)	34.	(C)	53.	(B)
16.	(B)	35.	(B)	54.	(D)
17.	(B)	36.	(C)	55.	(A)
18.	(B)	37.	(A)		
19.	(B)	38.	(B)		

Self-Assessment Guide
Science

Practice-test questions are sorted here by competency. To get an idea of your level of mastery, check the box under the question numbers that you answered correctly.

Competency 1: Knowledge of Effective Science Instruction   __/11

2	3	9	17	18	19	26	36	37	44

45

Competency 2: Knowledge of the Nature of Science   __/10

14	15	16	27	34	35	46	47	51	52

Competency 3: Knowledge of Physical Sciences   __/11

1	10	20	21	28	29	38	39	48	49

50

Competency 4: Knowledge of Earth and Space   __/10

4	5	11	22	23	30	31	40	41	53

Competency 5: Knowledge of Life Science   __/13

6	7	8	12	13	24	25	32	33	42

43	54	55

TOTAL   _____/55

Subtest 3: Science
Answer Explanations

1. (B)

    Choice (B) is the correct answer because heat is the energy of moving molecules.

2. (B)

    Choice (B) is the correct answer because the basic goals of science instruction are scientific literacy and application of the scientific method as they conduct simple experiments in much the same way that scientists do.

3. (B)

    Choice (B) is the correct answer because the remains or impression of a prehistoric organism preserved in petrified form as a mold or cast in rock is an example of a fossil. An arrowhead is man-made and therefore not considered a natural object.

4. (A)

    Choice (A) is the correct answer because Congress's establishment of the National Aeronautics and Space Administration was an immediate response to *Sputnik* being lofted as the first satellite to orbit the Earth. Although the United States launched *Explorer I* on January 31, 1958, the U.S. concern about lagging behind in technology was ongoing.

5. (A)

    Choice (A) is the correct answer because the water cycle begins with evaporation of water molecules that eventually condense into heavy droplets falling as rain into lakes, rivers, and the oceans.

6. (B)

    Choice (B) is the correct answer because viruses are much smaller than bacteria and and are not a kind of protozoa.

7. (C)

    Choice (C) is the correct answer because exteroceptors respond to pain, temperature, touch, and pressure.

8. (B)

    Choice (B) is the correct answer because bacteria live in the soil and in the roots of legumes (i.e., beans, peas, and clover). They change the nitrogen in the air, which plants cannot use, into nitrogen materials they can use.

9. (D)

    Choice (D) is the correct answer because having students prick their fingers could be hazardous.

10. (C)

    Choice (C) is the correct answer because to move an object, a magnet does not actually have to come into contact with the object. Therefore, it is considered a way of applying force at a distance.

11. (C)

    Choice (C) is the correct answer because dark, flat stratus clouds would suggest a storm is approaching.

12. (C)

    Choice (C) is the correct answer because only plants use chloroplasts for photosynthesis.

13. (A)

    Choice (A) is the correct answer because photosynthesis converts the Sun's energy to chemical energy to support biological life. Photosynthesis occurs in the chloroplasts of a plant's green cells within leaves.

14. (D)

    Choice (D) is the correct answer because the student is trying testing and verifying proposed answers to questions.

15. (A)

    Choice (A) is the correct answer because technology implies application to solve problems that benefit humankind.

16. (B)

    Choice (B) is the correct answer because a survey collects information.

17. (B)

Choice (B) is the correct answer because students assimilate new patterns of thinking by learning with and from individuals who are more proficient.

18. (B)

Choice (B) is the correct answer because the other responses illustrate informal methods, whereas lectures and tests are considered formal instruction.

19. (B)

Choice (B) is the correct answer because cooperative learning suggests an interdependency as students collaborate when solving problems.

20. (A)

Choice (A) is the correct answer because rust forms when oxygen atoms combine with the iron molecules in the frying pan.

21. (C)

Choice (C) is the correct answer because the yogurt mixture does not contain separate components.

22. (A)

Choice (A) is the correct answer because at one time, the continents were, if not touching, very close to each other to form a "supercontinent" called Pangaea. Continental drift explains how the continents moved across the Earth's surface.

23. (B)

Choice (B) is the correct answer because a seismograph measures earthquakes using the Richter scale.

24. (D)

Choice (D) is the correct answer because Carolus Linnaeus created a two-word naming system, which is still in use today for identifying a species.

25. (C)

Choice (C) is the correct answer because plants require the energy from the Sun for photosynthesis; the stems of plants grow toward the light. Since the Sun is in the sky, this generally means that the plant grows upward. If the source of the light differs (i.e., a houseplant near a window) the plants bend toward the light source. This occurs because hormones in the plant increase the number of stem cells on the side opposite from the light causing the stem to bend toward the light.

26. (A)

Choice (A) is the correct answer because scaffolding provides a structure for organizing information based on prior knowledge.

27. (A)

Choice (A) is the correct answer because identifying similarities and differences helps students focus traits by dividing groups into increasingly smaller groups based on finer distinctions that can also result in a serial continuum of related items in terms of one trait.

28. (B)

Choice (B) is the correct answer because the air molecules inside the balloon represent a gaseous state of matter with no definite volume or shape and no bonds among molecules that flow freely.

29. (A)

Choice (A) is the correct answer because molecules are formed when atoms combine. For example, two atoms of hydrogen that combine with one atom of oxygen form one molecule of water.

30. (C)

Choice (C) is the correct answer because mountains form when tectonic plates push rock through the crust. There are four types of mountains: folded, fault-block, domes, and volcanic.

31. (B)

Choice (B) is the correct answer because aquaculture is farming fish in artificial ponds and bays to help sustain fish populations and protect their role in ecosystems.

32. (A)

Choice (A) is the correct answer because new methods, such as genetic sequencing, now allow scientists to think about and classify organisms into three domains based on ribosomal RNA structure: archaea, bacteria, and eukarya.

33. (B)

Choice (B) is the correct answer because in the 1960s, organisms were classified into five kingdoms (Monera, Protista, Fungi, Plantae, and Animalia). Protista are microorganisms that don't fit into other categories (i.e., not bacteria; not animals, not plants; not fungi).

34. (C)

Choice (C) is the correct answer because theories must be proven before becoming a scientific law or principle.

35. (B)

Choice (B) is the correct answer because real-world decisions have social, political, and economic dimensions, and scientific information is often used to both support and refute those decisions. Scientific literacy helps us participate in the decision-making process of our society as well-informed and contributing members.

36. (C)

Choice (C) is the correct answer because the National Academy of Sciences focuses on what teachers need to know for effective science instruction rather than measuring learning.

37. (A)

Choice (A) is the correct answer because before a student can classify, hypothesize, and analyze, the scientific method requires observation that contributes to a reliable, consistent, and objective representation and understanding of our world in an authentic, relevant, and useful way.

38. (B)

Choice (B) is the correct answer because to move matter or produce a chemical change requires energy.

39. (D)

Choice (D) is the correct answer because potential energy is stored through chemical structure, position, or physical configuration (i.e., batteries). Objects that are higher and heavier store more potential energy that is released as the object falls.

40. (B)

Choice (B) is the correct answer because the Earth is composed of three layers: core, mantle, and crust. The mantle contains mostly magma, which is semi-molten rock.

41. (B)

Choice (B) is the correct answer because according to their method of formation, there are three types of rocks: igneous, sedimentary, and metamorphic. Individual pieces of rock are called grains. Metamorphic rocks change or "morph" into other kinds of rocks. Igneous or sedimentary rocks heated under tons of pressure change into metamorphic rocks. Geologists examining metamorphic rock samples found that some of the grains in the rocks are flattened (i.e., marble and slate).

42. (B)

Choice (B) is the correct answer because propagation occurs through the process of fission when the parent organism splits into two or more daughter organisms, thereby losing its original identity.

43. (A)

Choice (A) is the correct answer because the Punnett square is used to determine the probability of an offspring having a particular genotype or set of genes after reproducing offspring.

44. (C)

Choice (C) is the correct answer because differentiation of instruction accommodates students with disabilities. It also exemplifies universal design that benefits everyone.

45. (C)

Choice (C) is the correct answer because an anemometer is an instrument for measuring and indicating the force or speed and sometimes direction of the wind.

46. (D)

Choice (D) is the correct answer because various measurements of the plant height over a period of time would apply processes that make up the scientific method: observing and describing, formulating hypotheses, making predictions based on the hypotheses and testing those predictions (experimenting), and deriving conclusions.

47. (A)

Choice (A) is the correct answer because, while taking photographs, drawing sketches, and having discussions would prove beneficial, the information collected must be organized into a data table for analysis to verify hypotheses and reach a conclusion.

48. (B)

Choice (B) is the correct answer because objects sink in liquids if they are denser than the material that surrounds them. Archimedes' principle states that an object is buoyed up by a force equal to the mass of the material the object displaces. In other words, a rubber duck would float in the bathtub of water because it is less dense than the water.

49. (A)

Choice (A) is the correct answer because plasma occurs when matter is heated beyond its gaseous state to become ionized as a high-energy gas-like fluid of charged particles with no definite volume or shape.

50. (B)

Choice (B) is the correct answer because when an atom has more electrons than protons, the atom has a negative charge. When an atom has an equal number of protons and electrons, they cancel each other and the atom has no charge. If an atom has fewer electrons than protons, the atom has a positive charge.

51. (C)

Choice (C) is the correct answer because when scientific knowledge is durable, what has been learned has stood the test of time and experience, and can be replicated.

52. (A)

Choice (A) is the correct answer because the experiment tests an hypothesis about bean sprouts by manipulating the independent variable (the amount of water) to observe its effect on the dependent variable (the amount of time) and holding other variables constant (the location in the window, the amount of sunlight, etc.) So the y-axis shows the time of growth until a sprout appears and the x-axis shows the amount of water. Analysis might include varying the water to determine the optimal growing period for sprouts to appear.

53. (B)

Choice (B) is the correct answer because erosion occurs when water washes, glaciers push, or wind blows soil or rock away and deposits it in another area (deposition). Even a light rain shower can cause small amounts of soil to shift to another location. By planting horizontal rows, the effects of erosion would be reduced as water flows more slowly down a small gentle hill or when blocked by soil plowed in rows across the surface of the hill.

54. (D)

Choice (D) is the correct answer because the metabolic process releases energy from cells to support all life activities.

55. (A)

Choice (A) is the correct answer because organisms must be able to respond or react to physical or chemical stimuli either internally or in the environment. This function allows the organism to adjust to its environment to stay alive. Some reactions (i.e., pupil dilation) are immediate, while others occur over time (i.e., a plant bending toward sunlight).

PRACTICE TEST 1

FTCE Elementary Education K-6

Subtest 4: Mathematics

This practice test and an additional test are available at the online REA Study Center (*www.rea.com/studycenter*).

The FTCE Elementary Education K–6 (060) test is computer-based, so we strongly recommend that you take our online practice tests to simulate test-day conditions and to receive these added benefits:

- **Timed testing conditions**—Gauge how much time you can spend on each question.

- **Automatic scoring**—Find out how you did on the test, instantly.

- **On-screen detailed explanations of answers**—Learn not just the correct answer, but also why the other answers are incorrect.

- **Diagnostic score reports**—Pinpoint where you're strongest and where you need to focus your study.

Answer Sheet

1. Ⓐ Ⓑ Ⓒ Ⓓ
2. Ⓐ Ⓑ Ⓒ Ⓓ
3. Ⓐ Ⓑ Ⓒ Ⓓ
4. Ⓐ Ⓑ Ⓒ Ⓓ
5. Ⓐ Ⓑ Ⓒ Ⓓ
6. Ⓐ Ⓑ Ⓒ Ⓓ
7. Ⓐ Ⓑ Ⓒ Ⓓ
8. Ⓐ Ⓑ Ⓒ Ⓓ
9. Ⓐ Ⓑ Ⓒ Ⓓ
10. Ⓐ Ⓑ Ⓒ Ⓓ
11. Ⓐ Ⓑ Ⓒ Ⓓ
12. Ⓐ Ⓑ Ⓒ Ⓓ
13. Ⓐ Ⓑ Ⓒ Ⓓ
14. Ⓐ Ⓑ Ⓒ Ⓓ
15. Ⓐ Ⓑ Ⓒ Ⓓ
16. Ⓐ Ⓑ Ⓒ Ⓓ
17. Ⓐ Ⓑ Ⓒ Ⓓ

18. Ⓐ Ⓑ Ⓒ Ⓓ
19. Ⓐ Ⓑ Ⓒ Ⓓ
20. Ⓐ Ⓑ Ⓒ Ⓓ
21. Ⓐ Ⓑ Ⓒ Ⓓ
22. Ⓐ Ⓑ Ⓒ Ⓓ
23. Ⓐ Ⓑ Ⓒ Ⓓ
24. Ⓐ Ⓑ Ⓒ Ⓓ
25. Ⓐ Ⓑ Ⓒ Ⓓ
26. Ⓐ Ⓑ Ⓒ Ⓓ
27. Ⓐ Ⓑ Ⓒ Ⓓ
28. Ⓐ Ⓑ Ⓒ Ⓓ
29. Ⓐ Ⓑ Ⓒ Ⓓ
30. Ⓐ Ⓑ Ⓒ Ⓓ
31. Ⓐ Ⓑ Ⓒ Ⓓ
32. Ⓐ Ⓑ Ⓒ Ⓓ
33. Ⓐ Ⓑ Ⓒ Ⓓ
34. Ⓐ Ⓑ Ⓒ Ⓓ

35. Ⓐ Ⓑ Ⓒ Ⓓ
36. Ⓐ Ⓑ Ⓒ Ⓓ
37. Ⓐ Ⓑ Ⓒ Ⓓ
38. Ⓐ Ⓑ Ⓒ Ⓓ
39. Ⓐ Ⓑ Ⓒ Ⓓ
40. Ⓐ Ⓑ Ⓒ Ⓓ
41. Ⓐ Ⓑ Ⓒ Ⓓ
42. Ⓐ Ⓑ Ⓒ Ⓓ
43. Ⓐ Ⓑ Ⓒ Ⓓ
44. Ⓐ Ⓑ Ⓒ Ⓓ
45. Ⓐ Ⓑ Ⓒ Ⓓ
46. Ⓐ Ⓑ Ⓒ Ⓓ
47. Ⓐ Ⓑ Ⓒ Ⓓ
48. Ⓐ Ⓑ Ⓒ Ⓓ
49. Ⓐ Ⓑ Ⓒ Ⓓ
50. Ⓐ Ⓑ Ⓒ Ⓓ

K-6 Mathematics Reference Sheet

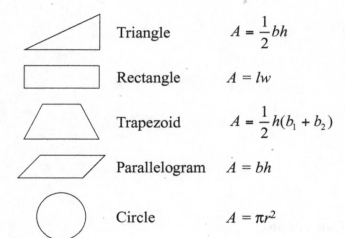

Triangle $A = \dfrac{1}{2}bh$

Rectangle $A = lw$

Trapezoid $A = \dfrac{1}{2}h(b_1 + b_2)$

Parallelogram $A = bh$

Circle $A = \pi r^2$

KEY	
b = base	d = diameter
h = height	r = radius
l = length	A = area
w = width	C = circumference
$S.A.$ = surface area	V = volume
	B = area of base

Use 3.14 or $\dfrac{22}{17}$ for π

Circumference
$C = \pi d = 2\pi r$

Surface Area
1. Surface area of a prism or pyramid equals the sum of the areas of all faces.

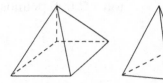

Volume
1. Volume of a triangular or rectangular prism equals the <u>Area of the Base</u> (B) times the height (h). $V = bh$.

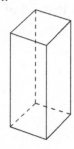 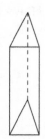

(continued)

2. Volume of a pyramid equals $\frac{1}{3}$ times the <u>Area of the Base</u> (B) times the height (h).

$$V = \frac{1}{3}bh$$

Pythagorean theorem: $a^2 + b^2 = c^2$

Conversions

1 yard = 3 feet = 36 inches
1 mile = 1,760 yards = 5,280 feet
1 acre = 43,560 square feet
1 hour = 60 minutes
1 minute = 60 seconds

1 liter = 1000 milliliters = 1000 cubic centimeters
1 meter = 100 centimeters = 1000 millimeters
1 kilometer = 1000 meters
1 gram = 1000 milligrams
1 kilogram = 1000 grams

1 cup = 8 fluid ounces
1 pint = 2 cups
1 quart = 2 pints
1 gallon = 4 quarts
1 pound = 16 ounces
ton = 2,000 pounds

Metric numbers with four digits are presented without a comma (e.g., 9960 kilometers). For metric numbers greater than four digits, a space is used instead of a comma (e.g., 12 500 liters).

Subtest 4: Mathematics

Questions: 50
Time: 1 hour and 10 minutes

Directions: Read each question and select the best response.

1. Mr. Sanders wrote the following on the board: $A^2 + B^2 = C^2$

    This is an example of

    (A) transitioning from concrete to abstract thinking.

    (B) thinking at an abstract level.

    (C) using a manipulative for conceptual understanding.

    (D) scaffolding a difficult concept.

2. Ellie has been asked to estimate how many items she sees. There are 3 groups of 5 cubes. What process is she most likely to be using?

    (A) subitizing

    (B) symbolic thinking

    (C) scaffolding

    (D) inventive strategies

3. Students in a fifth-grade class need to buy a protractor and a compass for math class. The combined cost for both items is $7.59 (without tax). The cost of the compass is $3.99 more than the protractor. Which of the following equations can a student use to determine the cost of the protractor?

    (A) $x = \$7.59 - \$3.99$

    (B) $\$7.59 = x - \$3.99$

    (C) $\$7.59 = x + (x + \$3.99)$

    (D) $\$3.99 + 7.59 = x$

4. Mr. Gleason is answering a question in math class. His answer is, "You do so by dividing the numerator by the denominator." What was the question?

   (A) How do you change a fraction into a decimal?

   (B) How do you change a decimal into a fraction?

   (C) How do you change a fraction into a percentage?

   (D) How do you change a decimal into a percentage?

5. Ms. Johnson's students have been learning about metric and customary units. Which of the following is correct?

   (A) A meter is longer than a yard.

   (B) A kilometer is longer than a mile.

   (C) A kilogram is less than a pound.

   (D) A liter is less than a quart.

6. Susan brought a water bottle from home. She wants to measure its capacity. What unit of measurement should she use?

   (A) kilogram

   (B) millimeter

   (C) liter

   (D) pound

7. Mr. Wood's class averaged 84 points on the last exam. What can be said about the class?

   (A) The mode of the class grades is 75.

   (B) The class mean is 84.

   (C) The standard deviation is 8.4.

   (D) The class median is 42.

8. Which math prefix and amount are correctly matched?

    (A) Deca = 10^2

    (B) Hecto = 10^{-3}

    (C) Milli = 10^{-1}

    (D) Kilo = 10^3

9. Which figure has the fewest number of parallel lines?

    (A) trapezoid

    (B) parallelogram

    (C) trapezium

    (D) rhombus

10. Which description best describes a scatter plot?

    (A) points on an x-axis and y-axis showing correlations

    (B) a frequency table of data

    (C) a tessellation of data

    (D) a transformation of data from one point in a coordinate plane from another

11. Mr. Anthony is using the following manipulative in his classroom: An oblong frame with rows of wires or grooves along which beads are moved. What is Mr. Anthony likely to be teaching?

    (A) operations on whole numbers

    (B) geometric shapes

    (C) capacity

    (D) comparisons of weights

12. In terms of developmental skills, Mrs. Camp's students are developing reasoning skills in concrete and real-life situations. What is most likely to be the age of students in Mrs. Camp's class?

(A) 1 year

(B) 3 years

(C) 8 years

(D) 14 years

13. Casey is learning about the property of reciprocals. Which of the following notations would exemplify what she is learning?

(A) $a \times \dfrac{1}{a} = 1$

(B) $a \times 1 = a$

(C) $a(b + c) = (a \times b) + (a \times c)$

(D) $a \times c = b \times c$

14. Which of the following is a composite number?

(A) 9

(B) 11

(C) 13

(D) 7

15. Which of the following concepts are correctly paired?

(A) hands-on math and scientific notation

(B) composite numbers and exponential notation

(C) integers and decimals

(D) ratio notation and fractions

16. Which of the following is a customary unit?

     (A) liter

     (B) ton

     (C) meter

     (D) gram

17. Ms. Carlisle gave her students a spelling test that had a maximum of 20 points. Students had the following scores: 5, 5, 5, 5, 5, 11, 12, 12, 13, 20. What measure of central tendency would be best to use?

     (A) mode

     (B) standard deviation

     (C) median

     (D) outlier

18. Kristin is solving a problem. She wants to cover the outside of her locker with an adhesive fabric. Which estimation strategy would be best to try?

     (A) make a sketch

     (B) make a list

     (C) look for patterns

     (D) act it out

19. What is true of the following figures?

     (A) They are similar.

     (B) They demonstrate tessellation.

     (C) They have the same radius.

     (D) They are rectilinear.

20. What is true of a coordinate plane?

    (A) It has 3 dimensions.

    (B) It has 4 quadrants.

    (C) It is a polygon.

    (D) It has obtuse angles.

21. Mrs. Castleberry uses a constructivist approach for teaching math in her second-grade classroom. What would you expect to see in the classroom?

    (A) an interactive whiteboard

    (B) a word wall with math vocabulary terms

    (C) examples of student work on a bulletin board

    (D) adherence to state standards in lesson plans

22. Mr. Marco has a large box of color tiles. He is using them to help students understand successive estimations as a problem-solving approach for larger groups of items. This reflects the concept of

    (A) tessellations.

    (B) reflections.

    (C) transformations.

    (D) iterations.

23. $(3^2)3^3 =$

    (A) 3^6

    (B) 3^5

    (C) 3^1

    (D) 3^0

24. Convert .875 to a fraction.

    (A) $\dfrac{2}{3}$

    (B) $\dfrac{7}{8}$

    (C) $\dfrac{4}{5}$

    (D) $\dfrac{5}{2}$

25. Convert .233 to a percentage.

    (A) 2.33%

    (B) 23.30%

    (C) 233%

    (D) .233%

26. Which of the following is factually *correct*?

    (A) Integers can be expressed as fractions.

    (B) There are more fractions than whole numbers.

    (C) Not all fractions can be expressed as integers.

    (D) All of the above are factually correct.

27. A truck container is 10 feet high, 10 feet wide, and 25 feet long. What is the volume of the container?

    (A) 2500 ft

    (B) 2500 ft^2

    (C) 2500 ft^3

    (D) 25000

28.   Kendra is plotting data on a coordinate plane. In which quadrant should she place (3, –2)?

(A)   Quadrant 1

(B)   Quadrant 2

(C)   Quadrant 3

(D)   Quadrant 4

29.   Mr. Fuqua wants to know if there is a relationship between the day of the week and the number of absences. He tracks this data over the course of a year. What should he use to present the data?

(A)   a frequency chart

(B)   an outlier identification

(C)   data skewing

(D)   scaling transformation

30.   Given the following shapes, what is the relationship between them?

(A)   The second figure is a scaled version of the first figure.

(B)   The second figure is a rotated version of the first figure.

(C)   The second figure is a reflection of the first figure

(D)   The second figure is a tessellation of the first figure.

31.   Principal Fitzmorris has put together a presentation. He wants to show the number of students in each grade as a proportion of the total number of students at the school. What should he use?

(A)   bar graph

(B)   line graph

(C)   scatter plot

(D)   pie chart

32. Cassie is solving the following math problem.

    > The number of people going to a movie on Monday is 95. If increased by a factor of 5 on Saturday night, what is the attendance at the movie on Saturday night?

    What process should Cassie use?

    (A) divide 95 by 5

    (B) add five to 95

    (C) find the mean of 5 and 95

    (D) multiply 5 by 95

33. Mrs. Foret told her class that the distance from the Earth to the sun is approximately 1.4959826×10^8 km. The number is equal to which of the following?

    (A) 14,959,826,000 km

    (B) 149,598,260,000,000,000 km

    (C) 14,959,826,000,000,000 km

    (D) 149,598,260 km

34. In terms of number theory, which of the following is true?

    (A) Parity describes a number that only has 2 factors—the number itself and 1.

    (B) Factors, when divided, result in a product.

    (C) Only whole numbers ending in 0, 2, 4, 6, and 8 are divisible by 2.

    (D) 0 is a prime number because it is divisible by itself.

35. Which of the following statements about numbers is true?

    (A) Multiplication is repeated subtraction

    (B) *Whole numbers* are the same as *counting numbers*.

    (C) A fraction is the same as a rational number

    (D) In the number 3^2, 3 is the exponent and 2 is the base.

36. Ms. Wood is using a contextual approach to teaching math to her first-grade class. What would you expect to see in her classroom?

    (A) students learning about measurements by making recipes

    (B) students using an abacus for counting

    (C) peer tutoring

    (D) students using drill and practice software to learning math facts

37. Kaitlyn is using *tans* in her class. What mathematical concept is Kaitlyn most likely to be learning?

    (A) estimation

    (B) spatial reasoning

    (C) counting

    (D) operations on whole numbers

38. Measures of central tendency

    (A) transform skewed data into data that is usable.

    (B) describe data as a single number.

    (C) assess learning style in terms of primary preferences.

    (D) also provide an estimate of variability.

39. In the following data set, 9 is which of the following?

    1, 4, 6, 7, 9, 13, 14, 14, 21

    (A) range

    (B) mean

    (C) mode

    (D) median

40. In a data set, what is the average distance from each data point in the set to the average?

    (A) an example of skewed data

    (B) a measure of central tendency

    (C) the absolute standard deviation

    (D) the range

41. Mr. Green is teaching his third-grade students about money and money management using "Green Bucks." Just as workers get paid to come to work, his students get "paid" to come to class and get there on time. His students also get paid for their "work" in class or for homework. Higher grades get more money; however, students can get paid "overtime" by correcting their work. He has a variety of ways in which students can spend their money. They can buy small items at the "Green Store" each week, purchase recess or free time, or save for monthly "Big Green Deals." What method is Mr. Green using?

    (A) collaborative learning

    (B) simulation

    (C) an instructional game

    (D) scaffolding

42. Each day, Mr. Varnado has a "problem of the day" as bellwork for his 5th grade class. In today's problem, he shows them how to use 8 toothpicks to make the shape of a fish. Then he challenges them to move 3 of the toothpicks so that the fish is going in the opposite direction. This type of problem would be classified as a

    (A) process.

    (B) translation.

    (C) application.

    (D) puzzle.

43. Which of the following is equal to 16?

    (A) 4^3

    (B) 16^1

    (C) 1.6×10^2

    (D) 16%

44. Ms. Cane's fifth-grade math class has been learning about expressions. Which student made the correct comment about expressions?

    (A) **Greg:** $3x + 12$ is an example of a number sentence.

    (B) **Collier:** Verbal expressions use the language of math.

    (C) **Luke:** Expressions and equations are the same things.

    (D) **Lola:** Variables are used in expressions, but not in equations.

45. Jennifer is sorting beads. She has made several groups. One group contains beads that are both red and round. One group contains beads that are both blue and round. One group contains beads that are both blue and square. One group contains beads that are both red and square. In Piagetian terms, Jennifer's ability to sort beads is at the

    (A) sensorimotor level.

    (B) pre-operational level.

    (C) formal operations level.

    (D) concrete level.

46. Mr. Morehouse is grading papers. He sees that Elsa incorrectly solved the following 4 problems:

18	95	73	22	88
23	18	27	29	66
311	1013	910	411	?

    If Elsa continues to make the same mistake, what would her answer be for the last problem?

    (A) 1414

    (B) 1544

    (C) 1514

    (D) 1644

47. Becky is learning about place value. Given the number, *1345.29*, which of the following is correctly matched with its place value?

    (A) 3, hundredths place

    (B) 2, tens place

    (C) 5, ones place

    (D) 9, hundreds place

48. Mr. Ellis is teaching his first-grade students subtraction and wants them to understand the correct vocabulary for each part of a problem. Given the problem $12 - 3 = 9$, which word would be used to label the *3*?

    (A) difference

    (B) subtrahend

    (C) minuend

    (D) dividend

49. $6(5 + 3) = (6 \times 5) + (6 \times 3)$ exemplifies

    (A) the distributive property of multiplication over addition.

    (B) the associative property for addition and multiplication.

    (C) the commutative property for addition and multiplication.

    (D) the properties of reciprocals.

50. *PEMDAS* is an acronym for remembering

    (A) the rules of divisibility.

    (B) invented strategies for solving word problems.

    (C) places in scientific notation.

    (D) the order of operations.

Practice Test 1, Subtest 4
Answer Key

1.	(B)	20.	(B)	39.	(D)
2.	(A)	21.	(A)	40.	(C)
3.	(C)	22.	(D)	41.	(B)
4.	(A)	23.	(B)	42.	(D)
5.	(A)	24.	(B)	43.	(B)
6.	(C)	25.	(B)	44.	(B)
7.	(B)	26.	(D)	45.	(D)
8.	(D)	27.	(C)	46.	(A)
9.	(C)	28.	(D)	47.	(C)
10.	(A)	29.	(A)	48.	(B)
11.	(A)	30.	(B)	49.	(A)
12.	(C)	31.	(D)	50.	(D)
13.	(A)	32.	(D)		
14.	(A)	33.	(D)		
15.	(D)	34.	(C)		
16.	(B)	35.	(C)		
17.	(C)	36.	(A)		
18.	(A)	37.	(B)		
19.	(A)	38.	(B)		

Self-Assessment Guide
Mathematics

Practice-test questions are sorted here by competency. To get an idea of your level of mastery, check the box under the question numbers that you answered correctly.

Competency 1: Knowledge of Student Thinking and Instructional Practices ___/12

1	2	11	12	21	22	36	37	41	42

45	46

Competency 2: Knowledge of Operations, Algebraic Thinking, Counting and Number Base 10 ___/13

3	5	13	14	31	32	34	43	44	47

48	49	50

Competency 3: Knowledge of Fractions, Ratios, and Integers ___/10

4	6	15	16	23	24	25	26	33	35

Competency 4: Knowledge of Measurement, Data and Statistics ___/9

7	8	10	17	18	29	38	39	40

Competency 5: Knowledge of Geometric Concepts ___/6

9	19	20	27	28	30

TOTAL _____/50

Subtest 4: Mathematics
Answer Explanations

1.   (B)

Choice (B) is correct because abstract thinking involves symbols, expressions, and formulas.

2.   (A)

Choice (A) is correct because subitizing is the skill to see and estimate the number of items (up to about 7).

3.   (C)

Choice (C) is correct because the cost of the protactor is x. The cost of the compass is x + \$3.99. The total (\$7.59) equals the cost of both items ($x + (x + \$3.99)$).

4.   (A)

Choice (A) is correct because a fraction has a numerator and a denominator. The starting point is a fraction and dividing the numerator by the denominator results in a decimal.

5.   (A)

Choice (A) is correct because a yard = 36 inches and a meter = 39.3701 inches, so a meter is more than a yard. A kilometer is about $\frac{2}{3}$ of a mile, so a kilometer is less than a mile. A kilogram is about 2.2 pounds, so a kilogram is more than a pound. A quart = 32 ounces. A liter = 33.814 ounces, so a liter is slightly more than a quart.

6.   (C)

Choice (C) is correct because liters are measures of volume or capacity. Kilograms and pounds are units of weight. Millimeters are units of length.

7.   (B)

Choice (B) is correct because *average* is another word for *mean*. You cannot tell mode (score that occurs most often) from the mean. You cannot tell the median (centermost score) from the average. You cannot determine a measure of variability from only the mean.

8.   (D)

Choice (D) is correct because kilo = 1000. The prefix hecto = 10^2 or 100. The prefix deca = 10^1 or 10. The prefix milli = 10^{-3} or .001.

9.   (C)

Choice (C) is correct because a trapezium has no parallel lines. A parallelogram and a rhombus each has two sets of parallel lines. A trapezoid has one set of parallel lines.

10.   (A)

Choice (A) is correct because scatter plots are specifically used to show correlations between two sets of data. A frequency table simply shows how many times a score or number is repeated in the data set. Tessellations do not apply to data. Transforming data points from one point to another is called translation.

11.   (A)

Choice (A) is correct because Mr. Anthony is using an abacus, which can show mathematical operations.

12.   (C)

Choice (C) is correct because the typical range for concrete operations is ages 7–11. The other ages are outside of the range.

13.   (A)

Choice (A) is correct because any number (except 0) multiplied by its reciprocal (1 divided by that number) equals 1.

14.   (A)

Choice (A) is correct because a composite number is one that can be expressed as several whole-number factors. 9 can be expressed as 3×3 or 9×1. All the other numbers are prime numbers, which can only be expressed as the number itself multiplied by 1.

15.   (D)

Choice (D) is correct because ratio notation is another way to show fractions. Each of the other pairs of concepts is not related.

16. (B)

Choice (B) is correct because a ton is a customary unit. All of the other terms are metric terms.

17. (C)

Choice (C) is correct. The mode is a measure of central tendency; however, the numbers with the highest frequency (5) would not clearly account for the higher numbers in terms of central tendency. Neither an outlier nor a standard deviation is a measure of central tendency.

18. (A)

Choice (A) is correct because a sketch would give her the best information for solving the problem. A list would not result in a resolution. There's no pattern to look for. Acting it out would not be helpful.

19. (A)

Choice (A) is correct. Tessellation is a repeated pattern. The figures do not have the same radius. A rectilinear figure has four, not five, sides.

20. (B)

Choice (B) is correct. A coordinate plane is two-dimensional. Polygons can be plotted on a coordinate plane, but a coordinate plane is not considered to be a polygon. Thus, it has no obtuse angles.

21. (A)

Choice (A) is correct because an interactive whiteboard allows the teacher and students to work with and manipulate math concepts. A word wall helps students learn vocabulary, but is not a constructivist approach that would result in mathematical conceptual understanding. Examples of student work do not always show constructivist learning. Sticking to state standards does not necessarily imply the use of a constructivist approach.

22. (D)

Choice (D) is correct because a successive approach means that an operation occurs multiple times.

23. (B)

Choice (B) is correct because when multiplying two numbers that consist of the same base and exponents, the exponents are added. In this example, $3^3 = 3 \times 3 \times 3$ and $3^2 = 3 \times 3$. Thus, the answer is $3 \times 3 \times 3 \times 3 \times 3$ or 3^5.

24. (B)

Choice (B) is correct because to convert a decimal to a fraction, the decimal is written as a fraction with the denominator as a power of ten and then reduced. Thus, $.875 = \dfrac{875}{1000}$. Reducing it to lowest terms $= \dfrac{7}{8}$.

25. (B)

Choice (B) is correct because to covert a decimal to a percentage, shift the decimal point 2 places to the right and add the percent symbol (%).

26. (D)

Choice (D) is correct because integers can be expressed as fractions, there are more fractions than integers, and not all fractions can be expressed as integers.

27. (C)

Choice (C) is correct because volume is expressed in cubic feet.

28. (D)

Choice (D) is correct because the coordinate pair will be to the right of the origin (0,0) and down. This places the point in quadrant 4.

29. (A)

Choice (A) is correct because Mr. Fuqua wants to show the frequency of absences by day.

30. (B)

Choice (B) is correct because the second figure is turned, but not changed. If it had been scaled, the second figure would be proportionally larger or smaller. If it had been reflected, the second figure would be flipped, but otherwise unchanged. To be a tessellation, there would need to be multiple plane figures that fill the plane with no overlaps and no gaps.

31.   (D)

Choice (D) is correct because Principal Fitzmorris wants to show each grade as part of the whole.

32.   (D)

Choice (D) is correct because the phrase "increase by a factor" means "to multiply."

33.   (D)

Choice (D) is correct because the exponent of 8 shows that the decimal has moved 8 places to the right. In converting from scientific to standard notation, the decimal place is moved to the right.

34.   (C)

Choice (C) is correct. Parity is the mathematical concept of classifying integers as even or odd. Factors, when multiplied, result in a product. 0 is not a prime number.

35.   (C)

Choice (C) is correct. Multiplication is repeated addition. Whole numbers include 0; counting numbers do not. In the number 3^2, 3 is the base and 2 is the exponent.

36.   (A)

Choice (A) is correct because contextual learning focuses on authentic situations such as preparing a recipe.

37.   (B)

Choice (B) is correct because tans are flat shapes in a dissection puzzle which facilitates the development of visual, spatial thinking.

38.   (B)

Choice (B) is correct. Measures of central tendency include mean, median and mode that can be reported as a single number.

39.   (D)

Choice (D) is correct because 9 is the center number in the data set. The range is the difference between 21 and 1 (20). The mean (average) is 9.88. The mode is 14.

40.   (C)

Choice (C) is correct. A measure of central tendency is a number that expresses a data set as one number. The range is the difference between the highest and lowest scores.

41.   (B)

Choice (B) is correct because the teacher has created a situation modeled on a workplace. Collaborative learning occurs when students work in interdependent groups. Instructional games provide learning activities that have game characteristics (e.g., competition, rules). Scaffolding is a teacher-directed strategy that provides students with an organizational or other structure to support learning until they can learn independently.

42.   (D)

Choice (D) is correct. A puzzle is a situation that requires ingenuity for the solution.

43.   (B)

Choice (B) is correct because 16^1 is 16×1. $4^3 = 4 \times 4 \times 4$ or 64. $1.6 \times 10^2 = 1.6 \times 100$ or 1600. $16\% = \dfrac{16}{100}$ or $\dfrac{4}{25}$.

44.   (B)

Choice (B) is correct. Choice (A), $3x + 12$, is not a number sentence because it includes a variable. Expressions can express greater than or less than relationships as well as equality. Equations, however, only express equality (Choice C). Variables can be used in expressions or equations (Choice D).

45.   (D)

Choice (D) is correct because the student can sort based on more than one dimension.

46.   (A)

Choice (A) is correct because Elsa is not carrying from the ones place to the tens place. She is adding each column independently and writing the answer.

47.   (C)

Choice (C) is correct. 3 is in the hundreds place, not the hundredths place. 2 is in the tenths place, not the tens place. 9 is in the hundredths place, not the hundreds place.

48.　(B)

　　　Choice (B) is correct because the subtrahend is the number that is being subtracted. 12 is the minuend. 9 is the difference. Dividend is related to division, not subtraction.

49.　(A)

　　　Choice (A) is correct because the distributive property of multiplication over addition states that a number multiplied by the sum of two other numbers can be handed out, or distributed, to both numbers, multiplied by each of them separately, and the products added together. In this problem, the 6 can be distributed to the 5 and the 3.

50.　(D)

　　　Choice (D) is correct. PEMDAS is the acronym for **P**arentheses, **E**xponents, **M**ultiplication, **D**ivision, **A**ddition, **S**ubtraction.

Index